Political Change in Modern South Asia

EDITED BY JOHN GALLAGHER AND ANIL SEAL

THE EMERGENCE OF INDIAN NATIONALISM

The Indian Statistical Institute has greatly
assisted the research on which the volumes
in this series have been based

THE
EMERGENCE OF
INDIAN NATIONALISM

COMPETITION AND COLLABORATION
IN THE LATER NINETEENTH
CENTURY

ANIL SEAL

Fellow of Trinity College, Cambridge

CAMBRIDGE
AT THE UNIVERSITY PRESS
1968

Published by the Syndics of the Cambridge University Press
Bentley House, P.O. Box 92, 200 Euston Road, London, N.W.1
American Branch: 32 East 57th Street, New York, N.Y. 10022

Standard Book Number: 521 06274 8

Printed in Great Britain
at the University Printing House, Cambridge
(Brooke Crutchley, University Printer)

To my parents

Contents

Maps and Tables

Maps and Tables

Preface

This book is the first in a series in which John Gallagher and I will examine the history of political change in south Asia from the 1870s to the 1940s. We have divided the period between us at about 1918, but neither of us promises not to stray across this boundary. The second volume will carry the analysis from 1888 to 1912; it will be the joint work of Gordon Johnson, Fellow of Trinity College, and myself. In all, there will be about five volumes.

In this book the chief task has been to study the emergence of national political organisation in India. This has led me to concentrate upon Indians educated in the western mode; for the same reason the stress has fallen upon the political experiments taking place within the three Presidencies of Bengal, Bombay and Madras during the viceroyalties of Lytton, Ripon and Dufferin. This simplification of the totality of Indian politics is deliberate. It omits for the time being much discussion of the confused stirrings of more traditional types of politics, and says little about the political scene in northern and central India. The reader need not be perturbed at these omissions. Occasionally in this series chronology will have to be sacrificed to coherence. These themes will be raised and placed in their historical context from the point in time when they became important weights in the Indian political balance.

In the research for this volume the unpublished records of government have been less important than for the later volumes. Since one of the tasks here has been to establish the background to early Indian politics, it is to official publications—the censuses, gazetteers, ethnographic surveys, and education reports—that I have turned most frequently. Nevertheless the private papers of the rulers of India have proved a useful source for tracking their attitudes and policies. But it is as true for the 1880s as for the 1940s that the best sources for Indian politics are the private papers of Indians.

Preface

In this volume there are many tables and statistics. They give an air of precision which is a little misleading since many of the statistical categories themselves are dubious and many of the returns pose baffling problems of comparison. The evidence they provide is by no means impeccable. But when used with caution, it can be highly suggestive.

The problem of spelling Indian place names and proper names is not easy to solve. For convenience, I have spelt the former according to the *Imperial Gazetteer* of 1907–9, and the latter I have spelt as they most commonly were spelt during the period.

This book took its first shape in a fellowship dissertation written in 1961. In its making I have incurred many debts of gratitude. In India, my researches have been greatly assisted by the generosity of the Indian Statistical Institute and its director, Professor P. C. Mahalanobis. I wish to thank Husain B. Tyabji, Sir Homi Mody, the Dadabhai Naoroji Memorial Trust, the Bombay Presidency Association, the British Indian Association, the Indian Association and the Servants of India Society for granting me access to papers and records in their possession. For his expert help I thank Sourin Roy at the National Archives. Sumit Sarkar and Professor D. K. Bedekar aided me in translations from some Bengali and Marathi texts. I have had much kindness and hospitality from many friends in India; my warmest thanks go to Premila and Nitya Waglé, B. Shiva Rao and Sir N. R. Pillai. I recall with particular pleasure the friendly encouragement of Jawaharlal Nehru.

For their courteous help I thank the custodians and staff of the India Office Library, the British Museum and the University Library, Cambridge. I am indebted to the Master and Fellows of Trinity College and to the Managers of the Smuts Memorial Fund for their support. To my friends and colleagues, Jeffrey Goldstone, Gordon Johnson, Gareth Jones, Ralph Leigh, Francis Robinson, Ronald Robinson, Edward Shils, Peter Swinnerton-Dyer and Tony Weir, and above all to Jack Gallagher, I owe a deep debt of gratitude. They have scrutinised one or other of the various versions from which this text has finally emerged; they have cast out many errors of style and judgement. Those which remain are mine alone.

TRINITY COLLEGE, CAMBRIDGE   ANIL SEAL

Abbreviations

Add.	Additional.
BG	*Gazetteer of the Bombay Presidency.*
BIA	Records and publications of the British Indian Association, Calcutta.
B.M. I.S.	British Museum, Indian State Papers.
C.P.	Central Provinces.
DP	Papers of the Marquis of Dufferin and Ava.
EC	*Report of the Indian Education Commission, 1882.*
HIG	W. W. Hunter, *Imperial Gazetteer of India.*
IA	Records and publications of the Indian Association, Calcutta.
I.N.C.	*Report of the Indian National Congress.*
LP	Papers of Robert, First Earl of Lytton.
MSS	Manuscripts.
Muslim Selections	*Correspondence on the subject of the education of the Muhammadan community in British India and their employment in the public service generally.*
NP	Papers of Dadabhai Naoroji.
N.W.P. & O.	North-western Provinces and Oudh.
P.P.	*Parliamentary Papers.*
PSC	*Report of the Public Service Commission, 1886–87* with appendices.
RDPI	*Report of the Director of Public Instruction; Report on Public Instruction.*
RNP	Report on Native Newspapers, published fortnightly by the provincial governments; incomplete series can be found both in the National Archives of India and in the India Office Library.
RP	Papers of George Frederick Samuel Robinson, First Marquis of Ripon.
Rs	Rupees.
SAB	W. W. Hunter, *A Statistical Account of Bengal.*

Wherever necessary these abbreviations are fully explained in the bibliography.

India: British Provinces and Native States

I

Political India

British rule in India became the most spectacular case of imperialism in modern times, but it was a special case as well. The early conquests seemed glittering to the men who made them, but half a century later the mid-Victorians, who relied on influence and looked askance on rule, were clear that they wanted no more Indias out of the bargain basements of Asia. Their Indian empire was not a millstone but neither had it turned out to be a treasure-trove. Only gradually was India made into a credible economic asset to the British economy as a whole rather than to a favoured few. Nevertheless the narrow interests originally confined to traders, shipping men and dabblers in stock broadened out to embrace cotton masters and railway builders. Railways also attracted the investor, and the flow of private capital increased with the growth of such cash crops as tea, indigo and jute. By the last quarter of the nineteenth century, the patterns of Indian trade were fitting conveniently into the international needs of the British economy.

Yet many of these new advantages might have been drawn from an India controlled informally, without the administrative loads, the diplomatic liabilities and the foreign wars to which Britain was committed by her oriental empire. On the logic of Cobdenism it was hard to justify so gigantic a possession in terms of the links between Britain and India alone. The advantages showed to the full only when they were placed in the larger context of British interests in Asia as a whole. Once it had been unified and rationally organised, India took its place beside the United Kingdom as a second nucleus of British expansion. In absolute terms her trade might not be massive; but it was large enough to throw her influence around her neighbours in Asia. Her systems of communication linked her far more tightly to the world market, and her activities were backed by far longer lines of credit. With the exception of the Russian Empire in Central Asia, no neighbouring state was impervious to her influence. From the Indian base, British influence flowed eastwards across Burma into Malaya, Siam and Indonesia; it moved into China, either through the shuttling of trade between Calcutta and the Yellow Sea, through diplomacy in Sinkiang, or through reconnaissance past the Irrawaddy into the south-west provinces. From the western flank of India, Bombay had spun a web of influence over the Persian Gulf and across the Trucial Coast to the Red Sea; and from there to Zanzibar, where it exploited the prestige of the client sultan to loom over the mainland of East Africa. These elegant and economical systems of informal control were typical of the Victorian mode of expansion through 'mere influence'; but what underpinned them was the formal empire in India. Much of the later influence depended on the fact of the earlier conquest. It was wise of Victorian statesmen to decide that they wanted no more Indias; but it was well for them that they possessed one already. As the British Empire became more and more an oriental empire, linking the Middle East, South-east Asia and the Far East, India had become its linchpin.

This second centre of British world power possessed formidable resources of its own. A nation of shopkeepers in Europe, in Asia the British were a militarist power. Here the Indian army guaranteed the security of the base, while providing the force to overawe or strike down its neighbours east or west. Its operations were largely outside the control of parliament, and their cost fell lightly upon the British taxpayer, who had a vote, while falling heavily upon the Indian taxpayer, who had not. Behind this unparliamentary army, an enormous reserve of manpower stood ready for British purposes, if the Sarkar was minded to stay. The events of 1857 showed that it was so minded. The armed challenge proved that the Indians could not turn the British out by force: not because the foreigners were the stronger, but because they were more united. As long as any internal crisis in the future was capable of a military solution, then they would be able to solve it. For some decades after 1857 this seemed to be the only type of internal crisis likely to threaten them; consequently the Raj sheltered behind a panoply of force which could evoke terror and inspire respect.

On the face of it, British dominion was an unabashed auto-cracy, tempered by the rule of law, but governing without any system of representation; the only open question in its consti-tution was whether to exercise the autocracy mainly from London or from Calcutta. In fact the mode of rule was much more subtle and conditional. But before going behind this outward appearance, it will be as well to look at the formal sys-tem of government as a whole.

Since the Act of 1858, government had lain partly in London with the Secretary of State for India, and partly in Calcutta with the Governor-General. Ultimate responsibility lay in parliament, but its members gave little heed to the problems of India. The taxpayers were not troubled. The parties were at one. The problems seemed far away. Furthermore, they were so arcane as to seem unintelligible. This freed the hands of the India Office, but its administrators were wary of asserting any detailed control over Indian affairs. In 1858 the Cabinet had agreed that 'the government of India must be, on the whole, carried out in India itself'.[1] In practice this meant that London was disinclined to intervene except in issues affecting the sub-continent as a whole or in provincial issues which had some bearing on general policy. But as communications quickened, London could keep in closer touch, and it grew harder to decide large issues in India. The Secretary of State did not discuss them entirely in the abstract since he was assisted by a council of retired Indian administrators, on whom he could draw for advice that was as skilled as it was sometimes dated. In theory, the India Council was merely a consultative body; in practice, it sometimes exercised an unofficial veto, either because the Secretary of State was weak or because he used its prestige to obstruct a Viceroy whose judgement he suspected.[2]

But the system still left great powers of initiation and control in the hands of the government of India. At the apex of this system stood the Governor-General of British India, who was Viceroy as the symbol of British paramountcy over the princes. With the exception of Lawrence, all nineteenth-century vice-

[1] Quoted in H. H. Dodwell (ed.), *The Indian Empire 1858–1918*. The Cambridge History of the British Empire, v (Cambridge, 1932), 211.
[2] For the role of the Council see S. N. Singh, *The Secretary of State for India and his Council (1858–1919)* (Delhi, 1962).

roys came to India as aristocrats, and with the exception of Curzon these aristocrats came with a sketchy knowledge of the country. Inevitably then, they were deeply dependent upon the advice of the Governor-General's Council, which came to consist of six members, dividing among themselves the main departments of government in a portfolio system. Of the members, both the commander-in-chief and the Finance member were sometimes brought in from outside. But it was the traditions of the Indian civil service which dominated the Council, and sometimes the Viceroy as well. In much the same way the service dominated the governors of the Madras and Bombay Presidencies, usually politicians or notables sent out from England. But the lieutenant-governors of Bengal, the North-western Provinces, and the Punjab,[1] together with the chief commissioners of the Central Provinces, Assam and Burma, were themselves officers of the covenanted civil service. Influential in policy-making, the service was supreme in the administration of British India.

In most provinces the main unit of administration was the division, controlled by a commissioner who had several districts in his charge. By common consent the district was the key unit of administration, and the deputy commissioner, collector or district officer who ruled the 250 districts of British India was the vital figure in the system. His charge exceptionally might contain more than three million people and might extend over as many as seventeen thousand square miles. Here his tasks were to keep the peace, to supervise the courts, to collect the land revenue, to contrive local improvements, to report on local conditions, and to administer statutes by the stack. In the classical theory of district administration which the British evolved in India and were later to take to Africa, the essential function of this man of all work was to discover and to mould the state of opinion in his district. To do this, he had to be constantly on tour, attentive to grievances, representing the Sarkar, acting, as the old phrase has it, as the Father and Mother of his district. But this was an idealised view. In the first place, the amount of touring depended on the type of

[1] Until 1911 Bengal included Bihar and Orissa; after 1902 the North-western Provinces and Oudh were known as the United Provinces of Agra and Oudh. Until 1901 the Punjab included what then became the North-west Frontier Province.

land settlement in his province. Where the revenue system called for a regular inspection of the crops by the district officer, then he would necessarily see more of the villages than an officer would see in another province, where the assessment of revenue had been permanently settled. Secondly, the pioneering style of rule was fast being replaced by a more sedentary administration, and it was a constant source of complaint that men who ought to be in camp were shut up in offices, grappling with the paper work forced on them by the growth of the secretariats, both at the centre and at provincial headquarters.

From the central secretariat at the top to the district officer at the bottom, the administration was reserved for the nine hundred or so members of the Indian civil service, the covenanted service.[1] In practice, this meant that it was reserved for the British. Indians were free to take the entrance examination for the service, but it was usually a freedom to fail.[2] By 1887 there were only sixteen Indians among the 890 members of the covenanted service, and not until the twentieth century did any of them rise higher than the commissionership of a division. Neither were matters easier for them in those branches of the executive where the top posts were not the preserve of the covenanted service; for here also the British still held the senior places. In government service, as in private practice, the career most open to Indian talents was the law. By an Act of 1861 the high courts at Bombay, Madras, Calcutta and Allahabad had been designated as supreme provincial courts; below them came the district and sessions courts. Here there were covenanted civilians on the bench, but Indians were joining them from the uncovenanted provincial services, and from the local bar.

In terms of formal constitutional analysis then, British India was ruled autocratically. At all levels from the Viceroy's Council

[1] The covenanted service consisted of those officers who had been duly examined and selected, then entered into a covenant with the Secretary of State, swearing loyalty to the crown and engaging themselves to accept the codes and discipline of the service. The Indian Civil Service Act 1861 (24 and 25 Vict. c. 54) expressly reserved to the service all the more important civil posts under the rank of member in council in the Regulation Provinces.

[2] By the end of the 1860s, only sixteen of them had attempted the examination, and only one had passed. See Argyll to Governor-General in Council, 8 April 1869, *Parliamentary Papers* [henceforth *P.P.*], 1878–9, LV, 305–6.

down to the district, the system spurned any recourse to respresentative government;[1] the first slow steps towards it in the districts and municipalities were not to come until the local government reforms of Ripon's viceroyalty, and in the provinces until the Indian Councils Act of 1892. As the heirs of despots, the British must be despots too, so the argument ran. The Indian Empire could not be governed by rosewater; on the contrary, the rulers of so vast, so various, so turbulent a land needed to keep their powder dry and their prestige intact. But if the price of India was eternal vigilance, then clearly the technique of decentralising the empire through responsible government, which the mid-Victorians had applied to the colonies of white settlement, could not apply to India.[2]

While inveighing against Oriental Despotisms, the British had created one of their own. The izzat, the prestige, of government was as matchless as that of the Mughals in their prime. Its interventions in the affairs of the Indian princes grew higher-handed. The protocol surrounding the Viceroy and Governor-General grew more complex. The prose of the administration might be as bland as that in any other of the Queen's dominions, yet its government ruled with a majesty all its own. Nevertheless, this administration, so renowned and peremptory, was hobbled by serious checks to its authority. Some of these limitations could be seen in the working of the system of government; others of a more fundamental kind were inherent in the

[1] In 1861 the Viceroy's Executive Council had been expanded by up to twelve additional members, of whom at least half had to be selected from unofficials. This body, which came to be known as the Legislative Council, had legislative powers over all persons and courts in British India. It was not of course a representative body; it was merely an extension of the Executive Council. The 1861 Act also provided that the Executive Councils of Madras and Bombay might be extended for legislative purposes. Legislative Councils were established for Bengal in 1862, and for the North-western Provinces and Oudh in 1886.

[2] The autocracy of the rulers of India was matched by the growing liberalism of Britain's attitude towards the 'Greater Britain' of her white settlements, striking a discord between these, the two most important modes, of British expansion. 'How can the same nation pursue two lines of policy so radically different without bewilderment, be despotic in Asia and democratic in Australia, be in the East...the greatest Mussulman Power in the world...and at the same time in the West be the foremost champion of free thought and spiritual religion, stand out as a great military Imperialism to resist the march of Russia in Central Asia at the same time that it fills Queensland and Manitoba with free settlers?' J. R. Seeley, *The Expansion of England* (London, 1883), p. 177.

very nature of British imperialism in India. As the structure of politics changed in Britain itself, the division of powers between London and Calcutta became a matter of more concern to the rulers of India. It might be self-evident to them that the country had to be ruled by command from above, not through representation from below. Yet how was this steadfast authoritarianism of the British overseas to be reconciled with the turn towards democracy of the British at home? After Disraeli had shot Niagara in 1867, it seemed that the traditional constants of British policy were imperilled by the unpredictable tastes of his new voters. In many ways these fears of Lord Cranborne and his circle turned out to be exaggerated; but in the later 1870s they both inhibited and irritated the Viceroy of India. Lytton wrote that 'England is fast losing the instinct and tact of Empire. The model English politician of the day...appears to me an exceedingly foul bird, who cannot help dirtying his own nest, and cackling over his own squitter';[1] behind the complaint lay his feeling of '...our great difficulty of working efficiently a despotic executive in India without bringing it into collision with a democratic legislature in England'.[2] Sure enough, Lytton's Afghan adventure was one of the targets in the Midlothian campaign, in which Gladstone's success seemed to show that a forward policy might be an electoral disaster.[3]

But this was not the only force tying the hands of the government of India. As the needs of defence and administration grew, so too did financial difficulties. British India was self-supporting: had it not been, the criticisms from the Little Englanders would have been much louder. Indian revenues were inelastic, since the bulk of them came from the land, and in spite of strict economy and decentralisation they balanced so uneasily that any sudden increase in expense, such as famine relief, a crisis on the frontier or a falling exchange, might threaten a deficit. With the failure of the thorough-going financial reform after the mutiny, the government of India delegated some of its general financial authority to the provincial administrations, for

[1] Lytton to Stephen, 28 January 1878, Stephen Papers, Additional Manuscripts (hereafter Add.), 7349.
[2] Lytton to Stanhope, 9 May 1878, quoted in M. J. Cowling, 'Lytton, the Cabinet, and the Russians, August to November 1878', *English Historical Review*, LXXVI (January 1961), 70 n. 4.
[3] This is not to say, however, that the election of 1880 was really won and lost over these overseas issues.

the sake of retrenchment.[1] From 1870, when Mayo launched this experiment in devolution, until 1887, when it was temporarily halted, Calcutta's total control over financial allocations to its subordinates was slowly reduced. During these vital years for Indian political growth, when the critics of the Raj were calling for social reform and economic expansion, the government was too poor to meet their demands.

But these divisions of authority and opinion between Calcutta and London, and between Calcutta and its provincial administrations, are less important than the power relations between the British rulers and their Indian subjects. Constitutions are poor guides to the realities of power in any colony, and this is particularly true of so complex a dependency as India. Whenever a Mr Mothercountry stated that the sub-continent was governed autocratically, he was producing a dramatised generalisation out of a special case. It might have needed the ironhanded methods of a Nicholson to launch the Punjab style of administration, and the cannon of Lord Clyde to batter flat a rebellion on the plains of Hindustan, but after the turbulences had been quelled, it was by the political methods of 'Clemency' Canning and John Lawrence that the talukdars of Oudh and the sardars of the Punjab had been won over. Self-interest, not self-abnegation, brought them to the side of the Raj. This argument was all the more true of the Presidencies of Madras, Bengal and Bombay. Here British power had been firm before its extension to upper India; here during the crisis of 1857 not a dog had barked; here there were districts and cities undergoing much more rapid economic and social change than any parts of Hindustan proper. If political devices diluted the autocracy in Lucknow and Lahore, then clearly they were still more influential in Calcutta and Bombay. Indeed this system of control by manipulation rather than by force extended far beyond the areas of pavements and street lighting. All the hills and jungles of Orissa were ruled by less than a hundred Englishmen.[2] Evidently there were large parts of British India where autocracy was tempered by consent.

By the consent of whom? Here the argument can be generalised. Colonial systems of government, in which the alien few

[1] Bisheshwar Prasad, *The Origins of Provincial Autonomy*... (Allahabad, 1941), p. 158.
[2] S. Gopal, *British Policy in India 1858–1905* (Cambridge, 1965), p. 7.

8

rule the native many, have tended to rely upon the support of some of their subjects, and the passivity of the majority; such a system is cheaper, and frequently less embarrassing. In India understandings between the Raj and some of its subjects were a necessity if an off-shore island in north-western Europe was to govern hundreds of millions in South Asia. But these collaborations themselves varied both in their nature and in their intensity. Collaboration is a slippery term which may apply at any level between acquiescence and resignation. Men who worked with the foreign regime did so from a variety of motives: the wish to keep a position of importance or the hope of gaining such a position, the intention of working for an attractive regime or the habit of working for any regime, however unattractive. But in the physiology of colonialism it is results not motives that matter; and all those groups may be classed as collaborators whose actions fell into line with the purposes of the British.

Such a system was not static, for yesterday's enemies might be tomorrow's allies. Neither was it uniform, because the unevenness of development throughout India called for different techniques in different regions. Nevertheless it is possible to identify certain broad groups as the allies or the enemies of the Raj in the decades after 1857. Collaboration in its most palpable form was embodied in those Indians who were employed by the state. Outside the charmed circle of the covenanted service, there was a multitude of Indians who held official positions under the central government, and in the service of the provincial governments. Many of the subdivisions, talukas and tahsils (the largest units inside a district) were administered by Indian officers who thus controlled another hierarchy of Indians down to the headman in charge of a village (the smallest unit inside a district). The British made no difficulty about employing Indians in the uncovenanted service; naturally enough, because India was too poor to justify the use of Europeans in close administration. Consequently, the government was never sure what the mass of its subjects were thinking.[1] It might exhort its European officers to tour their districts, but

[1] As Lyall put it after returning to a province from a term on the Viceroy's Council: 'the big Government people can only guess faintly and vaguely what will be the effect of their measures'; H. M. Durand, *Life of the Right Hon. Sir Alfred Comyn Lyall* (Edinburgh and London, 1913), p. 275.

their reports could be impressionistic at best. It was only at lower levels that opinion could realistically be tested, and here, as Sir Walter Lawrence recognised, 'the real administration was in the hands of the Indian officials'.[1]

There were other Indians standing outside the hierarchy of officials, whose support was of greater political importance to the Raj. During the first half of the century the British had often met resistance from landowners and notables, the traditional leaders of their localities, who were cut down for their pains.[2] But to dwell upon their resistance would be to pity the plumage and to forget the dying bird. For the most part, the Indian notables were moribund, and their resistance was scattered and spasmodic. Some of this old political elite had been blown into historical footnotes by the cannons of the redcoats, others had been shrunk into administrative agents by the pressures of British rule. For the princes the moment of truth had come in 1857, when the majority chose to be puppets rather than proto-martyrs. In any case all the great chiefs were brought into line after the Rising, when the British displaced the stiff-necked and cajoled the remainder. In a sense the Durbars of Lytton and Curzon, with plumes waving and swords flashing, were entertainments staged to impress the groundlings who had to pay for them. Most of these magnates became ineluctably committed to the Raj, although at the district level some of the local notables were more ambiguous collaborators. They had much to gain from collaboration. As landlords in the areas under permanent settlement, they enjoyed the prestige of collecting revenue for government; as talukdars or zemindars in upper India, they possessed tenurial rights certified by the Raj; wherever the government created them honorary magistrates, they were associated with the enforcement of its law. As landlords, they had an assured place in society; as men whom the Viceroy delighted to honour, as an unofficial local executive in the work of government, as the coadjutors of its official agents, their position was considerably enhanced. But if they gained from the connection, so too did the British. In a rural hierarchy founded on deference, the role of these local landowners could

[1] W. R. Lawrence, *The India We Served* (London, 1928), p. 113.
[2] These outbreaks are conveniently summarised in S. B. Chaudhuri, *Civil Disturbances during the British Rule in India (1765–1857)* (Calcutta, 1955), pp. 1–181, 198–219.

be pivotal. Not everywhere, however; for in some parts of India there were few large landowners, and here the political task might be the more difficult one of winning over powerful castes or educated men.

The British could look for collaboration of a more instructed sort from those men who were being educated in their schools and colleges. Like other alien regimes before them, the British required collaboration from a large body of native bureaucrats. Indian administration had always called for skills of a sort which traditional religious education could not by itself provide. In every generation, and under every empire, the learned Hindu castes who were the natural recruits for the bureaucracy had turned to whatever form of secular education the current regime had demanded. So in the nineteenth century, yesterday's scholars of Persian now became enthusiasts for English—first in the Presidency capitals and later up the country. This was not so much an enthusiasm for the cultural tidings about empiricism and induction as calculation of the material benefits which might accrue from learning the ways of the new rulers. For India was not merely an agglomeration of regions in uneven stages of development; it was also a league of submerged nations, a chaos of overlapping castes, a cockpit of rival religions. Between their tongues, sects and communities there were intense competitions, which under the circumstances of foreign rule mainly took the form of struggles for status. Education, which was a means to office, was a vital weapon in the effort either to conserve or to improve status; consequently much of the eagerness for the new learning which first gratified and then embarrassed the British, came from an Indian desire to surpass other Indians. Taking the new education was a method of defending an old primacy, or of challenging it.

When these educated men were Hindus for whom the coming of the British had meant emancipation from Muslim rule, their allegiance could sometimes be had for the asking. When, as in the exceptional case of the Parsis, they were compradors, their loyalty was spotless. But for many of the new educated, collaboration was likely to be a conditional bargain. So long as working with government seemed to benefit their regional, caste or communal aspirations, then they would do so. But once the benefits lessened, then so too did their pliancy.

Thus below an apparently autocratic system guided by a British bureaucracy and guarded by British redcoats there lay another system of Indian support and consent. This system mediated between the commands of Government House and the obedience of the men in the fields. It preserved an Indian role in the governance of the country. Most important of all, it set limits to the freedom of action which the regime could enjoy, if the support of one or other group of collaborators was not to be lost.

The supporters of the Raj ranged from the simple to the sophisticated. So did its enemies. If the attachment of its friends varied from the firm to the equivocal, so did the hostility of its opponents. Some of the simple societies of India had an inborn propensity to revolt, and throughout the century there was turbulence among them. Many of these movements such as the Santal rising of 1855 in Bihar and the Naikda rising of 1868 in Gujarat, were messianic in inspiration,[1] and they were hostile to the British not as foreigners but as rulers. But there was trouble from more complex religions as well. The Muslims were the largest example, but, on a smaller scale, the Kuka attempt to purify Sikhism led to violence in the Punjab in 1872.[2] In a land so fired by religious enthusiasm, there was as much danger of disturbance from those who wanted to reform their own faith as from those who wanted to do away with the faith of their neighbours.[3] There was also a constant danger of turbulence among the peasantry. Between 1859 and 1862 there were riots in Lower Bengal protesting against the terms on which indigo was grown.[4] In 1875 the Maratha peasants of Poona and Ahmadnagar broke heads and contracts in a series of free-for-alls.[5] But these were peasant risings of the traditional type, the reaching for sticks and stones as the only way of protesting against distress. Of specific political content they show

[1] These nineteenth-century movements are summarised in S. Fuchs, *Rebellious Prophets. A Study of Messianic Movements in Indian Religions* (London, 1965).
[2] M. M. Ahluwalia, *Kukas. The Freedom Fighters of the Panjab* (Bombay, 1965).
[3] Consequently the British Raj was careful to follow a policy of religious neutrality. But this limitation to its power was nothing new; it took it over from the Mughals and transmitted it to the Congress Raj.
[4] B. B. Kling, *The Blue Mutiny. The Indigo Disturbances in Bengal 1859–1862* (Philadelphia, 1966).
[5] Deccan Riots Commission, *P.P.* 1878, LVIII, 217–414.

little sign.¹ Faced with mounting debts and shrinking fields, they marched, not against the foreigner, but against the land-owner and the moneylender. The indigo rioters rose against agrarian oppression, not against alien control. The observation that the oppressors were foreigners was the contribution of the intellectuals of Calcutta.²

The scufflings produced by such religious and agrarian agitations might vex the Raj, but they could not alarm it. They were precisely the type of movement which the autocracy was equipped to confront: once brought into open resistance, they could be hunted, scattered and crushed. They were all grounded on local grievances and local aspirations, and they were all dependent on local leadership. The more they proclaimed their uniqueness, the more they restricted their appeal. Messiahs were hard to export from one tribe to another, and village Hampdens were unlikely to climb on an all-India platform. They appealed to other Indians over issues which could not have appealed to them less, and they used methods which the British could use better.

Muslim revivalism, on the other hand, was potentially an all-India movement. The efforts of the Wahhabi reformers to purge Islam of the faithless led them to try purging India of the infidel, and their resistance which extended over Bengal, Bihar, the Punjab and the North-west Frontier, was not quelled until 1871.³ The programme elaborated by the Wahhabis and by the theorists of Deoband,⁴ was of higher generality, founded on the common duties of all true believers in the Dar-ul-Harb⁵ to

---

¹ The 1879 rising in Maharashtra led by Phadke, a Brahmin, had political overtones. But it was mainly a rising of low-caste men who looted extensively; *Source Material for a History of the Freedom Movement in India (Collected from Bombay Government Records)*, vol. I (*1818–1885*) (Bombay, 1957), 73–129; V. S. Joshi, *Vasudeo Balwant Phadke* (Bombay, 1959).

² Kling, *The Blue Mutiny*, pp. 111–21.

³ *Selections from the Records of the Government of Bengal*, XLII (Calcutta, 1866); A. Ahmad, *Studies in Islamic Culture in the Indian Environment* (London, 1964), pp. 209–17.

⁴ The seminary at Deoband in the North-western Provinces was a centre of Muslim fundamentalism, hostile both to the British and to the modernising movements in Islam. In a later age, when the options had changed, it was to support the Congress Muslim cause against the demand for Pakistan; Ziya-ul-Hasan Faruqi, *The Deoband School and the Demand for Pakistan* (London, 1963).

⁵ 'The land of war', a territory in which it was a religious duty to fight for the faith. In 1870 Mayo induced a group of ulema to issue a fatwa pro-

13

band together for a political no less than a religious aim. But if this was an all-India movement, it was of an old-fashioned sort, likely to appeal to special tastes. Seeking to march backwards with fire and sword to the good old days of Aurangzeb, they were unlikely to attract those three-quarters of the population who were Hindu. Since their principles debarred them from treating the Raj neutrally, their tactics were limited to conspiracy and violence. Hence they were bound to fail in a land where both the informers and the big battalions were on the other side.

But neither friendship nor hostility to the Raj was a static relationship. The history of any colonial system is a series of permutations between government and different sets of allies and enemies. During the last quarter of the nineteenth century the terms of the connection between Britain and India were slowly changing. By this time the Indian commitment was beginning to weigh heavily upon British policy. Preoccupation with Indian security was driving Britain into deeper involvements all over Asia, just as it was helping to narrow the options of her diplomacy inside Europe. At this time again, there was a gradual change of themes inside British society, when the thrust of her economic expansion was slackening, and when it looked as though the coming of the mass vote might upset the imperial apple-cart. But it was the changes inside India itself which did most to recast the systems of collaboration. During the last decades of the century a gap began to open between the Raj and some of its educated subjects. As yet they were hardly moving into candid opposition, even if some Viceroys thought otherwise. Their first experiments in political organisation seemed to support government and yet to stand aside from it. But step by step, and with protestations of loyalty accompanying each move, their criticisms grew louder. Their new political associations, based in the Presidency capitals, were too moderate not to be tolerated; yet they claimed to voice the interests of the Presidencies in general, while hinting more and more directly that these interests were not pursued by the administration. These developments for the Indians meant dilemmas for the Raj. The new politicians were impeccably constitutional. Govern-

claiming that India was now a Dar-ul-Islam, or a land of Islam; but the Viceroy may have won his fatwa by methods similar to those used by Henry VIII in persuading his parliaments to change their mind.

ment might belittle them as lawyers on the make or Brahmins up to their tricks; it might define them as microscopic minorities or impecunious editors. But there was no way of bringing the weight of the autocracy upon men whose opposition was so ambiguous. Theirs were not movements which could be dealt with by a whiff of grapeshot; lawyers from the high court could hardly be ridden down or Surendranath Banerjea be blown from a gun. These men spoke highly of British justice. They asked God to bless the British Queen. They had friends inside the British parliament. But they spoke of the 'Un-Britishness of British Rule in India'.

This new technique of working through lawful associations was a vital tactic for the western educated as they moved into proto-politics. But they had no monopoly of it. As the competition grew sharper between castes and communities, many of these groups in hope of self-betterment took to this new technique as well. Caste associations could grow and wither as quickly as mushrooms, but their proliferation at this time indicates the passion for organisations which was beginning to sweep over parts of India. But associations founded on the solidarity of caste or community were not in themselves alone the stuff out of which political groupings could as yet be made. Their organising principles might be more effective than those they replaced, but they were equally limited in their appeal. Membership of these bodies was restricted to members of one caste or one community. Their sole reason for existence was to better the lot of these members. They could speak for no wider interests. Explicitly political action was limited to the associations of educated men. Since they were open groups, their members might belong to all castes and communities; since they commented on matters of concern to all, they claimed to stand for interests wider than those of their members. But although they worked at higher levels than the associations grounded on special interests, they were not cut off from them. An educated man continued to belong to a caste and a community, and hence he tended to belong to organisations of both kinds, one based on common kinship and religious persuasion and one based on common education and political persuasion. Behind the explicitly political and secular bodies concerned with general issues stood a parallel series of bodies limited to much narrower themes. What connected them was that each type of association penetrated the membership of the other. But as the only men who could play the two roles, the educated were the link between them.

From these simple preliminaries it is now possible to attack the general problem of this work, how modern politics in India began. All the arguments converge. Education was one of the chief determinants of these politics, and their genesis is clearly linked with those Indians who had been schooled by western methods.[1] Consequently the first step in the inquiry must be to discover from what parts of this competitive and unevenly-developed India these men had emerged.

Both higher and lower education of the western sort were distributed with great unevenness between the provinces of British India, and the history of public instruction makes clear why this was so. In 1835 the pressures of Evangelicals and Utilitarians had enabled Bentinck and Macaulay to win a clear victory for western education over the 'Orientalists' who would have preferred a much less sharp breach with the old syllabus. In 1854 Wood, President of the Board of Control, modified this policy by laying down that primary education in the vernaculars should be encouraged, but he also decided that the system of higher education in English should be crowned by the establishment of three universities. But Wood's plans for improving primary schooling came to little when funds ran low,[2] and India

[1] The historiographical dispute, whether the nationalist movement came from the western educated or from an indigenous tradition of revolt, misses the point. Both operated at the same time. Neither held to a constant position. Each had its defectors. Circumstances alter cases.

[2] On the history of Indian education, see H. Sharp and J. A. Richey, *Selections from Educational Records*, 2 parts (Calcutta, 1920–2); P. N. Kirpal (ed.), *Educational Reports, 1859–71*. Selections from Educational Records of the Government of India, I (Delhi, 1960); J. P. Naik, *Development of University Education, 1860–87*. Selections from Educational Records of the Government of India, II (Delhi, 1963); T. B. Macaulay, Minute on Education (1835), reprinted in G. M. Young (ed.), *Macaulay, Prose and Poetry* (London, 1952), pp. 719–30; C. E. Trevelyan, *On the Education of the People of India* (London, 1838); T. G. P. Spear, 'Bentinck and Education', *Cambridge Historical Journal*, VI, no. 1 (1938), 78–101; Syed Mahmood, *A History of English Education in India, (1781–1893)*, (Aligarh, 1895); Syed Nurullah and J. P. Naik, *History of Education in India during the British Period* (Bombay, 1943); B. T. McCully, *English Education and the*

was left with a top-heavy educational system. Moreover, administrative necessities were more potent than pedagogic theories in shaping the structure of the system. In principle there might be something to be said for educating mute, inglorious Miltons in the villages; in practice the pressing need was for clerks and public servants who could be hired at rates which the government could afford. Consequently, the decision to back higher education through the medium of English brought other changes in its train: English was made the language of administration, and increasingly the new education became the pass to employment in the public services.

But the impulse behind these educational changes did not flow from the calculations of the British alone. As early as 1817 the Hindus of Calcutta were so enthusiastic for the new learning that they founded Hindu College at their own expense. In 1823 when the Company opened a college to teach traditional studies, some Bengalis urged that European science and the English language should be taught there.[1] By now there was undoubtedly a strong demand for English education. Bishop Heber noticed it,[2] and in 1830 it was reported that the past decade had seen English 'cultivated with such wonderful success, that it would be easy at the present moment to point out between one and two hundred young native gentlemen in Calcutta to whom English is quite as familiar as their own tongue'.[3] Bengalis outside Calcutta also came to realise the utility of the new education. Lal Behari Dey was brought from Burdwan to Alexander Duff's school at Calcutta because his father could see that 'for secular purposes, for gaining a decent livelihood, a knowledge of the English language was absolutely necessary'.[4]

Origins of Indian Nationalism (New York, 1940); R. J. Moore, *Sir Charles Wood's Indian Policy 1853–66* (Manchester, 1966), pp. 108–23; E. Stokes, *The English Utilitarians and India* (Oxford, 1959), pp. 45, 57, 196.
[1] The Company refused Rammohan Roy's request that English be taught at Sanskrit College, but three years later had to accede to the popular demand.
[2] The bishop prophesied that this 'desire to learn and speak English... might... in fifty years time, make our language what the *Oordoo*, or *court* and *camp* language of the country (the Hindoostanee,) is at present'. R. Heber, *Narrative of a Journey through the Upper Provinces of India, from Calcutta to Bombay, 1824–1825...* (London, 1828), II, 307.
[3] *Samachar Darpan*, 27 February 1830, quoted in McCully, *English Education*, p. 60.
[4] L. B. Day, *Recollections of Alexander Duff...and of the Mission College which he founded in Calcutta* (London, 1879), p. 40.

In Bombay a similar enthusiasm brought the Elphinstone Institution into being in 1834.

When after 1835, the government at last began to set up western-style schools and colleges of its own, it could not cope with the demand. So in 1854 the role of private enterprise was recognised by Wood's grants-in-aid system, and this led to a remarkable expansion of privately-run schools staffed by Indians. In 1855 there were only forty-seven English schools in Bengal, but during the first eighteen months of the new system, seventy-nine English schools applied for grants.[1] By 1856 Duff commented not only on the schools that he and his fellow missionaries were running, but on 'several efficient seminaries established, and vigorously supported, by natives themselves, which supply a really superior English and vernacular education to thousands'.[2] Indians were showing self-help at the higher levels as well. Of the fourteen colleges affiliated to the new University at Calcutta in 1857, six were privately controlled. In these ways the needs of the British fell in with a reciprocal movement within Indian society. Tables 1 and 2 below set out the educational results of government encouragement combined

TABLE 1. *Number of educated (university entrance and higher examinations) by province, 1864–85*

	Entrance		First Arts		B.A.		M.A.	
	Passed	Failed	Passed	Failed	Passed	Failed	Passed	Failed
Bengal	16,639	21,151	5,252	8,027	2,153	2,776	491	330
Bombay	7,196	15,209	1,568	2,803	933	1,030	79	59
Madras	18,390	36,356	4,480	6,850	1,633	1,648	49	34
N.W.P. and Oudh	3,200	3,210	749	739	272	270	57	30
Punjab	1,944	2,614	341	375	107	129	32	11
C.P.	608	620	128	108	10	—	—	—
Assam	274	349	—	—	—	—	—	—
Total	48,251	79,509	12,518	18,902	5,108	5,853	708	464

Source: Tabulated from *Report of the Public Services Commission, 1886–87* (Calcutta, 1888) [henceforth *PSC*], appendix M, statement III and IV, pp. 81–2.

Calcutta, University Commission, 1917–19. Report. Vol. I, part I, *Analysis of Present Conditions* (Calcutta, 1919) [henceforth *Calcutta Commission*
[1] *Report*, I], 42.
[2] Quoted in McCully, *English Education*, p. 93.

with Indian enterprise: a steady expansion in the size of the western-educated class.

TABLE 2. *The growth of education in Arts colleges in British India, 1870–91*

	1870–1		1881–2		1886–7		1891–2	
	Colleges	Pupils	Colleges	Pupils	Colleges	Pupils	Colleges	Pupils
Bengal	16	1,374	21	2,738	27	3,215	34	5,225
Bombay	5	297	6	475	9	955	9	1,332
Madras	11	418	24	1,669	31	2,979	35	3,818
N.W.P. & O.	8	165*	6	349	12	478	12	1,311
Punjab	2	102	1	103	3	319	6	462
C.P.	—	—	1	65	3	100	3	232

Source: *Report of the Indian Education Commission...1882* (Calcutta, 1883) [henceforth *EC*], p. 274; A. M. Nash, *Progress of Education in India 1887–88 to 1891–92. Second Quinquennial Review* (Calcutta, 1893), p. 59.
* This excludes the pupils of attached collegiate schools.

Clearly the growth of the educated class was concentrated in the three coastal Presidencies where the impacts of British rule had worked much longer and gone much deeper than in those up-country provinces which had been organised during the nineteenth century. Muir College which in 1872 had been founded in Allahabad, and Canning College at Lucknow, were already creating a reasonable number of graduates, but many of these were Bengalis who had moved up to the North-western Provinces and Oudh.[1] Between the Presidencies themselves there were important variations. Madras had produced the largest number of candidates for university entrance, which reflects the greater concern for secondary education in the south. But at all levels of undergraduate and graduate performance, Bengal was as yet ahead either of Madras or of Bombay, although by the eighteen-seventies its lead was being whittled down. But the tables also illustrate two features that were common to university education in all the provinces of British India: the failure rate was high, and the amount of professional training was low.

[1] Bengalis were in the main 'a domestic, stay-at-home people'; but in 1881 there were just under 77,000 men from Bengal in the North-western Provinces, who in part were Biharis, in part sepoys in native regiments, but in part Bengali clerks, professional men, and government servants. *1881 Census, Bengal*, I, 151–2.

This general picture of expansion in higher education was qualified by the relatively stagnant condition of primary education. The aims of Wood's Despatch could only have succeeded if finances were buoyant, and they were not. In government's general financial straits, the best way of implementing the policy of 1854 was to build up the lower by depriving the higher; so in 1870 London instructed Calcutta that the bulk of public funds should go into 'elementary education for the mass of the people'.[1] More than a decade later the question was again raised by the Indian Education Commission of 1882. It rehearsed the arguments in favour of strengthening the educational base; and observed once again that if more was to be spent upon the schoolchild, less could be spent on the student. In line with nineteenth-century orthodoxy it went on to argue the merits of private enterprise in public education, recommending that government aid to higher education should be cut down, and private enterprise encouraged to take its place.[2] Calcutta accepted these recommendations and in 1888 the new dogma was proclaimed, that the government 'pioneers the way, but having shown the way, it recognises no responsibility to do for the people what it can do for itself'. Only a few government schools would be kept as models; for the rest, all should depend upon 'the vitality of local effort'.[3] As might have been expected, this decision was badly received by Indians who suspected that behind the reference to financial stringency lay the more sinister conclusion that the only good Indian was an uneducated one.[4]

[1] B. B. Misra, *The Indian Middle Classes* (London, 1961), p. 282. But Mayo's Director of Public Instruction was not happy about these proposed reductions of expenditure on education. Sir A. Grant, 'Some Observations on Education Administration in India', 16 November 1868. Mayo Papers, Add. 7490 (12).

[2] *EC*, pp. 455–69.

[3] Resolution of the Government of India on State-aided Education (18 June 1888), Home Department Proceedings (Education), *P.P.* 1888, LXXVII, 375–86.

[4] 'The Govt. of India has just published a Resolution which may be considered the death knell of higher education in the country. It distinctly instructs all administrations to retire gradually from higher education as private enterprise makes head...This is the *first* effect of the Indian National Congress. Educated natives must be less in India. So say the Govt. It is they who agitate. Let us diminish their number. As well may they try to stem the Atlantic. They cannot put back the hand of the dial. In fact the result will be that it will give natives greater stimulus to promote higher education. It will teach them greater self-reliance,' Wacha to Naoroji, 17 July 1888. NP.

Political India

If the aim of the policy was to discourage the growth of higher education, it was a flat failure; but if government meant what it said about wanting to stimulate private Indian enterprise, the policy was successful beyond all expectations. The singular result of the decisions of 1888 was that the government recommended changes that had already taken place, while gratuitously abandoning powers it still enjoyed. In the 1870s private enterprise was already sustaining much of the growth of education in Bengal. In the ten years after 1874 the number of college students in Bengal increased threefold; most of this increase happened in Calcutta, and almost all of it in privately-run colleges, whose small fees and large numbers enabled them to flourish without government grants.[1] In high and middle schools private enterprise had even greater success.[2] By 1882 there were seventeen times as many schools, and seven times as many pupils, in Bengal as there had been in 1871. Almost all this growth was in the private sector.[3] It was in Bengal that private enterprise had gone farthest, but private initiative was working to expand the system of higher education both in Madras and in western India.[4]

The government's new policy dramatically stimulated Indian enterprise, as table 3 overleaf shows. By the time that Dufferin left India in 1888, the Indian eagerness for western schooling had made the expansion of the educational system self-generating, so that it could grow with or without government favour. Between 1881–2 and 1901–2, there was a threefold increase in the

[1] In 1874 there were 633 Arts students in Calcutta colleges; in 1883, 1,649; the corresponding increase in the mofussil colleges was from 450 in 1874 to 1,250 in 1883. *RDPI (Bengal) 1882–3*, p. 12.
[2] In 1883 government high schools in Calcutta had 1,750 pupils; but Calcutta's twenty-one unaided schools had 8,088 pupils. The Metropolitan Institution, with 1,000 pupils, was the largest in Bengal. *RDPI (Bengal) 1883–4*, p. 48.
[3] *Report by the Bengal Provincial Committee...* Education Commission. (Calcutta, 1884) [henceforth, *EC (Bengal)*], pp. 67–8.
[4] See *Progress of Education in India 1887–88 to 1891–92*, pp. 79, 132–5. By 1885 over one-third of the total expansion of education in Bombay Presidency was in private hands. (*RDPI (Bombay) 1884–5*, p. 21.) There were eleven unaided secondary schools in Bombay city, while the Deccan Education Society maintained schools in Poona, Satara, and Dharwar. The school at Poona was a financial success, having 986 pupils by 1885. In the same year the Society launched Fergusson College, a striking example of the progress being made by private Indian enterprise. (*RDPI (Bombay) 1885–6*, subsidiary form no. 2, pp. lxxii–lxxxix.)

21

TABLE 3. *Growth of education, public and private, in British India, 1881–1901*

	1881–2				1901–2			
	Public	Private aided	Private unaided	Total	Public	Private aided	Private unaided	Total
English Arts colleges	31	21	11	*63*	32	55	53	*140*
Pupils	2,707	2,019	716	*5,442*	4,417	6,925	5,806	*17,148*
English secondary schools	562	1,080	491	*2,133*	696	1,573	828	*3,097*
Pupils	44,060	72,077	33,096	*149,233*	103,077	202,810	116,300	*422,187*

Source: A. Croft, *Review of Education in India in 1886, with special reference to the Report of the Education Commission* (Calcutta, 1888), pp. 32, 46. R. Nathan, *Progress of Education in India 1897–98 to 1901–02. Fourth Quinquennial Review* (Calcutta, 1904), II, 58, 62, 68, 73.

numbers of pupils being taught in English at high schools and colleges; but in both categories the highest rate of expansion was in the 'Private unaided' section. In the days when higher education was dependent on public funds, it had naturally expanded most where it had started first—in the three Presidencies. With the coming of a greater reliance on private enterprise, one of the effects was to lengthen their lead. In parts of Bengal, Bombay and Madras there was more reason to be eager for western education than elsewhere in India. Parents were more likely to pay for it. There were more graduates able to impart it. Among the great unevennesses in Indian development, the distribution of western education was among the most conspicuous, and the balance was tilted overwhelmingly in favour of the Presidencies.[1]

❧

Although British rule sharpened the competitive conditions in which they grew, the nationalist movements in India were not the creation of imperialism. Their development was so leisurely that the search for their genesis might be pushed back to the

[1] Inside the Presidencies themselves, the chances of educational expansion through private agency worked in favour of those districts which were already educationally advanced. In Bombay it was 'comparatively easy to enlist private enterprise in the districts of Poona, Thana and the advanced Collectorates of the Central Division'. Elsewhere it was not so easy; *RDPI (Bombay) 1884–5*, p. 22. The growth of the Universities at Calcutta, Bombay and Madras is illustrated by the tables in appendix I, below, pp. 355–6.

early decades of the nineteenth century. But the essence of historical analysis lies in explaining the timing of events. During the 1870s and 1880s came the beginnings of a mutation in Indian politics which was to convert many of the western-educated from collaborators into critics of the regime. This change was not dramatic or indeed irreversible. In the 1870s some Indians were experimenting with new methods of public expression which soon incurred the candid dislike of government; after 1880 they were groping for some form of all-India organisation; and towards the end of the decade, the nature and the implications of their demands were edging some of them into a certain detachment from British purposes. This slow, this reluctant, this portentous recognition of a division of interest first became apparent during the viceroyalties of Lytton, Ripon and Dufferin. What was happening to bring about so important a change at this time? Now some of the precise questions begin to pose themselves behind the generalities: who were these modernising men? From which parts of India did they come? What were their relations with other groups in their society? What impelled them to form their associations, and from there to work towards a unified political demand?

The highly uneven nature of development in India has been reflected in the highly uneven speeds of political mobilisation; indeed, the nationalisms of India might be defined as a process by which different parts of the country have been drawn into politics at different times and for different reasons. By concentrating upon those men who entered the politics of associations and then used them to move up to an all-India level, the method of conducting the inquiry then becomes plain. These men were the western-educated, and the western-educated were concentrated in the Presidencies. Their associations were based upon, or were derived from, the Presidencies. The impulses towards an all-India movement sprang from the Presidencies. Therefore it is with Bengal, Bombay and Madras that the discussion will be especially concerned—not because they were the only centres of Indian political organisation, but because they were the centres of Indian political organisation of a non-traditional type.

But since the Presidencies themselves were no more than administrative expressions, combinations of regions in every stage of development, the inquiry must be concentrated upon those sections of the Presidencies where education had gone furthest and associations had been most effective—that is to say, in the cities of Calcutta, Bombay, Poona and Madras, and in the regions of Bengal Proper, Maharashtra and Tamilnad.[1] Here the new educated classes must be related to the religious, the caste, the linguistic and the economic situations in which they lived. Their multifarious systems of local politics must be analysed from the point when they turned to the technique of association until they achieved a nominal all-India unity. But by examining the competitive circumstances in which they worked, the scope of the inquiry will extend beyond the Presidencies themselves and into the study of the only other all-India movement which was conceivable at this time, a movement which was to emerge as the Muslim breakaway.

[1] Since this book studies political associations in the places where their activity was sustained during this period, it will have much to say about local politics in Bengal and Bombay, where associations were effective, and little to say about local politics in Madras, where they were less so. But the role of Madras, together with the antecedents of its politics in the later nineteenth century, will be discussed in the next volume of this history.

2

The Political Arithmetic of the Presidencies

By the later nineteenth century the Indian Empire covered a sub-continent of one and a half million square miles, inhabited in 1881 by some 256 million people. More than one-third of India was composed of native states, with a population of fifty-six millions. In the remainder, the British directly ruled almost two hundred million subjects. British India consisted of the three old Presidencies of Madras, Bengal, and Bombay, and the more recently organised administrations of the North-western Provinces and Oudh, the Punjab, the Central Provinces, Assam and Burma.[1] Extending from Peshawar to Cape Comorin, the imperial sway covered some of the oldest civilisations of the world. It extended over deserts, vast regions of forest, and high mountains; and its peoples were in every stage of development from aborigines to sophisticated city dwellers. British dominion in India, which it has suited administrator and historian alike to regard as an entity, consisted in fact of different peoples inhabiting different regions, which had been pieced together at different times for different reasons.

All periods are periods of change, even in India. But colonial rule may well have accelerated the propensities towards change which had been forming in seventeenth- and eighteenth-century India. The impact of western government disturbed, and in some places upset, the traditional rankings of hierarchy and dominance in local society, thus increasing competitiveness between men of different communities and castes. Secondly, it produced a new unevenness of development between

---

[1] Assam was set up as a separate chief commissionership in 1874; Oudh was incorporated in the North-western Provinces in 1877. In addition there were three minor local administrations, Ajmer, Berar and Coorg. British Baluchistan was formed into a chief commissionership in 1887.

different regions, tilting the balance this time in favour of the three maritime provinces where British influence had first been felt and where its effects were most intensive. Through Bengal, Bombay and Madras British power had flowed across India, thus reversing the historic wave of invasions across the northern frontiers. Economically, they were the most highly developed parts of British India; but they were not uniformly developed within their boundaries. Because the critics of the Raj were most numerous and most vocal here, the anatomy of each Presidency must be dissected. But before looking at the factors of community, caste, language and economy in these regions, it is necessary to place these factors in their all-India setting.

In some parts of India the deepest social disunities came from

TABLE 4. *Distribution of religions in India, 1881*

	Hindus	Muslims	Sikhs	Parsis	Christians
Bengal					
Total	45,452,806	21,704,724	549	156	128,135
Per cent	65·4	31·2	—	—	0·18
Bombay					
Total	12,308,582	3,021,131	127,100	72,065	138,317
Per cent	74·8	18·4	0·75	0·4	0·8
Madras					
Total	28,497,678	1,933,561	—	143	711,080
Per cent	91·4	6·2	—	—	2·3
North-western Provinces and Oudh					
Total	38,053,394	5,922,886	3,644	114	47,664
Per cent	86·3	13·4	—	—	0·11
Punjab					
Total	7,130,528	10,525,150	1,121,004	462	33,420
Per cent	40·7	51·4	7·6	—	0·15
Central Provinces					
Total	7,317,830	275,773	97	399	11,949
Per cent	75·4	2·5	—	—	0·11
Assam					
Total	3,062,148	1,317,022	14	—	7,093
Per cent	62·7	27·0	—	—	0·15
All India (including native states)					
Total	187,937,450	50,121,585	1,853,426	85,397	1,862,634
Per cent	74·0	19·7	0·73	0·03	0·73

Source: *1881 Census, India*, I, 24–48; II, 10–15, 28–9.

religious rivalry. In each of the seven main provinces, the largest religious group was either Hindu or Muslim; among the minorities, the Sikhs were important in the Punjab and the Parsis in Bombay. The distribution of the Indian population by religion is given in table 4. In British India as a whole, one person out of five was a Muslim, and almost half of this community of more than forty millions lived in Bengal, a quarter in the Punjab. They were the majority community in Bengal Proper (excluding Bihar), in the Punjab, and in the Sind districts of Bombay; except in Sind, the Muslim majorities were not large. In Bombay, Assam and the North-western Provinces and Oudh the Hindus had a clear preponderance of numbers; their majorities in Madras and the Central Provinces were overwhelming.

Mere counting of heads, however, does not exhaust the complexity of the relationship between the two communities. Admittedly, differences of principle greatly separated most Hindus from most Muslims. Hindus believed in many gods and worshipped many images, while Muslims were monotheistic and rejected idols; Hindus were ranked in a hierarchy of castes, Muslims professed the equality of all true believers; the higher Hindu castes revered the cow, which Muslims killed and ate.[1] Hinduism was a religion specific to India, Indian Islam was but one sector of an œcumenical faith. From time to time and from place to place these differences sharply divided members of the two communities, but neither bloc was held together by a strong sense of solidarity. Indeed Hinduism and Indian Islam were so heterogeneous that it might seem that instead of discussing nineteenth-century India as the home of two nations, it would be more accurate to say that it was the home of none. Admittedly each of them was vaguely unified by the common ritual practices which were binding on all its members, and by the beliefs common to its scholars. In the twentieth century, these unifying forces produced political solidarities of the greatest importance, but there was little sign of this during the last quarter of the nineteenth century. During those years, the great religious communities were so internally divided, and their levels in the social hierarchy

---

[1] Naturally, in so complex a society, there are exceptions to these general statements. Some Hindus were monotheists. Many Muslims were ranked in castes.

so uneven in the country as a whole that religious rivalry cannot be seen either as a necessary or a sufficient factor in generating political activity in India.

Some three-quarters of India's population were Hindu—a term loose enough to include peoples of palpably different ethnical origin, separated from each other by language, customs, and religious rites. Upon all Hindus, however, caste and kinship imposed common systems of social discipline.[1] While they had considerable latitude in their beliefs, the social behaviour of Hindus was strictly regulated. The family,[2] not the individual, was the basis of Hindu society,[3] and caste regulated relations between families.[4] It laid down a ritually prescribed scheme of social status for the four classical orders, or varnas, into which society was ideally divided: at the top were the Brahmins, the priests and scholars; next came the Kshattriyas, the warriors; then the Vaisyas, the traders; and at the bottom the Sudras, the menials of Hindu society.[5] Below the caste system were the untouchables. In practice, however, this division counted for little. The groups that mattered were not the four varnas, but sub-castes, groups of families limited by occupation and language.[6] They were very numerous. In each main linguistic region there were about two hundred major, and about two thousand minor, caste groupings.[7] These sub-castes were usually endogamous, their membership was hereditary and they controlled their own affairs. A Hindu was born into his caste and could not change it through any action of his own. Its rules prescribed his social conduct in minute detail: they defined with whom he

[1] For a survey of the literature on caste, see 'Caste. A Trend Report and Bibliography', *Current Sociology*, VIII, no. 3 (1959), 135–83.
[2] The joint family, combining in one household all living members of the same direct line, was still the rule among the higher castes.
[3] L. Dumont, 'The Functional Equivalents of the Individual in Caste Society', *Contributions to India Sociology*, VIII (October 1965), 85–99.
[4] The village community, once an important instrument for regulation, no longer counted for much. See B. H. Baden-Powell, *The Indian Village Community* (reprint of London 1896 edition, New Haven, 1957), and H. S. Maine, *Village Communities in the East and West* (3rd edition, London, 1876), pp. 40, 104.
[5] Each varna includes a number of castes.
[6] On the connection between local systems of kinship and the local units of caste, see I. Karve, *Kinship Organisation in India* (2nd edition, Bombay, 1965), pp. 1–27.
[7] G. S. Ghurye, *Caste, Class and Occupation* (4th edition, Bombay, 1961), pp. 26–7.

might eat and have social intercourse, when he must marry and whom he might marry; they laid down the ritual of worship, they prohibited certain occupations and enjoined others. Failure to observe the rules of caste invited retribution in the next incarnation. It might also compel a man to do penance in the present. Where the breach was serious, it could lead to the outcasting of a member by the caste council.

The caste system was hierarchical but ambiguously so. In principle, the ritual order of status between castes was immutable, with the Brahmins enjoying a precedence over all others. In practice it was less rigid. Since the traditional fourfold division of the caste system was no more than an ideal construct, the hierarchies which it enjoined were no more than pious aspirations. Even among the higher castes, where ranking was fairly clear, a uniform basis of classification was difficult to establish.[1] Lower down the scale, precise ranking was impossible, since under the general designation of Sudras came a host of sub-castes of controversial rank. With these ambiguities of status, the ordering between castes was open to pressure, to argument and to change. But the ambiguities went further than this. Social ranking based on ritual had a necessary bearing upon a man's status, but often this status was confined to ritual occasions. By its side stood a leadership of a more worldly sort. Everywhere the ritual role of the Brahmins gave them the highest position in the orthodox caste hierarchy, but it did not necessarily give them social dominance. In many parts of India, there was a marked divergence between the ranking based upon ritual, and the dominance based upon local position. This might be determined by landownership, by holding posts in the administration, or by urban sources of income.[2] Such divergences between ritual ranking and material dominance have often led to efforts to bring them together. As a caste has prospered, so it has tried to raise its ritual status by claiming to belong to a higher varna than the one to which it was traditionally assigned; and by copying the customs generally held to be appropriate to the

[1] See M. Marriott, *Caste Ranking and Community Structure in Five Regions of India and Pakistan* (2nd reprint edition, Poona, 1965).

[2] In some regions, Brahmins were dominant in this sense; in others, non-Brahmins held this position—for example the Patidars and Rajputs in parts of Gujarat, and the Nayars in Malabar. See M. N. Srinivas, *Social Change in Modern India* (Berkeley and Los Angeles, 1966), pp. 10–14, 151–2; L. Dumont, *Homo Hierarchicus* (Paris, 1967), pp. 140–1, 204–8.

superior castes, it has advertised and consolidated its claim.[1] Among intermediate and lower castes there was much competitive reshuffling of this sort.

So pervasive a system as caste had profound implications for the making of Indian politics. It split Hindu society into innumerable units. It did little to bind together those who considered themselves members of the same varna. Even in regions with the same language and the same networks of kinship, wide differences in the standing and customs often separated Brahmins of one caste division from Brahmins of another. Between Brahmins of one region and Brahmins of another, these differences were likely to be wider still.[2] Among those who styled themselves Kshattriyas, Vaisyas and Sudras there were the same fragmentations.[3] In the race of competing aspirations which has characterised modern India, caste tended to sharpen rivalries between Hindus by marshalling the competitors into teams. Moreover, it cramped the development of individual mobility and took the place of the class solidarity of the west. When the Hindu climbed the social ladder, he carried with him much of his kin.[4] Yet at another level it was above all the common acceptance of caste which distinguished Hindus from men of other religions.

Another source of profound division within the sub-continent lay in its linguistic differences. Its peoples spoke a mass of mutually incomprehensible tongues. By the later nineteenth century some 179 separate languages and 544 dialects had been identified, which were in turn grouped into fifteen major literary languages belonging to five or six distinct families, with differences in structure, vocabulary, alphabet and script.[5] Hindustani

---

[1] For discussions of this process, see H. H. Risley, *The Tribes and Castes of Bengal. Ethnographic Glossary* (Calcutta, 1892), I, lxxxviii; II, 275, 280; I. Karve, *Hindu Society—An Interpretation* (Poona, 1961), pp. 45–9, 111–15; M. N. Srinivas, *Caste in Modern India and Other Essays* (Bombay, 1962), and Srinivas, *Social Change in Modern India*, pp. 1–45, 89–117.

[2] A Brahmin could not choose his spouse from all the Brahmin girls of India; as a rule she had to belong to his own endogamous group.

[3] There were exceptions, such as the Maratha-Kunbi cluster in western India.

[4] By changing his occupation, the Hindu did not change his caste. See N. K. Bose, *Modern Bengal* (Calcutta, 1959), p. 30.

[5] On the languages of India, see G. A. Grierson, *Linguistic Survey of India* (Calcutta, 1903–28); G. A. Greirson, *The Languages of India* (Calcutta, 1903), also reprinted in *General Report of the Census of India, 1901* (London, 1904), pp. 247–348; S. K. Chatterji, *Languages and Literatures of Modern*

was the main language of north India, serving as a *lingua franca* throughout the mid-Gangetic plain. But even here its unity was balanced by its divisions. In the form of Urdu, with its large number of Persian and Arabic words, the language had followed the expansion of the Mughal empire. In the form of Hindi, these Arabic and Persian borrowings were replaced by words derived from Sanskrit. Urdu was written in the Persian script, Hindi in Devanagari. Thus Hindustani was split into branches with separate scripts and vocabularies, and men spoke and wrote one or other of these variants according to their different religious and regional backgrounds. The languages of eastern and western India were allied at the level of technical linguistics to the languages of Hindustan but differed substantially from them. In the south, where the Madras Presidency lay, the languages belonged to a totally different family from the languages of north, east and west alike.

Amid this fragmentation, British dominion imposed upon the sub-continent a new official language, spoken by increasingly large numbers of Indians. English gave them a means of communication with their rulers, and with each other; but it also helped to widen the gulf between them and the mass of their countrymen. By bringing the Presidencies far in advance of Aryavarta, or north India, British rule increased the prestige of the languages of its most active collaborators in these regions. Bengali, Marathi and Tamil had followed the flag; and all three of them experienced renaissances during the nineteenth century.[1] Their rise in status did much to consolidate a sense of regional patriotism among their speakers. Renewed pride in these tongues was a sure sign of political awakening.

The politicising role of language was felt not only by those who benefited from linguistic expansion but by those who were threatened by it. The Bengalis, the Marathas and the Tamils were surrounded by submerged linguistic groups whose advancement and distinctive claims were neglected. A linguistic

India (Calcutta, 1963), a more recent survey which contains a useful bibliography; and R. Gopal, *Linguistic Affairs of India* (London, 1966).

[1] See D. C. Sen, *History of Bengali Language and Literature* (2nd edition, Calcutta, 1954), chapter VII; S. Sen, *History of Bengali Literature* (New Delhi, 1960), pp. 178–319; J. C. Ghosh, *Bengali Literature* (London, 1948), chapters IV and V; G. C. Bhate, *History of Modern Marathi Literature, 1800–1938* (Mahad, 1939); and C. and H. Jesudasan, *A History of Tamil Literature* (Calcutta, 1961).

revival of these depressed groups could provide both a symbol and a point of union for movements designed to challenge the pre-eminence of their neighbours.[1]

During the nineteenth century the economy of India, like that of medieval Europe, was composed of regions each with its own systems of growing and getting, without unified markets or the economic uniformities which industry and urbanisation can bring. The result was vast discrepancy between the economic sophistications of the Presidency capitals and the primitive agrarianism of much of the interior; Bengal included the economic extremes of Clive Street and the jungles of the Santal country. Unevenness of development had always been a feature of Indian economic life, but just as colonial rule had helped to upset traditional rankings in Indian society, so too it reshaped parts of its economic geography, and altered the inequality. From the innovations brought by oceanic trade it was Calcutta, and much later Bombay, which chiefly benefited. In these cities the docks, the harbour facilities, the banks and European Agencies were concentrated. Upon them converged the main railway lines and the road systems. In their hinterlands were grown most of the cash crops, and in their neighbourhoods jute and cotton mills gave India its first experience of modern industry. At the outset of British rule Madras city might have seemed equally likely to grow into a thriving commercial and industrial entrepôt, but by the later nineteenth century both Madras and its hinterland had lagged far behind the headlong growth of Calcutta and Bombay.

Despite the large hopes of some policy-makers in the early nineteenth century, British rule had signally failed to revitalise the Indian economies.[2] Only massive improvements in agriculture, which supported nine-tenths of its population, could have done so. But there had been no agrarian revolution. Indeed the later nineteenth century was a gloomy time of rising

---

[1] The Assamese, the Oriyas, and the Biharis eventually expressed their resentment against the Bengalis by urging the claims of their own languages; in Andhra the Telegus followed the same tactic against the claims of the Tamils; the intrusions of Marathi were denounced by Hindi-speakers in the Central Provinces and the Kanarese-speakers in the south of Bombay Presidency.

[2] See M. D. Morris and B. Stein, 'The Economic History of India: a Bibliographic Essay', *The Journal of Economic History*, XXI, no. 2 (June 1961), 179–207.

population, increased landless labour, subdivision of holdings, heavier indebtedness of the peasant and a disastrous series of famines.[1] Cultivation remained 'in the hands of small men, and the capital required for the cultivation of the soil is supplied in small sums by small capitalists to men of small commercial intelligence'.[2] In the infinite variety of tenures and modes of cultivation, the Indian peasant remained an illiterate man, short of capital, of fertiliser and of healthy livestock, tilling his few acres with implements unimproved since ancient times. Land revenue continued to be the backbone of government finance,[3] and the systems of collecting it remained as varied as the systems of tenures the British had inherited; they were no more than the latest touches added to the palimpsest.[4]

Yet the British were interested in developing their Empire, and here and there they did inject some dynamism into the Indian economies. British investment provided the funds for developing communications;[5] and these encouraged the growth of India's cash crops—jute in Bengal, cotton in western India, indigo in Bihar, tea in Assam; but these innovations were on far too small a scale to revolutionise the agrarian system as a whole. Moreover, the traditional industries of India did not survive the fierce blast of English competition, and the new industries failed to employ as many as were being displaced by the decline of the old.[6] Admittedly India's share of international trade was greatly expanding, but it was trade on a new pattern. Imports

---

[1] D. and A. Thorner, *Land and Labour in India* (London, 1962), pp. 70–81; and B. M. Bhatia, *Famines in India: a study in some aspects of the economic history of India, 1860–1945* (London, 1963) pp. 1–308.

[2] *Imperial Gazetteer of India* (new edition, Oxford, 1907–9), III, 90.

[3] In 1856 more than half of the public income of India came from land revenue; by 1886 about a third.

[4] See B. H. Baden-Powell, *The Land-systems of British India* (Oxford, 1892), 3 vols.

[5] By 1885, more than 12,000 miles of railway were open, and more than £153 million had been invested in them. The first line was opened in 1853; by 1871 Bombay was directly linked with Calcutta and Madras. W. W. Hunter, *The Imperial Gazetteer of India* (2nd edition, London, 1885–7) [henceforth *HIG*], VI, 545–50. Also see W. J. Macpherson, 'Investment in Indian Railways 1845–75', *Economic History Review*, 2nd series, VIII, no. 2 (1955), 177–86; and D. Thorner, *Investment in Empire* (Philadelphia, 1950), pp. 168–82.

[6] D. R. Gadgil, *The Industrial Evolution of India in Recent Times* (4th edition, Calcutta, 1942), pp. 1–193; D. H. Buchanan, *The Development of Capitalistic Enterprise in India* (New York, 1934); *Indian Industrial Commission 1916–18. Report* (Calcutta, 1918).

3   SEO

were mainly manufactures from Europe, and exports were raw materials, not the fabled silks and calicoes, sugar and spices which once had made their way to the marts of the world. India exported more than it imported and most of its foreign trade was controlled by Europeans.[1] Money for investment remained in short supply, and Indian wealth continued to seek the traditional security of precious metals, land and money-lending rather than the uncertainties of industry and commerce. These changes were not sufficient to give India social classes based on economic categories. Small comprador groups in the Presidency capitals did emerge, but they failed to forge strong links throughout the sub-continent.[2] Modern Indian capitalists did not spring ready-made from Britannia's helmet. For the most part Indian traders remained as they had always been, men following their hereditary vocations in the traditional way, both unwilling and unable to break down those barriers inside their society which inhibited more active development.

[1] Between 1840 and 1886 Indian foreign seaborne trade grew more than eight times, from £20 million to £163 million per annum. The growth is set out in the table:

Average foreign trade of India per quinquennium, 1840–89
(in lakhs of rupees)

Periods	Imports	Exports	Periods	Imports	Exports
1840–4	10,45	14,25	1865–9	49,31	57,66
1845–9	12,21	16,99	1870–4	41,30	57,84
1850–4	15,85	20,02	1875–9	48,22	63,13
1855–9	26,85	25,85	1880–4	61,81	80,41
1860–4	41,06	43,17	1885–9	75,13	90,28

Source: *The Imperial Gazetteer of India*, III, 268.

Cotton manufactures dominated imports—they were more than a third of the total imports over the whole period. Raw cotton took an increasingly large share of exports in the second half of the century; foodgrains, oil-seeds, jute, indigo, hides and tea were the other staples. See S. B. Saul, *Studies in British Overseas Trade, 1870–1914* (Liverpool, 1960), 188–207; *HIG*, VI, chapter XIX; J. Strachey, *India* (London, 1888), pp. 111–30; and R. Temple, *India in 1880* (3rd edition, London, 1881), chapter XVIII.

[2] For a Marxist view, see V. I. Pavlov, *The Indian Capitalist Class. A Historical Study* (New Delhi, 1964); for a less well-defined approach, see Misra, *The Indian Middle Classes*.

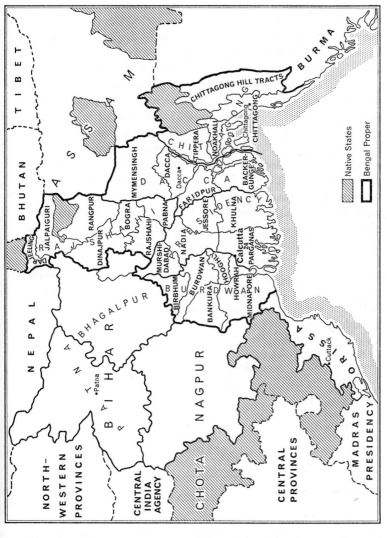

Bengal

The lieutenant-governorship of Bengal was the largest administrative division of British India, containing one-third of its total population and contributing one-third of its total revenues. By the time of Lytton's viceroyalty, Bengal contained forty-five districts in four distinct regions: Bengal Proper, the largest and most important, Bihar, Orissa and Chota Nagpur. Bounded on the north by the Himalayas and on the south by the Bay of Bengal, Bengal Proper encompassed the inland deltas of two great rivers, the Ganges and the Brahmaputra. A land of new mud, old mud and marsh, it was intersected by many rivers depositing a rich alluvium. Bengal Proper was united in language, but not in religion, for its population was almost equally divided into Hindus and Muslims. Bihar to the north-west, a flat and densely-inhabited country traversed by the Ganges, had a much greater degree of religious unity. Its people were predominantly Hindu, and their cultural affiliations were closer to north India, the heart of Hindu orthodoxy, than to Bengal. Orissa was a small region, whose population spoke the same language as their fellow-Oriyas of the northern parts of Madras Presidency. Chota Nagpur, the fourth region, was wild, hilly, and backward, dominated by the more advanced cultures of Bengal and Bihar. Statistics of area and population are set out in table 5:

TABLE 5. *Area and population of Bengal, 1881*

	Area in square miles	Population
Bengal Proper	70,430	35,607,628
Bihar	44,139	23,127,104
Orissa	9,053	3,730,735
Chota Nagpur	26,966	4,225,989
Total All Bengal	*150,588*	*66,691,456*
Feudatory States	36,634	2,845,405

Source: *HIG*, II, 285–6.

The Presidency of Bengal was thus an administrative convenience and not a genuine unity; Bihar, Chota Nagpur, and Orissa were segments of other races and linguistic groups, soldered to it for administrative purposes. It was in Bengal Proper that the wealth of the Presidency was concentrated. Here the British presence had bitten deepest, transforming its land tenures, galvanising its education and furnishing it with the largest city in Asia. It was here that Bengali civilisation, which for centuries had diverged from the pattern of Hindustan, was concentrated. It was from here that the Bengali, as trader, government servant or professional man, had moved up the country with the British advance.[1]

The communal distribution of the Presidency's population is given in table 6 below:

TABLE 6. *Hindus and Muslims in Bengal, by division, 1881*

(their numbers and proportion to the total population)

	Muslims	Percentage	Hindus	Percentage
Burdwan	957,630	12·95	6,208,208	83·96
Presidency	4,063,137	49·52	4,086,467	49·80
Rajshahi	4,885,165	63·16	2,818,858	36·44
Dacca	5,531,869	63·57	3,122,624	35·88
Chittagong	2,425,610	67·86	1,017,963	24·48
Bengal Proper	17,863,411	50·16	17,254,120	48·45
Bihar	3,312,697	14·32	19,169,327	82·88
Orissa	85,611	2·29	3,634,049	75·43
Chota Nagpur	231,282	5·47	3,187,710	48·45
All Bengal (excluding feudatory states)	21,493,002	33·22	43,245,206	64·84

Source: *HIG*, II, 285–6; *1881 Census, Bengal*, I, appendix A, A. no. 1.

In Bengal Proper, Muslims were in a bare majority, and they were especially numerous in eastern Bengal. Hindus, on the other hand, were by far the larger community in the western districts of Bengal, in Bihar, Orissa and Chota Nagpur. But these statistics give little indication of the relative standing and solidarity of the communities in the different regions.

Bengal Proper, insulated by its river barriers and its self-sufficient economy, lay outside the home of Brahminical culture

[1] According to a missionary estimate, there were about 6,000 Bengalis resident in the North-western Provinces in 1869, with colonies at Benares, Allahabad, Cawnpore, Lucknow, Agra, Meerut and Aligarh. (J. Welland, 'Educated Bengalis in the North Western Provinces', *The Christian Intelligencer*, XXXIX, new series, I (1869), 137–41, cited in McCully, *English Education*, pp. 196–7.) For evidence both here and in the Punjab of resentment against this Bengali intrusion, see the representation by the Sri Guru Singh Association (*EC (Punjab)*, p. 500) and chapter 7, below.

and the centre of the old empires of the mid-Gangetic plain. Consequently it had played a secondary role in the transmission of Sanskrit culture,[1] and orthodox Hinduism had been repeatedly challenged here by Buddhism, Jainism, Vaishnavism and finally by Islam.[2] Bengal's large Muslim population had been recruited mainly by local conversion. Yet in no other part of India outside Sind was the general condition of the Muslims so weak as in Bengal Proper. They were the majority community, but they were not the dominant one. The large Muslim landowners of the Punjab, the sophisticated talukdars of Oudh, or even the prosperous trading Bohras, Khojas and Memons of western India had few counterparts here. With the exception of a small clique of scholars in Persian, the community remained unlettered and poor. By origin most of them were low-caste Hindus, still scarcely distinguishable from their former caste fellows. Their backwardness was thus less a consequence of the decline of Muslim power since Plassey than a result of the poverty and lowly status of Bengali Muslims since time out of mind.[3]

In Bihar by contrast, Hinduism had been too strong to be swamped by Islam,[4] and centuries of Muslim rule had left the region with a small Muslim population. The standing of the community, however, was higher here than in Bengal Proper. More Muslims lived in towns,[5] more were educated and more were big landowners. In Patna nearly a half, and in Tirhut a quarter, of all landed proprietors in 1871 were Muslims.[6] In Orissa, Muslims were a still smaller part of the population, but here also more of them lived in towns and had a higher standing than their co-religionists in Bengal; in Chota Nagpur there were more Muslims, but they were not socially important.[7]

Bengal's relative isolation from Hindustan gave it a distinctive

[1] Bose, *Modern Bengal*, pp. 1–12.
[2] S. Dasgupta, *Obscure Religious Cults* (2nd edition, Calcutta, 1962), pp. 58–69; H. Sastri, *Bauddha Dharma* [Buddhism, in Bengali] (Calcutta, 1948), pp. 9–13.
[3] See chapter 7, below, pp. 300–2.
[4] *HIG*, ii, 294.
[5] In Saran district, for example, Muslims were 11·7 per cent of the total population, but were more than a third of the population of Sewan town. W. W. Hunter, *A Statistical Account of Bengal* (London, 1875–7) [henceforth *SAB*], xi, 256.
[6] *SAB*, xi, 135; xiii, 121.
[7] *Ibid.* xviii, 79–80; xvi, 83–4, 139.

caste structure which had a profound bearing upon its politics. Brahmins never bound upon Bengal the same orthodoxy they had imposed upon upper India. But here their secular position was not challenged by Kshattriyas and Rajputs. Instead they had to share pre-eminence with two other castes, the Kayasths and Baidyas. Between Brahmins, Kayasths and Baidyas on the one hand and the rest of Hindu society on the other there was a considerable gulf in social status and ritual ranking. Yet these three higher castes—sometimes corporately known as the bhadralok or respectable people—were not altogether cohesive. Caste boundaries in Bengal were not hard and fast. The bhadralok themselves were not an ascriptive group. Members of the higher castes vied one with another. But at the same time there were great efforts at self-betterment among the lower castes. These took the form of claiming higher ritual status and imitating the bhadralok way of life. Consequently the high castes had to compete with them as well; for all their squabbles among themselves, they still had a common interest in preventing these *arrivistes* from arriving.

Brahmins, traditionally the priests of the Aryan community, possessing a monopoly of religious instruction, had moved since time immemorial into a wide range of secular employment. In the later nineteenth century they were found in 'all respectable means of livelihood, except those involving personal or ceremonial pollution'.[1] As they scattered outside their traditional employments, their new occupations continued to be influenced by their traditional skills. They were government servants, and clerks, teachers and lawyers. But Brahmins also had a large place in the system of landownership and rent-receiving.[2] In eastern Bengal, one landlord in six was a Brahmin; and many estate managers and rent-collectors were men of this caste. In both east and north Bengal, one Brahmin in five lived on rents from land, and one in twelve was a manager of a zemindari estate or a landlord's agent.[3] When Brahmins were cultivators, they did not till the land themselves but employed lower caste labour.[4] They were found in 'all varieties of circum-

[1] Risley, *Tribes and Castes*, I, 141.
[2] See *SAB*, I, 53–8; II, 46, 194; III, 52, 293; IV, 46, 222, 329; V, 47, 52–5, 190, 286, 402–3; VI, 145; IX, 48.
[3] *1911 Census, Bengal*, V, 553, 571.
[4] *SAB*, IV, 46. Cultivating Brahmins were most numerous in Burdwan.

stance'; a few were wealthy, a good many were comfortably off, but the majority were poor.[1] However, Bengali Brahmins were not a homogeneous group. Divided into five main subcastes, they were further subdivided in the most intricate way.[2] In every district, moreover, there were 'degraded' Brahmins who had lost status for ministering to lower castes or for some other misdemeanour. Forming separate groups shunned by other Brahmins,[3] they further qualified any notion of Brahmin solidarity.

In Bengal Proper, there were no Kshattriyas native to the province.[4] The Rajputs, immigrants from upper India, were alone in claiming this status, but, humbly employed as watchmen, doorkeepers and policemen, they were few in number and uncertain in standing.[5] There were, however, two castes in Bengal, the Baidyas and Kayasths, who challenged the Brahmins in wealth and influence and had pretensions to be classed as twice-born. The Baidyas, a small caste peculiar to Bengal, lived mainly in the eastern districts. In social esteem they ranked next to the Brahmins,[6] while in education and wealth they were ahead of them. Once physicians, most of them had left their traditional calling.[7] In Dacca they were described as the 'upper middle class of the District',[8] and like the Brahmins they were strongly represented in government service, the professions and landownership. In eastern Bengal, one Baidya in three lived on rents from the land, and one in ten was an agent or manager of landed estates.[9] Although few in numbers, Baidyas were not a

---

[1] *SAB*, III, 285.

[2] In Bengal, Kulinism—a system of hypergamous divisions—was another divisive factor, leading to too many brides chasing too few Kulin bridegrooms. Cases were reported of Kulins with more than a hundred wives. These professional husbands could expect £200 with their first wife, less with subsequent ones. *SAB*, I, 53–5; V, 55; and N. K. Dutt, *Origin and Growth of Caste in India*, II: *Castes in Bengal* (Calcutta, 1965), pp. 5–13.

[3] *SAB*, I, 57–8.   [4] *Ibid.* III, 52.

[5] *Ibid.* I, 58; II, 46, 195; III, 52, 285–6; IV, 222; V, 47, 190, 403; VI, 145, 275, 380.

[6] In the eighteenth century Baidyas had purchased the right to wear the sacred thread; but their thread had two strings, while that of the Brahmins had three. Brahmins resisted Baidya pretensions to be ranked as twiceborn. See *SAB*, V, 47; and Dutt, *Caste*, II, 65–81.

[7] Risley, *Tribes and Castes*, I, 46–50.   [8] *SAB*, V, 47.

[9] *1911 Census, Bengal*, V, 553, 571. While some Brahmins, and many Kayasths, were cultivators, Baidyas were not found so close to the soil.

compact community; they were divided into four main sub-castes, and more than fifty gotras, with restrictions upon inter-marriage as severe as those among the Brahmins.

In Bengal there were many more Kayasths than Baidyas. Indeed the numbers and influence of this writer caste, greater here than in any other part of India, was one of the most striking features of Bengali society. Between Kayasths and Baidyas, there was a long-standing wrangle as to precedence. Risley, the census commissioner and author of the standard work on caste in Bengal, 'Putting aside the manifest futility of the discussion', awarded the superior place to the Baidyas,[1] but the Kayasths were quick to challenge his decision.[2] Although they were looked down upon as Sudras by the Brahmins, the Kayasths in Bengal were respected by other Hindus and deemed by them to belong to the higher castes. An adaptable, pioneering community, particularly numerous in the frontier districts of advancing Bengali civilisation, the Kayasths were traditionally administrators who had done well under the successive regimes of Bhuiyas, Muslims and British alike. Always

an ambitious and prosperous community...[the Kayasth caste] even under Muhammadan rule held most of the financial and revenue appointments throughout India; and since the English occupation of the country has almost secured the whole of the subordinate Government offices...every Kayath can read and write Bengali...[and] a large majority are versed in English.[3]

Kayasths also had a substantial stake in the land. In east Bengal there were more Kayasth landlords than Brahmin; 13·7 per cent of the caste were landed rentiers in east and north Bengal.[4] In the western districts of Midnapore and Hooghly many Kayasths were well-to-do landlords,[5] and in Nadia they were 'generally well off'.[6] Public servant and rent-receiver, the Kayasth, was also lawyer and trader. Like the Brahmin or

---

[1] Risley, *Tribes and Castes* I, 49–50.

[2] See C. K. N. Varma, *Criticisms on Mr Risley's Articles on Brahmans, Kayasthas and Vaidyas as published in his 'Tribes and Castes of Bengal'* (Calcutta, 1893).

[3] J. Wise, 'Notes on the Races, Castes, and Trades of Eastern Bengal' (privately printed, 1883), p. 313.

[4] *1911 Census, Bengal*, V, 553, 573. Wise however reported that 'None of the large Zamindars of Eastern Bengal are Kayaths, and few families are, as regards wealth, on an equality with the Brahman and Baidya houses'; and this was because Kayasths were 'extravagant and dissipated', Wise, 'Notes on Eastern Bengal', p. 313.   [5] *SAB*, III, 53.   [6] *Ibid.* II, 47.

Baidya, he was found in all 'respectable occupations', and the Kayasth who cultivated his own lands was equally careful not to hold the plough.[1] But Kayasths were not a well-defined caste. They were as subdivided as the Brahmins, and upstart castes were constantly trying to force their way into their ranks, and were resented for doing so. Further, Kayasths in Bengal had little in common with Kayasths in other parts of India.[2]

The numbers of Brahmins, Baidyas and Kayasths in the Presidency as a whole is given in table 7. Their distribution by district and division in Bengal Proper is set out in table 8.

T A B L E 7. *Brahmins, Baidyas and Kayasths in Bengal, 1881*

(Number and percentage of total Hindu population)

	Bengal		Bengal Proper	
Brahmins	2,754,100	6·05	1,076,854	6·21
Baidyas	84,990	0·18	77,120	0·44
Kayasths	1,450,843	3·18	1,056,093	6·12
Total	4,289,933	9·41	2,210,067	12·77

Source: *1881 Census, Bengal*, I, 143; II, 240, 249; III, 756.

In absolute numbers, the Brahmins, Baidyas and Kayasths together were as numerous in the western as in the eastern districts of Bengal Proper, but they were rare in most of north Bengal. In the east they were a larger proportion of the Hindu population as a whole than anywhere else in the Presidency. In Chittagong district, for example, one Hindu in three was a Brahmin, Baidya or Kayasth; in Dacca, one in five. It was in the eastern districts that most Kayasths and Baidyas lived, while the bulk of the Brahmins was concentrated in the western districts. But Calcutta and its suburbs had a high concentration of all three, and this shows how the opportunities offered by the metropolis attracted the high castes from east and west alike, and how far they had made it their city.

Just as there were no Kshattriyas in Bengal Proper, so also there was no Vaisya varna here. Vaisyas normally ranked after Kshattriyas and Brahmins. In Bengal, however, traders who elsewhere would have been Vaisyas were classed as Nabasaks, or clean Sudras.[3] From them a Brahmin could take water without

---

[1] *SAB*, IV, 46.   [2] Dutt, *Caste*, II, 51.   [3] *Ibid*. II, 114–24.

TABLE 8. *Distribution of Brahmins, Kayasths and Baidyas in Bengal Proper, 1881*

(with their percentage of the total Hindu population)

(1) District and Division	(2) Total Hindu population	(3) Brahmin	(4) Kayasth	(5) Baidya	(6) Totals (3)–(5)	(7) Percentage of (6) upon (2)
Burdwan	1,120,676	107,684	33,069	3,320	144,073	12·9
Bankura	910,845	84,322	20,575	3,881	108,778	11·9
Birbhum	617,310	39,724	8,902	1,834	50,460	8·2
Midnapore	2,235,535	117,414	92,178	3,762	213,354	9·6
Hooghly	822,972	76,271	25,484	2,462	104,217	12·7
Howrah	500,870	39,141	15,849	775	55,765	11·1
Total Burdwan	6,208,208	464,556	196,057	16,034	676,647	10·9
Twenty-four Parganas	1,003,110	62,670	30,013	1,260	93,943	9·4
Calcutta	278,762	38,868	37,570	2,684	79,122	28·4
Suburbs	149,930	13,373	14,781	644	28,798	19·2
Nadia	864,773	59,894	40,780	1,747	102,421	11·8
Jessore	631,439	37,752	62,611	1,972	102,335	16·2
Khulna	523,657	28,654	36,985	1,886	67,525	12·9
Murshidabad	634,796	33,935	15,655	1,474	51,064	8·0
Total Presidency	4,086,467	275,146	238,395	11,667	525,208	12·9
Dinajpur	716,630	8,913	6,024	655	15,592	2·2
Rajshahi	288,749	16,523	8,378	852	25,573	8·9
Rangpur	816,532	12,075	11,449	2,163	25,687	3·1
Bogra	140,860	4,614	3,759	213	8,586	6·1
Pabna	361,490	20,970	34,602	1,216	56,788	15·7
Darjeeling	126,717	3,882	406	20	4,308	3·4
Jalpaiguri	367,891	3,909	3,782	201	7,892	2·1
Total Rajshahi	2,818,858	70,886	68,400	5,320	144,606	5·1
Dacca	858,680	60,542	92,909	10,031	163,482	19·0
Faridpur	653,992	46,915	84,193	4,983	136,091	20·8
Backergunge	624,597	44,736	87,834	11,810	144,380	23·1
Mymensingh	987,355	50,152	108,409	4,615	163,176	16·5
Total Dacca	3,122,624	202,345	373,345	31,439	607,129	19·4
Chittagong	275,177	21,255	72,370	4,667	98,292	35·7
Noakhali	211,476	10,963	37,565	1,297	49,725	23·6
Tippera	511,025	31,502	69,373	6,470	107,345	21·0
Chittagong Hill Tracts	20,285	101	588	61	750	3·6
Total Chittagong	1,017,963	63,921	179,896	12,495	256,212	25·2
Total Bengal Proper	17,254,120	1,076,754	1,056,093	77,955	2,209,802	12·8

Source: Calculated from *1881 Census, Bengal*, II, table VIII, 240, 249; *1881 Census, Calcutta*, table XII, p. xxx; Risley, *Tribes and Castes*, I, 50; HIG, II, 285.

pollution and he could serve them as priest without degradation. It was a status to which lower castes aspired. Originally the Nabasaks were nine castes; by the later nineteenth century they were a larger and less clearly defined number, containing such castes as Telis, or oil-pressers, and Tambulis, or betel-sellers, who had succeeded in attaining this higher status.[1] All these gradations gave the caste structure a greater flexibility in Bengal than it had in most other parts of India. There were also differences between Bengal and upper India in the ranking of castes with similar occupations.[2] Moreover, inside Bengal itself caste ranking varied considerably from district to district.[3]

Beneath the Nabasaks there was a large number of 'intermediate' castes, which included castes of wealth and education such as the Subarnabaniks,[4] bankers and goldsmiths, and the Sahas, some of whom were prosperous traders. Naturally, they too strove to improve their standing. There were also signs that the largest cultivating castes of west and east Bengal, the Kaibarttas and Chandals, were trying to clamber up the caste ladder. In western Bengal, the Kaibarttas were divided between the farming and the fishing Jalikas. The former had a much higher status than the latter, and since the eighteenth century had been striving to dissociate themselves from their lower caste fellows by adopting Brahminical rules of life and new caste names.[5] In east Bengal, the largest caste was the Chandals or

[1] Influenced by the wealth and importance of many Telis, the Pandits of Nadia had recently confirmed their claim to be ranked as Nabasaks. See *SAB*, I, 61; III, 53, 287; IV, 51; V, 192.

[2] For example, whereas all Gopas, dairymen and keepers of cattle, were held to be clean Sudras in upper India, in Bengal only the Sadgops, who were not cowherds, as their caste name would imply, but one of the leading cultivating castes of western Bengal, had Nabasak status. Consequently, like any other caste intent on achieving bhadralok status, those Sadgops who had become men of influence 'now consider it degrading to touch a plough' (*SAB*, I, 62). In some districts a few Sadgops had ceased to cultivate and had turned to trade. (*SAB*, III, 287; IV, 51. Also see Dutt, *Caste*, II, 128–9.) On the other hand Napits or barbers, despised in upper India, were Nabasaks in Bengal.

[3] In Dacca the Tantis or weavers were deemed to be Nabasaks, but in other parts of Bengal they had a lower rank, and in Dacca, again, Gandhabaniks or spice-dealers, Nabasaks elsewhere, were considered an inferior caste. (*SAB*, V, 47–9.)

[4] The Subarnabanik caste contained 'some of the wealthiest men of the Metropolis as well as the Dacca district'. Maharaja Durga Charan Law (or Laha), a big zemindar and trader, president of the British Indian Association in 1885, 1888 and 1895, and twice a member of the Governor-General's Legislative Council, belonged to this caste. See C. E. Buckland, *Bengal under the Lieutenant-Governors* (Calcutta, 1901), II, 1089–90.

[5] *SAB*, I, 57, 63, 64; II, 47–8, 195; III, 54, 67, 288; Dutt, *Caste*, II, 131–5; Risley, *Tribes and Castes*, I, 375–82.

Namasudras who were despised by the higher castes as untouchables. They had expressed their resentment at this social discrimination by taking first to Buddhism and then to Islam.[1] The distribution of some Nabasak and cultivating castes is given below:

TABLE 9. *Distribution of selected Nabasak and cultivating castes in Bengal Proper, 1881*

Division	Selected Nabasaks			Selected cultivating castes	
	Teli	Napit	Sadgop	Kaibartta	Chandal
Burdwan	314,429	109,743	440,070	1,117,545	80,437
Presidency	115,752	105,430	100,635	498,838	397,572
Rajshahi	32,738	54,868	7,482	176,460	140,617
Dacca	47,684	106,866	4,121	176,729	863,002
Chittagong	15,226	50,381	623	60,990	108,542

Source: Risley, *Tribes and Castes*, I, 189, 382; II, 129, 214, 310; *1881 Census, Calcutta*, pp. xxx–xxxii.

The social dominance shared by Brahmins, Kayasths and Baidyas was based as much upon landownership, literary skills, administrative talents and a culture of their own as upon ritual status. Neither in Bengal nor in any other part of India did wealth by itself ensure social position; 'a very large portion of the Brahmins, Kayasths, and Baidyas of Bengal...even if not rich, take their place in the upper ranks; while men of wealth and position in the lower castes support the claims of high-caste men by the strenuous efforts they make to prove that the castes to which they severally belong are higher than the places accorded to them in public estimation'.[2] But the three high castes were not held together merely by the envy and respect of their social inferiors. They spoke and wrote the same language. They followed the same Sakta rituals.[3] Their customs —requiring infants to marry and forbidding widows to remarry —set the standards for castes below who aspired to rise in the social scale. By describing them as the bhadralok, the common-

---

[1] *SAB*, v, 50, 193, 259–60, 275, 285, 287, 406; vi, 381; Risley, *Tribes and Castes*, I, 183–9. In 1873 the Chandals of Faridpur 'made a general strike in the District, resolving not to serve any body of the upper class, in whatever capacity, unless a better position among the Hindu castes than what they at present occupy was given to them' (*SAB*, v, 285).
[2] *EC (Bengal)*, p. 67.   [3] Risley, *Tribes and Castes*, I, 442.

alty of Bengal recognised their superiority. Clearly these were the potential leaders of political Bengal, but it was less clear who would follow them. In Bengal the materials for inter-caste rivalry were abundant. But if the bhadralok had a remarkable proclivity to quarrel about status among themselves, they also had a common interest in resisting the pretensions of castes beneath them. Language and economic disparity widened this gulf still further and made improbable any concerted action between the learned and the rude.

In the Presidency as a whole there were three main vernaculars. Bengali was spoken by more than thirty-six millions. It was the language of Bengal Proper, but it was also spoken by substantial numbers in the Malda and Santal Parganas districts of Bhagalpur division in Bihar, in Chota Nagpur and in parts of Assam, as well as by smaller communities of expatriate Bengalis in upper India. Hindustani or Bihari was the language of another twenty-five millions, and Calcutta contained many up-country immigrants who spoke it. Another five millions spoke Oriya, and some Oriya-speakers had moved from Orissa to Burdwan. The distribution of these languages is shown below.

TABLE 10. *Languages in Bengal, 1881*

Division and Province	Percentage speaking		
	Bengali	Hindi, Urdu, Hindustani	Oriya
Burdwan	88·5	2·10	6·15
Presidency	94·5	4·47	0·45
Rajshahi	94·2	1·07	0·01
Dacca	96·6	0·50	—
Chittagong	95·2	0·11	—
Bengal Proper	*95·2*	*1·85*	*1·38*
Patna	0·02	99·90	—
Bhagalpur	11·65	79·85	0·01
Bihar	*4·07*	*92·91*	—
Orissa	0·77	2·44	96·34
Chota Nagpur	21·60	50·89	2·28
All Bengal (including feudatory states)	*52·37*	*35·65*	*7·83*
Total persons	36,416,970	24,799,081	5,450,818

Source: *1881 Census, Bengal*, I, 162, 165.

Bengali was less a unifying force inside Bengal Proper than the bare statistics suggest. Related to the languages of north India, Bengali originally was the vernacular the furthest removed from Sanskrit. But for more than a millennium Sanskrit words and usages had been imported into the literary language.[1] Yet in its early days Bengali literature had been religious and popular, influenced by medieval cults protesting against Aryan orthodoxy. In the nineteenth century, when Bengali experienced its renaissance, it became secular, losing its rustic tone and its popular appeal;[2] and the language was now shaped by English as well as Sanskrit models. This left it increasingly unintelligible to the mass of Bengalis who spoke dialects of a language which they could neither read nor write. Literary Bengali differed profoundly in vocabulary, in grammar, and even in pronunciation from these dialects. It was the language of formal speech, of books and newspapers. Educated Bengalis were thus equipped with a language which served well as a method of communicating among themselves, as a bond to unite them, and as a focus for their regional patriotism. But since 'In no other speech of India is the literary tongue so widely divorced from that of ordinary conversation as in Bengali',[3] their difficulties in addressing the people at large were great. Moreover, Bengali Muslims resented these Sanskritic and English borrowings.

The social dominance of Bengali-speaking people in Assam, Orissa, Chota Nagpur and parts of Bihar was reflected in the dominance of their language. As these areas, backward in the new education and professional training, came slowly to produce their own educated, eager for a share of opportunities snapped up by Bengalis, they attempted to redress the balance by stressing the claims of their own languages to be recognised as the languages of administration and the law courts. Bengali patriotism, and pride in language, came to be challenged by the patriotisms of the speakers of Assamese, Oriya and Bihari.[4]

[1] Sen, *History of Bengali Language and Literature*, p. 99.
[2] Ghosh, *Bengali Literature*, p. 167.
[3] *General Report of the Census of India, 1901*, p. 321. 'Bengal, too, is the province of all others in which there is the widest gap between the small literary castes and the masses of the people' (*1891 Census, India*, I, 143).
[4] For the beginnings of the demand: 'Bihar for the Biharis', see V. C. P. Chaudhary, *The Creation of Modern Bihar* (Patna and Khirar, 1964), pp. 24–43.

Bihari was 'a sister of Bengali, and only a distant cousin of the tongue spoken to the west', but the desire of Biharis to sever their connection with Bengalis was symbolised by the care they took over the pronunciation of sibilants, which was a literal shibboleth in Bengal and Hindustan.[1] Assamese also was 'a sister, not a daughter of Bengali'. Although its grammar was much the same as Bengali's, its pronunciation and its written literature helped Assamese 'to claim an independent existence as the speech of an independent nationality, and to have a standard of its own, different from that which a native of Calcutta would wish to impose on it'.[2] In 1889 Assamese educated in Calcutta brought out their own literary journal named *Jonaki*, which stressed the linguistic identity of Assamese. In the past Orissa had had little contact with Bengal, and its language, while related to Bengali, was not a dialect of it as 'Calcutta Pandits' claimed.[3] Oriya had a different script, and it had a literature of its own,[4] providing a focus for Orissa's claims against the Bengalis and against the Telegus whose domination had long historical roots. During the second half of the nineteenth century, the politicians of Calcutta were able to use the small but influential Bengali-speaking communities of Bihar, Assam, Orissa and upper India to support their claims to represent the Presidency and beyond. But step by step the new linguistic nationalisms of these areas refuted this claim.

Yet for all the obstructions which the Bengalis encountered on the frontiers of their expansion, they possessed a matchless advantage. The metropolis of Calcutta was the most conspicuous centre of their civilisation, and the city was at once the educational and cultural headquarters of the Presidency as a whole. Calcutta was the only large city in the Presidency.[5] It was the capital of British India as well as the administrative centre of Bengal. The University of Calcutta directed higher

---

[1] Unlike the men of the North-western Provinces, a Bengali pronounces his 's's' as if they were 'sh'; Biharis succeeded in pronouncing their 's's' like their western neighbours, but 'it is a modern innovation'. See *General Report of the Census of India, 1901*, p. 318.

[2] *Ibid.* p. 324.   [3] *Ibid.* p. 317.   [4] *Ibid.* p. 318.

[5] Bengal's urban population was proportionately the smallest among India's main provinces. Dacca, the only large city in Bengal Proper besides Calcutta, had a population one tenth as large as the metropolis. In all Bengal there were only eleven towns with a population of more than 50,000, and town-dwellers were a mere 5·26 per cent of the total population. *1881 Census, Bengal*, I, 32–3.

education throughout Bengal and upper India. Its high court possessed the most extensive jurisdiction and dealt with the largest amount of litigation of all the courts of India. It is a striking fact that more than a quarter of the city's Hindu population belonged to the bhadralok.[1] Some had been attracted by the opportunities it offered in the new education, in the public services and in the professions. Others, in particular the wealthy landed proprietors and rent-receivers of the province had been drawn by a city life which they found more enticing than the domestic quiet of the mofussil.[2] With their ornate mansions and English carriages these absentee zemindars joined the successful babus in demonstrating that Calcutta, whatever its other pretensions, was undoubtedly the centre of Bengali bhadralok civilisation.

Yet Calcutta had to house other groups as well. In 1881 the city and its suburbs possessed a population of 790,286. Less than two-thirds of this population were Hindu; less than two-thirds spoke Bengali, and one person in eight had come to the city from outside the Presidency.[3] Nearly a third of the population was Muslim; one third spoke Hindi or Hindustani (an index of the immigration from Bihar and upper India) and more than 20,000 spoke Oriya. There was a European population of about 16,000. Moreover, whatever the cultural stamp which the bhadralok imposed upon Calcutta, they possessed very few of the levers of dominance inside it. Calcutta was above all a commercial city. It was the main port of India and the focus of the vigorous internal commerce of Bengal. It provided an

---

[1] See table 8, above, p. 43.

[2] In the town and suburbs of Calcutta, 2,088 men were returned as 'zemindars or landowners'. In comparison, there were 892 employed in the law, 893 'physicians and surgeons' (besides some medical practitioners of the old sort), and 1,752 teachers and professors. *1881 Census, Calcutta*, table XIX, pp. xliii–xlvii.

[3] Hindus were 62·6 per cent, Muslims 32·2 per cent, and Christians 4·4 per cent of the city's population. Less than 500 described themselves as Brahmos. Besides the European population, there were 4,670 Eurasians (although this figure was known to be a serious underestimate). 26·5 per cent of Calcutta's citizens had been born in the city, 12·5 per cent in the surrounding district of Twenty-four Parganas, 47·6 per cent elsewhere in Bengal, Bihar, Orissa and Chota Nagpur, and 12·3 per cent outside the province. *1881 Census, Calcutta*, pp. 24, 34–5, 38–9, xxxiii–xlii. It was the boast of Bengalis that whereas they went outside their province as white-collar workers, men from upper India came to Calcutta in search of manual employment.

admirable maritime outlet from the areas of greatest agricultural productivity, particularly for the export staples of indigo, opium, jute and tea. The processing of jute had made it an industrial centre as well.[1] But it was not Bengalis who, for the most part, conducted this lively city trade. Calcutta's foreign trade, its shipping, banking and insurance were run by European Agency Houses.[2] The bhadralok complained of this exclusion, but they did little to remedy it. Similarly, internal trade was kept out of their hands and was dominated by men from other Indian provinces.[3] Again, the bhadralok had no share of the little manufacturing that was developing on Hooghlyside in the late nineteenth century. It was European capital which launched these jute and cotton mills. Calcutta's handful of Europeans had an impact upon the city quite out of proportion to their numbers. Not only did they hold the reins of power in administrative, economic and academic affairs, they also controlled the municipality of Calcutta itself. Indeed the bhadralok had less control over the affairs of their city than did the Indian inhabitants of Bombay. In the Corporation constituted in 1876 twenty-four of the seventy-two municipal commissioners were nominated, while the remainder were elected on a very narrow franchise. By the time of the reforms of 1888, the bhadralok had come to appreciate the advantages of sharing in local administration. Even so, they were denied effective control over the reconstituted Corporations. More of their members gained the vote; but the European community nominated fifteen commissioners, and it was the large property-owners of the city who had the predominant voice in its government.[4]

[1] The first power-driven jute mill was set up in the 1850s; by 1882 there were twenty large jute factories in and around Calcutta, with more than 5,000 power looms and 38,000 employees. See *HIG*, II, 309 and C. W. E. Cotton, *Handbook of Commercial Information for India* (Calcutta, 1919), p. 108.

[2] *Indian Industrial Commission, 1916–18. Report*, pp. 8–9, 14.

[3] Already in the nineteenth century, the Marwaris were beginning to get a hold upon the local retail and exchange trade of Bengal. See *SAB*, I, 63; VII, 124, 308; XI, 45, 161; XIV, 65–6; B. Ghose, 'The Economic Character of the Urban Middle Class in 19th century Bengal', in B. N. Ganguli (ed.), *Readings in Indian Economic History* (Bombay, 1964), p. 145; Pavlov, *The Indian Capitalist Class*, pp. 313–17.

[4] G. A. Grierson, *The Administration of the Lower Provinces of Bengal, 1882–83 to 1886–87, being a supplement to the Annual General Administration Report for 1885–86* (Calcutta, 1887), pp. 36–8; and H. Tinker, *The Foundations of Local Self-Government in India, Pakistan and Burma* (London, 1954), pp. 27, 40–2, 52.

In so far as the bhadralok played a role in the economic leadership of Bengal, they did so not through trading which they despised, but through landholding which they respected. This role was the consequence of institutional rather than economic change. In 1793 Cornwallis' Permanent Settlement in Bengal had fixed in perpetuity the government's share of revenue from each estate.[1] It had declared the tax-collector or zemindar to be the proprietor of the soil, and had given him all the property rights unless the tenant could prove prescription or custom. The Settlement was intended to insure the punctual receipt of land revenue, and to bring confidence back to the countryside. By securing to the landowners the increment from the improvement of their estates, it aimed to create a class of landlords who would provide the land with capital. Its results, however, were quite different. The original revenue demand was too high, and estates were liable to be sold for arrears. Many estates were sold or broken up, and Cornwallis' zemindars were replaced by men described by Mill as 'useless drones'[2]—a judgement which more recent experience has not upset. Some were men who had done well out of the British occupation of Bengal. And when British rule failed to deepen the economic changes it had encouraged, they put their money back into the land. A conspicuous example is the Tagore family. After having worked impartially for the French and British alike, it used some of its earnings in trade and administration to buy up the zemindari of Rajshahi,[3] just as some of the old retainers of Clive and Hastings went on to found other dynasties of landlords.

For three or four decades after the Settlement, when land

---

[1] On the Permanent Settlement in Bengal, see Baden-Powell, *Land-systems of British India*, I, 389–699; and Baden-Powell, *A Short Account of the Land Revenue and its Administration in British India; with a Sketch of the Land Tenures* (Oxford, 1894), pp. 154–61; S. Gopal, *The Permanent Settlement in Bengal and its Results* (London, 1949); H. R. C. Wright, 'Some Aspects of the Permanent Settlement in Bengal', *Economic History Review*, 2nd series, VII, no. 2 (1954), 204–15; R. Guha, *A Rule of Property for Bengal. An Essay on the Idea of a Permanent Settlement* (The Hague, 1963); N. K. Sinha, *The Economic History of Bengal; from Plassey to the Permanent Settlement* (Calcutta, 1956 and 1962), II, 1–22, 119–82; *Report of the Land Revenue Commission Bengal* (Alipore, 1940–41), I, 5–39.

[2] J. S. Mill, *Principles of Political Economy* (3rd edition, London, 1852), I, 394.

[3] L. N. Ghose, *The Modern History of the Indian Chiefs, Rajas, Zamindars, etc.* (Calcutta, 1879–81), II, 160–2.

was more available than labour, revenue demands pressed hard. But after the 1820s, agricultural prices and rent rolls rose steadily. The permanence of the Settlement meant that while the government's share of the produce remained much the same, an increasing surplus was left in the hands of the landlords. On the face of it, this should have led to a marked increase in the prosperity of the small body of zemindars. But by the third quarter of the century, only a small proportion of the permanently settled area remained in their direct possession, since many zemindaris had been sold to sub-proprietors. At first this had been a device to spread the load of paying the revenue. For example, early in the century the Raja of Burdwan, finding the state implacable and his tenants unwilling, divided some of his zemindari into lots called patnis, and sold them, together with his rights as zemindar, on condition that the purchaser paid the revenue assessed on them. The purchaser or patnidar, who became a permanent tenure holder, sometimes sold lots to others known as dar-patnidars, and they too sold lots to still others below them, known as das-dar-patnidars. This system, officially recognised and guaranteed in 1819, led to the creation of a vast class of intermediate tenure holders.[1]

As the margin widened between the fixed land revenue demand and the economic rent of the land, investment in the purchase of these subordinate tenures and shares in the land became more profitable, particularly since incomes from land were not subject to other taxation.[2] By 1855 it was estimated that some two-thirds of Bengal were held on tenures of this sort, and there is a presumption that many of the purchasers had urban connections.[3] As one lieutenant-governor of Bengal put it: 'The territorial circumstance most noteworthy in recent times is the increase of small properties; during the last two genera-

[1] In this way, many zemindars were reduced 'like the Raja of Burdwan, to the position of annuitants receiving every year the fixed sums due from *patnidars*', L. S. S. O'Malley and M. Chakravarti, *Bengal District Gazetteers. Hooghly* (Calcutta, 1912), pp. 211–13; in Backergunge, 'Subinfeudation is the characteristic feature…Not only are the tenures extremely numerous, but the degrees of subinfeudation are very great; thus in many estates there are eight grades of intermediate tenures between the proprietors and actual cultivators of the soil and the number very often extends to twelve grades and sometimes to twenty'. (J. C. Jack, *Bengal District Gazetteers. Bakarganj* (Calcutta, 1918), p. 94.)

[2] But see below, p. 211.

[3] Misra, *The Indian Middle Classes*, p. 134.

tions the tendency has been for the large estates to split up; and the Bengali barrister, lawyer, official, litterateur, trader, while following diligently his calling in the city, contrives to acquire his bit of land.'[1]

This proliferation of tenures was assisted by the operation of the laws of inheritance in Bengal, both Hindu and Muslim. Hindu law prescribed equal division among sons, while Muslim law laid down that two-thirds of the property must be equally divided among the sons, and one-third among the daughters. Sometimes these tenures and subtenures comprised definite units of land, but frequently they did not. A tenure might be split into any number of shares, which resulted in the tenants paying their rents to many different landlords—a fraction, calculated at so many annas or so many pice in the rupee, to each.[2] These titles could become so complex that the holder of a share might sometimes be quite unaware of what he was sharing and where it was.[3]

The Permanent Settlement thus gave Bengal a labyrinthine revenue system. It produced a few large zemindars, most of whom were absentee.[4] It also led to the subdivision of estates and the proliferation of proprietors and co-parceners.[5] Large numbers of these zemindars and rent-receivers were members

---

[1] R. Temple, *Men and Events of My Time in India* (London, 1882), p. 435. 'Large savings are generally invested in the purchase of landed property.' (*SAB*, III, 376.) [2] *HIG*, II, 306.

[3] One settlement report noticed that 'Those who owned land very often did not know what land it was they owned...The settlement camps were indeed regarded somewhat as lost property offices. Landlords came to find their lands and tenants came to find their landlords', Jack, *Bakarganj*, p. 98.

[4] For details about Bengal's absentee landlords, see *SAB*, I, 163; II, 93, 278; III, 146, 368; IV, 105, 275, 372; V, 106, 214, 333, 458; VI, 185, 319, 416–17; VII, 93, 301–2, 409; VIII, 81, 277; IX, 140, 141, 328; X, 127, 294; XI, 135; XII, 111–12, 255; XIII, 121, 288; XV, 135; XVI, 139, 411; XVII, 98–9; XIX, 31. The two thousand or so persons outside Calcutta with annual incomes from land of £500 and over 'in fact constitute the landed gentry of Bengal —its squirearchy and its nobility'. (*EC (Bengal)*, p. 66.) Yet, as one Bengali contemporary commented, these wealthy and sometimes titled men of property were 'entirely the creatures of the state'. Extravagance, the laws of succession and endless partitions were constantly breaking up their estates. So 'we have no aristocracy...unless we call by that name the ever-changing, unhistoric class composed of wealthy men of all grades and descriptions'. (N. N. Ghose, *Kristo Das Pal: a Study* (Calcutta, 1887), pp. 117–18.)

[5] The *Statistical Account of Bengal* observed 'the tendency towards the subdivision of property, which is now noticeable in nearly every District

of the three higher castes, and it was in part this unearned increment from the land which financed their incursions into literary and political pursuits. But contrary to Cornwallis' hopes, these men were unlikely candidates for the role of rural entrepreneur. In fact the Settlement stifled agrarian enterprise. Marked by 'the evils of absenteeism, of management of estates by unsympathetic agents, of unhappy relations between landlord and tenant, and of the multiplication of tenure-holders, or middlemen, between zemindar and cultivator in many and various degrees',[1] the land system of Bengal rendered almost impossible the co-ordination necessary for the improvement of property, and prevented the consolidation of holdings which was equally needed.[2]

The Settlement was also intended to encourage a healthy relationship between landlords and tenants. It had the opposite effect. Although tenant rights were supposed to be protected in the Settlement, the Regulations had not defined them. The Company merely reserved the right of intervention, and by the

of Bengal' (*SAB*, v, 130–1). The following table shows this process in five districts:

	1850		1870		1911	
	Estates	Proprietors/ Co-parceners	Estates	Proprietors/ Co-parceners	Estates	Proprietors/ Co-parceners
Hooghly	2,784	5,775	3,850	8,215	7,953	27,685
Midnapore	2,561	4,735	2,808	6,358	3,013	20,405
Dacca	8,606	9,731	8,739	16,688		
Faridpur	165	448	2,307	3,126	N.A.	
Backergunge	4,208	5,160	4,729	5,960		

Source: *SAB*, III, 378–80; v, 130, 226, 343; L. S. S. O'Malley, *Bengal District Gazetteers. Midnapore* (Calcutta, 1911), p. 136; O'Malley and Chakravarti, *Hooghly*, p. 213.

In a survey for the assessment of the Road Cess made between 1871 and 1873, it was found that in sixteen districts of Bengal there were 80,951 estates and 304,656 tenures; two-thirds of the entire valuations of £4,721,332 were due to these under-tenures. The average ratio of the government revenue demand to the valuation of estates was less than one third of the annual rental value; but there was considerable variation, and in some districts the valuation of the estates was as high as nine and a half times the revenue paid to the government. (*Report on the Administration of Bengal, 1873–74* (Calcutta, 1875), p. 17.)

[1] *Land Revenue Policy of the Indian Government* (being the Resolution issued by the Governor-General in Council on the 16th January 1902) (Calcutta, 1902), p. 8.

[2] *Royal Commission on Agriculture in India. Evidence taken in the Bengal Presidency* (Calcutta, 1927), IV, 136, 274, 290, 345.

time this power came reluctantly and timidly to be exercised in the second half of the nineteenth century, the old rights of the tenantry had virtually been effaced. For the first few decades after 1793 when the revenue demands pressed hard upon the zemindars, they were given special powers of distraint over their tenants. But as their economic position improved, the rights granted to them when weak became an instrument for exploitation when playing from strength. In this way landlord right became tenant wrong. Moreover, middlemen had much the same interests as zemindars in screwing what they could out of the cultivators. Since it was mainly the lower castes who tilled and the higher who took, this economic division reinforced the social division which existed between the bhadralok and their inferiors.

However, by the later nineteenth century the returns from the land were not growing fast enough to maintain the zemindars in the style to which they had become accustomed and the bhadralok in the situation their status required. It has been estimated that the profit of the rent-receivers increased almost thirteen times in the first eighty years after the Settlement; after 1872, when their numbers continued to grow, their incomes increased hardly at all.[1] District officers noticed the change:

It must be admitted that the zemindars, taken as a body, are not in a prosperous or flourishing state. A few of the distinguished houses have been utterly ruined, while others are in state of rapid decay. This sad state has resulted partly from their own acts and partly from other causes. The laws of inheritance lead to the rapid multiplication of shares in joint property. An imaginary estate which yielded a handsome income to the original owner is but a modest competence to his six successors, and will be but a pittance to, say, 36 grandchildren. The present management of the property, however, requires the consent of the six owners, who are suspicious of each other, and can agree to nothing. Mismanagement results, and sooner or later ruin is inevitable. It is generally accelerated by habits of extravagance...[and] the maintenance of a scale of expenditure which, consistent enough with the means of the original owner, is altogether beyond the competence of his successors.[2]

[1] See J. M. Datta, 'Banglar Jamidarder Katha' ['The story of the zemindars of Bengal', in Bengali], *Bharatvarsha*, XXXI, part 2, no. 6, (1951), 401–35. One factor was the increased power of the tenancy to combine against their landlords; another was the Tenancy Act of 1885.

[2] Annual General Report of the Presidency Division, 1875–6, dated 17 August 1876. Bengal General and Miscellaneous Proceedings, September 1876, vol. 871.

Similarly, rentier incomes from subsidiary shares were not increasing fast enough to sustain the growing numbers of shareholders. The condition of the middle class, according to the collector of Noahkali, was 'becoming more and more deplorable every year'.[1] In Presidency division, officials doubted 'whether the status of the people of the higher classes is generally improving', and warned that 'a large and increasing class of discontented (and not unnaturally discontented) respectable people is growing up'; the difficulty was 'the social system, under which early marriage is universal and poor relations are not ashamed to live in a state of dependence on the wealthier members of the family...In many a family...there is a real struggle for life, and these instances will become more and more numerous till the caste prejudices are weakened which restrict the range of occupations open to the *bhudrolok*'.[2] These gloomy prognostications were to become a feature of reports from Bengal for the next half century. In 1887 the government realised that 'Throughout the Province the only class whose condition does not appear to be improving is that composed of the educated and semi-educated scions of the higher castes'.[3]

Although the takings of the bhadralok from this once profitable land system were considerable,[4] they had never been large enough to support all its members. From the earliest times, the literary castes had used their traditional skills in service and profession to supplement their landed incomes. In Dacca for

[1] Annual General Report of the Chittagong Division, 1875–6, dated 10 August 1876, *ibid.*

[2] Annual General Report of the Presidency Division for 1876–7, dated 1 August 1877, *ibid.* August 1877, vol. 871. In a survey made thirty years later, it was found that the bhadralok of Faridpur 'generally speaking...lives in a condition of considerable comfort upon an average income which is much higher than the average in any other class of the community, although this is very largely due to the big incomes which the more successful enjoy. On the other hand, too large a proportion of the class lives in grinding poverty'. (J. C. Jack, *The Economic Life of a Bengal District. A Study* (Oxford, 1916), p. 89.)

[3] Grierson, *The Administration of the Lower Provinces of Bengal from 1882–83 to 1886–87*, p. 13.

[4] In 1881 their gross receipts from land were estimated at almost thirteen and a half million pounds. After paying the land revenue and cesses, the rent receivers kept nearly nine millions. (*1881 Census, Bengal*, II, table XXI, 538–41.) It was calculated that there were not more than 2,000 persons outside Calcutta with annual incomes from land of £500 and above. Including them, there were 100,000 persons in Bengal with annual incomes from land of £20 or more. (*EC (Bengal)*, p. 62.)

example these castes were 'very numerous... and generally have a minute share in a landed estate, on which it would be impossible to support life. Hence they throng our high schools, and gain a smattering of English, in the hope... of obtaining some Governmental post.'[1] In 1876 the lieutenant-governor of Bengal noted:

most of the small zemindars, not only by hundreds, but by thousands, whose income from the land does not suffice for their support, betake themselves to other professions, Let anyone count up the members of the professional classes in Bengal—solicitors, barristers, judicial and administrative officers, clerks and other ministerial officials, literary men, traders and merchants, who own some land, more or less,—and he will perceive the intellectual activity and the spirit of self-help which pervade the land-owning community...[2]

Yet by 1891 the great majority of educated and professional men had clearly cut loose from dependence on agriculture; only about 7 per cent of government officers and clerks, 10 per cent of lawyers, 10 per cent of teachers, and less than one per cent of literary men had a connection with the land.[3] For most of them education had become the means of survival.

Just as Bengal was far in advance of most regions of India in its schooling, so some regions of Bengal were far in advance of others. The map illustrates how wide these discrepancies were. The first impulse towards western education had been felt inside Calcutta itself, and even when the localities began to have colleges and high schools of their own,[4] the metropolis continued

[1] Memorandum on the Material Condition of the Lower Orders in Bengal during the ten years from 1881–2 to 1891–2, p. 15, quoted in Misra, *The Indian Middle Classes*, pp. 266–7.

[2] Minute by R. Temple, 14 January 1876, p. 15, *Report on the Administration of Bengal, 1874–75* (Calcutta, 1876).

[3] *1891 Census, Bengal*, IV, table XVII, 836–52. In the early twentieth century, it was reported that of 'the respectable classes' in Faridpur district 'nearly one-half (12,771 families) are landlords who support themselves partly or wholly upon the rents paid by their tenants, another quarter (6,935 families) are maintained by the professions, law, medicine or the priesthood, and the remainder (7,629 families) are clerks, either in Government employ or in the employ of landlords or traders.' (Jack, *Bengal District*, p. 89.)

[4] Colleges were founded in 1836 at Hooghly, in 1845 at Krishnagar, in 1846 at Dacca, and in 1853 at Berhampore. By 1870 there were eighteen colleges in the Lower Provinces. Presidency College in Calcutta was the largest in India; there were four aided missionary colleges in or near Calcutta, and three unaided, besides St Xaviers. In addition there were nine government colleges in the mofussil. See *RDPI* (*Bengal*) *1870–1*, p. 65.

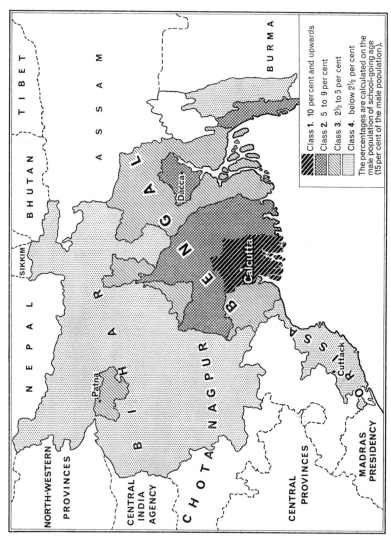

Collegiate and secondary education in Bengal
(Source: *RDPI (Bengal) 1886–7*, Map 2, opposite p. 30.)

Class **1.** 10 per cent and upwards
Class **2.** 5 to 9 per cent
Class **3.** 2½ to 5 per cent
Class **4.** below 2½ per cent

The percentages are calculated on the male population of school-going age (15 per cent of the male population).

to dominate Bengal's educational life. 'Calcutta has the reputation,' the Director of Public Instruction reported in 1872, 'of giving the best education, not only in law but also generally; and clever boys are sent there from all parts of the country'.[1] In 1883 of the 3,756 pupils in Bengal colleges, 2,445 were in Calcutta.[2] Again it was in Calcutta that many graduates found employment. The metropolitan area and the surrounding districts of Howrah, Hooghly and Twenty-four Parganas contained more than half the Indians in Bengal who knew English. Burdwan and Presidency divisions contained more educated men than Dacca, although this was only because they included Calcutta and its suburbs.[3] North Bengal was far behind western and eastern Bengal, but even it was more advanced in than Bihar, Orissa, and Chota Nagpur.[4]

These unevennesses of educational distribution through the different regions of Bengal were matched by educational inequalities among its communities. Muslims were a third of Bengal's population and more than a half of the population of Bengal Proper,[5] but very few of them went to school. Between 1836 and 1886 only 5·2 per cent of the students who passed examinations at Calcutta University were Muslims, while 85·3 per cent were Hindus.[6] The number of Muslim pupils being publicly educated in 1884 is given below:

TABLE 11. *Muslim education, Bengal, 1883–4*

Public institutions	Total pupils	Number of Muslims	Muslim percentage
Arts colleges	2,826	132	4·6
High English schools	53,991	5,186	9·6
Middle English schools	46,445	5,756	12·3
Middle vernacular	62,209	8,251	13·2
Upper primary	99,476	14,897	14·9
Lower primary	1,097,116	348,286	31·7

Source: *RDPI* (*Bengal*) *1883–4*, p. 149.

[1] *RDPI* (*Bengal*) *1871–2*, p. 102.   [2] *RDPI* (*Bengal*) *1883–4*, p. 11.
[3] In 1891 of 158,414 males (European and Indian) literate in English in the Lower Provinces, 80,108 came from the metropolitan area. *1891 Census, Bengal*, III, 227–8.   [4] *Ibid.* 223–5.
[5] For the communal distribution in Bengal, see above, table 6, p. 37.
[6] Calculated from Annual Return by religion of candidates successful in the Entrance, First Arts, B.A., and M.A. examinations, 1876–86, *PSC*, appendix M, statement I, pp. 78–9.

The higher the education, the rarer were the Muslims. At the same time, Muslim backwardness in education was more marked in some parts of the province than in others. In eastern Bengal, where Muslims were the bulk of the agricultural population and by far the larger community, they were the least educated. On the other hand, in those parts of the Presidency where there were fewer Muslims, they tended to be better educated. In Burdwan division, for example, they filled seven per cent of all school places; in Midnapore district they had a fair *per capita* proportion of scholars.[1]

But when Bihar, Chota Nagpur and Orissa are considered in isolation from Bengal Proper, a quite different picture emerges. These were regions backward in the new education; and here, as in the North-western Provinces and Oudh, although Muslims were a minority, in the main they belonged to higher and more literate strata of society.[2] In the Patna division of Bihar, Muslims received proportionately more schooling than Hindus; in every district but two of the Bhagalpur division they did not lag behind.[3] In Orissa, where Muslims were only 2·29 per cent of the population, belonging mainly to 'the better classes', the proportion of illiterates among them was 'actually less than among the Hindus',[4] and it was in high and English schools that they were proportionately the strongest. Here there was little evidence of Muslim backwardness. In eastern Bengal where Muslims were conspicuously absent from college and high school, this was because they were poor and lowly not because they were prejudiced by their religion against the new learning.

It was obviously the Hindus who were taking the predominant share in high schools and colleges.[5] Tables 12, 13

[1] *RDPI (Bengal) 1883–4*, pp. 149–50.

[2] '...in the great Hindu countries of Orissa and Bihar, the small Muhammadan communities quite hold their own in the field of education, whilst in South Bihar they have decidedly the advantage.' *1891 Census, Bengal*, III, 225. In Patna, the large number of Muslims at high school belonged to 'the rich and respectable classes of society'.

[3] In Bhagalpur the exceptions were the Bengali-speaking districts of the Santal Parganas and Malda. *RDPI (Bengal) 1883–4*, pp. 149–50. Two years later, the number of Muslim pupils had increased in high and middle English schools, although it had decreased in lower primary schools. (*RDPI (Bengal) 1885–6*, pp. 105–6.)   [4] *1881 Census, Bengal*, I, 194.

[5] In 1881, 92·41 per cent of college pupils, and 86·55 per cent of high and middle school pupils in Bengal were Hindus (*EC*, pp. 227, 275).

TABLE 12. *Caste of Hindu students in all Bengal, 1883–4*

	Colleges	High schools	Middle English	Middle vernacular	Primary upper	Lower
Brahmins, Kayasths, etc.	84·7	73·4	67·3	56·8	42·2	34·5
Nabasaks	9·3	14·2	16·9	20·0	24·6	28·8
Trading and intermediate castes	6·0	11·6	14·5	20·8	28·3	29·3
Others	—	0·8	1·3	2·4	4·9	7·4

Source: Calculated from *RDPI (Bengal) 1883–4*, Subsidiary table I, xii.

TABLE 13. *Learning and literacy by caste among male Hindus in Bengal Proper, 1891*

	Northern Bengal		Eastern Bengal		Western Bengal	
	(1) Learning and literate	(2) Percentage of (1) of caste population	(1)	(2)	(1)	(2)
Brahmin	25,628	68·1	133,631	80·3	203,432	65·2
Kayasth	19,909	61·4	162,095	50·7	90,862	67·8
Baidya	N.A.		16,999	74·3	N.A.	
Selected Nabasaks						
Teli	6,324	39·1	16,668	37·2	40,908	21·6
Napit	4,025	14·4	19,992	13·5	16,365	20·9
Sadgop	N.A.		N.A.		60,800	24·5
Selected trading castes						
Bania	3,908	25·8	15,856	43·1	45,307	53·2
Sunri	9,864	39·7	57,670	47·1	11,570	23·0
Selected agricultural and other castes						
Kaibartta	12,631	12·6	14,521	8·0	222,525	29·3
Chandal	2,353	3·5	17,956	2·5	N.A.	

Source: *1891 Census, Bengal*, III, 229.

and 14 show which Hindu castes were being educated. Clearly the Brahmins, Kayasths and Baidyas dominated higher education. Next came the Banias and other trading castes of whom many were literate, but few knew English, a language

TABLE 14. *Knowledge of English by caste among literate male Hindus in Bengal Proper, 1891*

	Northern Bengal		Eastern Bengal		Western Bengal	
	(1) English-knowing	(2) Proportion to literate	(1)	(2)	(1)	(2)
Brahmin	2,513	12·8	5,548	5·7	17,173	11·8
Kayasth	1,219	8·2	7,181	6·3	12,547	18·6
Baidya		N.A.	2,200	20·5	N.A.	
Selected Nabasaks						
Teli	115	2·4	143	1·1	1,635	5·8
Napit	35	1·2	93	0·6	821	7·2
Sadgop		N.A.	N.A.		2,627	6·4
Selected trading castes						
Bania	98	3·2	238	1·9	2,215	6·6
Sunri	128	1·7	591	1·3	349	4·1
Selected agricultural and other castes						
Kaibartta	145	1·5	157	1·4	3,842	2·2
Chandal	11	0·6	62	0·4	N.A.	

Source: *1891 Census, Bengal*, III, 229.

hardly necessary for careers in the bazaar.[1] Except in Calcutta, 'native merchants have not much cultivated English learning'.[2] When well-to-do shopkeepers and gomastas in the villages sought education, they went to vernacular schools.[3]

The bhadralok's grip on higher education can be illustrated in another way. The provincial administration's records of the occupations followed by the parents of students show that, in 1870, the vast preponderance of college students were sons of professional men, government servants and rent receivers in that order. Very few were drawn from the commercial classes. In the larger category of students learning English, the sons of rent-receivers were more numerous than the sons of government servants. Only one in ten was the son of a trader.[4] In

---

[1] Traders and money-lenders, described in Faridpur as 'the richest residents of the district' were 'a very miserly...class, who consider their children only require to obtain the small acquaintance with writing and arithmetic necessary to keep shop'. *SAB*, v, 348.

[2] *RDPI (Bengal) 1870–1*, p. 69.

[3] *RDPI (Bengal) 1875–6*, p. 42.

[4] *RDPI (Bengal) 1870–1*, pp. 60–81.

1883–4 more than half the students at college and high school had fathers employed by the government or in private service and the professions, and about a fifth came from families dependent on rents. Only about 7 per cent of the college students and 13 per cent of the high school boys had a background of trade. Even fewer had emerged from the peasantry—one per cent of the college and 6 per cent of the high school pupils.[1] As the Calcutta University Commission noted,

it is not from the agricultural classes, any more than from the commercial or industrial classes, that the eager demand for educational opportunities has come... The classes whose sons have filled the colleges... are the middle or professional classes, commonly known as the *bhadralok*; and it is their needs, and their traditions, which have more than any other cause, dictated the character of university development in Bengal.[2]

Even when well-to-do families were extensively defined so as to include the five thousand persons enjoying annual incomes of £500 and above,[3] few of the scholars came from families of this sort. 'Riches,' one Director of Public Instructio sadly concluded 'are evidently antagonistic to persevering study.'[4] Parental incomes in 1883–4 are set out in table 15.

[1] Calculated from returns, *RDPI (Bengal) 1883–4*, pp. 10–11 and General Statistics, p. xii.

[2] *Calcutta Commission Report*, I, part 1, 27–8.

[3] This figure includes 2,000 persons outside Calcutta with incomes from land, and 3,000 with incomes of this order from other sources, including service, the professions and trade. (*EC (Bengal)*, p. 66.) The income structure of Bengal according to this estimate, was as follows (*ibid.* pp. 66–7):

> 9,500,000 families earned £7·3 per annum (average)
> 200,000 families earned £20–50 per annum
> 50,000 families earned £50–500 per annum
> 5,000 families earned £500 and over per annum.

In 1886 there were only 149 Indians employed by the government of Bengal earning incomes of Rs 5,000 and over, and another twenty employed by the government of India; 10,026 were employed by Bengal earning between Rs 250 and Rs 5,000, and another 2,379 in the same income brackets were employed by the imperial government. Government servants sent 893 boys to college and 12,270 to high and middle schools in 1885. On average each government employee had one son at college or English school. (*RDPI (Bengal) 1884–5*, p. 8, and *Abstract of Returns of Indian Civil Establishments on 31st March 1886* (Calcutta, 1887).)

[4] *RDPI (Bengal) 1870–1*, p. 67. In 1870–1, only twenty-five of a total of 1,374 students at 'General Colleges' belonged to families with annual incomes from land of Rs 20,000 and over; of the rich property owners of Calcutta there was one solitary scion (*ibid.* p. 60).

TABLE 15. *Parental income groups of Bengal students, 1883–4*

	Rs 5,000 per annum and over (%)	Rs 200–5,000 (%)	Under Rs 200 (%)
Colleges	13	78	9
High schools	7	67	26
Middle English	2·5	48	49
Middle vernacular	1·5	38	61
Upper primary	0·7	20	79
Lower primary	0·3	12	88

Source: Calculated from *RDPI* (*Bengal*) *1883–4*, p. 10.

Many of the bhadralok families who educated their sons must have had a struggle to pay the fees.[1]

We know well [wrote Sir Alfred Croft in 1881] that any considerable increase in the fees now paid by college students would compel many to withdraw. It seems not to be fully understood...how poor the middle classes that flock to our colleges really are. Half the students live from hand to mouth...Not five per cent of the students belong to what are called the higher classes; and but few are 'well able to pay for their own education'. And yet, though far behind in point of wealth, they correspond to, and are in fact the only representatives of, our professional classes at home; and the pressure among them for the means of subsistence is so great, that they must either be educated or go to the wall.[2]

Until the overthrow of the Marathas, Bombay had been the smallest and the least successful of the three Presidencies. But the vast accessions of territory it received after 1818, the annexation of Sind in 1843, and the acquisition of Kanara in 1862, brought the Presidency to the size and shape it was to retain during the rest of the British period.[3] By the later nineteenth century those regions of Bombay which were directly ruled by the British extended over 124,000 square miles, were divided into twenty-four districts, and contained some sixteen

[1] Fees at Bengal's departmental colleges varied between Rs 3 and 12 per month, and between Rs 3 and 6 at private colleges; at government high schools, the tuition fees were between Rs 1 and 5 per month. (*EC*, pp. lviii, lxv.)

[2] Sir A. Croft, Director of Public Instruction in Bengal, to the Rev. J. Johnston, 26 June 1881. RP, Add. MSS 43575.

[3] Sind became a separate province under the Government of India Act, 1935.

Bombay Presidency (excluding Sind)

and a half million people. The area and population of the Presidency in 1881 are given in table 16 below.

TABLE 16. *Bombay Presidency, 1881: area and population by province, division and district*

Province, district or division	Total area in square miles	Population
Ahmadabad	3,821	856,324
Kaira	1,609	804,800
Panch Mahals	1,613	255,479
Broach	1,453	326,930
Surat	1,662	614,198
Total, Gujarat	*10,158*	*2,857,731*
Thana	4,243	908,548
Kolaba	1,496	381,649
Ratnagiri	3,922	997,090
Total, Konkan	*9,661*	*2,287,287*
Khandesh	9,944	1,237,231
Nasik	5,940	781,206
Ahmadnagar	6,666	751,228
Poona	5,348	900,621
Sholapur	4,521	582,487
Satara	4,988	1,062,350
Total, Deccan	*37,407*	*5,315,123*
Belgaum	4,657	864,014
Dharwar	4,535	882,907
Bijapur	5,757	638,493
Kanara	3,911	421,840
Total, Karnatak	*18,860*	*2,807,254*
Karachi	14,115	478,688
Hyderabad	9,030	754,624
Shikarpur	10,001	852,986
Thar and Parkar	12,729	203,344
Upper Sind Frontier	2,139	124,181
Total, Sind	*48,014*	*2,413,823*
City and Island of Bombay	22	773,196
Total, Presidency	*124,122*	*16,454,414*

Source: *1881 Census, Bombay*, II, I.

Interspersed with the British districts were numerous native states, with a population of almost seven millions, ranging from tiny enclaves to the larger principalities of Baroda and Kolhapur.[1] Obviously, the Presidency differed markedly from Ben-

---

[1] Baroda, however, was not the charge of Bombay; it was ruled from Calcutta.

gal. Its population was much smaller. Most of its territories had been acquired much more recently. Its princely states were more numerous and some of them much more important. Again, there was much less linguistic and ethnic unity. Stretching through fifteen degrees of latitude, Bombay Presidency consisted of four well-defined regions, each with a language of its own: Sind in the north-west, Gujarat, the Deccan-Konkan region, and the Karnatak areas in the south. In addition, the city and island of Bombay had a character of its own.

In 1881 the chief languages in the Presidency were distributed in the following manner:

TABLE 17. *Languages in Bombay Presidency, 1881: percentage distribution by divisions*

	Marathi	Gujarati	Kanarese	Sindi	Hindustani
Gujarat	0·73	94·26	—	0·01	4·41
Konkan	93·34	2·63	0·05	—	3·55
Deccan	89·32	1·52	1·05	—	6·02
Karnatak	16·08	0·17	72·81	—	8·52
Sind	0·36	2·34	—	84·93	0·65
Bombay city	50·17	26·80	0·15	0·18	11·56
Total Presidency	47·11	18·86	12·77	12·47	5·30
Total persons	7,751,497	3,103,310	2,101,931	2,051,727	871,421

Source: *1881 Census, Bombay*, I, 106; II, 38–41.

In 1881 almost three-quarters of the population of Bombay Presidency were Hindu. Table 18 gives the distribution of the two main communities:

TABLE 18. *Distribution of Hindus and Muslims, Bombay Presidency, 1881*

	Hindus	Percentage	Muslims	Percentage
Gujarat	2,247,852	78·7	295,751	10·3
Konkan	2,087,968	83·5	131,333	5·7
Deccan	4,699,773	87·5	289,898	5·5
Karnatak	2,465,059	87·8	258,232	9·2
Bombay city	502,851	65·0	158,713	20·5
Sind	305,079	12·6	1,857,204	78·2
Presidency	12,308,582	73·4	3,021,131	18·4

Source: *1881 Census, Bombay*, I, 44.

If Sind, where more than half of Bombay's Muslims lived, is excepted, just over 8 per cent of the total population was Muslim. About one-fifth of Bombay city's population was Muslim, but elsewhere they were a much smaller minority. Before the British conquest, the Marathas had dominated all parts of the Presidency except Sind and had rooted out Muslim influence wherever they could. Hence it is hardly surprising that in Gujarat, the Konkan, the Deccan and the Karnatak the Muslim notables were few. Consequently, not only was the community a minority, it was also for the most part inert. Even in the towns Muslims were mainly small traders, artisans and labourers.[1] Their poverty stood in the way of their taking up the new educational opportunities, and to this handicap was added that of language. Outside Sind, most Muslims spoke Hindustani, and as yet government had made little provision for education through the medium of this tongue.[2]

Despite the efforts to develop its port of Karachi,[3] Sind remained largely inaccessible across its borders of mountains, deserts, salt flats and swamps. This large area supported only two and a half million people. Eleven centuries of Islamic rule had produced a population of whom four-fifths were Muslims, and these were loosely organised under the sway of large landowners. Hindus formed one-eighth of the population, and most of them were town-dwellers, whose ability to read and count made them as indispensable to the administration of Sind as they were to its trade.[4] But Sind remained a backwater, out of touch with the rest of the Presidency and out of sympathy with it.[5] Sindi, the regional language, had little currency outside its native districts, whose isolation had left it heavily

---

[1] But some members of the unorthodox Muslim sects such as the Bohras and Khojas were wealthy traders.

[2] *Gazetteer of the Bombay Presidency* (Bombay, 1877–1904) [henceforth *BG*], II, 55, 376–7; III, 36, 226; IV, 40; X, 131–4; XIII, 216–46; XV, part I, 400–11; XVI, 26, 75–84; XVII, 214–35; XVIII, part I, 481–506; XIX, 124–47, XX, 199–211; XXI, 196–226; XXII, 222–49; XXIII, 282–305.

[3] In 1838, Karachi's population was 14,000; in 1881, 73,560. Its sea-borne trade increased from £121,150 in 1843 to over £7 million in 1882–3. W. W. Hunter, *Bombay 1885 to 1890. A Study in Indian Administration* (London, 1892), 25; *HIG*, VII, 455.

[4] In 1881, only 1·4 per cent of the Muslims of Sind were 'educated in any sense of the word', while 15 per cent of the Hindus were literate. *Report of the Bombay Provincial Committee*. Education Commission, Bombay, I (Calcutta, 1884) [henceforth *EC (Bombay)*, I], 59.

[5] *HIG*, XII, 517–19; *1881 Census, Bombay*, I, 3.

studded with 'archaic features' and its literature undeveloped.[1] The administrative system recognised, and reinforced, this segregation. Sind had a separate system of government, a judicial system that was largely independent, and many of the enactments of the Bombay Legislative Council did not apply to its districts.[2]

Gujarat, on the other hand, had experienced more involvement with the rest of the Presidency.[3] After four and a half centuries of Muslim rule it had fallen to the Marathas, and Baroda became one of the branches of the Confederacy. One of the legacies of Maratha rule in Gujarat was the large number of Hindu states which survived to complicate the map and the politics of the Presidency.[4] Another consequence was to depress the position of the Muslims. In the third place, the exactions and upheavals of the Marathas made the settled conditions of British rule a not unwelcome prospect for the Gujarati Hindus, who were without any tradition of ruling themselves. Much of Gujarat was fertile; more people there lived in towns than in any other part of the Presidency,[5] and this, together with its active trading which took Gujaratis to every port and mart of western India, rendered the population 'the most wealthy and contented in the Presidency'.[6] Yet for all its commercial activity and linguistic revival there were few overt signs of political activity in Gujarat in the later nineteenth century.

The Kanarese-speaking districts of Belgaum, Bijapur, Dharwar and North Kanara were dormant as well, although it was the quiet more of submersion than of contentment. These districts, lying south of the Konkan and Deccan, were sections of the Karnatak which time and chance had bundled into the Bombay Presidency. Much of the Karnatak had been occupied by the Marathas, and during the nineteenth century remained under the domination of Marathi-speakers, although the bulk

[1] Chatterji, *Languages and Literatures*, 348–9.
[2] Hunter, *Bombay*, 23–7, 466–7. In 1888, and again under Curzon, there were proposals to transfer Sind to the Punjab.
[3] On Gujarat's history, see *BG*, I, part I.
[4] Out of the Gujarati territory which fell into their hands, the British organised about one-seventh of its area into five districts, leaving the rest under native rule.
[5] In Gujarat, the percentage of the urban population was 19·9, in the Konkan it was 9·0, and in the Deccan, 14·3, *1881 Census, Bombay*, II, 2.
[6] *EC (Bombay)*, I, 55.

of the population spoke Kanarese. The inertia of the region at this time is reflected by the smallness of its trade and the self-sufficiency of its agriculture. Some 35 per cent of the Hindu population of these four districts belonged to the Lingayat sect,[1] whose members disliked Brahmins and the Brahminical tenets of transmigration of souls, child marriage and the veto on widow remarriage. It may well have been the unifying force of the Lingayat religion which kept the Kanarese language alive,[2] just as it was to provide a focus for non-Brahmin hostility towards the Brahmins.

The main region of the Presidency was Maharashtra.[3] In addition to the Deccan, it included the Konkan, the lowland maritime strip which had been the home of Shivaji, the Maratha hero. In minor details of dialect, customs, dress and agriculture the people of the Konkan, insulated by the sea on one side and the Western Ghats on the other, were different from their neighbours in the Deccan. But from the Konkan several tortuous routes ran over the Ghats to the Deccan or desh, 'the middle country', which was both the cultural and political heart of Maharashtra, containing Poona, the historic capital of the Peshwas, and the important religious centres of Pandharpur and Nasik. So far from being dormant, Maharashtra had been politically active since the seventeenth century. From this harsh plateau the Marathas had organised an empire which at its height extended to the Indian Ocean in the east and to Delhi in the north. But after the final destruction of Maratha power in 1818, the rulers of the old Confederacy became either clients or exiles, and the Marathi regions were thereafter organised into British districts or native states.

Many of the British thrusts in India had the effect of breaking Muslim rule, and hence of bringing indirect advantages to the Hindus, as in Bengal. But the fall of the Maratha empire ex-

---

[1] *BG*, XXI, 149–51; XXIII, 219–80. There were also strong Lingayat groups in North Kanara, Poona, Sholapur, and Satara districts. *BG*, XV, part 2, 89–90; XVIII, part I, 270–2; XIX, 59–60; XX, 75–85.

[2] *Ibid*. I, part 2, 477.

[3] Maharashtra, as such, does not appear on British maps in the nineteenth century. It corresponds to the Marathi-speaking area in western and central India, and extended through the Konkan and Deccan along the Tapti and Purna valleys on its northern boundary, into the Marathi-speaking districts of the Central Provinces to the east. In its more restricted sense, it refers to the Deccan.

tinguished the major Hindu power in India. Its collapse had sombre consequences for Maharashtra's population. For the Brahmins whose spiritual authority and secular talents had won them the direction of the empire under the Peshwas, and for the Maratha warriors who had sustained it, the loss was dramatic. Once British rule was imposed upon Poona, the conquered conquerors found their occupation gone. Cut off from the plunder of other regions, they were forced to cultivate their own garden. Working on this unrewarding soil, the Brahmins were unlikely to forget the days of their greatness, and the sturdy Maratha peasantry were unlikely to become sleek. After 1818 the British were well aware that they were holding a wolf by the ears. That is why Elphinstone took the greatest care to preserve the institutions of the country. Much as he would have liked to apply the policy of Bentham, it was the practice of Burke that he followed. In Bengal the British conquest had knocked flat the central institutions of the country together with its Muslim overlords, and Cornwallis had transformed the land tenures. No-one dared risk this social engineering in Maharashtra. Believing that the best security for the new regime lay in conciliating the ablest supporters of the old, Elphinstone treated them suavely, salvaging many of the Maratha states, and interfering as little as possible with the structure of land-holding and native institutions.[1]

Subject to influences from both north and south, Maharashtra had been the meeting ground of many cultures. Its marriage customs followed the pattern of the south, but its language belonged to the Indo-Aryan family of the north.[2] Yet despite these influences Maharashtra and its people had remained distinct from their neighbours. They were united by a language which was a tongue with few variations between the high and the low and between place and place.[3] The religious poets of old who had done much to create the tradition of Maharashtra had

[1] K. Ballhatchet, *Social Policy and Social Change in Western India 1817–30* (London, 1957), pp. 34–6, 91–9; also see E. Stokes, *The English Utilitarians and India* (Oxford, 1959), pp. 148–50.

[2] D. D. Karve, *The New Brahmans. Five Maharashtrian Families* (Berkeley and Los Angeles, 1963), p. 1.

[3] Although tatsamas (words borrowed from Sanskrit) were used by Marathi scholars who tried to heighten the style of the language, they did not gain that complete mastery over the literary language that they had in Bengali. *General Report of the Census of India, 1901*, p. 315.

written in a demotic style which penetrated deep into society. Later in the nineteenth century it was the boast of Maharashtrian reformers that both priest and ploughman in their country had the same religious understandings in the same tongue. In the second half of the century Marathi, like the languages of its neighbours, began to enjoy a literary renaissance, but whereas some of these had for long been culturally submerged, Marathi itself had been the language of conquerors. Just as the renaissance of Oriya, Bihari, Assamese and Hindi had been largely directed against the cultural dominance of Bengali, so too the renaissances of Kanarese and Hindi were in large part intended to throw off the yoke of Marathi on the frontiers of its expansion.

This linguistic solidarity of Maharashtra was connected with its religious uniformity. The overwhelming proportion of its population was Hindu, and the result of their long struggles against Islam had been to construct a militantly Hindu Raj inside which Muslim influence had been largely extirpated. There was no solid population of Muslim converts in the Deccan and Konkan to match those in Sind or in Bengal Proper. Here there was no Muslim aristocracy; and successful Muslim traders could be found mainly in Bombay city.

The structure of caste in Maharashtra was marked by its comparative simplicity.[1] It was built in three tiers, with a thin layer of Brahmins at the top, the bulk of the non-Brahmin castes in an intermediate position, and below them the 'depressed' castes. In Maharashtra the Brahmins were far less subdivided than in Gujarat. Whereas there were more than eighty different local divisions or sub-castes among Gujarati Brahmins,[2] in Maharashtra there were only twelve,[3] and the two largest, the Deshaths and Chitpavans or Konkanasths, were more than three-quarters of the Brahmin population of the Deccan and Konkan as a whole.[4] In Maharashtra Brahmins had an incomparably higher standing than in Gujarat, where,

---

[1] For a perceptive discussion, see Karve, *Hindu Society—An Interpretation*, pp. 15–49.

[2] *BG*, IX, part 1, 2–54. According to another estimate, there were ninety-three endogamous divisions, and as many subdivisions again, among Gujarati Brahmins. (R. E. Enthoven, *The Tribes and Castes of Bombay* (Bombay, 1920–2), I, 217).

[3] Enthoven, *Tribes and Castes*, I, 214.

[4] See tables 19 and 20, below, pp. 74–5.

despite their traditionally high status, they were not the best educated, the most prosperous or the most influential community. Many Gujarati Brahmins still followed their traditional occupation as priests; about 40 per cent were agriculturists, some of whom tilled the soil with their own hands like any cultivator;[1] and they were commonly the clients of lowlier if richer Hindus. They did not show the same talent or enthusiasm for employment in public service as their castemen in Maharashtra.[2]

In contrast, the Brahmins of Maharashtra clearly possessed social as well as ritual dominance. Of the twelve Brahmin sub-castes the largest were the Deshaths, but the most forceful and enterprising were the Chitpavans. In the distant past they had settled along the coast of Ratnagiri from where many had climbed inland over the Ghats to the Deccan. Here they seized power from the non-Brahmin descendants of Shivaji, established the Peshwai, and brought the fortunes of the Confederacy to a pinnacle from which they were dashed first by the Afghans and then by the Marquis of Hastings. After 1818 they determined to accept the accomplished fact rather than to resist it, and they now turned their formidable talents to an equivocal collaboration with their new rulers. Under the British as under the Peshwas, the Brahmins continued to enter the administration, and once they discovered that under the new Raj education was the key to office, they went to school and college in their determination to maintain by new methods the old aims of Brahminical pre-eminence.[3] *fluctuat nec mergitur.*

Chitpavans were concentrated in Ratnagiri and Poona districts, and there mainly in the towns; but they retained their old supremacy in the Marathi districts as a whole. Government

---

[1] Bengali and Maharashtrian Brahmins seldom engaged in manual labour of this sort.

[2] On the educational attainments of Gujarati Brahmins see below, pp. 88–9. Six local trading castes ranked higher in literacy than the best educated Gujarati Brahmin sub-caste. (*1881 Census, Bombay*, I, 164.) 38·7 per cent were priests, whose education 'was simply the learning by rote of the ritual required for everyday ceremonies'; the condition of the Audichyas, the largest sub-caste, was typical: 'Most...live on alms; a few...are cultivators; the rest are cooks or...village priests.' Sixty-one per cent of Gujarati Brahmins followed secular professions (including cultivation), but less than 8 per cent were professional men, government servants or clerks. (*BG*, IX, part I, 4–22.)

[3] See Temple, *Men and Events of My time in India*, p. 497.

service was not their only occupation; they were also lawyers, writers, engineers, doctors, merchants and moneylenders. In Ratnagiri they owned the best land; in Poona they owned the big estates. Chitpavans were generally deemed the ablest Hindus in western India, hard, pushing, crafty and stingy. They moved readily where opportunity beckoned in Bombay city, in the British districts, the states, and further afield in the Central Provinces.[1] Deshath Brahmins, a quarter of a million strong, had much in common with the Chitpavans. As the *Poona Gazetteer* remarked, 'in all walks of life the Deccan Brahmans press Chitpavans close'.[2] Distributed throughout Maharashtra, the Deshaths were especially strong in the villages where many of them held the post of kulkarni or deshpande. On the other hand, some of them were writers, bankers, moneylenders and traders. But in no district did they have as tight a grip as the Chitpavans upon administration and the professions.[3] Table 19 sets out the distribution of all Brahmins throughout the Presidency, while the distribution of Deshaths and Chitpavans is given in Table 20.

TABLE 19. *Distribution of Brahmins in Bombay Presidency, by division, 1881*

Division	Total Brahmins	Percentage of Hindu population
Gujarat	143,808	6·4
Konkan	106,262	5·1
Deccan	226,574	4·8
Karnatak	143,037	5·8
Bombay city	31,199	6·2
Presidency including Sind	664,411	5·5

Source: Calculated from *1881 Census, Bombay*, I, 118; II, 3, 34*b*.

In contrast to Bengal where Brahmins shared predominance with the writer caste and Baidyas, the Brahmins of Maharash-

---

[1] On the Chitpavans, see *BG*, XVIII, part 1, 99–158; XIX, 54–5; X, 111–13, 138; and Enthoven, *Tribes and Castes*, I, 241–4.
[2] *BG*, XVIII, part 1, 108 n.
[3] See Enthoven, *Tribes and Castes*, I, 244–5; *BG*, XVIII, part 1, 108; in Satara Deshaths were described as 'neither hardworking nor enterprising', content with their quit-rent lands and government grants (*BG*, XIX, 51).

TABLE 20. *Distribution of Deshaths and Chitpavans in Bombay Presidency, 1881*

	Deshaths	Chitpavans
Thana	7,470	9,426
Kolaba	1,940	8,336
Ratnagiri	983	28,611
Konkan	*10,393*	*46,373*
Khandesh	27,578	1,712
Nasik	21,766	3,496
Ahmadnagar	27,249	1,255
Poona	32,673	11,581
Sholapur	23,360	1,627
Satara	34,046	8,359
Deccan	*116,672*	*28,030*
Gujarat	*996*	*197*
Karnatak	*64,743*	*4,583*
Bombay city	N.A.	N.A.
Presidency total	*242,804*	*79,183*

Source: Calculated from *1881 Census, Bombay,* II, lxiv, lxvii.

tra were in a position of solitary, and indeed perilous, pre-eminence. Here there were very few members of writer castes. Their distribution throughout the Presidency can be seen in the following table. Western India did not have many Prabhus

TABLE 21. *Distribution of Hindu writer castes in Bombay Presidency, 1881*

	Brahma-Kshattriya	Kayasth Prabhu	Kayasth	Kayasth Patane Prabhu	Total
Gujarat	2,164	261	1,057	50	3,532
Konkan	46	10,188	15	223	10,472
Deccan	410	1,750	125	325	2,610
Karnatak	—	—	6	—	6
Bombay city	575	1,464	94	4,756	6,889
Presidency excluding Sind.	3,195	13,663	1,297	5,354	23,509

Source: *1881 Census, Bombay,* II, lxiv–lxix.

and Kayasths, and the Deccan had hardly any at all. The advantage which this gave to the Brahmins of the Deccan can be seen from the disadvantage which the presence in the Konkan of these born bureaucrats meant for the Brahmins there. The Kayasth Prabhus of the Thana and Kolaba districts of the Konkan had a long tradition of administrative service as writers and accountants, both under the Muslims and under the Marathas. They proceeded to serve under the British, and their rivalries with the Brahmins persisted as fiercely as ever.[1] Kayasths clung together for mutual protection, and in Kolaba priests who officiated for them were summarily out-casted by the Brahmins. In Pen matters had gone further—no Brahmin could accept alms from a Prabhu on pain of excommunication, and no Prabhu was allowed into a Mahadev temple.[2] Another small but talented caste of writers were the Patane Prabhus almost all of whom had moved into the city of Bombay.[3]

The predominant Brahmins in the Deccan were also free from another challenge which confronted Brahmins elsewhere in the Presidency. The poor lands of the Deccan offered little scope to the trader. In contrast Gujarat was a thriving centre of trade and industry. Even when Bombay city drained away some of the business of its ports, Gujarati traders had moved there and won a share of its commerce. The East African trade was virtually a Gujarati monopoly, and railways and cotton helped to keep the Gujarati districts commercially alive.[4] In consequence, the trading castes, in number no larger than the Brahmins, were by reason of their wealth and intelligence one of the most important sections of the population of Gujarat.[5] In Maharashtra, on the other hand, the few indigenous trading castes that there were had to compete for what business there was against groups from outside, Marwaris from Rajputana,

[1] *BG*, XIII, part 1, 87–108.
[2] *Ibid.* XI, 46.
[3] These Patane Prabhus, less than 5,000 strong in the city, made their mark upon the metropolis; 'All their boys know English, most of them up to the University entrance test'. In 1881 they had thirty-five undergraduates and twelve graduates among their number; they held some of the top posts in government. The first Indian appointed as judge to the Bombay high court was a Patane Prabhu and in the professions three high court barristers, five solicitors, ten pleaders, five doctors, and three civil engineers were men of this caste, while others had embarked successfully on business careers. (*BG*, XIII, part 1, 89–108.)
[4] *HIG*, III, 51.
[5] One possible reason for the large numbers of Brahmins in Gujarat was the 'comparative wealth of the upper classes which allows of an increased number of temples and of larger endowments' (*1881 Census, Bombay*, I, 128).

Banias from Gujarat, and Lingayats from the Karnatak, as well as against Brahmins trading for themselves.[1] There was no question here of the Banias becoming the patrons of the Brahmins.

In Maharashtra there were two large intermediate castes of peasants, the Marathas and Kunbis, so alike as to be almost one caste and so numerous and so solid as to be almost a 'distinct nationality'. In 1881 there were almost three and a half million Maratha-Kunbis in the Presidency, of whom some two-thirds lived in the Deccan, chiefly in the districts of Poona, Khandesh, Satara and the state of Kolhapur.[2] Yet the status of so large a group could not be the same throughout the caste. The highest sections, the Assal Marathas or Marathas Proper, claimed Kshattriya status, and some were local chiefs, such as the ruler of Kolhapur, while others had provided the Deccan with its soldiers and some of its landlords. Since they regarded themselves as superior to all other non-Brahmins, these Assal Marathas followed Brahminical precepts about widow-remarriage.[3] But the vast bulk of Maratha-Kunbis had no such pretensions and were cultivators pure and simple.[4] While the patels, or headmen, of the Deccan were invariably Marathas, they were overshadowed in the village by the Brahmin kulkarni or accountant,[5] since few of the patels had any education at all.[6] In Gujarat, on the other hand, the patels and patidars were men of considerable standing, recruited from the Kunbis of that region who were both powerful and well-educated in the vernacular.[7] Table 22 shows the main castes.

[1] *BG*, XVIII, part 1, 261–79; XVIII, part 2, 99.
[2] *1881 Census, Bombay*, II, 118, 125–6; *BG*, XII, 62; XVIII, part 1, 279; XIX, 64.
[3] Enthoven, *Tribes and Castes*, III, 19.
[4] 'Kunbis and Marathas are differentiated rather by wealth and social status than by any hard and fast caste distinction. Socially the Maratha is the superior of the Kunbi.' *Ibid.* III, 9.
[5] Although authority in the village was invested both in the patel and the kulkarni, 'the superior education and intelligence of the accountant who has to write all the reports...give him almost the whole power'. (*BG*, XVIII, part 1, 97.)
[6] See table 25, below, p. 88.
[7] The Kunbis of Gujarat, one and a half million strong in 1881, or about 14 per cent of Gujarat's Hindu population, were organised into four divisions. Each local unit of Anjna, Kadwa and Matia Kunbis had its patel. Lewa Kunbis, the largest division of the four, were dominated by patidars, who were chiefly found in the district of Kaira. *BG*, VII, 74–5; IX, part 1,

TABLE 22. *Size of some main Hindu caste groups in Bombay Presidency, 1881*

Castes	Percentage of total Hindu population	Numbers
Brahmins	5·53	*650,880*
Rajputs	1·82	*214,186*
Writer castes	0·21	*24,622*
Trading castes	3·70	*435,451*
Artisan castes	10·87	*1,280,648*
Agricultural castes	55·25	*6,507,691*
including		
Maratha-Kunbi*		3,403,059
Depressed castes	9·31	*1,096,542*
including		
Mahar*		852,523
Mang*		161,970

Source: *1881 Census, Bombay*, I, 118–19, 127; II, 34*b*–35.

*More than 86 per cent of the Maratha-Kunbis lived in the Deccan and the Konkan. About 70 per cent of the Mahars lived in the Konkan and Deccan, while half the Mangs were in the Deccan and the rest mainly in the Karnatak.

Between Brahmins and these non-Brahmins there was a long history of rancour which the nepotism of the Peshwas had only exacerbated. Elphinstone's policies may possibly have saved British dominion in western India; they certainly postponed the decline of Brahminical pre-eminence in Maharashtra. After 1818 the resentments of non-Brahmins though banked, still burned, as is shown by the anxiety of the Brahmins to argue that they had never been lit, and that in so solid a society as theirs the gap between castes was bridged by a common language, religion, culture and history. The fact remains that in terms of status neither Prabhu nor Bania, Assal Maratha nor Kunbi could as yet challenge the superiority of Maharashtra's Brahmins.

Brahmins possessed advantages in the economy of the region as well. Since 1836 land tenures in Maharashtra, as in most of

154, 163; Enthoven, *Tribes and Castes*, II, 144–55. These patels and patidars 'retain to the present day much of their former influence. They are in many cases rich, and possess a strong hold over the villagers.' (*HIG*, III, 106.)

the Presidency, had gradually been organised on a raiyatwari system in which settlements were fixed with individual land-holders for a period of thirty years. They were given rights of occupancy, together with a transferable and heritable property in the land.[1] Many of the largest agricultural castes of Maharash-tra—the Marathas, Kunbis, Kolis and Malis—were themselves smallholders with revenue obligations to government. None of the Deccan districts had large estates resembling the latifundia of Bengal.[2] Neither did anything like the huge Bengali web of intermediate tenures and rent receivers exist here.[3] Yet in this agrarian structure the Brahmins had an ample place as land-holders in their own right, usually tilling the land with hired labour.[4] Others were in the process of becoming landowners. Once they had scraped together some capital, they were pur-chasing a stake in the land both as an investment and as a means of consolidating their local position. 'Professional classes have a marked fondness for land investment', the *Satara Gazetteer* observed. 'Few successful pleaders, Government servants, or even priests...will be found who do not own some land. The fondness for land investment has undoubtedly increased under British rule.'[5] Again Brahmins played a leading role in the villages as the kulkarni or the moneylender. In this last capacity the Brahmin, like usurers of other castes, acquired his bit of the peasant's land. For the Deccan peasantry had always lived close to subsistence and were notoriously thriftless, and now their condition experienced violent ups and downs. During the boom years of the American Civil War, cotton and railway building brought new prosperity to the Deccan districts.[6] Using as collateral the legal right acquired under raiyatwari, the peasant contracted heavy debts, and the end of the boom in the late 1860s, a series of bad harvests and a new and higher revenue

[1] Baden-Powell, *The Land-Systems of British India*, III, 197–320.
 and Baden-Powell: *A Short Account of the Land Revenue*, 206–13.
[2] In 1881, of 227,871 holdings in Poona district, only one was over 300 acres, and another eighty-nine were over 100 acres. More than a third were under five acres. *BG*, XVIII, part 2, 6.
[3] *HIG*, III, 56–8.
[4] *BG*, XVIII, part 2, 1–2, 99, 100, 106, 124.
[5] *Ibid.* XIX, 180.
[6] The development of cotton as a cash crop received an enormous fillip during the war; and although prices slumped after 1865, production held firm. A. W. Silver, *Manchester Men and Indian Cotton 1847–72* (Manchester, 1966), appendix K, pp. 314–17.

assessment all combined to drag him down. When the money-lender hurriedly called in loans which the peasant had no hope of repaying, his land was put into jeopardy. He expressed his resentment in the Deccan Riots of 1875. Much of this resentment was against Marwari and Gujarati moneylenders, but some of it spilled over against the Deccani Brahmin who, as large land-owner or village accountant, dabbling in moneylending and grain-trading, had taken a hand in this exploitation.[1] But for all their difficulties the large peasant castes in the Deccan continued to hold most of the soil, and the Brahmins found that under the British no less than under the Peshwas there were few fortunes to be made by possessing the land of that infertile plateau. In the nineteenth century as before there could be no substitute for office. And for office education was increasingly becoming essential.

However, the towns of the Deccan had little to offer the ambitious Brahmin. Although Poona could look back to the glories of the Balajis, it was now merely the mofussil head-quarters of a British district of little prosperity. Apart from the district administration, it could offer no great expectations. There was little trade, less industry, and small scope for the professional man. But after the engineers had linked Poona with Bombay in 1863, it began to look forwards as well as back-wards. Once again it could become the nodal point of the Dec-can, and by 1880, its population had grown to almost 100,000. At the same time, Poona was again becoming a centre of learn-ing, and its new schools and colleges teaching in English were attracting the Brahmin youths from the Deccan districts.[2] But it still remained no more than a university town—notoriously no places for satisfying the ambitions of graduates. It was to the city of Bombay that they had to turn.

By the 1880s the city of Bombay had all the marks of a modern metropolis. It had been one of the chief beneficiaries of the fall of the Marathas which had opened the hinterland to develop-ment. It was the administrative headquarters of the Presidency, the seat of the central law courts and of the University. In addition, it enjoyed the advantage of being the natural terminus of the routes to India from the West. By the later nineteenth

---

[1] *BG*, xviii, part ii, 106–33; Deccan Riots Commission, *P.P.* 1878, lviii, 237–55.   [2] *BG*, xviii, part iii, 48–64.

century, the port had become the commercial hub of western India, the headquarters of the cotton and bullion trades, and the rival of Calcutta as a money market. The 1850s had seen the establishment of textile mills and the city became an industrial centre. The foreign trade of Bombay, which supported these multifarious activities, had expanded sharply since the 1860s. By 1881 cotton to the value of nine and three-quarter million pounds was being exported annually, and the total foreign trade of the Presidency came to more than fifty-seven millions. In addition there was a valuable coasting trade.[1] In contrast to Calcutta, native Indian enterprise was very active and powerful in Bombay. Indians controlled most of the cotton-buying up country; they had a large share of the foreign cotton trade of Bombay; they were active in the bullion market, and dominated the traditional foreign marts, although Europeans kept the lion's share of the city's trade with Europe.[2] Their most striking commercial success had been to move from their command of the cotton trade to develop the mills. From their tentative beginnings in 1857 Bombay's mills had by 1881 grown to be forty-nine in number, employing nearly 40,000 persons.[3]

So wide a range of opportunities had attracted Indians from all parts of the Presidency, and so the city was not the clear preserve of any one linguistic or ethnic group.[4] Half its population spoke Marathi, another fifth Gujarati, and over one-tenth Hindustani. Less than one man in twenty was a Kanarese-speaker.[5] Similarly the city contained many different communities. Among the Muslims, who formed a larger proportion of the population here than in any other part of the Presidency outside Sind, the influential section were the well-to-do traders. They were for the most part Memons, Bohras and Khojas, whose trade lay with the traditional markets of western India—the Persian Gulf and the east coast of Africa. Perhaps the most enterprising group among them was the tiny Sulaimani sect of

---

[1] *HIG*, III, 65, 81.

[2] Among Indian trade associations were the Bombay Cotton Trade Association, founded in 1876, and the Bombay Native Piece-goods Merchants Association founded in 1881.

[3] Of these, thirty-six mills employing almost 32,000 people were in the city. *HIG*, III, 60, 81.

[4] *1881 Census, Bombay City*, pp. 63–5.

[5] *Ibid.* p. 58.

Bohras, from whose ranks came the first Muslim barrister, solicitor, doctor and civil engineer of western India.[1]

But the most spectacular partakers in Bombay's prosperity were the Parsis, a small community of Zoroastrians who had immigrated to western India. They spoke Gujarati, and it was from Gujarat, where the only other large Parsi community still lived, that they had originally moved to the city.[2] But unlike other communities, most Parsis by this period were not immigrants from outlying districts but had been born in the city.[3] They had achieved great success in all of the city's most active commercial and industrial affairs. They were far more than business men of the old school. Their trading operations extended beyond Asia and Africa, making them the active competitors of the British in European markets as well. The Parsis were among the biggest property-owners in the city. They were also its leading citizens, who had played an active part in public affairs from the early days of municipal politics. Indeed this close-knit community of Zoroastrians embraced the British connection so fervently that the first Indian baronet belonged to the Parsi dynasty of Jeejeebhoy.[4]

Among their Hindu competitors in the city's trade and property-holding, Gujaratis were the most important group. Banias from Gujarat had achieved great success along the more traditional lines of foreign trade and on the Bombay cotton exchange. Gujarati Brahmins in the city were chiefly there as priestly clients of the traders, and were as little inclined towards the new educational opportunities here as in their native districts. The main thrust of Brahmin immigration into the city came from Maharashtra.[5] By the second half of the century Chitpavans and Deshaths were proving much readier to turn to the new education than their fathers had been. Consequently

---

[1] *1881 Census, Bombay City*, p. 46. The Tyabji family were Sulaimani Bohras.

[2] Parsis were 0·4 per cent of the Presidency's population in 1881; in Bombay city they were 6·3 per cent of the population and in Surat district, 2·1. Elsewhere their numbers were insignificant. *1881 Census, Bombay*, I, 44.

[3] 70·3 per cent of the Parsi population were born in the city. *1881 Census, Bombay City*, p. 63.

[4] D. F. Karaka, *History of the Parsis* (London, 1884), II, 109.

[5] Eighteen per cent of the city's Brahmins were born in Bombay, another 18 per cent were natives of Ratnagari district, 7·5 of Poona, 3·7 of Thana and 3·1 of Satara. *1881 Census, Bombay City*, pp. 63–4.

they filled the schools, colleges, offices and courtrooms of Bombay.[1] But the bulk of the Maharashtrian immigration was composed of Marathas and Kunbis of whom there were more than 175,000 in the city in 1881. At first they had come from nearby districts, often as seasonal labourers,[2] later they were to provide India's first disciplined labour force in the cotton mills.[3]

For all the activities that made Bombay a metropolis, dominating the Presidency as an agent of westernisation, it was not able to impose upon its hinterlands the same unmistakable stamp which Calcutta had pressed upon its mofussil. Whereas native Calcutta was undeniably Bengali in tone and temper, the ethos of Bombay was both more ambiguous and more eclectic. Of the numerous groups jostling inside the city none enjoyed a clear primacy. Parsis—city-born, wealthy and educated—could do little more than ingratiate themselves with their rulers while coming to terms with their more numerous fellow-citizens. The Muslims had no hinterland from which they could influence the city. The Gujarati seths, another strong monied interest, were far away from their homeland. Moreover they were split by caste and by faith, and they had little tradition of public life. At first sight, then, it might seem that the best chance to dominate the city was left to the Marathi-speakers. They were the most numerous of its citizens, Maharashtra was close at hand, and they had as leaders the able Brahmins who were becoming the province's administrators and professional men. But the early politics of the city were controlled by a coalition among oligarchies where wealth and property counted most; and most Maratha Brahmins had neither qualification. Later the basis of politics was to change as educated and professional groups began to assert themselves. But the Chitpavans and Deshaths could never monopolise classroom and college as the bhadralok could in Calcutta.[4] In a city not their own and pullulating with ambitious and able men who also saw the advantages

---

[1] In 1837 a missionary had reported that 'in Puna, and through the whole of the Dakkan, a knowledge of English is not particularly an object of desire, even with the great and wealthy...The case is very different at the great emporium of the country', quoted in McCully, *English Education*, p. 114.

[2] *1881 Census, Bombay City*, pp. 58, 64.

[3] M. D. Morris, *The Emergence of an Industrial Labor Force in India* (Berkeley and Los Angeles, 1965), pp. 39–83.

[4] See below, pp. 85–6, 89.

6-2

of education, they had to be content with an uneasy partnership. So when the revival of their aspirations called for a centre of Maharashtrian civilisation, it was to Poona that they returned.

🦚

In the Presidency of Bombay, education was distributed very unevenly. The level of literacy was highest in Bombay city.[1] In the hinterland, it was highest in Gujarat where there was 'a healthy division of trades and occupations; the fruits of agriculture are assured, and everywhere there are signs of prosperity and contentment. With a rich soil and abundant openings for educated talent in trade and commerce the upper classes are independent, and the middle classes ready to improve their position.'[2] Of the Marathi-speaking districts, Poona was the best educated, but in general literacy these districts were behind Gujarat, and on a par with the Karnatak. Sind was the most backward region, and its population was almost wholly illiterate.[3] Statistics on literacy in the most advanced district in each division are given in table 23.

TABLE 23. *Percentage of males either learning or literate, Bombay Presidency, 1881 and 1891*

	1881	1891
Bombay city	32·5	31·9
Gujarat		
Broach	20·9	27·9
Konkan		
Kanara	12·4	15·7
Deccan		
Poona	12·1	14·1
Karnatak		
Dharwar	11·6	15·7
Sind		
Karachi	9·3	10·9
Bombay Presidency	11·4	12·6

Source: *1891 Census, Bombay*, VII, 104.

[1] In 1881, one-third of the city's male population was either learning or literate. *1891 Census, Bombay*, VII, 194.
[2] *EC (Bombay)*, I, 60. Even Gujarat's Muslims were 'not strangers' to this 'general and active spirit of enterprise'.
[3] Of Sind's Muslims, who were 78 per cent of the population, 'only 1·4 per cent are educated in any sense of the word', *ibid.* 59.

Statistics of literacy alone are misleading, for they say nothing about what kinds of education were received. In secondary English education Gujarat was not clearly ahead of the Marathi-speaking districts,[1] and in college education it was far behind. The citizens of Ahmadabad had indeed set up the Gujarat College to supply the region with administrators and thus prevent the influx of 'foreigners from the Deccan or other provinces' which the shortage of Gujarati graduates had encouraged. But in 1882 this College had nine pupils in all, and only two of them were successful in the university examinations.[2] In contrast, the Deccan College at Poona had 121 students and was the only flourishing college outside Bombay city. Moreover, a large proportion of the undergraduates in Bombay city's three colleges came from 'the Marathi-speaking section of the Hindu community'.[3] Fergusson College, set up in Poona in 1885, soon became one of the largest colleges in the Presidency.[4] College education was thus concentrated in the cities of Bombay and Poona.

In terms of communities the picture was more complex. Although college education in Poona, and to a lesser extent in Bombay, was sustained by the enthusiasm of Maharashtrian Brahmins, there was another community in western India still better educated than they. By 1891 more than three-quarters of male Parsis were either at school or literate; more than a quarter knew English.[5] This small community, a mere 0·4 per cent of the Presidency's population, contained 21·69 per cent

---

[1] The Northern (or Gujarat) division had ten high schools in 1877; in the Central, or Marathi-speaking division there were six, and there were another three in the Marathi-speaking North-eastern division, and four in the Southern division, which was partly Marathi-speaking and partly Kanarese. Bombay city had one government and fourteen aided high schools. (*RDPI (Bombay) 1877–8*, p. 17.) Of 400 successful pupils in the 1879 matriculation examination, Gujarat sent ninety-eight, the Marathi-speaking districts (together with the Kanarese) 123, and 158 came from the city of Bombay; from Sind there were only fifteen. (*RDPI (Bombay) 1879–80*, p. 32.)

[2] *EC (Bombay)*, I, 135–7.

[3] *Ibid.* A decade before, of sixty-nine Brahmins at Elphinstone College, forty-one were Maharashtrians, nineteen Gujaratis, and nine Saraswats. (*RDPI (Bombay) 1869–70*, appendix B, no. 1, 254–5.)

[4] See P. M. Limaye, *The History of the Deccan Education Society (1880–1935)* (Poona, 1935), appendix XXVII. By 1897, the year of the plague, the College had 348 pupils.

[5] See table 25, below, p. 88.

of all college students and 13·25 per cent of all high and middle school pupils in 1881. The absolute number of Parsi students receiving a higher education was second only to that of the Brahmins.[1] In all the main university examinations held from 1858 to 1876 they contributed 26·1 per cent of the successful candidates and in the next decade they were to contribute 21·4 per cent.[2] Parsis were 'far more advanced in educational interest than even the Brahmans'.[3]

In marked contrast, few Muslims received an English education and fewer still went to university. In Sind where two-thirds of them lived, illiteracy was so widespread as to drag down the community's average educational attainments in the Presidency as a whole. In college, Muslims were only 1·47 per cent of the students, and in high and middle schools they were 4·39 per cent in 1881.[4] In university examinations too they were falling behind. Before 1876, 2·05 per cent of the successful candidates were Muslims; between 1876 and 1886 only 1·3 per cent.[5] In these ten years only ten Muslims became Bachelors of Arts. But at the lower levels the educational backwardness of the community was less striking. In fact, outside Sind, the community was proportionately more literate than the Hindu. It was not religious prejudice and language difficulties which kept them out of the higher schools so much as the lack of incentive. In none of the occupations they usually followed—ranging from unskilled jobs as porters, cart-drivers, constables, watchmen and messengers to more lucrative employment as traders—was higher education necessary.[6]

It was natural in a Presidency so dominated by the Hindu community that Hindus should dominate higher education. They were almost 80 per cent of the population, and in 1881–2 they were three-quarters of the students and scholars in college, high and middle school.[7] Their percentage of university suc-

[1] *EC*, pp. 227, 275.
[2] Calculated from *RDPI (Bombay) 1878–9*, p. 22; and Annual Return by Religion of Successful Candidates (Entrance, First Arts, B.A. and M.A.) 1876–86, *PSC*, appendix M, statement I, pp. 78–9.
[3] *RDPI (Bombay) 1884–5*, p. 121.   [4] *EC*, pp. 227, 275.
[5] Calculated from *RDPI (Bombay) 1878–9*, p. 22; and *PSC*, appendix M, statement I, pp. 78–9.
[6] *1881 Census, Bombay*, I, 158–60.
[7] The precise figures are 73·48 per cent in college, 72·08 per cent in the schools. Besides Parsis, the only other community to dent the Hindu

cesses was rising: 64·9 per cent before 1876, and 72·6 per cent between 1876 and 1886.[1] Table 24 gives the caste of Hindu students in 1875 and, in a roughly comparable form, in 1881.[2]

TABLE 24. *Caste of Hindu students in 1875 and 1881, Bombay Presidency*

(Percentage of total Hindu students)

| 1875 | College | High school | Middle school | | Primary school |
			First grade	Second grade	
Brahmins	66·1	61·3	46·6	37·2	27·3
Prabhus and other writer castes	11·6	7·3	10·0	3·9	3·4
Trading castes	16·0	13·0	18·1	18·6	12·3
All others	6·3	18·4	25·3	40·3	57·0

Source: Calculated from *RDPI* (*Bombay*) *1875-6*, pp. 106–7.

1881	College	High and middle school	Primary school
Brahmins	66·1	50·5	36·8
Kshattris	4·2	3·0	4·3
Other writers	9·7	12·6	2·4
Traders	14·4	16·1	17·0
Shopkeepers	0·0	1·7	5·0
All others	5·6	16·1	34·5

Source: Calculated from figures returned by the Director of Public Instruction, *1881 Census, Bombay*, I, 168.

Table 25 shows the extent of literacy and knowledge of English among the various castes of the Hindu community and compares it with the educational attainments of the other communities.

preponderance was the Indian Christians, who had 1·89 per cent of college and 8·14 per cent of the high and middle school places. (*EC*, pp. 227, 275.) In the Presidency, there were 138,317 Christians (including Europeans and Eurasians) of whom almost two-thirds lived in the city or in the neighbouring district of Thana. (*1881 Census, Bombay*, I, 44; II, table III, 3.)

[1] Calculated from *RDPI* (*Bombay*) *1878–9*, p. 22; and *PSC*, appendix M, statement I, pp. 78–9.

[2] The caste percentages in 1884–5 were much the same. Brahmins were 60·1 per cent of all Hindus at college, and 54·6 per cent of Hindus at high school. But other castes were slowly increasing their share of higher education. Calculated from *RDPI* (*Bombay*) *1884–5*, pp. 122–3.

TABLE 25. *Literacy and knowledge of English by caste and community, Bombay Presidency, 1891*

Caste	Total males in caste	Total males literate	Percentage of male literates	Total males knowing English (excluding pupils)	Percentage of males knowing English
All Brahmins	*570,885*	*272,170*	*47·6*	*20,544*	*3·6*
Deshasth	148,968	83,584	56·5	5,197	3·5
Konkanasth or Chitpavan	60,371	32,586	54·0	5,810	9·6
Audich	82,742	34,188	41·2	1,087	1·3
Gaud	17,603	8,876	50·0	1,007	5·7
Nagar	10,457	5,698	54·5	942	9·0
Karhada	17,362	9,589	55·4	913	5·3
Saraswat	10,627	5,100	48·2	790	7·0
Kshattriya	*24,664*	*7,166*	*29·0*	*1,429*	*5·8*
Writer castes	*15,483*	*8,101*	*52·3*	*2,541*	*16·4*
Prabhu Kayasth	9,185	4,795	52·0	832	9·0
Prabhu unspecified	2,996	1,716	57·3	1,272	42·4
Trading castes Hindu, Muslim and Jain	*654,120*	*270,939*	*41·3*	*4,513*	*0·7*
Agricultural castes					
Maratha	1,084,036	41,395	3·8	1,167	0·1
Kunbi Deccani	820,949	18,391	2·2	157	—
Mali	152,560	4,602	3·0	277	0·2
Kunbi Lewa	284,937	28,792	10·1	173	0·6
Kunbi Kadwa	140,968	13,842	9·9	62	0·4
Lingayat	290,451	31,836	10·9	201	0·6
Other communities					
Parsis	38,442	22,611	58·8	10,462	27·2
Eurasians	4,079	1,935	47·4	1,805	44·2
Indian Christians	71,417	16,286	22·8	8,945	12·5

Source: Calculated from *1891 Census, Bombay*, VII, appendix A, table no. 4, vii; VIII, tables C and D, Castes, by Education, 394–420.

Among Hindus, the Brahmins took by far the largest share of the new educational opportunities; and it was in college and high school that their superiority was most marked. Among the Brahmins, the Chitpavans and Deshaths had done best. In Maharashtra, 'higher secular education' had always been 'the monopoly of the Brahman caste... Its object was to fit the scholar for the public service... The exclusive right of the Brahman caste to higher education was a tradition sanctioned by religion and enforced by public opinion.' For other castes in Maharashtra traditional education was 'practical instruction in such special subjects as would engage in after life the attention of the schoolboy, whose career was already irrevocably mapped out for him by caste'.[1] In 1882, at Deccan College in Poona, 93 per cent of the Hindus were Brahmins.[2] In Maharashtra, where writers were few, traders poor and agrarian castes illiterate, the Brahmins had the educational field almost to themselves. But they were not equally pre-eminent in every part of the Presidency. In Gujarat they were less well educated than the trading castes.[3] In the city of Bombay trading and writer castes alike were also active in higher education. In 1882 less than half the Hindus (46·4 per cent) at Elphinstone College were Brahmins, 30 per cent were members of trading castes, mainly Gujaratis, and 14·1 per cent were Prabhus.[4] It was only in the city that the writer castes, a mere 0·21 per cent of the Presidency's population, challenged Brahmins seriously, for this was 'the point apparently, to which these classes tend, as in the free competition of a commercial city the hereditary qualification of the Brahman as the educated class is postponed in favour of personal merit'.[5] But here they forced the Brahmins to share their educational advantages with others who differed from them not only in community and caste but also in economic standing.

[1] *EC (Bombay)*, I, 216.
[2] Calculated from *EC (Bombay)*, I, 136.
[3] Of thirty-six castes with the highest literacy in the Presidency, twenty-one were Brahmin, nine were trading castes, and four were writer castes. Chitpavans headed the list. Five castes from Gujarat had a place among the top twelve, but none was Brahmin. Nagars, highest among Gujarati Brahmins, were sixteenth in the serial order, and no less than five Gujarati trading castes were ahead of them. *1881 Census, Bombay*, I, 164.
[4] Calculated from *EC (Bombay)*, I, 136. At Deccan College there were only three Prabhus and one solitary Bania at this date.
[5] *1881 Census, Bombay*, I, 129.

This can be illustrated by considering next the occupations and incomes of the parents of the students. Table 26 sets out parental occupations in the Presidency's six arts colleges in 1882.

TABLE 26. *Occupation of parents of students in Arts colleges, Bombay Presidency, 1881–2*

Government servants	149
Professional persons	52
Clerks	77
Merchants and traders	72
Persons of property	35
Government pensioners	27
Priests	14
Cultivators	16
Zemindars	10
Others	23
Total	475

Source: *EC* (*Bombay*), 1, 136.

At all colleges, government servants were the largest group among the parents. But Bombay and Poona differed sharply in their ability to attract pupils from commerce. More than

TABLE 27. *Occupation of parents of students in government colleges, high schools and first-grade Anglo-vernacular schools, Bombay Presidency, 1877–8*

	Number	Percentage
Government officials	*1,778*	
Government officials (native states)	*360*	
Village officers	*149*	
Pensioners	*110*	
Soldiers	*17*	
Total government servants	2,414	30·0
Private clerks	1,443	14·5
Professional persons	668	8·2
Priests	321	3·3
Commercial classes	1,483	18·0
Others	1,799	26·0
Total	*8,128*	*100·0*

Source: Calculated from *RDPI* (*Bombay*), *1877–8*, p. 47.

20 per cent of Elphinstone's pupils were the sons of business-men, but at Deccan College less than 10 per cent came from a similar background.[1]

Parental occupations of all college, high and middle school students in 1877–8 are set out in table 27 above. It will be seen that at high and middle schools the pattern was much the same. In Gujarat merchants sent more children to school than did government servants, whereas in Maharashtra government servants were by far the largest parental group. Sons of professional men and of 'persons of property' were most numerous in the city of Bombay.[2] In the Presidency as a whole sons of government officials, clerks, professional men and 'persons of property' were clearly preponderant. Evidence taken by the Education Commission in 1882 supports these conclusions. According to the Superintendent of the New English School at Poona, most of its pupils were the sons of public servants, clerks or small landholders. R. G. Bhandarkar pointed out that while education had made some progress among merchants in Bombay city, most students were from castes 'whose occupation under the old regime was writing'. A. B. Desai stressed that both lawyers and men employed in the ad-ministration of native states were seeking education for their sons.[3] The high proportion of parents belonging to the 'commercial classes' reflected the educational attainments of Parsis and of Gujarati traders both here and in their native districts.

Yet over the Presidency as a whole it was the case that 'the wealthy classes...furnish but a small proportion of the students', and this was mainly, as one Parsi observer noticed in 1882, because 'learning has been looked upon only as a means for obtaining a livelihood'. It was 'the struggling but

[1] *EC (Bombay)*, I, 136.
[2] In 1877 at Elphinstone High School in Bombay there were 711 pupils; of these 328 were sons of 'persons of property or professional men', 275 of 'government officials and private clerks', and sixty-nine of traders. At Poona High School, 268 of its 482 pupils, or more than 55 per cent, were sons of government servants, ninety-six of professional men or persons of property, and thirty-seven of tradesmen. In high schools in the Deccan an interesting feature was the large number of sons of impoverished Brahmin priests and mendicants: sixty-five in Dhulia High School, twenty-four at Nasik, twenty in Satara and seven in Poona. *RDPI (Bombay) 1877–8*, pp. 30–8.
[3] *EC (Bombay)*, II, 233, 266, 285.

respectable' classes who wanted education.[1] In Maharashtra the parents of college and high school boys were manifestly poor. Of 105 parents of pupils at Deccan College in 1882, only five had monthly incomes of Rs 500 and over; eleven earned between Rs 250 and 500, nineteen between Rs 100 and 200, thirty-one between Rs 50 and 100, and thirty-nine under Rs 50 per month. Obviously many of them could ill afford college fees amounting to Rs 22 a month.[2] More striking still was the financial standing of those parents who sent their children to the New English School, Poona:

TABLE 28. *Parental incomes, New English School, Poona, 1882*

Annual income	Number of parents
Nil (beggars)	19
Under Rs 100	70
Rs 100–200	95
Rs 200–400	112
Rs 400–600	87
Rs 600–1,000	78
Rs 1,000–3,000	92
Rs 3,000 and over	20
Total	573

Source: *EC (Bombay)*, II, 234.

Thus more than two-thirds of the parents had incomes of under Rs 600 per year, or Rs 50 per month, just 3·5 per cent had monthly incomes above Rs 250, and the same percentage were beggars. 'As a general rule', was the official conclusion,

the only students who can be said to belong to wealthy families are Parsis and a few of the Gujarathi Hindus. But the students drawn from the Marathi-speaking portion of the Hindu community are, as a rule, poor and dependent on scholarships, or on stipends earned for private tuition or on private charity. It is from this class that most of the students in Deccan College and a considerable portion of the Hindu students in Elphinstone College are drawn.[3]

Thus the social groups in Bombay Presidency who obtained higher education at this time were not as homogeneous as those of Bengal. Western India was producing two different types of

---

[1] See *EC (Bombay)*, II, 249, 256, 266, 285. In 1867 the Principal of Elphinstone had warned that 'the rich will be able to afford their ignorance until they feel pressure from below' (*RDPI (Bombay)*, *1867–8*, appendix B, no. 1, p. 172).   [2] *Ibid.* p. 233.   [3] *EC (Bombay)*, I, 137.

educated elite. Those emerging from the colleges of Poona belonged overwhelmingly to the Maharashtrian Brahmin castes who were themselves a dominant group in their local society. But of those emerging from the colleges of Bombay city, Maharashtrian Brahmins were a much smaller proportion, and inside the metropolis they were far from being the pre-eminent group.

🎗

The twenty-two British districts of Madras Presidency extended over an area of almost 120,000 square miles with a population of just under thirty millions. They comprised four distinct regions. In the north lay the Telegu country, or Andhra, roughly covered by the British districts of Vizagapatam, Godavari, Kistna, Nellore, Kurnool, Cuddapah, Anantapur, and part of North Arcot. To the south-east lay Tamilnad, the home of one of the oldest civilisations in India, extending through North Arcot, South Arcot, Chingleput, Salem, Coimbatore, Tanjore, Trichinopoly, Tinnevelly and Madura. In Tamilnad there were large numbers of Telegu speakers, but the Tamils themselves showed little propensity to move into the Telegu area.[1] On the west coast, Malabar extended beyond the district of that name into the native states of Travancore and Cochin. In South Kanara were the Kanarese-speaking people whose affinities lay with the state of Mysore and with the southern districts of Bombay Presidency. Besides these main divisions, Ganjam and Vizagapatam contained large Oriya-speaking minorities.

The people of these regions had little contact with north India. The rivers and hills of central India hampered easy communications, and the sharp differences in language and social systems accentuated the isolation of the south from Hindustan. Yet since the fall of the empire of Vijayanagar in 1565, the internal divisiveness of south India had enabled northern empires to conquer it. Mughal lieutenants came to power along the Coromandel Coast and in Hyderabad, while other parts of the country passed under Maratha rule. In the second half of the eighteenth century the struggle for power developed into a series of wars between the Europeans, the Nizam of Hyderabad, the Marathas and the Muslim rulers of

[1] This trend goes back to the days of the Vijayanagar empire.

Madras Presidency

Mysore. The peoples of south India, the prize for which these struggles were fought, had little connection with any of them. When the British emerged as victors, they thus controlled a population inured to alien government, and one British ruler after another was to comment upon their docility. The upheavals of the wars had devastated the land. A foot-loose soldiery had trampled over it. Many of its peasants had fled. Pressed financially, the Company pitched its revenue assessments high and did its utmost to prevent the peasantry from moving freely from one locality to another. But although the Presidency passed through hard times, it was little disturbed by civil commotion. Later in the century, when southern agriculture was beginning to recover, the Presidency was struck by the famines of the 1870s and 1880s.[1]

Of the three Presidencies, Madras had the least complicated communal structure, by reason of the overwhelming Hindu majority. There were only a few Muslims: on the west coast there were the fanatical Moplahs; other Muslims were concentrated in the central districts and Madras city. They were mostly poor converts, with only a handful of influential men to lead them. Most of the Christian converts in India lived in the Presidency, the Catholics mainly in Malabar, and the Protestants along the east coast. By 1881 there were almost three-quarters of a million Christians in Madras. They were drawn mainly from the lowest Hindu classes, but the educational work of the missions did much to improve their position. Table 29 sets out the districts of Madras and the communal distribution of their population.

In the south the caste system was far more rigid than in other parts of India. Although they were a smaller proportion of the Hindu population than in other provinces,[2] Brahmins commanded status and respect to a greater degree than elsewhere. Apart from a few castes of dubious Kshattriya status,[3] they and

[1] S. Srinivasa Raghavaiyangar, *Memorandum on the Progress of the Madras Presidency during the last forty years of British Administration* (2nd edition, Madras, 1893), pp. 1–43. But see D. Kumar, *Land and Caste in South India* (Cambridge, 1965), pp. 168–93.

[2] In 1881 the percentage of Brahmins of the total Hindu population was 3·9 in Madras compared with 6·1 in Bengal, 4·8 in Bombay, 12·2 in the North-western Provinces and Oudh, and 11·6 in the Punjab. *1881 Census, Madras*, I, 111.

[3] Just under two hundred thousand persons were returned as Kshattriyas. *Ibid.* I, 110.

TABLE 29. *Area, population and communal distribution, Madras Presidency, 1881*

District	Total area in square miles	Total population	Hindus (%)	Muslims (%)	Christians (%)
Ganjam	3,106	1,503,301	99·5	0·4	0·1
Vizagapatam	3,477	1,790,468	98·7	1·1	0·2
Godavari	6,525	1,780,613	97·6	2·2	0·2
Kistna	8,471	1,548,480	92·0	5·6	2·3
Nellore	8,739	1,220,236	93·3	5·0	1·2
Cuddapah	8,745	1,121,038	90·7	8·7	0·5
Kurnool	7,788	709,305	86·8	11·5	1·6
Bellary	11,007	1,336,696	91·3	8·2	0·4
Chingleput	2,842	981,381	95·7	2·6	1·7
North Arcot	7,256	1,817,814	94·5	4·5	0·6
South Arcot	4,873	1,814,738	94·9	2·7	2·2
Tanjore	3,654	2,130,383	91·0	5·3	3·7
Trichinopoly	3,561	1,215,033	92·1	2·8	5·1
Madura	8,401	2,168,680	89·6	6·5	3·9
Tinnevelly	5,381	1,699,747	86·4	5·3	8·3
Salem	7,653	1,599,595	95·8	3·2	1·0
Coimbatore	7,842	1,657,690	96·9	2·3	0·8
Nilgiris	957	91,034	86·8	3·9	9·3
Malabar	5,765	2,365,035	70·6	27·6	1·8
South Kanara	3,902	959,514	83·1	9·8	6·1
Madras city	27	405,848	77·8	12·4	9·8
Total	119,972	29,916,629	91·1	6·4	2·3
Pudukota Territory	1,101	302,127	93·3	3·0	3·7
Agency tracts specially censused					
Ganjam	5,205	246,303	99·9	0·1	—
Vizagapatam	13,903	694,673	99·9	0·1	—
Godavari	820	10,899	99·8	0·1	0·1
Grand total for the Presidency	141,001	31,170,631	91·4	6·2	2·3

Source: *1881 Census, Madras*, II, 2, 3, 40.

they alone were considered Aryans among the local Dravidian population. But the position of the Brahmins varied from region to region. In Malabar, the Nambudris might have seemed the most highly respected Brahmins in all India. They exercised dreaded powers of social interdict and excommunication over other castes, were courted by the flower of Nayar womanhood, and revered as practically divine.[1] They were affluent into the

---

[1] Secure from the pricks of necessity, the Nambudris remained the most conservative of castes. C. A. Innes, *Madras District Gazetteers, Malabar*

bargain, but it was not with them but with the non-Brahmin Nayars that effective social dominance lay. Originally a military caste of invaders claiming Kshattriya status, the Nayars owned most of the land and commanded unquestioned subservience from the peasantry. They were also the best educated community on the west coast. As the intellectual equals of the Brahmins of the east coast, they successfully competed with them in the professions and public services of the south.

In Tamilnad the Brahmins maintained their high ritual status while increasing their social and economic power. Split into two religious sects, the Smarthas and Vaishnavites, Tamil Brahmins were broken into a multitude of sub-castes.[1] About half of them lived in the three districts of Tanjore, Trichinopoly and Tinnevelly,[2] where they possessed an unquestioned pre-eminence. In Tanjore, the Brahmin district *par excellence*, hardly a family among them did not possess land, and some had valuable estates. Nominally a raiyatwari area,[3] much of Tamilnad was in fact organised more like a squirearchy. Although they had the legal status of raiyats, Brahmin landholders were not humble peasants. Many of them had been mirasidars, the traditional large landholders, and they divided their lands into lots cultivated at rack rents by tenants.[4]

Tamil Brahmins, and the Aiyengars especially, were as famous for their ambition and adaptability as the Chitpavans of Maharashtra. An official manual noted 'there is hardly a pursuit, literary, industrial or professional, to which they do not apply themselves with remarkable success'.[5] There were also a number of Deshath Brahmins marooned after the Maratha

and Anjengo (Madras, 1915), pp. 104–15; E. Thurston, *Castes and Tribes of Southern India* (Madras, 1909), V, 152–241, 283–413.

[1] See Thurston, *Castes and Tribes*, I, 269, 333–56; *1881 Census, Madras*, I, 107 and A. Béteille, *Caste, Class and Power: Changing Patterns of Stratification in a Tanjore Village* (Berkeley and Los Angeles, 1965), pp. 46–69.

[2] In Tanjore district, Brahmins were 6·94 per cent of the Hindu population; in Tinnevelly, 4·03; in Chingleput, 3·41; in Trichinopoly, 3·04 per cent; and in every other Tamil-speaking district less than 3 per cent. *1881 Census, Madras*, I, 253–300.

[3] The raiyatwari system of land settlement in the south was different from that in Bombay in the important respect that settlements were made annually. See Baden-Powell, *Land-systems of British India*, III, 3–194.

[4] G. Slater, *Southern India. Its Political and Economic Problems* (1936), pp. 117–18.

[5] T. Venkaswami Row, *A Manual of the District of Tanjore, in the Madras Presidency* (Madras, 1883), p. 170.

invasions in Tamilnad where they still enjoyed something of their old reputation for administrative skill and intellectual superiority. They dominated the lower grades of the administration when it passed to the British, and as late as 1855 they supplied most of the sherestidars, naib sherestidars and tahsildars throughout Madras.[1] But in the second half of the century competition from Tamil Brahmins was gradually depriving them both of their prestige and of their positions. The Tamil Brahmins, by securing a tight grip on the new educational system, rapidly infiltrated government service and the law. To a strong ritual and economic position they thus added new sources of social prestige and wealth. Telegu Brahmins, both Vaidikis, or priests, and Niyogis, or laymen,[2] were slower in adapting to the new conditions and less successful in pushing out the Maratha Brahmins from the local administration in Andhra.

In the south the gulf between Brahmins and non-Brahmins, whether in status, ritual or language, was immense. There were few Kshattriyas and Vaisyas.[3] No large writer caste challenged the Brahmins in the administrative field, as it did in Bengal.[4] But among the 80 per cent of the Hindu population classified as Sudras,[5] there were several castes of importance, the Vellalas and the Chettis among the Tamils, and the Kapus, Kamas and Balija Naidus among the Telegus. Yet none of these had much solidarity. Among the Vellalas, for example, there were divisions of ritual, of sect and of sub-caste. Most of them were cultivators but some had started going to school and seeking

[1] R. E. Frykenberg, *Guntur District, 1788–1848* (Oxford, 1965), p. 77. In 1891 there were 33,274 Deshath Brahmins in the Presidency, equally divided between the Tamil and Telegu country (*1891 Census, Madras*, XIV, 311). The role of the Maratha Brahmin in the early politics of the south is important; it will be examined in a later volume.

[2] In 1891 there were 113,427 Vaidikis and 100,942 Niyogis in the Telegu districts. *1891 Census, Madras*, XIV, 312–13. The Niyogis were more adaptable and better educated than the Vaidikis, and they shared with the Tamil Brahmins some of the new opportunities. See table 35, below, p. 108.

[3] Some Kapus or Reddis claimed to have once possessed Kshattriya status, while the Telegu Komatis and the Tamil Vellalas and some Chettis aspired to Vaisya ranking.

[4] The Kanakans and Karnams, or writers, were just over a hundred thousand in number, or 0·34 per cent of the Hindu population (*1881 Census, Madras*, I, 110); and they were not as enterprising or as learned as the Prabhus of Bombay. See Thurston, *Castes and Tribes*, III, 150–9; IV, 1–3.

[5] *1881 Census, Madras*, I, 104.

public employment. Some were village accountants, and a few were public servants of higher standing. By 1871, at least one Vellala had taken his M.A. degree.[1] The Chettis were the main Tamil trading caste, so numerous in the district of Ramnad that it was sometimes known as Chettinad; but the caste was found throughout the Presidency and further afield in south-east Asia.[2] In the Telegu country, the Kapus or Reddis were cultivators, farmers and small landlords, with a firm grip on the land. They were the largest single caste in the Presidency. Ranking next to the Brahmins in the social scale, and pro-hibiting widow remarriage, they were as yet still reluctant to move from their position of rural dominance to classroom and office.[3] Kamas, who were closely allied to them, were also cultivators who owned many of the zemindaris in the per-manently settled districts of the north. Recalling with pride their alleged Kshattriya origins, they shunned any form of domestic service and were punctilious in religious matters.[4] The chief Telegu trading caste was the Balija Naidu, who were found in every part of the Presidency. Affiliated to the Kapus, they too possessed 'a high place in the social system'; most of them were traders, a few were landowners, and they evinced greater enthusiasm for learning than the Kapus.[5] Towards the end of the nineteenth century Tamil and Telegu non-Brahmins alike began to trespass upon the preserve of the Brahmins, setting the pattern for the later politics of Madras.[6] But it was at the bottom of society that the caste system of south India showed its full rigour; here the Pariahs, or untouchables, were more numerous than in other parts of the country and their disabilities were more crippling.[7]

[1] Thurston, *Castes and Tribes*, VII, 361–89.
[2] *Ibid.* II, 91–7.
[3] *Ibid.* III, 222–48. Thurston reported a 'common saying among the Kapus that they can easily enumerate all the varieties of rice, but it is impossible to give the names of all the sections into which the caste is split up' (*Ibid.* III, 226).   [4] *Ibid.* III, 94–105.   [5] *Ibid.* I, 134–45.
[6] Among the Sudras, the Census Commissioners in 1881 confessed that 'the question of status becomes hopeless'. Acquired wealth and education was 'a factor in the change going on in respect of social pre-eminence. And it is not to be understood that this change has made great way yet. It is in the large towns that it is chiefly noticeable...' (*1881 Census, Madras*, I, 104–5.)
[7] In 1881 there were about three and a quarter million Pariahs in the Presi-dency, that is to say, 15·5 per cent of the Hindu population, *ibid.* I, 109–10.

In Madras Presidency, five main languages were spoken. Table 30 shows their regional distribution.

TABLE 30. *Distribution of main languages in Madras Presidency, 1881*

	Tamil (%)	Telugu (%)	Malayalam (%)	Kanarese (%)	Oriya (%)	Others (%)
Ganjam	—	39·6	—	—	44·4	—
Vizagapatam	—	82·6	—	—	14·0	—
Godavari	—	96·5	—	—	—	—
Kistna	—	93·8	—	—	—	5·1*
Nellore	—	93·7	—	—	—	—
Cuddapah	—	90·4	—	—	—	—
Bellary and Anantapur	—	52·4	—	37·7	—	—
Chingleput	74·5	22·6	—	—	—	—
North Arcot	54·3	40·4	—	—	—	—
South Arcot	86·7	—	—	—	—	—
Tanjore	93·5	—	—	—	—	—
Trichinopoly	83·8	—	—	—	—	—
Madura	80·0	14·4	—	—	—	—
Tinnevelly	84·4	13·8	—	—	—	—
Salem	70·8	18·4	—	7·4	—	—
Coimbatore	65·6	20·8	—	12·2	—	—
Malabar	—	—	93·0	—	—	—
South Kanara	—	16·9	—	21·3	—	44·4†
Madras city	59·0	23·3	—	—	—	—
Total Presidency	39·7	38·8	7·6	4·2	3·6	
Total numbers	12,413,517	12,104,394	2,369,671	1,303,345	1,128,560	

Source: Calculated from *1881 Census, Madras*, I, 117–20, 195–325.

* Hindustani.   † Tulu.

Oriya apart, all these were Dravidian languages with long histories. The Tamil spoken by the Brahmins was heavily influenced by Sanskrit and differed both in vocabulary and accent from the Tamil spoken by non-Brahmins. By the 1860s the language was undergoing reform.[1] Telegu followed the same pattern somewhat later; by the end of the century the first generation speaking a modernised Telegu was already in-

[1] In modern times the champions of a Tamil free from Aryan influence have been the non-Brahmins.

fluential.[1] So far from there being a dominant language in the Presidency, both these tongues were spoken by about the same number of south Indians and although each was firmly based in its regional setting, nevertheless there was sharp competition between them. Their rivalry chiefly turned on the relative shares of Tamil and Telegu speakers in the administrative and professional posts for which the new education qualified them. Here the Tamils possessed an advantage. The capital of the Presidency was also their own chief city; western education was more actively developed in Tamilnad than in the Telegu country.[2] In time Telegu complaints became vocal; but they conveniently neglected the dominance of Telegu itself over those Oriya and Kanarese speakers who lived within predominantly Telegu districts. In this picture of linguistic rivalries, as in most other respects, Malabar presents a special case. Insulated by geography from the general movements inside the Presidency, and in any case greatly assisted in their educational progress both by the enterprise of the Nayars and by the large amount of Christian missionary activity, Malayalam speakers took their fair share of government posts.

The economy of Madras was in no sense unified, and of all the three Presidencies its agricultural system was the closest to subsistence and the furthest from exchange. It had few cash crops and no export staple of importance. This weakness was reflected in its trade, which both externally and internally was much less active than in Bengal or in Bombay.[3] There had been less pressure upon the Madras trader to modernise his affairs and little incentive for more alert Indian groups to try and supplant him. No effort had been made to challenge the European monopoly in the carrying trade to the west, and Indian enterprise continued to work only on the fringes of the Indian Ocean trade. Similarly, Madras had the weakest industrial sector. The early establishment of a few mills in Madras

---

[1] *General Report of the Census of India, 1901*, pp. 184–287; *Contemporary Indian Literature, A Symposium* (2nd edition, New Delhi, 1959), pp. 101, 106–7, 134–6, 285–6.

[2] See below, pp. 104–6.

[3] The total seaborne trade of Madras Presidency in 1871–2 was £18,767,506; in 1882–3, it was only £20,083,187; *HIG*, IX, 63. Whereas about 84 per cent of India's exports and imports were handled by Bombay and Calcutta, only 10 per cent moved through Madras. (Misra, *The Indian Middle Classes*, p. 42.)

city had not led to an expansion of the factory system, since the Presidency had no staples whose processing could sustain industrial development.[1] European capital and European management dominated what manufactures there were.[2] The transport system remained as underdeveloped as the economy it was designed to serve: the railways of the south had fallen far behind those in the other two Presidencies. Of India's 10,144 miles of railway in 1882, only 1,515 miles ran through Madras, and of nearly fifteen million tons of freight carried annually by rail in India, only 1,600,000 tons moved across the southern Presidency.[3] Indeed, its isolation was faithfully reflected in the pattern of its steel lines. Madras had a direct line to Bombay, but only a loop through central India gave it access to Calcutta.

Whereas Calcutta and Bombay had grown rapidly in the nineteenth century, Madras city had not. In 1881 it had a population of just over 400,000. It was a predominantly Hindu city, yet 12 per cent of its population was Muslim, a proportion considerably above the average for the Presidency, and nearly 10 per cent was Christian. Telegu Brahmins and traders, Malayalam-speaking Nayars, and some people from Kanara came to the city, but Madras remained primarily the capital of Tamilnad. It possessed nothing like the pulling power of Calcutta or Bombay. Three-quarters of its population were natives of the city, and of its immigrants, three-quarters came from adjoining districts, while a mere 9 per cent had travelled 'any appreciable distance'.[4] The city had not attracted a disproportionately large number of Brahmins. In 1881 they were returned as 13,469, or 4·2 per cent, of a Hindu population of 315,517.[5] In addition there were a few Kanakans, or accountants (2,450), about 6,000 Kshattriyas, and 22,000 traders. A striking index of the city's unbalanced nature is that whereas its male population was returned as containing a total of 17,424 in

[1] *HIG*, IX, 53–60.
[2] *Imperial Gazetteer of India, Provincial Series, Madras*, I (Calcutta, 1908), 68–70.
[3] Statistical Abstract relating to British India for 1873/4 to 1882/3, Eighteenth Number, *P.P.* 1884, LXXXIV, 481, 484.
[4] *1881 Census, Madras*, I, 128–9.
[5] In 1891, there were 17,749 Brahmins in Madras city and district. Of these, 9,400 came from four main Tamil Brahmin groups, Tengalai, Vadagalai, Vadama, and Smarta, and less than 2,500 from the Telegu Niyogi and Vaidiki. There were 979 Deshaths. *1891 Census, Madras*, XIV, 362, 364.

'professional' classes and 18,488 in 'commercial' classes, no fewer than 170,000 were returned as having 'indefinite and non-productive' occupations.[1]

Madras was the third largest city in India, the administrative headquarters of a Presidency, but it was not a rapidly expanding metropolis capable of dominating and galvanising its hinterland.[2] While Calcutta and Bombay were already modern cities, Madras remained a congeries of rural villages. Apart from Fort St George and a small area of Blacktown, it had no centre. Lack of industry was not compensated by an abundant trade; it had no natural harbour, and goods and passengers had to disembark by hazardous surf-boats on to an old iron jetty and roadstead.[3] The real activity of the city lay in its colleges and schoolrooms. It was the best-educated city in India, with one literate person in every four. In 1882 Madras had a university, five Arts colleges with 786 pupils, three colleges for professional training with 217 pupils, as well as a medical and an engineering college, fourteen English high schools with 1,263 students, and fifty-five middle and 154 primary schools, where English was taught to 3,461 and 9,627 boys respectively. In all there were more than 25,000 children at school, of whom about three-fifths were learning English.[4] Deprived of the excitement of Clive or Forbes Street, Madras enjoyed the consolations of Academe.

Despite its reputation as the 'benighted' Presidency, Madras possessed a level of literacy higher than any other province.[5] By 1886 it had five more English colleges than Bengal, and it had as many arts students. With twenty-three more colleges, and three times as many students, it was far ahead of Bombay.[6]

[1] *HIG*, IX, 108–9.
[2] The three most active Tamil districts all had natural centres of their own. In Tanjore district, both Tanjore town, Negapatam and Kumbakonam had populations of more than 50,000 in 1881; Trichinopoly, with a population of about 85,000, was the second largest city in the Presidency, and in Tinnevelly district where the towns were smaller, one person in five was a town dweller. *1881 Census, Madras*, I, 192–4.
[3] The first steps to provide a harbour were taken in 1871.
[4] *HIG*, IX, 115–16.
[5] Burma excepted. *1891 Census, Madras*, XIII, 178.
[6] *RDPI (Madras) 1886–7*, p. 102. But 'As regards Professional colleges... both Presidencies are greatly in advance of Madras, a state of things resulting from their greater wealth and industrial development' (*ibid.*).

Between 1864 and 1886, 61,124 candidates in Madras sat for
the university entrance examinations; in Bengal, 37,790 and in
Bombay, 24,857.[1] The number of arts graduates in this period
was as large in Madras as in Bengal.[2] The viceroyalties of
Lytton, Ripon and Dufferin coincided with a time of rapid
expansion of higher education in the south. In 1876 the only
arts colleges had been in the city of Madras and in the Tamil
district of Tanjore; by 1888 every district of the province had
its own. However, the 'enormous advantage...to the Tamil
population of the Presidency', which accrued from the location
of its early colleges, was not lost;[3] in higher education the Tamil
districts remained far ahead.[4] Table 31 shows the relative advance of the districts. More than 80 per cent of the undergraduates, and 70 per cent of the high school boys came from
Tamil districts, while the Telegu districts provided only 10 and
14 per cent respectively. Malabar, on the west coast, was relatively
advanced. Tanjore, Trichinopoly and Tinnevelly together had
about as many students as Madras city.

While college education in Bengal was dominated by Calcutta,
and in western India by Bombay and Poona, there was no such
dominance by Madras in the south. By 1883–4, of a total of
2,175 college pupils, 689, or a third, were in Madras city, but

[1] The failure rate in Madras and Bombay was higher than in Bengal; the
number of successful candidates was: Madras, 20,555; Bengal, 16,639;
Bombay, 7,723. *PSC*, appendix M, statements III and IV, pp. 81–2.

[2] Madras, 2,158; Bengal, 2,153; Bombay, 1,014, *ibid.*

[3] *RDPI (Madras) 1875–6*, p. 120, and *RDPI (Madras) 1887–8*, map facing
p. 50.

[4] In 1877–8, of the total of 196 college students, 144, or almost three-
quarters, came from Tamil districts, while only 13 per cent came from the
predominantly Telegu-speaking districts. Madras led with thirty-eight
pupils; Tanjore came next with twenty-eight, then Chingleput with
twenty-one, South Arcot with seventeen, and Malabar with fifteen. *RDPI*
(*Madras*) *1877–8*, p. 21.

The lead of the Tamil districts is also suggested by the statistics for
optional languages taken in university examinations by successful candidates. More than half the candidates in 1876 offered Tamil:

	Matriculation	First Arts	B.A.	Total
Tamil	1,048	181	56	1,285
Telegu	489	71	19	579
Kanarese	205	38	8	251
Malayalam	217	48	18	285

Source: *RDPI (Madras) 1876–7*, pp. 15–16.

TABLE 31. *Distribution of colleges and high schools in Madras Presidency, 1879–80*

District	Arts colleges		High schools	
	Institutions	Pupils	Institutions	Pupils
Predominantly Tamil-speaking				
Tanjore	3	301	10	684
Trichinopoly	1	56	1	225
Tinnevelly	3	52	6	382
South Arcot	1	19	4	121
Madura	1	10	3	95
		438		1,507
Mainly Tamil-speaking				
Madras city	4	461	16	1,352
Chingleput	–	–	5	143
Salem	1	18	1	49
Coimbatore	1	26	2	138
North Arcot	–	–	2	57
		505		1,740
Predominantly or mainly Telegu-speaking				
Godavari	1	49	4	208
Vizagapatam	2	25	3	146
Kistna	1	16	5	120
Bellary	1	7	2	65
Cuddapah	–	–	1	21
Nellore	–	–	2	112
Kurnool	–	–	1	17
		97		689
Oriya/Telegu-speaking				
Ganjam	1	5	2	97
Malayalam-speaking				
Malabar	2	90	6	372
Kanarese-speaking				
South Kanara	1	31	1	95

Source: *RDPI (Madras) 1879–80*, p. 5.

only 284 of them were natives of it. If the undergraduates belonging to a district are defined as those who went from it to study at the capital as well as those who remained behind at local colleges, then Tanjore and Trichinopoly were clearly in the lead, and Godavari, the Telegu district with the most undergraduates, ranked only sixth, behind Malabar, Madras city, and

Tamil-speaking Tinnevelly.[1] That the people of the Telegu districts were noticeably less instructed than those of the south and the west, is borne out by table 32 on learning and literacy in 1881.

TABLE 32. *Percentage of population under instruction or instructed, Madras Presidency, 1881*

Madras	26·0	Madura	8·7	Kistna	5·5
Tinnevelly	12·1	South Arcot	8·3	Kurnool	5·1
Tanjore	11·7	North Arcot	7·6	Cuddapah	4·8
Chingleput	10·8	Bellary	6·1	Salem	4·7
Malabar	10·7	Nellore	5·9	Godavari	4·5
Nilgiris	9·0	South Kanara	5·8	Ganjam	3·7
Trichinopoly	8·8	Coimbatore	5·7	Vizagapatam	2·5

Source: *RDPI* (*Madras*) *1881–2*, p. 7.

In Madras the Hindus had a tighter hold upon education than in Bengal or Bombay. Muslims in the south were badly educated beyond the primary stage; there was no enterprising minority such as the Parsis of Bombay capable of challenging the Hindus. Indian Christians were relatively well educated as a consequence of missionary efforts, but the missions alone could not give them the wealth and the standing to make the most of their advantage.

TABLE 33. *Percentage by community of students at college, and high and middle schools, Madras Presidency, 1881–2*

	Population percentage	College	High and middle school
Hindus	91·4	90·0	85·6
Muslims	6·2	1·8	3·5
Indian Christians	2·3	7·0	9·3

Source: *EC*, Statistical Tables, pp. liv, lxi.

Of 17,115 successful candidates in university examinations between 1876 and 1886, 85·8 per cent were Hindu, 1·2 per cent Muslim, and 8 per cent Indian Christian.[2] The caste of Hindu pupils is given in table 34.

[1] Tanjore had 409 undergraduates, of whom 334 were in local colleges in the district; Trichinopoly had 323, of whom 309 were in the district; of Malabar's 180, 117 went to local colleges; Tinnevelly had thirty-four of its 141 at Madras, but only nine of Godavari's 106 undergraduates studied at the metropolis. *RDPI* (*Madras*) *1883–4*, pp. 48–9.

[2] *PSC*, appendix M, statement 1, pp. 78–9.

TABLE 34. *Caste of Hindu male pupils, Madras Presidency, 1883–4*

(Percentages of total Hindus)

	Brahmins	Vaisyas	Sudras	Others (including Pariahs)
Colleges	74·6	3·2	21·7	0·5
Secondary schools	45·5	5·6	45·8	3·1
Primary	14·4	10·0	68·4	7·2

Source: Calculated from *RDPI* (*Madras*) *1883–4*, Subsidiary Tables, pp. 2–139.

Seventy-three per cent of all successful Hindu candidates in Madras University examinations between 1876 and 1886 were Brahmins.[1] As education spread, the Directors of Public Instruction were impressed by 'the energy with which the Brahmans are endeavouring to keep the lead in the higher education throughout the country',[2] and by their growing enthusiasm for 'Western knowledge'.[3] In 'the vast preponderance of the Brahman element in the Arts course', they saw 'one of the chief reasons why the *alumni* of the University adopt callings of a learned or clerical as opposed to those of a scientific or practical character, as such professions are in sympathy with the traditions and aspirations of the race as it is found in Southern India'.[4] In secondary schools, however, Brahmins had less than half the places, and the share of Vaisyas and Sudras was growing faster. Equally, between 1879 and 1884 when the number of college students doubled, lower caste matriculates increased by 67 per cent while the Brahmins increased by 33 per cent—hardly 'the marvellous advance' claimed by the reports, but a clear indication that non-Brahmins were coming to realise the advantages of education.[5]

[1] *PSC*, appendix M, statement I, pp. 78–9.
[2] *RDPI* (*Madras*) *1880–1*, p. 61.
[3] *RDPI* (*Madras*) *1883–4*, p. 45.   [4] *RDPI* (*Madras*) *1881–2*, p. 53.
[5] In 1879 seven out of ten candidates for matriculation were Brahmins; in 1884–5 they were only six out of ten. *RDPI* (*Madras*) *1884–5*, p. 54. In 1888 one in forty-one Brahmins of school-going age was at college; yet only one Vaisya or Sudra (who were half the Hindu population) in 2,004, and one low-caste Hindu in 46,300. By contrast, one Indian Christian in 215, and one Muslim in 3,092 were at college. (*RDPI* (*Madras*) *1887–8*, p. 61.)

Table 35 compares the educational attainments of Brahmins with some of the other castes and communities.

TABLE 35. *Literacy and knowledge of English by caste and community, Madras Presidency, 1891*

Caste or community	Total number of males in caste	Percentage illiterate	Number knowing English	Number of literate males among whom one knows English
Brahmin Deshath	16,036	—	2,290	—
Vadama	68,170	18·99	4,184	10
Niyogi	54,082	19·10	2,878	12
Tengalai	22,898	19·65	1,844	8
Vadagalai	32,080	19·98	2,342	8
Vaidiki	56,778	24·69	1,674	19
All Brahmins	*551,951*	*27·79*	*24,976*	*12*
Kanakan	19,908	34·19	198	53
Karnam	26,800	41·34	200	59
Komati	144,223	39·54	549	126
Chetti	312,389	55·24	1,781	63
Vadugan	87,475	75·55	240	72
Balija	352,604	79·88	4,545	12
Nayar	189,830	51·02	1,405	49
Vellala	1,043,426	72·78	9,514	22
Kapu or Reddi	1,222,546	90·55	1,291	67
Pariah (Paraiyan)	997,319	97·25	706	23
All non-Brahmin Hindus	—	—	*30,531*	—
Labbai	155,794	71·70	114	304
Saiyid	55,849	79·26	439	19
Moplah	413,085	87·75	97	406
All Muslims	—	—	*3,138*	—
Native Christian	359,751	78·24	8,806	6
Eurasian	13,138	21·36	6,639	—
European	—	—	5,918	—
All Groups	*17,619,395*	*85·12*	*81,472*	—

Source: *1891 Census, Madras*, XIII, 179, 181; XIV, table XVI, 306–28; XV, table c, 26–64.

Those who sent their sons to school in Madras were mainly landholders and officials. Details for 1883–4 are given in table 36. As more boys went to school, the 'bulk of the entire increase, nearly two-thirds of it, is made up...of the children of land-

TABLE 36. *Occupation of parents of students, Madras Presidency, 1883–4*

	Colleges (excluding professional colleges) (100)	Secondary schools (100)
Landholders	38·4	30·0
Officials	28·5	17·5
Petty officials	11·8	17·0
Traders	7·0	14·0
Others and not known	14·3	21·5

Source: Calculated from *RDPI (Madras) 1883–4*, p. 47, and Statistical Tables, 2–3, 54–5.

holders',[1] a comment both upon the undiversified economy of Madras and upon the close connection that its literati had with the land. In Malabar, Brahmins and Nayars filled the colleges and schools; most of them were sons of officials and relatively big landlords.[2] However, in the Presidency as a whole 'Native Chiefs, Zemindars, and other wealthy classes, considering that education and the passing of public examinations are only necessary to those seeking employment, do not generally resort to the

TABLE 37. *Parental incomes of male students, Madras Presidency, 1883–4*

	Colleges		Secondary schools	
	Total	Percentage	Total	Percentage
Less than Rs 200 per annum	905	41·6	38,246	62·1
Rs 200–5,000 per annum	1,189	54·7	22,428	36·4
Rs 5,000 and upwards	81	3·7	935	1·5

Source: Calculated from *RDPI (Madras) 1883–4*, p. 47, and Statistical Tables, pp. 2–3, 54–5.

public institutions'.[3] Since half the boys at Presidency College in Madras city were sons of officials, and since few officials earned large salaries, the Principal thought it wrong 'to designate as wealthy' the parents of his undergraduates. According to the Principal of Christian College, the best comparison was

---

[1] *RDPI (Madras) 1885–6*, p. 7.   [2] *EC (Madras)*, Report, p. 113.
[3] *Ibid*. Evidence, p. 177.

with Scottish universities where most of the parents were poor and could pay the fees 'only at the cost of a struggle'.[1] In the Telegu districts it was the sons of officials and of 'Brahmin beggars' who were keenest to go to school.[2] Just how modest were parental means can be seen from table 37 above. Clearly the incentives for the Brahmins to seek education as a method of self-betterment were at least as great in the south as in any other part of the country.

☙

After these surveys of the first phase of Indian educational expansion, it is possible to come to grips with the main problems. Who were the men taking advantage of the new education? From what regions and districts did they come? What were their social backgrounds and their relationships with other groups inside their own society?

In Bengal, Brahmins, Kayasths and Baidyas, the bhadralok, coming from the eastern and western districts of Bengal Proper, and bunching inside the metropolis of Calcutta, had taken the largest share of higher education. In Bombay it was the Brahmins of Maharashtra and the Parsis of the city who had done so. Here the literati had concentrated not in one centre but in two: the metropolis of Bombay and the Maharashtrian capital of Poona. In Madras, the Brahmins of Tamilnad, and to a lesser extent of the Telegu regions, were in the lead. Here the Tamil districts had been the first to take these opportunities. The city of Madras itself was little more than an educational centre to which students flocked, but from which many later returned to the districts.

The emergence of these groups was not a direct result of economic change. Nineteenth-century India had seen no extensive industrial development, and it is apparent that the graduates had little connection with trade or business. With their commercial links and their educational interests, the Parsis were the only approximation to a bourgeoisie in India at this time.[3] But they were ill-equipped to play the *beau rôle*

---

[1] *EC (Madras)*, Report, p. 113.   [2] *Ibid.* Evidence, pp. 20–4.

[3] There has also been a tendency to define the substantial landed proprietors of Bengal as a middle class in the western mode. In terms of nineteenth-century India this seems to sacrifice social reality to sociological elegance. What produced these men was institutional rather than economic change.

which some historiographers demand of their bourgeoisies. For they were too few and too alien. Apart from this handful of compradors, the matriculates and graduates were generally men of high status but frequently of low income. Some had urban connections; many of them came from families traditionally associated with administrative and professional work; but in all three Presidencies many belonged to families which owned land.

Between one Presidency and another there were considerable differences in the social cohesion of the educated. Equally, there were great dissimilarities in their relations with the rest of society. In Bengal Proper the bhadralok were tolerably well united by a common religion and language, as well as by the social dominance which they enjoyed. Nevertheless there were differences of caste and regional origin between them, and there was a certain disunity of interest between big zemindars and intermediate tenure holders, between those primarily dependent on rents and those who had carved out an independence from agrarian means of support. Moreover, the factors which tended to hold the bhadralok together were precisely those which isolated them from the rest of Bengali society. The community to which they belonged was the minority community in Bengal Proper. Their triad of castes was contemptuous of the castes below them. The sophisticated language which was so powerful a force in uniting their sentiments was barely intelligible to the mass of their countrymen. Their very profits from the land settlement divorced them from the tillers of the soil whose labours supported their activities.

In western India, there was little cohesiveness among the graduates in Bombay city. Here the Maharashtrian Brahmins had to come to terms with men from other castes, communities and regions. In Maharashtra, however, almost all the educated were local Brahmins. At first sight there seemed to be considerable solidarity between them and the rest of Maharashtrian society. Here there was no sophisticated version of the language to divide them. There were no great latifundia to split the interests of landlord and tenant. All social groups had been deeply influenced by the same religious inspirations and by the same historical achievements. For these reasons, the Brahmins were quick to claim the fundamental unity of their society. But perhaps they protested too much. Below them, the non-Brahmin caste of Marathas had traditions and aspirations which could readily be turned against the pre-eminence of their Brahmin leaders. Like the bhadralok in upper India, however, these Brahmins had networks of influence beyond the desh. As the notables in parts of the Karnatak and the Central Provinces, they did much to bring these regions under the sway of Poona and to submerge their speech under Poona's tongue.[1]

In Madras where the Brahmins had as yet no serious competitors in the advance towards western education, the intelligentsia possessed a unity based on caste status. In so far as it was Tamil Brahmins who had made most successful use of their opportunities, there was the further unity of language and race. But since the Tamils were forced more and more to share their educational advantages with other regions and other castes, the educated of the south were split by linguistic and ethnic divisions, and to some extent by caste divisions as well. Neither solidarity nor sympathy linked these elites with the societies to which they belonged. Throughout most of the Presidency the Hindus had the field to themselves, and within the regions there were some linguistic unities. But these were trifles compared with the powerful divisive effects of caste. In much of south India the gulfs between Brahmins and the rest of the community were so wide, and the natural antipathies so bitter, that society here was divided at least as effectively by caste as elsewhere it was divided by religion. Protected by the British inside this system of exclusiveness and associated by them in the administration of the province, the Brahmins of south India had less incentive than the bhadralok or the Maharashtrian Brahmins to launch into political dissent.[2]

The uneven development between different regions and the competitiveness between different groups meant that there was little possibility of unity between the graduates and their societies. The advantages of one group meant the drawbacks of the rest. The successes of the advanced regions blocked the aspira-

---

[1] This expansiveness, unlike that of the bhadralok, had been in evidence before the British occupation, since it owed much to an earlier and indigenous imperialism.

[2] Among the literati of Madras, dissent began at home but it took the uncharitable form of complaints against the activities of Christians which seemed to be disturbing the docility of their poor.

tions of the backward. With all these local rivalries and the glaring national differences between east, west and south, there was still a level at which the elites of Bengal, Bombay and Madras could work together—and this was the level of all-India. In so doing, their main purpose may well have been to strengthen their position inside their local societies. Yet, possessing the unity of a common education, they could be brought to think in national terms by similar ambitions and resentments within the framework of the Raj. These ambitions and resentments can only be understood by considering their opportunities under the British, and the restraints which they feared their rulers might impose upon them.

3

The Rewards of Education

Both the hopes and fears of the educated were concerned with
the chances of gaining employment at what they thought was the
right level. Some avenues were barred to them outright, and
others offered meagre prospects. The army would not have them
as officers. Caste restrictions and lack of capital stood between
them and any business career better than clerking. In 1882 the
Education Commission noticed that 'Some engage in trade.
They are, however, comparatively few in number. For commerce needs capital, and hereditary aptitude for business,
neither of which is usually possessed in any sufficient degree
by those educated in our colleges.'[1] In a survey of the careers
of over 1,700 Calcutta graduates made in 1882, only one was
returned a 'merchant', and two were termed 'planters'.[2] 'We
should take our proper share in the field of new enterprize',[3]
was the Poona Sarvajanik Sabha's exhortation to the educated.
But this was mere theorising from the side lines. Business was
one career not generally open to the talents.

The agrarian sector could not supply the missing opportunities. Nowhere in India was there a class of enlightened
farmers putting into the land the seeds of their learning. The
high schools and colleges did not teach about manures and
rotation, silage and soil-banking. In the Deccan, the land was

[1] *EC*, p. 302; 'For the middle professional classes...the outlook is not
encouraging. The corresponding classes in England, when they find the
liberal professions and public service overstocked, take to business or
manufacture. But for these pursuits (putting aside the calling of clerks or
artisans) capital is generally required, and the professional classes of
Bengal are miserably poor—much poorer, it is certain, than the corresponding classes in England. It is not the want of enterprise but want of capital,
that is at the root of the present difficulties.' (*RDPI (Bengal) 1876–7*, p. 65.)
[2] See appendix 2, table 51, below, p. 358.
[3] 'A Note on Economic Reform', *The Quarterly Journal of the Poona
Sarvajanik Sabha*, VIII, no. 1 (July 1885), Independent Section, p. 2.

farmed by a peasantry deep in debt, not by substantial land-lords. It was the constant complaint of the Poona elite that without a permanent settlement of the revenue Bombay's farm land would remain starved of capital. Such a settlement would 'provide that the thrifty and hard-working classes will succeed to the ownership of the land...The monied classes, having at present no interest in the land, cannot occupy the position, nor enjoy the status, nor discharge the function of landlords. The absence of such a class retards progress in all directions. The Presidency of Bengal enjoys this advantage over the rest of India and this circumstance alone accounts for its prosperous and progressive condition.'[1] But in Bengal, where matters were different, the net result was much the same. The zemindars and intermediate tenure holders were often absentees; in any case they had no hand in farming. The mirasidars of Tanjore let their lands at rack-rents, and showed little interest in improvement. However much the terms and tenures of agriculture might vary from one Presidency to another, the educated elite was either divorced from landholding, or, more frequently, was receiving an alimony by virtue of its growing separation from it.

That left the public services and the professions. For both, education was required. Thus all roads led to the schools, and from the schools back to the public services and professions. From ancient times the higher castes of India had been the administrators and literati of their communities. Since higher education under the British was primarily a course offering its pupils the new qualifications now demanded for just those employments which were traditionally theirs, the new elites moved unswervingly down these two avenues of advancement.[2]

In societies with an autocratic constitution and a backward economy, the will and working of government is the mainspring of enterprise. This has been particularly clear in large oriental states with an age-long tradition of despotism. In India government had always been the largest employer, and

---

[1] 'The agrarian problem and its solution', *ibid.* II, no. I (July 1879), Independent Section, pp. 17–18.

[2] For details about the careers of Indian graduates, see appendix 2, tables 50–4, below, pp. 357–60.

service under it the main avenue of employment for the literate and professional classes of the country. Again, in all dependent societies in modern times, a desk in the government office has been a solid claim to esteem. Since it is from the administration that all blessings flow, membership of the regime offers local influence and security of employment; more important, it is the first rung on the ladder of power. All over the world, nationalist leaders have been formed out of government subordinates, men who put their working hours to good use in studying the mechanics of power, and devoted their leisure to studying the obstacles barring their own promotion.

In the administrative hierarchy which ruled India, ranging from the village officials at the bottom, through the uncovenanted services, to the covenanted service at the top, Indians filled the lower ranks and supplied the vast majority of the officials. Yet most of them were humbly employed and poorly paid; perhaps only one in ten was paid Rs 75 a month or over. In 1867 there were 13,431 appointments with salaries of this order, and more than half of them were held by Europeans, who had all the best paid jobs, and by Eurasians. Between 1867 and 1887 opportunities in the public services for Indians increased. By 1887 the Hindu share—38 per cent in 1867—had risen to 45 per cent of the 21,466 posts now available. But Europeans and Eurasians still held almost half the appointments. In Bengal and in Bombay, Indians were taking over most swiftly, but even here, in the myriad departments of the bureaucracy, responsibility and reward were still mainly for Europeans.[1]

The highest posts under government were reserved by law to the covenanted members of the Indian civil service, of whom there were about a thousand. In theory Indians were not debarred from this service, but in practice every difficulty stood in their way—the expense of going to England for the examinations, the prejudice against crossing the 'black water', the nature of the syllabus, and the official reluctance to admit Indians into this vital service.[2] By 1887 only a dozen Indians had entered

[1] See appendix 3, tables 55–9, below, pp. 361–3.
[2] For the official policy on the admission of Indians into the service, see chapter 4, below; also see note on the limit of age prescribed for candidates for admission into the Indian civil service by R. C. Dutt, 6 May 1884, appended to Minute by Ripon, 10 September 1884. B.M., State Papers, *B.P.* 1/8 (4).

the covenanted ranks by open competition.[1] Others had tried to get in but had failed. Some of these were men who were to make their mark in the politics of Indian nationalism. Manmohan Ghose, the Calcutta barrister, a leader in the Indian Association and later in the Bengal Congress, failed both his attempts in the examination. His brother Lalmohan had also sat it before taking to the law.[2] Ananda Mohan Bose, the first Indian Wrangler at Cambridge, successfully took all the intellectual hurdles, only to be unseated in the riding test. Ratnavilu Chetty graduated at sixteen from Madras, won top marks in mathematics in the competitive examination of 1874, but died soon after joining the service.[3] Surendranath Banerjea was one of the few to get in, but he did not get on, since he was soon dismissed on what he claimed were trumped-up charges.[4] Many fathers suffered like an influential Parsi editor, Kabraji, who told the Public Service Commission how he had been ruined in the unsuccessful attempt to get his son into the service. When the Maharashtrian fire-brand, Bal Gangadhar Tilak, stated that he had never tried for the examination, this astonished the commission, for everyone now acknowledged, if they did not applaud, the ambition of able Indians to enter this *corps d'élite*.[5] Wherever there were men in India with degrees to their name, there were aggrieved people eager to make common cause in pressing for easier entry into the service.[6] As Surendranath said: 'The question is likely to come again and again until this concession is made. We attach much greater importance to it than to any other question connected with the administration of the country.'[7] Lytton's statutory service was meant as a concession, but since it was recruited by nomina-

---

[1] *PSC*, p. 53.

[2] Styled 'the Dacca Orator', Lalmohan was a delegate of the Indian Association to England in 1879 and 1880, and the first Indian to stand for parliament.

[3] History of the five Natives of India who have passed successfully in the London Competitive Examinations for the Indian Civil Service when under the age of 19, Appendix to Minute by Ripon, 10 September 1884. B.M., State Papers, *B.P.* 1/8(4).

[4] S. Banerjea, *A Nation in Making. Being the Reminiscences of Fifty Years of Public Life* (London, 1925), pp. 28–9.

[5] *PSC (Bombay)*, IV, section 2, pp. 114–20, 326.

[6] Syed Ahmed Khan warned the Viceroy about 'political discontent... among the educated classes of the Natives' over the age limit. See Minute by Ripon, 10 September 1884. (B.M., State Papers, *B.P.* 1/8 (4).)

[7] *PSC (Bengal)*, VI, section 2, p. 74.

tion and lacked the rewards or the standing of the covenanted service, it satisfied no-one, not even the men of good family and social position whom it aimed to patronise. By 1886 twenty-seven Hindus, fifteen Muslims, two Parsis and two Sikhs had been appointed under the statutory rules of 1879.[1]

This left the uncovenanted service as the best opening for Indians. But here promotion and pay went so far and no further. Bankim Chandra Chatterjee swiftly scaled the ladder as high as deputy collector, but here he stopped for eighteen years. The iron of this rung so entered his soul that he took to novel writing. Yet there had been a sharp increase in the number of Indians in this service; Mayo's efforts in this direction had been

TABLE 38. *Number of persons employed in the executive and judicial branches of the uncovenanted service; their religion, caste and educational attainments, 1886–7*

| | Total em-ployed | Hindus* | | Muslims | | Number who passed | | | | |
						Entrance	First Arts	B.A.s	M.A.s	Total
Bengal	623	522	83·7	53	8·5	173	94	215	60	542
Bombay (and Sind)	384	328	85·4	21	5·4	88	21	50	7	166
Madras	345	297	86·0	14	4·0	86	37	43	2	168
N.W.P. and Oudh	521	262	50·2	235	45·1	43	17	27	7	94
All India	2,588	1,866	72·1	514	19·8	449	185	370	87	1,091

| | Caste of Hindus | | | | | |
	Brahmins	Kshatt-riyas	Kayasths, Prabhus	Banias, Vaisyas	Sudras	Others
Bengal	178	—	219	12	54	59
Bombay (and Sind)	211	26	37	38	1	15
Madras	202	2	—	13	74	6
N.W.P. and Oudh	89	37	107	25	1	3
All India	904	147	454	113	146	102

Source: Calculated from *PSC*, pp. 34–41.

* The figures on Hindus in Bombay include Parsis.

[1] *PSC*, p. 27.

followed by the rules of 1879, which laid down that thereafter Indians alone were to be appointed to uncovenanted offices with salaries of over Rs 200 per month. This had gradually forced out the Europeans, and by 1887 there were only 139 left in the executive and judicial branches of the uncovenanted service. Table 38 gives details about the religion, caste and education of Indians in this service. Since men were not often employed outside their own provinces, less than two thousand jobs were available in the uncovenanted executive and judicial branches in Bengal, Bombay and Madras. Not all of them were given to the educated; in Bombay and in Madras less than half of the uncovenanted civilians had qualifications in the new education. With so little fruit from the pagoda tree, there would be many Indians who would go away hungry.

During the eighteenth and nineteenth centuries, the development of the professions as well-organised, self-regulating, groups made considerable strides in Europe.[1] This was not the case in India. For one thing, the practices of medicine and law were still wrapped in an oriental esotericism far removed from the prejudices of the new regime. But side by side with the ayurveds and hakims, the traditional doctors, the pandits and kazis, who were the exponents of a partly codified Hindu and Muslim law, and the professors in the Sanskrit tols and Muslim madrassas, there slowly emerged in the nineteenth century groups of men trained in the western professional skills of medicine, law, engineering and education. In India, however, even when the Raj had begun to provide facilities for professional education, the line dividing professional employment under the government from professional self-employment was still hard to establish. Some Indian engineers and doctors were employed in the public services, and many of the arts graduates, who might have practised law or taught in private schools, were similarly attracted into the service of the regime. Men educated to the new professional standards and setting up in practice for themselves were at first few in number and of an uncertain standing. Since they lacked any central organisation

---

[1] See W. J. Reader, *Professional Men. The Rise of the Professional Classes in Nineteenth-century England* (London, 1966).

to regulate their entry and professional conduct, there was no obvious way in which members of the same profession throughout the three Presidencies could be united. This fact alone helps to explain why political practices were slow to start in nineteenth-century India.

Of all the professions, medicine had perhaps the sturdiest indigenous tradition.[1] But like most other professions, it had remained a hereditary one. Its modern history dates from the opening of the Calcutta Medical College in 1835, the Grant Medical College at Bombay in 1845, and the school in Madras in 1852; graduates from these schools were appointed as sub-assistant surgeons; some went into private practice and found an increasing demand for their talents among well-to-do Indians. Once the universities began to award degrees in medicine, the most rapid development was in Calcutta and the slowest in Madras. It is interesting that in this profession, where the new training with its emphasis on anatomy and surgery would seem to have offended against high caste prejudices, the higher castes of Bengal established a dominant position. For example, of 244 students at the Dacca Medical College in 1875–6 only six were low caste men, while there were seventy Brahmins, one hundred and twenty-eight Kayasths and thirty-six Baidyas.[2]

By 1882 the government of Bombay felt that the new medical profession had developed sufficiently to require proper regulations to improve its status, and that the time had come to register its qualified practitioners and regulate their practice. It might have seemed so in Bombay. In the 1850s only thirty-nine men qualified at the Grant Medical College; but the following decade had produced 131 graduates in medicine, and 'a far wider sphere of practice has developed in this city, and some of the smaller cities of this Presidency'.[3] But in Bengal where the new doctors were most numerous, the government thought that legislation was premature since the profession was in its infancy, and '...that section of the community which employs medical

---

[1] T. A. Wise, *Commentary on the Hindu System of Medicine* (Calcutta, 1845); and J. F. Royle, *An Essay on the Antiquity of Hindoo Medicine* (London, 1837).

[2] *RDPI (Bengal) 1875–6*, p. 78. Only four were Muslims.

[3] Government of Bombay to Government of India, 18 May 1882; and Principal, Grant Medical College to Secretary, General Department, Government of Bombay, 22 December 1882; Home Department (Medical) Proceedings, no. 44, May 1883. RP, Add. MSS 43578.

practitioners of English schools...forms as yet but a small proportion of the population of these provinces.'[1] Madras was even less sanguine about the possibility of organising and regulating the doctors. Since its establishment, the Medical College there had produced only fifty graduates. Of these some went into government service, '...a few are at Madras endeavouring to obtain a livelihood by practice, but would prefer...Government appointments'. How hard the going still was in Madras was shown by the case of one medical graduate who tried to start a private practice, but 'gave it up very soon as unprofitable work, and is now seeking employment as a schoolmaster'.[2] In fact such private practice as existed was handled by less qualified apothecaries or hospital assistants and by practitioners of the old sort. So the government of India decided against any general legislation for the profession.[3] In the later nineteenth century, the profession made considerable strides; some Indian doctors won big reputations and handsome incomes; their services were increasingly in demand,[4] but it was not until the next century that the doctors captured the cities of India, and to this day they have not invaded the countryside.

Of all the recognised professions, engineering remained the most backward. Since there was so little industry and technology in India, this was understandable enough. But because the government built roads, bridges, canals and railways, it always needed some civil engineers. Its main supply did not come from the colleges of the Presidency capitals. An engineer-

[1] Government of Bengal to Government of India, 7 December 1882, Home Department (Medical) Proceedings, no. 45, May 1883, RP, Add. MSS 43578.
[2] Acting Principal, Madras Medical College, to Director of Public Instruction, 26 July 1882, *ibid.* In 1881 there were 'hardly any qualified private practitioners [surgeons and physicians] outside the Madras City' (*1881 Census, Madras*, I, 141).
[3] Government of India to Government of Bombay, 8 May 1883, Home Department (Medical) Proceedings, May 1883, RP, Add. MSS 43578.
[4] 'The Natives...educated in the medical colleges and schools, have already acquired the confidence, and are still further rising in the estimation, of their countrymen. They are extensively employed not only by the Government, but also by municipal corporations and local committees separate from the State. They are fast obtaining a private practice, of a large and lucrative character, superseding the ancient profession of medicine according to the Oriental method. There is not as yet any regulation prohibiting men from practising medicine unless they possess diplomas from British authorities, and thus the practitioners under the Oriental system are still free to practise their art.' Temple, *India in 1880*, pp. 150–1.

ing class which was opened at Elphinstone in 1854 soon closed for lack of candidates, and Calcutta did not have an engineering school of its own until 1856. Not until Ripon's viceroyalty did most of the universities have full degree classes in civil engineering, and it was only then that the first inroads were made into the higher grades of the profession and into the monopoly of Anglo-Indians at Thomason College in the North-western Provinces.[1]

Teaching was the occupation where the new educated were most frequently employed and least well paid. Here the opportunities ranged from the comparatively respected and remunerative positions in the Departments of Education as deputy-inspectors of schools and as principals and professors in government colleges and high schools down to the humble position of schoolmaster in the village. Many graduates went back to the classroom as teachers, and many others with lesser qualifications also found employment in satisfying the growing demand for an English education.[2] In Madras, where the range of openings was less ample than in Bengal or Bombay, the Education Department took more than half the graduates recruited by government between 1871 and 1882, and 'a very large number of those not in the public service are engaged in educational work'.[3] In 1887 Bombay decided that in future it would employ in government schools no teacher who had not passed the First Arts examination.[4] In 1882 there were sixty-two graduates, forty-four men who had passed the First Arts, and 209 matriculates on the government's payroll of 448 teachers at its high and middle schools. Only 133 of them, mainly instructors in 'special subjects', were without any university education.[5] In Bengal, the trend was much the same, and here private entrepreneurs discovered that the business of schooling was profitable for the owners, if not for the teachers. Despite their low salaries,[6] they continued to command the

---

[1] Temple, *India in 1880*, pp. 151–2; Misra, *The Indian Middle Classes*, pp. 184–5, 289.

[2] See, for example, *RDPI (Madras) 1881–2*, p. 3.   [3] *Ibid.* p. 163.

[4] *RDPI (Bombay) 1877–8*, pp. 30–1. In 1877, there were 161 teachers paid monthly salaries of Rs 50 to 300 by government: 134 were matriculates and thirty-nine of them were graduates.   [5] *EC (Bombay)*, I, 126.

[6] A headmaster at a government high school in Bombay earned on average Rs 462 per month in 1882; an assistant master, Rs 90 per month. At government middle schools, the average pay was about Rs 87 and Rs 45

traditional respect accorded to them in India. Nevertheless, teaching would not rank as a profession in many of the accepted senses of the word. There was scant control over qualifications, particularly in private schools, little organisation to set and maintain standards, and as yet few schools specifically trained teachers.

Journalists were even less a well-defined profession since India's growing press employed few of them full-time,[1] and most editors and contributors combined their journalism with some other employment. Attempts to create an all-India organisation of editors had no success in the nineteenth century,[2] and not even at a provincial level was there a press association of journalists to lay down professional standards.

The most vigorous developments were in the legal profession. Following the transformation of the Indian legal system by the Codes, by the high courts founded in 1861 and by the right accorded in criminal and civil suits alike to employ pleaders, it became necessary first to regulate the qualifications for pleaders and afterwards to organise a radically different system of legal training. In the Indian legal profession, where large numbers had necessarily to work independently of government and had increasingly to master foreign doctrines, there were two striking developments. Its numbers rose steadily. So did its standing. By the later nineteenth century there were almost 14,000 persons returned as belonging to the profession in the three Presidencies.[3] Although these figures greatly exaggerate the size of the profession viewed as a new group, the growth of its

respectively. (*EC (Bombay)*, I, 126.) In private schools and colleges the pay was usually considerably less; a top professor in an unaided Calcutta college normally earned between Rs 60 and 225 per month. (*EC (Bengal)*, p. 100). In Madras, trained graduates could earn between Rs 40 and 75 per month, while trained matriculates and men with First Arts earned between Rs 15 and 40. Untrained, these men earned between Rs 10 and 50, while primary schoolteachers were paid not more than Rs 15 or Rs 8 per month, depending whether they were trained or not. Despite the low rewards the profession had attracted in Madras 160 Hindus teaching at colleges, 2,500 at secondary schools for boys and more than 20,000 in primary schools (*RDPI (Madras) 1888–9*, pp. 157–62).

[1] On the growth of the press, see appendix 5, below, pp. 366–72.
[2] See chapter 6, below.
[3] These figures of course include legal practitioners of every rank and sort as well as all those who supplied ancillary services such as law stationers and stamp dealers, and by no means all of them had been educated in the legal systems of the west. According to the 1881 census, Bombay had 1,904, Madras, 4,705, and Bengal Proper, 7,261 employed in the legal

new elements can readily be gauged by the expansion of the number of law graduates at the three universities. More than 1,500 law graduates had qualified at Calcutta by 1888, and already by 1882 more than 500 graduates had entered the profession to take up private practice. In Bombay the most rapid growth took place in the later 1880s; Madras came second to Calcutta in the size of its law schools.[1]

The profession was bound to grow rapidly in the later nineteenth century by reason both of the growing volume and complexity of the regulations, and of the increase in litigation, particularly over land. Between 1856 and 1886, the number of civil suits in India almost trebled.[2] More than a third of these suits were in Bengal,[3] where the absence of 'that certainty as to the respective rights and obligations of the parties which a sound and satisfactory system of land tenure should provide'[4] encouraged an immense volume of litigation, and supported the largest legal profession in India.[5] Here zemindar sued

profession. *1881 Census, Bombay*, II, table XII, pp. 50–6; *1881 Census, Madras*, II, 198–9; *1881 Census, Bengal*, II, 368–72. For example, in Madras the total included many who were 'not even locally recognised as authorised practitioners'. 'There are only 32 barristers, and these, with 32 solicitors and attorneys are the only lawyers according to the English standard.' Although 2,835 vakils were returned, some were petition-writers; by 1882, 2,516 had been officially admitted as vakils, and of these only eighty-three were vakils of the high court (*1881 Census, Madras*, I, 141); Bengal's figures were particularly inflated, and notoriously unreliable.

[1] See appendix 1, below, pp. 355–6.
[2] In 1856 there were 730,000 civil suits; in 1886, 1,908,869. Memorandum on some of the Results of Indian Administration during the past thirty years of British rule in India, February 1889, *P.P.* 1889, LVIII, 8. In 1866 Maine, Law member of the Viceroy's Council, spoke of 'the immense multiplication of legal practitioners', and noted that 'the great addition... is due to the numbers and influence of the Native Bar. Practically, a young educated Native, pretending to anything above a clerkship, adopts one of two occupations—either he goes into the service of Government, or he joins the Native Bar... the Bar is getting more and more preferred to Government service by the educated youth of the country, both on the score of its gainfulness and on the score of its independence.' (M. E. Grant Duff, *Sir Henry Maine. A Brief Memoir of his Life...with some of his Indian Speeches and Minutes* (London, 1892), p. 243.)
[3] In 1881 the number of original suits in British India was about 1,600,000 of which well over 500,000 were in Bengal. Statistical Abstract...from 1879–80 to 1888–9, Twenty-fourth number, *P.P.* 1890, LXXVIII, 284–5.
[4] *Report of the Land Revenue Commission Bengal*, I, 38.
[5] In the early twentieth century, it was still true that 'The lawyers are the spoilt children of Bengal life. They make an income entirely dispropor-

zemindar; together they sued their intermediate tenure-holders and tenants, and the lawyers, sometimes cadets of these litigious landlords and often rent receivers in their own right, were ready at hand to coax them into the courts. Thus in Bengal the expansion of the profession spread far beyond the limits of Calcutta. Already by 1875 they were active in every district headquarters of Bengal.[1] In western India, by 1881 there were more men employed in the law in Gujarat and the Deccan than in the city of Bombay;[2] in Madras the district bars were in fact larger, if less influential, than the bar in the Presidency capital.[3]

The rise in status of the profession was as remarkable as its growth in numbers. One factor enhancing the standing of lawyers was that by necessity many of them were now being trained along western lines, and their legal training and knowledge of English gave them the opportunity to win a share in the practice of the high courts. From the 1860s a few Indians had qualified as barristers-at-law of the Inns of Court, and they joined the first generation of graduates from the Indian universities in an assault upon the European monopoly of advocacy in the high courts. By 1886 Indians had succeeded in getting a large share of this practice in Bombay and Calcutta, and to a lesser extent in Madras, as table 39 demonstrates.

Their rise in the independent sector of the profession was

tionate to their abilities; thus an able lawyer will make five or ten times as much in a year as an equally able doctor, and even an incapable lawyer will make a better income than most capable members of other professions'. Jack, *Economic Life*, p. 91.

[1] In Dacca division, for example, there were three barristers, 372 pleaders, and 470 law agents in addition to stamp-vendors and Muslim 'law doctors'; Dacca district had the most pleaders, but Backergunge had 261 law agents as well as seventy-one pleaders. (*SAB*, v, 35, 185–6, 282, 396.) Burdwan district had 210 pleaders and 214 law agents, while Midnapore had ninety-six pleaders, and 388 law agents. Howrah and Hooghly, suburbs of Calcutta, had many lawyers, and Nadia also had an active local bar. Calcutta's lawyers were returned together with those of Twenty-four Parganas: there were twenty-six barristers, 127 attorneys, 531 pleaders, and 784 law agents. (*SAB*, IV, 40; III, 45, 277; II, 39; I, 46.)

[2] There were 440 men employed in law in Gujarat, of whom 148 were in Ahmadabad and 114 in Surat; 579 in the Deccan, 153 in Poona; and 360 in Bombay city, *1881 Census, Bombay*, II, table XII, pp. 50–6.

[3] While Madras city had fifty-nine vakils in 1881, there were 357 in Tanjore district, 198 in Tinevelly, 186 in Madura, 146 in Trichinopoly and 116 in Coimbatore; Godavari, Vizagapatam and Kistna had 241, 161 and 124 respectively, while Malabar had 407. *1881 Census, Madras*, II, 198–9.

TABLE 39. *Indian advocates, attorneys and solicitors at the high courts of Calcutta, Bombay and Madras, 1877 and 1886*

	1877		1886	
	Indian	Total	Indian	Total
Bengal				
Advocates	4	72	37†	128
Attorneys and solicitors	38	116	65	150
Bombay				
Advocates	12*	42	27	62
Attorneys and solicitors	20	50	28	64
Madras				
Advocates	5	51	12	64
Attorneys and solicitors	2	33	15	60

Source: *India List, Civil and Military, March 1877* (London, 1877), pp. 32–3, 124, 144–5; and *ibid. January 1886* (London, 1886), pp. 32–6, 124, 144–5.

* P. M. Mehta, Badruddin Tyabji, B. M. Waglé, and K. T. Telang were among them.
† Eight of these were Muslims.

paralleled by the better opportunities afforded to Indians in the judicial branches of government service. All seven of the Indians who entered the covenanted service between 1871 and 1876 were barristers-at-law, and all of them except Romesh Chandra Dutt, who became the first Indian collector, made their careers on the judicial side.[1] By 1888 there was at least one Indian judge at each of the high courts; with hardly an exception the subordinate judges and magistrates were Indians; nine-tenths of the original civil suits as well as three-quarters of the magisterial business of the courts of India came before Indian judges and magistrates.[2] Surveying the changes of a generation, an official memorandum published in 1889 noted 'the advance made by the great majority of Native Judges and Magistrates in education, in legal training and in uprightness of character'. Thirty years ago 'few of these officers knew English, none of them had obtained a University degree, and hardly any enjoyed any legal training. At the present time nearly all Civil Judges in the older provinces know English, and many are University graduates in Arts or Law, while in most provinces all salaried magistrates appointed in recent years are men of

[1] *PSC*, p. 53.   [2] Memorandum, *P.P.* 1889, LVIII, 7.

education.'[1] Once a gaggle of unqualified practitioners, lawyers were now increasingly men of education, fluent in English and with some learning in the law. 'The Pleaders of the High Court of the present day', wrote the Chief Justice of Bombay in 1873, 'stand in highly favourable contrast to the old practitioners of the late Sudder Adawlut.' In 1854 when Westropp had arrived in Bombay, there was only one pleader who could speak English and who 'had any knowledge of his business'. But after English had become the language of the court, the old pleaders were slowly replaced by 'the new native practitioners, all of whom could speak English...and had passed an examination in law'.[2] This was as true of lawyers practising in criminal as in civil courts. The rise in the standards of the profession was not confined to the Presidency capitals, although here it was most striking. The same process could be discerned up country, where some of the high court lawyers extended their practice, and where increasingly large numbers of the local lawyers had been educated at university. In 1882 the Bombay Provincial Committee of the Education Commission learnt that the 'old practitioners' still had 'a stronghold' in the mofussil, but that 'their place was being gradually filled by the alumni of the Elphinstone High School and of the University of Bombay'.[3] Indeed the trend had already been obvious in 1865. In that year, out of a total of 673 pleaders in the regulation courts of the Bombay Presidency, forty-eight knew English and sixty-seven had certificates of legal education. The previous year, there had been only thirty-eight who knew English and forty-five with certificates.[4] Similarly in Bengal, Sir Richard Temple remarked in 1875 that whereas the Calcutta bar had 'enjoyed a high repute for more than one generation', now 'the native Bar in the interior of the country is fast rising above the humbler level it once occupied, and is becoming popular and respectable: its members at the remote and scattered stations of the rural districts take social rank together with the native officials'.[5] In Madras, too, it was clear that 'Barristers, vakils

[1] Memorandum, *P.P.* 1889, LVIII, 7.
[2] Memorandum by M. Westropp, Chief Justice, Bombay, 16 May 1873 enclosed in Wodehouse to Argyll, 19 May 1873, Argyll Papers (Reel 316).
[3] M. Westropp, evidence, *EC (Bombay)*, I, 144–5.
[4] *P.P.* 1866, LII, 449.
[5] Minute by Temple, 14 January 1876, p. 33; *Report on the Administration of Bengal 1874–5* (Calcutta, 1876).

and other legal practitioners are rising in importance'.[1] As their standing rose, so did their incomes. Table 40 gives some idea of the incomes of lawyers in the three presidencies. Great fortunes in the law were not to be had for the asking, but the income of Badruddin Tyabji of Bombay shows what a leading Indian lawyer could earn.[2] Less successful men could still scrape a competence which compared well with the pittances earned by most of their fellows in the public services.

Since the supply of lawyers was beginning to outstrip demand,[3] it became relatively easy in the law, as in the public services, to raise standards. In 1873 the Calcutta high court ruled that whereas previously a man passing the Entrance examination had qualified for admission as a pleader, now he must pass the First Arts examination. In 1876 the Director of Public Instruction noticed that matriculates were finding it increasingly difficult to 'qualify themselves for any profession unless they go forward to a University degree'. Year by year both the high court and government were imposing more stringent educational standards, and now 'none but an educated person can hope to enter the public service in any except its menial branches'.[4] As qualifications rose, those lawyers who possessed them came to view themselves more and more as a group with specialist needs and demanding specialist privi-

---

[1] Raghavaiyangar, *Memorandum on the Progress of the Madras Presidency*, p. 161.

[2] *Badruddin Tyabji's income from the law, 1868–90*

	Rs		Rs	
1868	7,170	1880	27,245	
1869	8,325	1881	30,130	
1870	11,906	1882	30,170	
1871	15,470	1883	33,365	
1872	18,195	1884	51,700	
1873	30,065	1885	53,700	
1874	34,685	1886	85,200	
1875	43,265	1887	44,480	(Tyabji was in England
1876	29,945			for part of the year)
1877	31,845	1888	61,220	
1878	39,695	1889	87,095	
1879	24,015	1890	122,360	

Source: MSS Fee Book, 1868–90, Tyabji Papers.

[3] In 1876, the Bengal government noted that both the public services and the law were 'overcrowded'; Temple's Minute, 14 January 1876, p. 87, *Report on the Administration of Bengal, 1874–5*; also see *RDPI (Bengal) 1876–7*, p. 64.

[4] *RDPI (Bengal) 1878–9*, p. 101.

leges. Here again it is developments up country which are suggestive—in the district towns members of the local bar began to organise themselves into professional associations which, after the manner of caste groups, claimed a social precedence which they had not previously enjoyed.

TABLE 40. *Incomes of the legal profession, Bengal and Bombay, 1888–9, and Madras, 1890–1*

	Bengal		Bombay*		Madras†
	Barristers and pleaders	Other legal practitioners	Barristers and pleaders	Other legal practitioners	Barristers, pleaders and other legal practitioners
Incomes between Rs 500 and 2,000 per annum	1,404	1,809	413	53	1,034
Incomes of Rs 2,000 and over per annum	551	229	129	5	267

Source: *Report on the Financial Results of the Income Tax Administration in the Lower Provinces for the year 1888–9* (Calcutta, 1889), pp. iv–v; *Reports on the operations in connection with the Income Tax in the Bombay Presidency for the year 1888–9* (Bombay, 1889), pp. 12–13, 18–19, 33, 38, 55, 60–1; Raghavaiyangar, *Memorandum on the Progress of the Madras Presidency*, pp. cxc–cxci.

* These figures exclude Bombay city.
† The distribution of assessees between Madras city and the districts is revealing. Of the total of 1,301 lawyers paying tax only sixty-one were in the city. But of these, forty-seven earned more than Rs 2,000 per annum, and their assessment came to Rs 15,435, while the assessment on the remaining 220 in the districts earning over Rs 2,000 was Rs 24,607. Modest incomes were the rule in the hinterland, while the big incomes were in the city. In Bengal, Calcutta had 121 barristers, and fifty-seven other legal practitioners earning over Rs 2,000 per annum, and another 158 and 104 earning less than that. Here the largest incomes were earned in the city, but good incomes could be had outside.

Forming an independent status group, confident in their new skills, able to conduct the constitutional dialogue with their rulers, lawyers marched in the van of politics in later nineteenth-century India, just as they had for centuries managed the politics of revolt in the Occident. Since government servants were cramped by dependence on the goodwill of their employers, it was the lawyer who became the spokesman for the educated. Because the frontiers between his profession and the services were so fluid, there was a community of interest between him and those other educated men who were looking for advancement under the government. With means of his own, living in the administrative centres, he was admirably fitted to take the lead.[1] In the Presidency capitals it was the successful high court lawyer who was the backbone of politics; in the mofussil it was the pleader at the district bar. In the early 1880s, Bipin Chandra Pal noticed the lawyers 'advancing rapidly into considerable power and influence over their countrymen in every district through their position at the Bar. This was the beginning of what came to be subsequently characterised as "Vakil Raj"'.[2]

[1] Yet Indian lawyers from the different provinces met each other as politicians and not in a professional capacity.

[2] B. C. Pal, *Memories of My Life and Times* (*1886–1900*), II (Calcutta, 1951), xxxiv.

4

The Policies of the Rulers

The notions and policies of the British remain of crucial importance at this time, because Indian attitudes were still reactions to official measures rather than independent initiatives. Indeed, only the government of India was in any position to take a comprehensive view of Indian affairs, because the only unity of India lay in the supremacy of that government over the British provinces and native states alike. The apex of this system of government was the Governor-General and Viceroy. Accordingly, however much it might please the Old India Hands to dismiss him as the Great Ornamental,[1] it was the policies enunciated by him or in his name which reflected the official attitudes towards educated Indians all over India. It was this that brought these Indians together and determined whether they would unite in favour of the Raj or not. Lytton was the first Viceroy to be urgently confronted with this problem; his solutions were reversed by Ripon; Dufferin took a middle course. Yet all three were trying to protect the Raj against the onslaught of change.[2]

When Lytton arrived in 1876, he was soon complaining that 'Northbrook really settled nothing of importance, and has bequeathed to me all the biggest questions of Indian Government, greatly embarrassed by the previous systematic evasion of their accumulating difficulties.'[3] He was by no means the only Viceroy to lament the policy of the man he replaced;

---

[1] G. Aberigh-Mackay, *Twenty-one days in India, or the tour of Sir Ali Baba, K.C.B.* (new edition, London, 1882), pp. 3–8.

[2] The days are past when histories of modern India can be defined as histories of British policy alone. But volumes which exclude it would be equally bizarre.

[3] Lytton to Stephen, 28 May 1877, Stephen Papers, Add. 7349.

but in this case the difference in aims and methods was striking. Northbrook was one of the Whig Barings with no great fondness for state action. Disturbed by the widespread unrest he found in India, he had tried to allay it by doing as little as possible; his plan was 'to take off taxes and stop unnecessary legislation'.[1] He gratified educated Indians by resisting plans for a more active frontier policy and a new press law, abolishing income tax and declining to scrap the import duties on British cottons. Thus they could almost forgive the famine and the Baroda difficulties, and Northbrook could fairly claim that his masterly inactivity had made him a popular Viceroy.

Lytton, on the other hand, began his rule with his imagination excited by the possibilities of action. He had gone to India with the 'fancy prospect...painted on the blank wall of the Future of bequeathing to India the supremacy of Central Asia and the revenues of a first-class Power'.[2] The literary man was now to play the statesman, but his foreign policy suffered from the singular disadvantage that he believed his own rhetoric. To Lytton the great game on the northern and north-western frontiers of India was a simple matter of treating the local rulers like cab-drivers, who would trot forward when they were called for. Intent on pinning the Russians north of the outer rim of Kashmir or back on the Oxus, he tried to control Chitral and Yasin and the whole quadrilateral between the rivers Indus and Kunar; but in the event the rulers would not move to his command.[3] Afghanistan was a pivotal point in this strategy, and Lytton's missions and troop movements were intended to reduce it to a client state.[4] This was another oversimplification which failed to reckon with the local reaction, and

[1] Northbrook to Grenfell, n.d. April 1873, B. Mallet, *Thomas George, Earl of Northbrook...A Memoir* (London, 1908), p. 69; compare Northbrook to Argyll, 3 October 1872, Northbrook Papers, MSS Eur. C. 114 (9). For an explanation of this policy, see G.R.G. Hambly, 'Unrest in Northern India during the Viceroyalty of Lord Mayo, 1869–72; the Background to Lord Northbrook's Policy of Inactivity', *Journal of the Royal Central Asian Society*, XLVIII, part 1 (January 1961), pp. 37–55.
[2] Lytton to Stephen, 7 April 1880, Lady Betty Balfour (ed.), *Personal and Literary Letters of Robert First Earl of Lytton* (London, 1906), II, 200.
[3] G. J. Alder, *British India's Northern Frontier 1865–95* (London, 1963), pp. 114–37.
[4] D. K. Ghose, *England and Afghanistan* (Calcutta, 1960), chapters I–IV; W. K. Fraser-Tytler, *Afghanistan* (2nd edition, London, 1962), pp. 138–50.

his hopes of dominating Kabul ended in ruins. On the north-eastern frontier he was as eager for action as on the north-western, and in 1879 when the Afghan difficulties were piling up, he pressed London to sanction severe measures against Upper Burma.

Audacity on the frontiers demanded tranquillity inside them, but in fact the external uncertainties were heightened by a growing doubt over domestic security. Here Lytton felt that not only Northbrook but also the senior administrators had been much to blame. Coming from England with a fresh eye, he could see little political sagacity in the Indian civil service, and he told the Secretary of State: 'I am convinced that the fundamental political mistake of able and experienced Indian officials is a belief that we can hold India securely by what they call good government; that is to say, by improving the condition of the ryot, strictly administering justice, spending immense amounts on irrigation works, etc.'[1] Lytton had not come to rule an Oriental empire by jog-trot administration, but with creative policy, which the civilians seemed reluctant to create; as he again complained to Salisbury: 'Neither in my own Council, nor in any member of the official class here, whom I have yet met (with the exception of John Strachey), have I found a grain of statesmanship.'[2] So there was nothing for it except to turn to the happy few who possessed the statesman's instincts, to Salisbury in the India Office, to John Strachey, the Finance member, and to Fitzjames Stephen, who had returned from Calcutta to the English Bench. Their distrust for liberalism matched Lytton's own, and he quickly accepted their views about the spread of western education in India. Already in 1868 Strachey had been arguing that 'Some people seem to think that education will make the people of India loyal and contented. I believe this opinion to be altogether erroneous.'[3] Such a judgement was bound to appeal to Salisbury's sardonic realism; his comminations about the spread of knowledge, like Strachey's, might have applied to England no less than to India, where the newly educated, 'a deadly legacy from Metcalfe and Macaulay

[1] Lytton to Salisbury, 11 May 1876, LP, (3/1).
[2] Lytton to Salisbury, 18 May 1876, LP (3/1).
[3] Minute, 17 December 1868; appended to Note on the Admission of Natives to Appointments hitherto reserved to the Covenanted Civil Service, 21 October 1872, LP (23/1).

...cannot be anything else than an opposition in quiet times, rebels in time of trouble'.[1] Lytton, with his contempt for the trend in British politics, took the point as well, and he was soon denouncing '...the Baboos, whom we have educated to write semi-seditious articles in the Native Press, and who really represent nothing but the social anomaly of their own position'.[2] Clearly, it was useless seeking internal security through the babus. Where then might it be found?

To the Viceroy's mind, it could be found among the Indian aristocracy. Others had looked for it there already, for one of the lessons of the 1857 rising had seemed to be that it was necessary to conciliate the princes, indeed all the traditional notables in Indian society.[3] But if this was an aristocratic reaction, it was a brief one, for the social ills of India which were already apparent by the 1860s slowly drove government to legislate for the peasant's protection against the landowner.[4] Once again, Lytton's large vision of the East simplified the problem by overlooking the difficulties. He thought he saw '...a great feudal aristocracy which we cannot get rid of, which we are avowedly anxious to conciliate and command, but which we have, as yet, done next to nothing to rally round the British Crown as its *feudal* head'.[5] On the Viceroy's assumptions, rallying it would produce two political gains. The loyalty of the notables would ensure the loyalty of the people. The direct association of the Queen with India would capture their hearts. Hence the task was plain: 'To secure completely, and efficiently utilise, the Indian aristocracy is...the most important problem now before us.'[6]

The frivolity of this reasoning marked it as Lytton's own, not that of his mentors. Salisbury thought little of the plan,

[1] Salisbury to Lytton, 9 June 1876, LP (516/1).
[2] Lytton to Salisbury, 11 May 1876, LP (3/1).
[3] T. R. Metcalf, *The Aftermath of Revolt. India, 1857-70* (Princeton, 1965), pp. 222-37.
[4] Tenant law was defined by a Rent Recovery Act (Madras) VIII of 1865; Revenue Code (Bombay Act V of 1879); the North-western Provinces XII of 1881; the Central Provinces IX of 1883; the Bengal Tenancy Act VIII of 1885 (in addition to the older (Bengal) Act X of 1859); Oudh XXII of 1886 (in addition to the Oudh special Act XXVI of 1866 which prescribed the conditions under which the talukdars' privileged position was conceded); and Punjab XVI of 1887.
[5] Lytton to Disraeli, 30 April 1876, LP (3/1).
[6] Lytton to Salisbury, 11 May 1876, LP (3/1).

although he did not oppose it.[1] Stephen had warned the Viceroy that the princes would always be 'a set of most dangerous and reluctant allies...no more fit to share in the Government of India than to sit in the House of Lords'.[2] But the vision of a thousand swords leaping from their scabbards in defence of the throne charmed the novelist in Disraeli as well as the poet in Lytton, and they decided to bid for the imagination of the East by proclaiming the Queen as Empress of India. At the Delhi Durbar where the Indian aristocracy vowed fealty to their liege lady, they were rewarded with new banners, together with more guns to their salutes, honours that were distributed on a more lavish scale than the rations being doled out in the famine tracts of southern and western India. Obviously it would take more than a little bunting and gun-cotton to win the magnates but equally obviously they could not be given a share in real power. After examining the concessions which lay in his gift, Lytton suggested that there should be an Indian peerage and an Imperial Privy Council, 'to be composed exclusively of only the greatest and most important native princes... for purely consultative purposes';[3] at the same time the magnates were to take a larger place in the existing Legislative Councils.

The whole of this programme went to pieces. In London the India Council was strongly opposed to the scheme for a Privy Council; moreover, it would have required legislation, and after the storm over the Royal Titles Bill, the Cabinet was not prepared to risk more trouble in parliament.[4] That was the end of the Imperial Privy Council scheme. All that came of it was the empty title of 'Counsellor of the Empress', conferred on eight rulers and twelve officials. This meant the end of the Indian peerage proposals as well. As for the Legislative Councils, Lytton learned that he could not find the right magnates to nominate. This set of fiascos suggested that there were growing constraints on the power of the government of India, and that policy could not be made merely by a Viceroy in Calcutta exchanging ideas with a few correspondents back in

[1] Salisbury to Disraeli, 7 June 1876, Salisbury Papers (Beaconsfield). I owe this reference to Mr James Cornford.
[2] Stephen to Lytton, 6 March 1876, Stephen Papers, Add. 7349.
[3] Lytton to the Queen, 12 August 1876, LP (3/1).
[4] Salisbury to Lytton, 10 November 1876, LP (3/1).

England. Lytton chafed at the restraints in London, inveighing against 'the coalesced stupidities' of the India Council[1] and 'that deformed and abortive offspring of perennial political fornication, the present British constitution';[2] but he was soon to find that some of the restraints were in India as well.

As Lytton's experience of the East grew longer, he came to change his mind about the Indian civil service. At first, when his chief inspiration had come from the powerful minds of Salisbury and Stephen in London, he had found the civilians too narrow; but by 1877 he was professing 'an immense faith in the energy, ability, and ruling instinct of the men on the spot'.[3] The new faith still included the generalised theories of authoritarianism which Stephen had developed, so that Lytton saw India as 'a field of administration which furnishes us with the practical confutation of a great many liberal fallacies'.[4] But it now embraced many of the assumptions of the administrators themselves. These assumptions have often been described in too sweeping a way.[5] By the last quarter of the century a new trend in their thinking was becoming clear. In 1870 Mayo had proclaimed that 'the age of improvement has begun',[6] and the role of government became more complex. The tasks of compiling statistics, of revising land settlements, of extending cultivation, of grappling with famine, and of ruling the municipalities all fell on the administration. Inevitably, the organisation and the procedures of the bureaucracy grew more elaborate, and more and more they became a closed group whose skills none but they could understand. It was not that a gulf between rulers and ruled was any new thing; but now that gulf was widened by the change of function. If India was to be improved,

[1] Lytton to Salisbury, 4 October 1877, LP (518/2).
[2] Lytton to Cranbrook, 27 May 1878, LP (518/3); also cited in Cowling, 'Lytton, the Cabinet and the Russians', *English Historical Review*, LXXVI (January 1961), 70 n. 4.
[3] Lytton to Morley, 9 November 1877, Balfour, *Personal and Literary Letters*, II, 94.
[4] Lytton to Cranbrook, 30 April 1878, LP (518/3); cf. 'Happily, people don't really believe...in heaven or hell or liberalism as applied to India.' Stephen to Lytton, 17 April 1876, Stephen Papers, Add. 7349.
[5] Some members of the service were iron-fisted rulers, but it also included supporters of Indian aspirations, such as Hume, Wedderburn and Cotton. Civilians in general have been accused of a contempt for Indians, but it was civilians who worked to establish much of the ancient history and the ethnology of India.
[6] W. W. Hunter *Life of the Earl of Mayo* (London, 1876), I, 209.

136

who could improve it but the civilians? And who could understand the methods of the civilians but the civilians? Two conclusions would follow. First, entrance into this vital service
should be rigorously controlled. Secondly, the izzat, the prestige of the administration, must be maintained at all costs. Lytton was not the first Viceroy to accept these doctrines; but he
was the first to accept them explicitly; in so doing, he was to
bring them into public dispute, and thereby to speed up the
growth of Indian nationalism. The interaction of his views and
those of the civilians can be seen in controversies over Indian
entry into the services and Indian conduct of newspapers.

In the 1860s the problem of how to employ educated Indians had already been stated. Since their education might
qualify them for high rank, the issue of entry into the covenanted
service came into the open. By law the main posts in the Regulation provinces[1] were restricted to members of the covenanted
service, and only in the non-Regulation provinces, which were
further afield, where education was least advanced and the demand least insistent, was the government prepared to sanction
similar openings for Indians.[2] But meanwhile the infant
political associations in India urged that a proportion of the
covenanted posts should be reserved for Indians and that the
entrance examinations should be held in India as well as in
England.[3] The government would have none of this, but as a
consolation it offered scholarships to send nine Indians a year
to Britain, where they might study for the examination, if they
wished.[4] A year later, under pressure from the India Council, this
minor boon was withdrawn.[5] In withdrawing it, the India Office
committed itself to doing something to remedy the problem.

In 1870 it passed a measure which it was to take all the in-

---

[1] The Regulation provinces were the Presidencies of Madras and Bombay,
and the lieutenant-governorships of Bengal and the North-western
Provinces.
[2] Government of India, Foreign Department (General), 19 August 1867,
P.P. 1878–9, LV, 303.
[3] J. M. Tagore to Secretary of State for India, 16 March 1868, enclosing
Memorial of the British Indian Association; also Memorial of the Bombay
Association, forwarded 5 March 1868, LP (23/1).
[4] Government of India, Home Department (Education) to Secretary of
State, 7 July 1868, *P.P.* 1878–9, LV, 303–4.
[5] The India Council were 'violently opposed to the Scholarships cheme and
...jealous of its possible revival', Argyll to Mayo, 17 September 1869,
Mayo Papers, Add. 7490 (47).

genuity of Calcutta to interpret out of existence during the next ten years. This Act enabled the government of India to appoint Indians to posts previously reserved by law for the covenanted service.[1] After this new demarcation, all that was needed were rules and regulations to work the Act. But it was the covenanted service itself which was to draft them; and it was reluctant to do so, taking refuge in legal niceties.[2] Argyll had expected 'adverse opinion, and adverse advice in India'.[3] To allay these fears, in 1872 he enunciated three principles to guide Calcutta in making the new rules: a high proportion of the top posts must remain in British hands; Indians could be considered for senior judicial but not for executive appointments; and they should be paid less than Englishmen.[4] In December 1873 draft rules were ready, but with their restrictive provisions came a call for caution,[5] and it took another two years of prompting from London before the rules were finally passed.

It was clear to everyone that the 1875 rules had not solved the problem of employing Indians. Stephen believed that on its solution 'lies practically the fate of the empire'.[6] In Salisbury's view the principles laid down in 1870 solved nothing, because of the opposition of the services.

Competition has made all the services into which it has been introduced much more difficult to manage; in fact they will soon be more fitly called 'masteries' than 'services'. They look upon their posts and their prospects as property which they have won with their bow and spear; and the good things whereof they have right to defend...by the use of any weapon within reach.[7]

[1] C. Ilbert, *The Government of India* (Oxford, 1898), pp. 127, 239–40. The plan was to free the government of India 'from the Competitive Examination system here, as regards the appointment of Natives' Argyll to Mayo, 12 March 1869, Mayo Papers, Add. 7490 (47).

[2] See Note by John Strachey on the admission of natives of India to appointments hitherto reserved to the Covenanted Civil Service, 21 October 1872, LP (23/1).

[3] Argyll to Mayo, 4 October 1871, Mayo Papers, Add. 7490 (49).

[4] Argyll to Governor-General in Council, Public Despatch no. 113, 22 October 1872, *P.P.* 1878–9, LV, 310–11.

[5] 'The legislation...tends beyond question to diminish British ascendancy ...to destroy...the privileges which the covenanted civil servants have hitherto enjoyed...It may be too late to discuss now the general policy of this legislation, and it is, therefore, all the more desirable to scrutinize very carefully the way by which it is proposed to regulate it in detail.' Minute by Sir P. E. Wodehouse, 6 January 1874, LP (23/1).

[6] Stephen to Lytton, 6 July 1876, Stephen Papers, Add. 7349.

[7] Salisbury to Lytton, 27 October 1876, LP (516/1).

Lytton soon discovered this for himself. The moment any specific proposal was made there was '*instans tyrannus*, that Argus, the Covenanted Service, occupying the whole ground, and fiercely complaining that the ground is not large enough for its own accommodation'.[1] But as his sympathies warmed towards the covenanted service, Lytton became persuaded that its reluctance to surrender its perquisites was not the real difficulty. There was no question of giving Indians high executive posts, but merely a few of the higher judicial appointments and some jobs in the uncovenanted service. The problem now was to decide who these Indians were to be, and how so limited a concession could be reconciled with the more generous pronouncements of the Raj.

Lytton had the happy knack of believing that whatever topic his mind was working on should be the crucial topic for others as well. By 1878 the question of the services had become 'by far, the gravest, and most important, we have yet to deal with';[2] and so it would have to be settled by the usual dashing methods. Government was saddled with the pledges in the 1833 Charter, the Proclamation of 1858 and the Act of 1870; they were equally bound by custom to appoint Europeans to all higher posts; no small modification of this practice could satisfy the aspirations of the Indians encouraged by the pledges; no large modification could be agreeable to the interests of the covenanted services, sustained by the custom. If government was to shake itself free of these constraints, one or other of these irreconcilables had to be scrapped, and Lytton was clear that it was the pledges which would have to go. In a secret note he justified this course:

We all know that these claims and expectations never can, or will, be fulfilled. We have to choose between prohibiting them or cheating them: and we have chosen the least straight-forward course...both the Governments of England and of India appear to me, up to the present moment, unable to answer satisfactorily the charge of having taken every means in their power of breaking to the heart the word of promise they have uttered to the ear.[3]

The more straightforward course would be to circumscribe the pledges, to cut them down, but to make them realities within their new limits.

[1] Lytton to Salisbury, 28 September 1876, LP (3/1).
[2] Lytton to Salisbury, 27 March 1878, LP (518/3).
[3] Note by Lytton, 30 May 1877, Notes in Home Department (Public) Proceedings, May 1879, nos. 287–328, RP, Add. MSS 43580.

Lytton's plan was to classify government service into two categories. From one of them Indians would be excluded, and they would be 'plainly and publicly' warned that 'natives must never aspire' to it; it 'would include all important administrative posts'.[1] In other words, the covenanted service would be reserved strictly and exclusively for Europeans. 'It is one thing', Lytton wrote to his member for Public Works, a simple engineer,

to admit the public into your park, and quite another thing to admit it into your drawing room...Already great mischief has been done by the deplorable tendency of second-rate Indian officials, and superficial English philanthropists to ignore the essential and insurmountable distinctions of race qualities, which are fundamental to our position in India; and thus, unintentionally, to pamper the conceit and vanity of half-educated natives, to the serious detriment of commonsense, and of the wholesome recognition of realities.[2]

Among the realities was the fact that 'we hold India as a conquered country...which must be governed in all essentials by the strong, unchallenged, hand of the conquering power'.[3]

Convinced by such officials as Sir John Strachey, Sir Ashley Eden and Sir George Couper that 'the natives are not fitted for important and responsible administrative offices',[4] Lytton conceived his plan for a closed native service, 'organised on a footing entirely distinct from the present Covenanted Service'.[5] To it would be transferred some of the lesser judicial posts hitherto reserved for the covenanted service as well as the better paid posts in the uncovenanted service. This would be the second category. It would be inferior in standing and in remuneration to the covenanted service. It would not be recruited by competition. It would be for Indians only.

But which Indians? It was palpably true that the demand for better employment opportunities in the public service was coming from the graduates of Calcutta, Madras and Bombay. Since this was a complicating fact, Lytton chose to ignore it, speaking loftily about the semi-educated natives. Parroting the Old India Hands, his most contemptuous phrases were about the Bengalis.

[1] Lytton to Salisbury, 9 February 1877, LP (518/2).
[2] Lytton to Col. Sir A. Clarke, 26 April 1878, LP (518/3).
[3] Lytton to Sir E. Perry, 18 April 1877, LP (518/2).
[4] Eden to Lytton, 23 April 1877, LP (519/5). Also see Strachey to Lytton, 4 March 1877; and Couper to Lytton, 22 April 1877, LP (519/4).
[5] Lytton to Salisbury, 10 May 1877, LP (3/2).

As he put it: '...the Baboodom of Lower Bengal, though disloyal is fortunately cowardly and its only revolver is its ink bottle; which though dirty, is not dangerous.'[1] But his impartial scorn fell upon the educated Indian in the other Presidencies as well:

For most forms of administrative employment he appears to me quite unfit...The educated, and educable, natives of Bengal, Madras, and Bombay, are probably unfit for employment out of their own Presidencies, and the hardier and more energetic races of the north will not submit to any educational process imposed by us as qualification for Government employment.[2]

This was a convenient finding, for at least it enabled Lytton to support the Indian aristocracy,[3] natural administrators to a man. Admittedly, they would hardly do well in the dry-as-dust scrutiny of competitive examination, but these sombre Gladstonian methods might be dispensed with in a more romantic setting. Appointments to the new closed service should be by patronage, and preference should be given to good social standing, not mere educational qualifications.[4] This would produce—eventually—'...a better class of Native Civil Servants than the Bengalee Baboos. If you get hold of young men of good family, you will secure along with them all the members, and all the influence, of their families; and this will ramify far and wide'.[5] This time Lytton would slam two doors at once, for educated Indians would be shut out of the covenanted service and would find it hard to squeeze into the closed service. But for so elegant a solution there would be a price to pay. Since it would mean amending the Queen's Proclamation, revising several Acts of Parliament and breaking a good many pledges, it would require legislation. Cranbrook, who was Secretary of

[1] Lytton to Caird, 12 December 1879, LP (518/4), cf. 'Physical peculiarities of race render the political opinions of Bengalees of comparatively little importance', Minute by Strachey, 17 December 1868, appended to Note by Strachey, 21 October 1872, LP (23/1).
[2] Lytton to Sir E. Perry, 18 April 1877, LP (518/2).
[3] The Indian Army commanders had refused to consider commissioning them.
[4] For details of the scheme see Public Despatch no. 35, 2 May 1878, Home Department (Public) Proceedings, May 1879, no. 321, RP, Add. MSS 43580. A blunt civilian comment was made by Lepel Griffin: 'In a competitive examination, the scum would assuredly rise to the top', *ibid.* nos. 287–328, RP, Add. MSS 43580.
[5] Lytton to Salisbury, 10 May 1877, LP (3/2).

State in 1878, saw the political impossibility of going to parliament with such a bill.[1] Defending Lytton's policies had caused enough trouble already. Cranbrook refused point blank to introduce the measure. Once again Lytton had been foiled by the quirks of democracy in England, with its suspicions of patronage. It was all very well for the ennobled literary men of the Beaconsfield regime to suggest these traditional methods, but they were now dealing with a House of Commons elected by householders, lodgers and other persons not far removed from babus. How kindly would they take to the methods of the Pelhams? Or even to the ideals of Coningsby?

So the Secretary of State proposed that Calcutta should stick to the code as it stood; each year a few Indians should enter the covenanted service under the 1870 Act, but they should be kept out of top offices.[2] That was as far as London would go. On this basis new rules were formulated,[3] and the statutory civil service was created in 1879. Social status was to be the criterion for selection to it.[4] It opened what Sir Charles Aitchison called 'the side door of charity, nomination, and patronage'.[5] It had followed three years after the reduction of the age limit for the covenanted service examination. Ostensibly this had been to enable successful candidates to go to university before coming to India; in effect, the new age limit 'virtually excluded Indians'.[6] 'It was then [in Lytton's viceroyalty] well known, and is not now disputed', Ripon was told later on, 'that while opening to Natives the door of nomination, that of open competition in England was practically closed'.[7] In the dead-end occupations of the uncovenanted service Indians had been given a more generous scope by Lytton's government. But when

[1] Lytton had earlier been warned by his service advisors that no Secretary of State would countenance the legislation his scheme demanded. Note by A. J. Arbuthnot, 20 January 1878, RP, Add. MSS 43580.

[2] Cranbrook to Lytton, 25 August 1878, LP (516/3). Also see Public Despatch to India, 7 November 1878, Home Department (Public) Proceedings, May 1879, no. 322, RP, Add. MSS 43580.

[3] Public Despatch from India, no. 31, 1 May 1879; and Resolution, 24 December 1879, Home Department (Public) Proceedings, December 1879, no. 371.

[4] See Lytton to Buckingham and Chandos, 25 December 1879, LP (518/4).

[5] Cited in Minute by Ripon, 10 September 1884, B.M., *B.P.* 1/8 (4).

[6] *PSC*, pp. 54–5.

[7] Note by T. C. Hope, 24 August 1883, RP, Add. MSS 43578.

they dreamt of preferment or reflected on the fate of their press, educated Indians had reason to feel themselves the victims of a contrived discrimination.

The staple of the new Indian journalism was to hold up specific targets for the widespread sense of grievance that an unsympathetic foreign rule engendered. Indian-owned newspapers had begun to move beyond merely reporting news to the more ambitious and less costly task of creating a climate of opinion about it. More of them were political in scope and they backed the organised political demands of the educated Indians. In their efforts to capture a circulation, and with it a revenue from advertisers, editors soon found that exaggerated attacks on government, the reporting of incidents with overtones of racial injustice, were what their readers wanted. They found too that blackmail might be more profitable than exposure. In Bengal, where education was most advanced, the trend had gone furthest, and the most virulent was the vernacular press. Not only were many of the Bengalis who became journalists well educated, but in Bengal the competition between the papers was fiercest; consequently, it was here that the excesses were most marked. It was here too that British officials and businessmen were most vulnerable to organised muckraking, since the government was close at hand in Calcutta to take note.

The question of curbing the press had already been raised in Northbrook's time. Sir George Campbell, the lieutenant-governor of Bengal, had pressed for a gagging act,[1] since under the existing law, successful prosecution of a newspaper was all but impossible. 'My own opinion has always been', he later wrote, 'that an entirely free press is inconsistent with a despotic form of government, even if it be a paternal despotism.'[2] Northbrook would have none of this, arguing that 'We are very ignorant of the feelings of the people…and the press may to a certain extent supplement the deficiency'.[3]

Here was an argument that would have appealed to Metcalfe and his generation. It did not appeal to Lytton. In India, as in Ireland, where there was a danger to British rule, *salus imperii*

[1] Campbell to Northbrook, n.d. July 1872, Northbrook Papers, MSS Eur. C. 144 (13).
[2] G. Campbell, *Memoirs of My Indian Career* (London, 1893), II, 315.
[3] Northbrook to Campbell, 20 July 1872, Northbrook Papers, MSS Eur. C. 144 (13).

143

suprema lex. Since the English-language newspapers knew their place and many of them were owned and run by Englishmen, they could go their way; what was needed was an act to curb vernacular journalism. Consequently, he circulated a minute suggesting 'a Press-law on the lines of the Irish Act—applicable only to the Native Press'.[1] Every provincial government concurred except Madras, which traditionally disliked interference from the centre. Bengal, of course, was enthusiastic; and in Bombay Sir Richard Temple went one better: 'If anything at all is required in Bengal, it would be still more required in Bombay.'[2]

The opinions elicited by this openly discriminatory proposal show the differences in attitude between the more liberal and the more authoritarian of the civilians when they were confronted with a question of pure policy-making rather than administration. Hobhouse, the Law member, warned the Viceroy that a legal distinction between the English and the vernacular papers would be 'at variance with the whole tenour of our policy...raising a still deeper and wider question, viz. whether it is right to promote the education of the native'.[3] On the other side, Lepel Griffin had long been urging a press law,[4] and Ashburner of the Bombay Council wanted to ban Indian political associations into the bargain.[5] But the most lucid statement of the authoritarian view was made by Sir George Couper, the lieutenant-governor of the North-western Provinces:

...it seems to me the time has come for us to cease from putting our heads in a bush and shouting that black is white. We all know that in point of fact black is *not* white; and the sooner we plainly recognize and act upon that fact the better it will be for our influence and hold on the millions we govern. That there should be one law alike for the European and Native is an excellent thing in theory, but if it could really be introduced in practice we should have no business in the country...To me there is nothing more remarkable than the reluctance we evince to admit we have gone too far, especially in the direction of so-called progress. I think most men who have anxiously considered the subject will agree that we have carried State education too far...

[1] Lytton to Eden, 20 October 1877, LP (518/2).
[2] Temple to Lytton, 12 January 1878, LP (519/7).
[3] Note by A. Hobhouse, 10 August 1876, *P.P.* 1878, LVII, 475–9.
[4] See Note by Griffin, August 1877, Notes in Home Department (Public) Proceedings, May 1879, nos. 278–328, RP, Add. MSS 43580.
[5] Note by Ashburner, 7 February 1878, *P.P.* 1878, LVII, 495–6.
[6] Note by Couper, January 1878, *ibid.* 498.

With this support, Lytton could ignore the opinions of Madras. He wasted no time, and passed the Vernacular Press Act with 'unusual haste'.[1] Various reasons for the haste and secrecy were put forward publicly by Lytton; the triumph of Russian arms in the war with Turkey, and the imminent departure of the Viceroy for Simla.[2] To Stephen he was franker. The Press Act, he admitted, was virtually an executive act, though in legislative form.[3] Speed was essential to prevent criticism in India and obstruction by parliament. 'Such are our reformed...institutions', wrote the unrepentant proconsul; 'We can only work them by a series of subterfuges.'[4]

The Act had two objects—to suppress or punish seditious writings, and to prevent editors using their columns for blackmail. Restricted to publications in the vernacular, it specifically excluded English-owned and English-language papers from its provisions. In London there were a few dissenters in the India Council. They spoke of Britain's mission to educate the people of India to 'self-government in their own affairs'; they condemned the Act as a repudiation of 'the large and liberal policy we have pursued in India for the last fifty years'; they compared the Dutch and British systems of colonial government, and saw this as a belated attempt to change course.[5] But these seemed outmoded views. In endorsing the bill, Lytton himself said he trusted in 'the spread of education and enlightenment' to make it eventually unnecessary. But he immediately regretted his remarks. 'For the province we have most "educated and enlightened"', he pointed out, 'is undoubtedly Lower Bengal, and it is probably in this province that the character of the Vernacular Press has been worst'.[6] He told the Council that

[1] Lytton to Stephen, 26 May 1878, Stephen Papers, Add. 7349. On 13 March Lytton cabled London, pleading the case for immediate legislation, and sketching the heads of a bill he intended to pass at a single sitting of the Legislative Council the very next day. He promised in due course to forward its proceedings to the Secretary of State. London's approval was cabled on the 14th, and on that day the Act became law.
[2] Lytton to the Queen, 21 March 1878; Lytton to Northbrook, 25 April 1878, and Lytton to Cranbrook, 25 April 1878, LP (518/3).
[3] Lytton to Stephen, 20 April 1878, Stephen Papers, Add. 7349.
[4] Lytton to Stephen, 26 May 1878, Stephen Papers, Add. 7349.
[5] *P.P.* 1878, LVII, 410–19.
[6] Lytton to Maine, 21 March 1878, LP (518/3).

the Act was a measure of public safety; and it was his prime duty permanently to maintain British ascendancy in India.[1]

In choosing the ways of maintaining that ascendancy, Lytton had been guided, partly by his ambition to leave a strong India as the monument to his rule, and partly by his impatience at the obstacles which baffled his ambition. His talent for the swift, strong phrase reflected his penchant for the swift, strong policy. But frequently the phrase had to do duty for the policy. The Viceroy lacked the craft and understanding to deal with the forces which hampered him in Britain no less than in India. He ridiculed the democracy which was to bring about his replacement in 1880 and the prompt repeal of his Press Act; he failed to see that parliament would never endorse his plans for the civil service. In India, there was something unreal about dealing with the problem of employing educated Indians by ratiocinating it out of existence and by asserting that the true problem was how to employ the notables. There was something foolish about passing the Press Act and the Arms Act, both of them justifiable in principle, but drafted to discriminate openly against Indians. There was something provocative about scrapping the tariffs which protected Indian textiles against Lancashire. In each of these matters Lytton had extenuating circumstances on his side,[2] but in them all, this gifted and in some ways generous man thought Indian opinion so negligible that he could risk open discrimination. He was wrong. Educated Indians in the Presidencies bitterly resented these slights, and this feeling of victimisation gave a fillip to their political organisations.

It was not only that his rule saw sporadic violence here and there inside the frontiers, such as the Deccan Riots and the rising of Phadke in Bombay. These were small affairs, grounded in local discontents. Much more important was the slow growth of aspiration on what seemed to be an all-India scale. This process was already apparent to a perceptive civilian in the backwater of Hyderabad:

[1] Abstract of Proceedings of the Governor-General's Council, 14 March 1878, *P.P.* 1878, LVII, 461–6.
[2] Lady Betty Balfour, *The History of Lord Lytton's Indian Administration, 1876 to 1880: compiled from Letters and Official Papers* (London, 1899), pp. 475–85, 502–85.

within the last...20 years...a feeling of nationality, which formerly had no existence...has grown up, and the...Press can now, for the first time in the history of our rule, appeal to the *whole Native population* of India against their foreign rulers. Twenty years ago...we had to take account of local nationalities and particular races. The resentment of the Mahratta did not involve that of the Bengalee...*Now*...we have changed all that, and are beginning to find ourselves face to face, not with the population of individual provinces, but with 200 millions of people united by sympathies and intercourse which we have ourselves created and fostered. This seems...the great political fact of the day.[1]

In India, as in Ireland and South Africa, the forming of the second Gladstone administration in April 1880 upset the thinking both of the governed and of Government House. To a statesman reared on the strategy of the mid-nineteenth century it was clear that the most effective, and the most elegant, method of maintaining the imperial connection was through the device of self-government. But how were these principles to be applied to India? Even if Gladstonian liberalism might apply to the white colonies, was it not irrelevant to India, that classical colony of exploitation?[2] Nevertheless, to the Whigs who dominated the Liberal government of 1880 it seemed clear enough—especially before they took office—that the methods of Disraeli, Salisbury and Lytton were as pernicious as they were imprudent for the governing of the sub-continent. It is easy to see why the defeat of the Conservatives was hailed by India as a prelude to better times.

Gladstone's first moves seemed to bode well for India. Lytton was immediately recalled. In Afghanistan his forward policy was stopped. In his place arrived a Viceroy of impeccable liberalism, who wished to put it into practice. But this was more than could be said of the Secretary of State. Once in office, both Hartington and Kimberley, who succeeded him, were less eager to embark on a wholesale reversal of the policies of the previous regime. It was enough to do the essential—to move out of Afghanistan. After some prodding, they were prepared to allow the repeal of the Vernacular Press Act. But when it came to the issue of the cotton duties, there was no question

---

[1] W. B. Jones, Commissioner, Hyderabad Assigned Districts, Memorandum, 28 February 1878, *P.P.* 1878, LVII, 504–5.

[2] P. Leroy-Beaulieu, *De la Colonisation chez les Peuples Modernes* (5th edition, Paris, 1902), II, 188–216.

of antagonising Lancashire to please India. Nor was the India Office willing to countenance Ripon's schemes to reform the Legislative Councils or to amend the Arms Act; even less was it prepared to re-open the thorny question of the civil service.

Twenty years had passed since Ripon had helped to administer India as Wood's Under Secretary of State. Now, as the new Viceroy surveyed his charge in the light of the 'broad liberal principles'[1] which he brought with him to each new office, he was convinced that his predecessor's attitudes were detestable and his policies dangerous. Their sum effect had been to convince Indians that their interests had always been sacrificed to England's. This impression had been given at an unfortunate time, for Ripon discovered in India an increasingly articulate public opinion and new aspirations.[2] A policy was needed to win over the 'daily growing body of Natives educated by us in western ideas and western learning'. 'Unless we are prepared to afford to these men', he wrote, 'legitimate openings for their aspirations and ambitions, we had better at once abolish our Universities and close our Colleges, for they will only serve to turn out year by year in ever-increasing numbers men who must inevitably become the most dangerous and influential enemies of our rule.'[3] It was the authoritarian argument, turned inside out. During the past decade educated Indians had begun to shape India's public opinion.[4] To alienate them seemed to Ripon the height of political folly. The future belonged to them. Their leadership over the Indian peoples, their influence and power, would inevitably grow.[5] Admittedly, most Englishmen in India did not like the educated native. Lytton had shared this 'vulgar' distaste, and had designed a policy around it,[6] disowning the heritage of Metcalfe, Macaulay and Ripon's old chief, Sir Charles Wood. But the new Viceroy believed that only by the infusion of earlier Victorian ideals could modern India be reconciled to British rule.

It was not merely his liberal creed that precipitated this re-

[1] Ripon to John Bright, 19 July 1882, RP (B.M. I.S. 290/7).
[2] Ripon, Memorandum...on Local Self-Government, 26 December 1882, enclosed in Ripon to Kimberley, 26 December 1882, RP (B.M. I.S. 290/5).
[3] Ripon to Kimberley, 4 April 1884, RP (B.M. I.S. 290/5).
[4] Ripon to Kimberley, 10 July 1883, RP (B.M. I.S. 290/5).
[5] Ripon to Kimberley, 9 May 1884, RP (B.M. I.S. 290/5).
[6] Ripon to Kimberley, 11 June 1883, RP (B.M. I.S. 290/5).

appraisal, it was rather 'the hourly increasing...necessity of making the educated natives the friends, instead of the enemies, of our rule'.[1] 'There are', the Viceroy concluded,

...two policies lying before the choice of the Government of India; the one is the policy of those who have established a free press, who have promoted education, who have admitted natives more and more largely to the public service in various forms, and who have favoured the extension of self-government; the other is that of those who hate the freedom of the press, who dread the progress of education, and who watch with jealousy and alarm every thing which tends, in however limited a degree, to give the natives of India a larger share in the management of their own affairs. Between these two policies we must choose; the one means progress, the other means repression. Lord Lytton chose the latter. I have chosen the former...[2]

Here was an analysis on classical Victorian lines charged with an undertone of urgency. Yet the Viceroy's actual programme was modest enough. He hoped to re-open the civil service question, but London would not allow him to do so.[3] Among his immediate plans was a small extension of the elective principle to the Legislative Councils. This would enable the government to consult representative Indians. He failed. Turning to local government as a way of associating educated Indians more closely with their rulers and of giving them some elementary political training, Ripon promised much but could deliver little. The uproar over the Ilbert bill further illustrates

[1] Ripon to W. E. Forster, 19 May 1883, RP (B.M. I.S. 290/7).
[2] Ripon, Memorandum...on Local Self-Government, 26 December 1882, enclosed in Ripon to Kimberley, 26 December 1882, RP (B.M. I.S. 290/5).
[3] Ripon's plan was to raise the age-limit for the covenanted service examination. During the Ilbert bill crisis, most of the Viceroy's counsellors opposed any measure to increase the number of Indians in the civil service (Notes by Bayley, 4 August 1883; Baring, 6 August 1883; Hope, 24 August 1883; Wilson, 30 August 1883, RP, Add. MSS 43578). After the uproar had died down, Ripon again pressed London to raise the limit (Viceroy to Secretary of State, telegram, 17 April 1884, RP, Add. MSS 43580), but Kimberley would not move (Kimberley to Ripon, 2 May and 22 May 1884, RP (B.M. I.S. 290/5)); in September, Ripon combined the proposal that the age limit be raised to twenty-one with a plan to limit the total Indian intake into both the covenanted and the statutory services to 18 per cent (Letter of the Government of India, Home Department (Public), no. 51, 12 September 1884, *P.P.* 1884-5, LVIII, 130-3). London remained adamant (Despatch of Secretary of State, no. 1, Public, 8 January 1885, *ibid.* 153-4 and Kimberley to Dufferin, 8 January 1885, DP 18 (Reel 517)).

the weakness of the Viceroy, the limitations on his authority and the growing tension between rulers and ruled.

Reversing the trend in India depended in the last resort on support from London and co-operation in India. In London, where the India Council disliked changes, everything depended on how much support the Viceroy received from the Secretary of State and the Cabinet. Ripon was unlucky. India was not one of Gladstone's interests; Ireland and Egypt preoccupied him. In them this ill-starred government had troubles enough; neither Hartington nor Kimberley wanted to add Indian policy to the list of party conflicts. But tampering with the Legislative Councils could only mean more trouble for the government. When Ripon judged that his Secretary of State would control the India Council, and that he himself could trample over the bureaucracy, he was wrong.

In India, the conservative school of thought which found Ripon's viceroyalty dangerous included most European officials and non-officials.[1] Sir James Fergusson, the governor of Bombay, was the most intransigent of Tories, both 'narrow minded and injudicious, and...as local...as if he had been born in a Bombay office'.[2] In Bengal, Rivers Thompson, the lieutenant-governor, a civilian in the same mould as his predecessor, Sir Ashley Eden, who now mounted an attack upon Ripon from the India Council, was at best an uncertain ally, at worst one of the instigators of agitation against the Viceroy.[3] Grant Duff of Madras, once the Liberal Under-Secretary of State for Colonies, was another disappointment since he soon 'surrendered himself to the guidance of his very narrow surroundings',[4] rapidly persuaded by his Indian experience that liberalism was not for export.[5] Sir Alfred Lyall, in the North-western Provinces, proved slow and deliberate in implementing the Viceroy's schemes.[6] Yet it is misleading to

[1] Baron de Hübner, *A Travers L'Empire Britannique* (*1883–1884*) (Paris, 1886), II, 258.
[2] Ripon to Northbrook, 1 July 1881, RP (B.M. I.S. 290/7).
[3] Ripon to Baring, 16 July 1883, RP (B.M. I.S. 290/8).
[4] Ripon to Kimberley, 29 August 1884, RP (B.M. I.S. 290/5).
[5] See Duff's memorandum, 24 June 1885, enclosed in Duff to Dufferin, 24 June 1885. DP, 47 (Reel 528), and Duff to Dufferin, 2 January 1885. DP, 47 (Reel 528).
[6] See Ripon to Lyall, 10 January 1883. RP (B.M. I.S. 290/8). Lyall himself confessed in 1882: 'I am driving my own coach cautiously, and trying to

picture Ripon as fighting this just battle for India single-handed. Among his liberal supporters was Major Evelyn Baring, once Northbrook's private secretary in India and now Strachey's successor as Finance member. Whatever his doubts may have been about the wisdom of the old policy of stimulating higher education,[1] he saw that 'Having put our hand to the plough we cannot turn back'.[2] Courtney Ilbert, the Law member sent out in response to Ripon's plea for 'a good wide-minded constitutional lawyer and a sound Liberal',[3] together with Sir Charles Umpherston Aitchison, one of the first 'competition-wallahs' and a 'real good man of the best Scotch type',[4] were two others who stood loyally by the Viceroy.

As for the mass of the officials, Ripon generously conceded that India had 'the best bureaucracy that the world has ever seen', though it had 'the faults and the dangers which belong to every institution of that kind...conspicuously a jealousy of allowing non-officials to interfere in any way whatever with any portion, however restricted, of the administration of the country'.[5]

Another of Ripon's burdens was the unrelenting opposition of the India Council, which he described to Gladstone as 'the most Conservative body now existing in Europe'.[6] In vain the Viceroy asked Hartington:

What is the use of a Liberal Government, so far as India is concerned, if it is to give itself up, bound hand and foot, to the guidance of a set of old gentlemen, whose energies are relaxed by age, and who, having excellent salaries and no responsibility, amuse themselves by criticising the proposals and obstructing the plans of those, who have the most recent knowledge of the real state of India, and who have upon their shoulders the whole responsibility for the good government of that country.[7]

But there was more to the opposition of the India Council than the conservatism of the old. The Council, whose distinguished membership included Sir Henry Maine, Sir Ashley Eden and General Richard Strachey, considered the new Viceroy a

prevent the Government of India from driving me', quoted in Durand, *Life of Lyall*, p. 266.
[1] See Note by Baring, 15 April 1881, RP, Add. MSS 43575.
[2] Baring to Mallet, 25 September 1882, enclosed in Baring to Ripon, 25 September 1882, RP (B.M. I.S. 290/8).
[3] Ripon to Hartington, 4 August 1881, RP (B.M. I.S. 290/5).
[4] Ripon to Hughes, 25 May 1883, RP (B.M. I.S. 290/7).
[5] Ripon to Gladstone, 6 October 1882, RP (B.M. I.S. 290/7).
[6] *Ibid.*   [7] Ripon to Hartington, 14 September 1882, RP (B.M. I.S. 290/5).

'dangerous Radical, second only in wickedness to Gladstone',[1] and saw it their duty to prevent him tampering with the imperial structure that they, and generations of officials before them, had so carefully constructed. By the end of his viceroyalty, as he contemplated the wreckage of his plans, Ripon bitterly let London know that his experience had at last taught him to expect 'almost anything in the shape of opposition on the part of the Members of your Council'.[2] So it was with some justice that Hübner thus summed up his views on India under Ripon: 'C'est un spectacle curieux et peut-être unique que celui d'une immense administration dirigée d'après des doctrines répudiées par la grande majorité de ceux qui la composent. C'est cependant en ce moment le cas de l'Inde.'[3]

This was the setting for Ripon's first foray into liberal reform. Educated Indians had long been asking for elected representation in the Imperial and Provincial Legislative Councils, and the new Viceroy, ebulliently declaring that 'I get more Radical every day',[4] was prepared to grant it. Whereas Lytton had hoped to nominate his magnates, Ripon, on the other hand, wanted the larger municipalities to elect Indians to the Legislative Councils, which would be reorganised to admit ten such elected members, one each from Calcutta, Bombay and Madras, and seven from the other main cities. This would 'advance the political education of the people, and would be a real step towards giving them a larger share in the management of their own affairs'. Associating responsible Indians with the work of legislation, Ripon argued, would do more to secure British rule than Lytton's policy of excluding them. He could not resist adding that eventually his scheme would probably lead to 'a further advance along the same road of extended self-government...but then according to my way of thinking that is the road along which we ought to travel'.[5] This comment was a work of supererogation, so far as the India Office and its advisers were concerned, for it seemed all too plain to them that here might be Home Rule on the instalment plan. So when Ripon put up his scheme to the India Office, it was a year before

[1] Ripon to Hughes, 8 December 1882, RP (B.M. I.S. 290/7).
[2] Ripon to Kimberley, 16 May 1884, RP (B.M. I.S. 290/5).
[3] Hübner, *A Travers l'Empire Britannique*, II, 259.
[4] Ripon to W. E. Forster, 26 May 1881, RP (B.M. I.S. 290/7).
[5] Ripon to Hartington, 31 December 1881, RP (B.M. I.S. 290/5).

Hartington replied, and then merely to say that the proposal was premature. Lord Hartington was not perhaps the most energetic or impetuous of Queen Victoria's Ministers; and his Whiggish caution had been strongly reinforced by the forebodings of the Old India Hands. Maine, Lyall and even Aitchison concurred that this was not the time for such a plan, nor India the place.[1]

Frustrated in his large plan, the Viceroy now turned to a more modest project, the development of local self-government. If there was no scope for liberalism at the top of the representative system, there might well be at its base. Lawrence had suggested, and Mayo had begun, a policy of financial decentralisation and local taxation, on the grounds that the best way of raising local taxes was to associate tax-payers with the levying and spending of their money. With the new financial approach had come a small measure of local self-government. In 1873, legislation was passed sanctioning for other towns municipal powers long enjoyed by the Presidency capitals, and also allowing the ratepayers in the districts to elect members to the district committees. This legislation was merely permissive, and by Ripon's time little effect had been given to it, since the officials still regarded municipalities and district committees as administrative conveniences, not schools for training Indians in the arts of self-government, and Indians themselves had remained apathetic to their limited opportunities. The origin of Ripon's policy of local self-government lies in the plans of the Finance Department which in 1880 was faced by the quinquennial revision of Mayo's provincial settlements.[2] To extend financial devolution and to simplify the task of taxing at the local level, Baring, the Finance member, planned to put the elective principle to work by letting municipalities and rural districts administer local receipts and charges.[3] 'The credit is yours', Ripon told Baring, 'I feel convinced that you have laid the foundation of a system of municipal self-government which will confer increasing benefits upon India as time goes on.'[4]

[1] Hartington to Ripon, 26 December 1882, RP, Add. MSS 43569.
[2] See Baring to Ripon, 29 July 1880, RP, Add. MSS 43596.
[3] Resolution of the Government of India (Department of Finance and Commerce), no. 3353, 30 September 1881, *P.P.* 1883, LI, 8–13.
[4] Ripon to Baring, 7 October 1881, RP (B.M. I.S. 290/8); also see Ripon to Baring, 14 August 1882, RP (B.M. I.S. 290/8).

During 1881 Ripon's thoughts on local government had slowly been maturing. In April when the Viceroy was asked to ratify the appointment of a deputy collector to manage the Ahmadabad Municipality, the Finance Department argued that in western India there were plenty of intelligent and educated Indians capable of managing their own municipal affairs without officials to direct them.[1] Ripon was impressed by this argument; reluctantly ratifying the appointment, he urged Bombay to encourage 'the independence and real self-government of municipalities, and to restrict direct administrative interference ...as much as possible'.[2] It was clear to him that if municipalities and district boards were 'to be of any use for the purpose of training the natives to manage their own affairs, they must not be overshadowed by the constant presence of the *Burra Sahib*'.[3] Later that year, when the Calcutta Municipality Amendment Act took from the municipality and gave to the Bengal government the power to extend the water supply to the suburbs, Ripon agreed to the change 'with regret'.[4] By now his article of faith that self-government was better than good government was donning its Indian dress. '...the political end to be attained by the development of self-government in this country', the Viceroy reasoned, 'is so important as to render a very patient and forbearing mode of dealing with the shortcomings and even with the follies of local bodies most desirable.'[5] He suspected that local self-government in India had not been given a fair trial, and called for information.[6] What he now learnt about the workings of the elective system confirmed his worst suspicion.

Bengal reported that forty-eight of Calcutta's Commissioners were elected; yet in its opinion those who voted were a 'wretchedly small' number, and those who were elected were

---

[1] See Note by T. C. Hope, 19 April 1881, and Note by Baring, 21 April 1881, RP, Add. MSS 43575.

[2] Note by Ripon, 30 April 1881, RP, Add. MSS 43575.

[3] Quoted in L. Wolf, *Life of the First Marquess of Ripon* (London, 1921), II, 99.

[4] What finally persuaded the Viceroy was the Home member's plea that such was the incompetence of Calcutta's municipality that 'if the law be left as at present, the suburbs of Calcutta may wait for their water-supply until the next decade or longer!' Note by Gibbs, 4 July 1881, RP, Add. MSS 43575.   [5] Note by Ripon, 8 August 1881, RP, Add. MSS 43575.

[6] The initiative was taken in May. See Note by Ripon, 2 May 1881, RP, Add. MSS 43575; and Circular from Government of India (Home Department) to Local Governments, 10 May 1881, *P.P.* 1883, LI, 145.

'nobodies'; the only enthusiasts for the municipal franchise were a handful of ambitious young men of advanced notions; and they simply discouraged the better type of Bengali as well as the European from seeking a place in the Corporation. In the mofussil only three small municipalities had elected members, and in two of them there was no enthusiasm for elections. On this limited evidence the lieutenant-governor came to the conclusion that the elective system had been tried prematurely, was now discredited, and should be scrapped.[1] The government of Madras also reported disparagingly about the voting system. By 1881 there were nine municipalities with the right of election, but only four of them had exercised it and men who mattered shied away from the hustings where success would depend upon the votes of their inferiors.[2] In the western Presidency, Bombay city alone had elected representatives. Here a seat on the Corporation was prized by the city's notables, and the municipality was famous for its enterprise and efficiency, but the government of Bombay was unhappy about its growing impatience of control. Several of the larger mofussil towns—Poona and Ahmadabad among them—had shown that they too wanted to elect their municipal representatives, but the government of Bombay was against it. Poona, for one, was notorious for sedition and restless Brahmin sentiment, and it would be rash to relax the official hold.[3] On this evidence the Home Secretary concluded with some justification that 'it was impossible to say on the facts that self-government had anywhere been fairly tried and failed'; in most cases, 'the principle of local self-government has been... discredited and evaded...no proper effort is made to work municipal government as it was intended it should be'.[4]

These findings made a deep impression on the Viceroy. Here was a potentially powerful 'instrument of political education', which he thought could bring 'fresh life into the somewhat torpid system which at present exists' by training Indians to manage their local affairs by themselves. Since provincial

[1] Note by A. Mackenzie, Home Secretary, 29 November 1881, RP, Add. MSS 43576; and Letter from the Government of Bengal, 12 July 1881, *P.P.* 1883, LI, 148–9.
[2] Letter from the Government of Madras, 3 August 1881, *ibid.* 145.
[3] See Letter from the Government of Bombay, no. 3510, 20 October 1881, *ibid.* 146.
[4] Note by A. Mackenzie, Home Secretary, 29 November 1881, RP, Add. MSS 43576.

governments were unlikely to take kindly to a 'new departure', the main lines of advance would have to be laid down by the central government.[1] This was the aim of Ripon's famous Resolution on Local Self-Government of 18 May 1882, which bore all the marks of the Viceroy's good intentions. Humdrum matters were now dressed up as a great experiment in freedom; the Resolution stated that the extension of local self-government was not meant primarily to improve the administration but rather to foster the political education of that growing class of public-spirited men whom it would be bad policy not to utilise. Municipal and local rural boards should be established wherever possible, with a large preponderance of elected non-official members. Government control of these bodies should be exerted from without rather than from within, official chairmen being avoided, so that they should be encouraged to manage their own affairs. Rural boards should be given control of all local rates and taxes; perhaps the assessment and collection of the unpopular licence tax might be one of their useful tasks; and they should be allowed to initiate and direct the construction of local works. But everywhere Ripon played safe by reserving large discretionary powers to government and by giving the local administrations considerable latitude over the details of their provincial scheme. In any case the Resolution was merely permissive; it carried no statutory force.[2]

Baring's comment on this policy was typically frank.

...I do not see how we could move more cautiously and tentatively than we are moving. We are not pressing any hard and fast system on the different provinces of India. We are leaving a great deal to local judgement...We are not forming a number of political associations throughout the country to discuss political matters. We are forming Boards and Committees to discuss local requirements in the way of education, sanitation, roads & etc. And we shall see that they adhere to their proper business...What, however, we want to do is to... make realities of institutions which, under existing circumstances, are often little better than shams...The idea that we are going too fast is a phantom...We shall not subvert the British Empire by allowing the Bengali Baboo to discuss his own schools and drains. Rather shall we afford him a safety-valve if we can turn his attention to such innocuous subjects...[3]

[1] Note by Ripon, 27 April 1882, RP, Add. MSS 43576.
[2] Resolution of the Government of India, 18 May 1882, *P.P.* 1883, LI, 25–32.
[3] Baring to Mallet, 25 September 1882, enclosed in Baring to Ripon, 25 September 1882, RP (B.M. I.S. 290/8).

It was not these pragmatic arguments but the Viceroy's incantation of diffuse generalities from the liberal textbooks which were read by the Indian public, and that is why it welcomed the Resolution. Even so, its enthusiasm was restrained.[1] In some parts of India and in some of the larger towns, there was a growing demand for an extension of the elective system, and some Indians were prepared to agree that local self-government was a necessary preliminary for the grant of something more substantial. Already in 1880 the Indian Association of Calcutta had resolved that 'local self-government must precede national self-government'.[2] But when it came to the point most Indians were bored by drains and dismayed at the prospect of taxing themselves. They liked the spirit of Ripon's Resolution, with its hint of better things to come, but local self-government interested them as the prelude to the reform of the Legislative Councils, not as an alternative to it. Just after Ripon left India, the Secretary of the Home Department summed up the Indian reaction to the scheme: 'The experiment is still practically untried', he reported; 'The Native papers cry out "huzza", and say "we have got this, give us more".'[3]

For the same reason that the Resolution was popular in India, it was disliked in London. Salisbury and Lytton attacked the Viceroy for his doctrinaire approach. But the India Council and the India Office under a Liberal ministry were equally critical.[4] Seeing Ripon's plans running into heavy weather, Hartington advised the Viceroy to err on the side of caution. With conscious irony he added that the provincial governments would no doubt help him with this task of self-restraint.[5] Kimberley, Hartington's successor at the India Office, agreed with the critics on the India Council that there was too little official control and that the district magistrates were being unwisely excluded 'from all direct participation in...[local]

---

[1] One reason for this was given by A. O. Hume. 'I do not wonder that natives are timid and slow to move. The curse of India is on them— today you are with us tomorrow we have a man utterly opposed to your views. The natives have seen this so often, that they are shy of taking boldly even what a friend like yourself may offer...', Hume to Ripon, 30 December 1882, RP, Add. MSS 43616.

[2] Fourth Annual Report of the Indian Association, 1879–80, p. 5, IA.

[3] Gibbs to Dufferin, 4 February 1885, DP, 47 (Reel 528).

[4] Ripon had not taken the precaution of getting his Resolution approved by London before issuing it; to this the India Council took grave exception.

[5] Hartington to Ripon, 23 June 1882, RP, Add. MSS 43568.

affairs'.[1] London's criticisms grew louder when the Resolution came into effect. Even the timid Local Self-Government bill of the Central Provinces, the first of the new measures, with its strictly limited franchise and its cautious extension of power to the boards and municipal committees,[2] appeared too radical. Official control, Kimberley told the Viceroy, was essential, and elections were foreign to India, and should be introduced with the utmost circumspection to a few localities only.[3] This was tantamount to repudiating the Viceroy's policy. When Ripon threatened to resign, Kimberley relented, promising to support Calcutta even though he might criticise and disagree with its plans.[4] But this exchange came to be known in India,[5] and it sapped the Viceroy's power to push through his policy.

The obstacles in India were formidable enough already. When issuing his Resolution Ripon had told Baring that it would not surprise him 'if some of the Local Governments kick',[6] and he realised that most officials would hesitate over measures that impinged upon their absolute control over the districts.[7] Admittedly in the Punjab, where Aitchison ruled, Ripon got his 'model Bill'.[8] But from Lyall, whose schemes looked fairly satisfactory, the Viceroy had hoped for a more vigorous response.[9] In Madras, Grant Duff was prompt enough in pledging his support, but when it came to the point, the Madras civilians won the day. The governor was persuaded to permit as an experimental measure non-official presidents in only three municipalities. Elections were allowed only in municipalities with populations of over 25,000. It took much badgering from Calcutta before the Madras bills were made a little less constricting.

[1] Kimberley to Ripon, 15 June 1883, RP (B.M. I.S. 290/5).
[2] *Report on the Administration of the Central Provinces for the Year 1883–4* (Nagpur, 1884); and Ripon to Aitchison, 12 January 1883, RP (B.M. I.S. 290/8).
[3] Despatch of the Secretary of State, Legislative no. 15, 10 April 1883, Legislative Department, Proceedings, September to November 1883, no. 3.
[4] Kimberley to Ripon, 15 June 1883, RP (B.M. I.S. 290/5).
[5] *Pioneer*, 7 May 1883.
[6] Ripon to Baring, 18 May 1882, RP (B.M. I.S. 290/8).
[7] Gibbs to Ripon, 24 June 1882, RP (B.M. I.S. 290/8).
[8] Ripon to Kimberley, 27 July 1883, RP (B.M. I.S. 290/5).
[9] Resolution of the Government of North-western Provinces and Oudh, no. 358, 5 December 1882, *P.P.* 1883, LI, 200–14; and Ripon to Lyall, 10 January 1883, RP (B.M. I.S. 290/8).

But it was precisely in those provinces where Ripon's schemes were intended to pay the largest political dividends that they were most fiercely resisted by the local administration. In Bombay, Sir James Fergusson publicly accused Calcutta of subverting an efficient system by this ill-advised insistence on self-government.[1] Urging 'the necessity of caution and the inexpedience of hurrying a change which is utterly novel', he admitted that there was a cry for self-government in his Presidency, but it came 'chiefly from the agitating Brahmin class and is chiefly political'. Giving the larger cities elections was risky; and an 'early and complete realisation' of the Viceroy's policy was out of the question.[2] In his draft bills on local self-government, collectors were to be kept as *ex officio* members of the local bodies. Not less than half the members were to be officials. The president would be a government nominee; in practice he would usually be the collector. Even after Ripon and the Home Department forced Bombay to recast the bills, official control of the local bodies remained rigorous. There was no provision that elected members should be a majority or that non-officials should normally be the chairmen.[3] Hope and Gibbs, moderate men who had careers in the Bombay service behind them, saw that in so developed a province there was clearly a case for working Ripon's new policy whole-heartedly. To give the Maratha Brahmin a chance to occupy himself with his local affairs would be an excellent antidote to sedition in Poona and the Deccan.[4] But Fergusson, supported by his Council, thought otherwise. 'It is not in the Native character', he warned the Viceroy, 'to be satisfied; and whatever we propose will be as far from satisfying the ambitious Brahmin party as the measures of H.M. Govt. are from satisfying the Land League...why should we plunge so deeply and hastily into untried waters, risking perhaps the good government of local interests for years to come, and creating any amount of trouble, difficulty and *odium* for Government...?'[5] The Bombay Local Self-Government bills which finally received Ripon's consent did not

[1] Resolution of the Government of Bombay, no. 3583, 19 September 1882, *P.P.* 1883, LI, 39–57.
[2] Fergusson to Ripon, 31 May 1882, RP (B.M. I.S. 290/8).
[3] S. Gopal, *The Viceroyalty of Lord Ripon 1880–4* (London, 1953), pp. 107–8.
[4] Note by Gibbs, 9 December 1881, RP, Add. MSS 43576.
[5] Fergusson to Ripon, 7 October 1883, RP (B.M. I.S. 290/8)

actually preclude further progress; they contained the possibility at some distant date of a wholly elected local body presided over by a man who was neither an official nor a European. But they did not then and there give educated Indians the responsibility and power Ripon wanted them to assume.

In Bengal, the lieutenant-governor, Rivers Thompson, resourcefully used the latitude allowed him to devise schemes that neither Calcutta nor London would accept. As a result, by the end of Ripon's viceroyalty only a Municipalities bill had been passed in Bengal, while the Local Boards bill was indefinitely postponed. Thompson's predecessor, Sir Ashley Eden, whose views about local self-government were notoriously illiberal,[1] warned the Viceroy from London that 'with the remembrance of the Mutiny, and of several famines ever present in my mind, and with my knowledge of the shallowness and unreality of the cry of the so-called educated Bengalis, their extreme selfishness and unfitness to manage their own affairs, I do feel very strongly the importance of maintaining as strongly as possible the dignity, position, and influence of the representative of Government in the district'.[2] Much the same attitude lay behind the Bengal government's circular of July 1882 on local self-government. The Home Department noted 'a want of genuine tone in the Bengal Resolution', its concern to keep 'the district officers...as leaders', and concluded that 'it would appear as if the Resolution had been drafted by an opponent of the scheme...'[3] But Rivers Thompson stuck to the traditional civilian view that control by government was essential. District committees, without the restraining hand of the magistrate,

would...very soon find objects more attractive than roads and bridges and schools and ferries; and by the necessity of their position and the instigations of professional politicians they would be quickly arrayed against all official authority. The position would be worked for purposes of a distinct political character...I, for one, do not consider Bengal at least (where the danger is greatest from the comparative advance in Education) prepared for this.[4]

[1] See Note by Hope, 14 April 1882, and Note by Mackenzie, 25 April 1882, RP, Add. MSS 43577.
[2] Eden to Ripon, 17 August 1882, RP (B.M. I.S. 290/7).
[3] Note by Gibbs, 31 July 1882, RP, Add. MSS 43579; for Ripon's view of the circular, see his Note, 12 August 1882, RP, Add. MSS 43577.
[4] Thompson to Ripon, 1 May 1883, RP, Add. MSS 43594.

Baring condemned this policy as shortsighted. Its object was 'manifestly to exclude the "penniless, spouting University student"'. Such a course had no future. 'Whether we like or dislike the typical Baboo', Baring argued, 'the fact of his existence has to be recognized.' If the Bengalis were not allowed to spout in local bodies, they would do so on more dangerous platforms.

> The attempt to exclude the Baboo from political life is...not practicable; and if it were practicable...would be a political error. We had much better recognize his existence and give him a safety valve for his spouting—descending upon him, and his Committee, mercilessly if he spouts *haute politique* instead of confining his attention to road and drains.
>
> My own belief is that 10 years hence the political development of the country will have got on a long way further than Thompson—or for the matter of that, most people in this country—imagine. When once the ball of political reform is set rolling, it is apt to gather speed as it goes on. All history teaches this.[1]

Ripon's disputes over local government, like Lytton's disputes over the press, were at bottom an argument over the nature and the effects of western education in India. Manifestly, the stream of graduates was increasing, and would become either a political danger or an asset to the Raj. It was in the three Presidencies of Bengal, Bombay and Madras that this educational process had gone the farthest; but it was precisely here that the provincial governments were most reluctant to put Ripon's local government proposals into effect. The debate between Ripon and the Presidencies turned on this: should the political stirrings of the educated be mobilised in the interests of the Raj by associating them with government at a local level, or would it be safer to maintain official control by keeping the graduates out? It is clear that the dominant trend in official thinking was pessimistic about the probable results of the whole experiment. For every assertion that the government should make good use of it, there was a counter-statement that the Indians were making bad use of it, that it was strengthening the seditious Bengalis, the implacable Maharashtrians and the selfish Tamils. On this line of reasoning the spread of western education might well bring the Raj into jeopardy. In opposing these assertions Ripon was not denying their conclusions, for it was as clear to him as to his

[1] Baring to Ripon, 3 August 1883, RP, Add. MSS 43597.

opponents that the activities of the graduates might end by imperilling the Empire with which he was entrusted—unless he could find a way of channelling them into becoming an asset. He thought that he could do so; if not through the councils, then through local government. But this was not much to offer. As one of his advisors put it:

Take the fullest measure of our latest scheme, and what does it really amount to when stripped of the tinsel draperies with which it was hung? It is simply to let the people manage their own water-supply, drainage, roads, dispensaries and primary schools, giving them greater freedom in so doing...[1]

It was not enough; and once Indian opinion realised that reform of the Councils was not to be the corollary, they lost interest. By 1884 Ripon was admitting that the real danger to his local government scheme was that it might 'fail from the apathy, not the activity of the people'.[2] But this was a Ripon wiser by four years' experience of rule and more aware of the limitations which cramped his freedom of action in India.

By his liberal creed, Ripon was opposed to any kind of racial discrimination by law. The Vernacular Press Act—'that wretched piece of legislation'[3]—was repealed,[4] but Lytton's Arms Act, which had introduced a system of licensing firearms into India while exempting Europeans from it, and which Ripon also disliked, could not be dealt with so simply. For good or ill, the exemption of Europeans was now an accomplished fact, and 'its withdrawal...as far as concerns residents in India, would be...calculated...to excite that very controversy between different races of Her Majesty's subjects which it should be our endeavour to avoid'. At this stage, the Viceroy was against fresh legislation, and prepared to improve the working of the Act in practice.[5] In this he got little help from the provincial governments, and by 1882 their obstruction had convinced him that administrative action alone could not end 'the

---

[1] Gibbs to Dufferin, 4 February 1885, DP, 47 (Reel 528); and see W. S. Blunt, *India Under Ripon. A Private Diary* (London, 1909), p. 271.

[2] Ripon to Kimberley, 27 January 1884, RP (B.M. I.S. 290/5).

[3] Ripon to Hartington, 29 October 1881, RP (B.M. I.S. 290/5).

[4] Here Ripon had the rare advantage of the Prime Minister's support, for ever since 1878 Gladstone had been denouncing the Act as one of the crimes of the Beaconsfield government. See Ripon to Hartington, 12 July 1880, RP (B.M. I.S. 290/5).

[5] Minute by Ripon, 11 April 1881, RP, Add. MSS 43575.

anomalies, inequalities, and unnecessary hardships to which the Arms Act, as at present administered, gives rise'. What he now proposed was legislation to compel Europeans and Indians alike to take out licences if they wanted to bear arms.[1] But the India Office was not prepared to bell this cat, and Ripon had to drop his plan.

By so doing, he was spared a dress-rehearsal for the uproar caused by the Ilbert bill.[2] This bill was not an integral part of Ripon's reforming policy, and if the Viceroy had suspected the furore it would unleash he would undoubtedly have held it back. It was simply the outcome of administrative change—changes in legal procedure, and the admission of Indians to more responsible posts in the public services. Until 1872 judicial officers up country had no power to try European British subjects except for some minor offences; they could only commit them for trial before a high court. This was a privilege highly valued by the planters and other unofficials, and increasingly useful to them as their growing community moved deeper into the interior. In 1872 the Criminal Procedure Code had been amended so as to give first class magistrates, sessions judges and justices of the peace limited powers to fine or imprison members of the white community in the mofussil. It conciliated them by granting a new privilege: namely the right to trial by white magistrates. In 1877 an Act vesting in magistrates, irrespective of their race, jurisdiction within the limits of the Presidency towns over Europeans and Indians alike added point to the anomaly. Of course, Indians could become high court judges; but until they attained the office of district magistrate and sessions judge—which were senior posts in the hierarchy of the service and usually held by the civilians—it did not become a practical problem. It was only when Indians began to enter the covenanted service by open competition that the whole question came to life. Already in 1864 one Indian had passed into the service; in 1871 there were another three. The trickle had continued thereafter. By now these Indians had become district magistrates and sessions judges, but could not try European British subjects as their British colleagues in the service were entitled to do. The anomaly was palpable.

[1] Note by Ripon, 21 April 1882, RP, Add. MSS 43577.
[2] For a recent study see C. E. Dobbin, 'The Ilbert Bill', *Historical Studies, Australia and New Zealand*, XII, no. 45, October 1965, pp. 87–102.

So in 1882 Behari Lal Gupta, one of these Bengal civilians, advocated an amendment of the law to give Indian district magistrates and sessions judges the same powers as their European counterparts. This note of Gupta's was strongly supported by the government of Bengal.[1] These representations did not reach the government of India in time to be taken into account in the revision of the Criminal Procedure Code that was passed early in 1882; but the Home Department recorded that 'a change must be made',[2] and Mackenzie, the Home Secretary, anticipated nothing more than 'a slight and temporary outcry among the more bigoted Europeans'.[3] When the Bengal proposal was circulated to the other provincial governments, they generally agreed with it.[4] So did nearly all members of the Viceroy's Council.[5] In October 1882 proposals embodying the changes were put before the Secretary of State; in February 1883 Ilbert introduced a bill to give them effect.[6] At this point the storm broke, bringing down upon the Viceroy a hail of opposition and abuse.

[1] Note by Gupta, 30 January 1882, *P.P.* 1883, LI, 653–4. Gupta himself while officiating as Presidency magistrate had powers of jurisdiction which he lost when he received a more responsible appointment in the mofussil.

[2] Note by Gibbs, 6 April 1882, RP, Add. MSS 43577.

[3] Note by Mackenzie, 5 April 1882, RP, Add. MSS 43577.

[4] Note by P. Roy, 17 August 1882, RP, Add. MSS 43577; and Despatch of the Government of India, Judicial no. 33 of 1882, 9 September 1882, *P.P.* 1883, LI, 649–52.

[5] The Military member, General Wilson, was alone in Council against any change. Note by T. F. Wilson, 5 September 1882, RP, Add. MSS 43577.

[6] Both in the timing and the scope of his measure, Ripon miscalculated. Since everyone was agreed that there must be a change, he decided that it would be better to go one step further, and settle the matter once and for all: 'I do not think that it is advisable to be continually tinkering with these race questions.' Those who had raised the issue would have been satisfied by the grant of jurisdiction to those first class magistrates who were also district magistrates and sessions judges, but Ripon was attracted by Aitchison's larger proposal to give jurisdiction to *all* first class magistrates. In Council, Ilbert and Baring supported the larger scheme while Hope, Bayley and Gibbs supported the smaller. Ripon backed the wrong horse. Things were made worse by the bill's defective drafting; it was particularly unwise and unnecessary to vest the local governments with discretionary powers to grant jurisdiction to judicial officers of lower standing. Such powers should have been statutory, not left to the executive; in any case they were premature. These provisions lent colour to Anglo-Indian fears and also gave the local governments a pretext to qualify or withdraw their approval from a measure they had originally backed. See Note by Ripon, 28 August 1882; Note by Bayley, 28 August 1882; Note by Gibbs, 24

The agitation against the bill is one of the most unsavoury episodes in modern Anglo-Indian history. It united the entire unofficial European community—the planters and merchants of eastern India, and the Calcutta bench and bar in particular—into an hysterical condemnation of the Viceroy and an unrestrained attack on the educated Indians whose fitness to sit in judgement over white men and women in the mofussil the bill had dared to suggest.[1] A European and Anglo-Indian Defence Association was formed; it gave Indians an object lesson in the arts of unprincipled, but highly organised, agitation. There was wild talk of a white mutiny,[2] of packing the Viceroy off to England by force, of getting the European Volunteer Corps to disband. These attacks on Indians rapidly undid the gradual improvement in race relations since Canning's time; the cry of 'our women in danger' revived fears and passions latent since the Mutiny. They were not confined to India. In England, too, the controversy evoked an outspoken attack on liberal policy towards India and an uncompromising assertion of the doctrine of racial superiority. *The Times* took the lead. The case was put bluntly by Fitzjames Stephen. It was not the bill alone, but the entire tenor of Ripon's policy that he found disturbing: 'it is impossible to imagine any policy more fearfully dangerous and more certain, in case of failure, to lead to results to which the Mutiny would be child's play than the policy of shifting the foundations on which the British Government of India rests. It is essentially an absolute government, founded, not on consent, but on conquest.'[3]

But there was more to the Indian agitation than the fulminations of the 'd — d nigger party'.[4] In addition there were a

August 1882; Note by Baring, 28 August 1882, and Note by Ilbert, 4 September 1882, RP, Add. MSS 43577.

[1] The best single source on the Anglo-Indian agitation is the *Englishman*, 1883–4. For typical memorials and representations for and against the bill, see *P.P.* 1884, LX, 119–683. A concise account of the whole affair will be found in Wolf, *Life of Ripon*, II, 119–50, and Gopal, *The Viceroyalty of Lord Ripon*, pp. 113–66.

[2] See J. Lambert to Primrose, Viceroy's Private Secretary, 22 September 1883, RP (B.M. I.S. 290/8).

[3] Letter to *The Times*, 1 March 1883; also see J. F. Stephen, 'Foundations of the Government of India', *The Nineteenth Century*, XIV, no. 80 (October 1883), 548–68; and Stokes, *The English Utilitarians and India*, pp. 287–309.

[4] Northbrook to Ripon, 24 October 1883, quoted in Gopal, *The Viceroyalty of Lord Ripon*, p. 116.

number of separate causes that converged into a general suspicion and dislike for the course that Ripon seemed to be setting. Modest and ineffectual though they were, his reforming policies struck many of the post-Mutiny generation of Anglo-Indians as dangerous in the extreme. Some of them feared that the liberal Viceroy had been sent out 'simply to "put the native on the *gadi*" (throne)...and benefit them at the cost of the Europeans'.[1] The leading English-owned paper in Calcutta, the *Englishman*, put the matter in a nutshell in its call to arms: 'Mr Ilbert's Bill is...nothing more than the first instalment of a series of laws to enable the Government to pursue its plan of rapidly Indianising the entire administration of the country... In fighting against Mr Ilbert's Bill...the European community are fighting against their own ruin and the destruction of British rule in India.'[2] The Viceroy learnt to his cost that the opposition was not 'so much an opposition to that particular measure as to the whole policy of Parliament by which Natives have been admitted to the Covenanted Service'.[3]

It was common knowledge that Ripon was for this policy; but in no sense was it his invention. In fact Lytton's measure—the statutory service and the rules about the uncovenanted service—had done more to let Indians into the higher ranks than anything Ripon was to achieve. But the real impact of the statutory service began to be felt only under Ripon's regime,[4] when Lytton's regulations became a continuing source of irritation to Englishmen in India who were looking for employment in the government. To this grievance another was added in 1883 when, prompted by London, Ripon's government had lowered the qualification for admission to Indian engineering colleges, and had laid down that 'only natives pure and simple' were henceforth to be eligible for the handful of guaranteed appointments in the Public Works Department reserved for these students. Ripon perhaps had misunderstood London when he

[1] Gibbs to Ripon, 23 March 1883, enclosed in Ripon to Kimberley, 26 March 1883, RP (B.M. I.S. 290/5).

[2] *Englishman*, 28 April 1883.

[3] Memorandum by Ripon, 6 March 1883, enclosed in Ripon to Halifax, 6 March 1883, RP (B.M. I.S. 290/7).

[4] On 1 January 1880 there were only eleven native civilians ('Competition-wallahs' as well as statutory service men); on 1 January 1883 there were thirty-three. W. W. Hunter to Ripon, 30 August 1883, RP (B.M. I.S. 290/8).

interpreted the term 'native' in its colloquial rather than its statutory sense, but the effect of these Roorkee resolutions was to exclude Eurasian and European residents of India from the civil engineering colleges which previously had been their preserve. Still other factors contributed to the general unease. Against the Viceroy's advice, Hartington had decided to reduce the salaries of the puisne judges on the Calcutta bench, thus bringing them in line with other high courts in India.[1] A Tory Secretary of State had urged this economy, and the Liberal Ministry had insisted upon it in spite of Ripon's objections. But this parsimony had not gone down well with the Calcutta bench and bar, especially when they compared it with the Viceroy's efforts to raise the pay of Indians in the uncovenanted service. Their resentment increased in 1882, when Ripon appointed an Indian judge to officiate as chief justice of the Calcutta high court for the first time in its history, despite the fulminations and protests of Sir Richard Garth, the chief justice who was going on leave. The planters, who were most numerous in Bengal, Bihar and Assam, had their complaints as well; together with other landowners, they disliked the way the Bengal Tenancy bill proposed to restrict their powers over tenants.[2] Thus various discontents were ready at hand. What was needed was an issue general enough to unite the different elements into a combined assault on the Viceroy's policy. This the Ilbert bill provided. 'On looking about for support', the Officiating General Superintendent of Operations for the Suppression of Thugee and Dacoity reported,

they found one portion of the European community which disliked a Native Chief Justice, another which disliked Native Civilians, another which disliked the Local Self-Government scheme, and all the Eurasians who disliked the Rurki Bill. These disconnected atoms all flew together, while those with no interest in any of these questions at least were sensitive on anything affecting European women. So it happens that the Government has hit off the only one subject on which all classes, for different reasons are of one mind. Hence the agitation.[3]

[1] Ripon to Kimberley, 10 February 1883, RP (B.M. I.S. 290/5).
[2] 'If you add these grievances of the lawyers to those of the planters... you have the secret of the whole affair.' Ripon to Grant Duff, 27 March 1883, RP (B.M. I.S. 290/8).
[3] J. Lambert, A review of the situation in Calcutta, 18 July 1883, enclosed in Lambert to Primrose, 18 July 1883, RP (B.M. I.S. 290/8).

By March 1883, the Viceroy had realised that the bill was 'the excuse for the present outbreak of feeling, and not its main cause',[1] noting with regret that 'the whole of my work here is at stake'.[2]

The uproar over the bill was largely confined to Bengal, where race relations were more acrimonious than in other parts of India.[3] Nevertheless, issues of the greatest importance to the whole sub-continent were raised by the measure. This point did not escape the well-meaning Viceroy. He realised that it was not the bill alone that was in jeopardy but 'the maintenance of a truly liberal policy in India'.[4] When Fitzjames Stephen joined in the attack, the point became clearer still, for education and local self-government were included in Stephen's reappraisals.[5] An entire philosophy divided the Viceroy from the former Law member; their policies, Ripon could see, were irreconcilable.[6] So far as he was personally concerned, the Viceroy was unwilling to govern India for a day if it was decided that Indians could not be educated and permitted a share in the management of their affairs. 'If India is to be governed on such principles', he told Forster, 'I am certainly not the person to govern it'.[7] Either the Queen's Proclamation—'the Indian Magna Carta', as Aitchison described it[8]—would be swept aside or it would be respected.[9] The real issue, Ripon asserted, was 'whether natives are, or are not to continue, in accordance with the repeatedly declared policy of Parliament, to be admitted in considerable numbers to the Covenanted Civil Service. If they are, the existing law about the trial of Europeans *must* be altered, if not now, at all events in a few years.'[10] In that sense, the Ilbert bill was a touchstone of Ripon's whole work in India.[11] Indians, whose studied moderation during the controversy contrasted

[1] Ripon to Kimberley, 18 March 1883, RP (B.M. I.S. 290/5).
[2] Ripon to Hughes, 6 March 1883, RP (B.M. I.S. 290/7).
[3] There were exceptions. A junior policeman in a Bombay district noted: 'We were keenly excited about it at Bijapur'; E. C. Cox, *My Thirty Years in India* (London, 1909), p. 88.
[4] Ripon to Northbrook, 31 March 1883, RP (B.M. I.S. 290/7).
[5] See Ripon to Kimberley, 4 May 1883, RP (B.M. I.S. 290/5).
[6] Ripon to Hughes, 7 April 1883, RP (B.M. I.S. 290/7).
[7] Ripon to W. E. Forster, 26 March 1883, RP (B.M. I.S. 290/7).
[8] Aitchison to Ripon, 10 December 1883, RP (B.M. I.S. 290/8).
[9] Ripon to Northbrook, 31 March 1883, RP (B.M. I.S. 290/7).
[10] Ripon to J. K. Cross, 6 March 1883, RP (B.M. I.S. 290/5).
[11] Ripon to Hughes, 6 March 1883, RP (B.M. I.S. 290/7).

well with Anglo-Indian attitudes,[1] were as clear as their rulers that the bill was a 'test question, the decision of which will prove whether the promises of the British Government are realities or shams'.[2] So everyone, whether they were for the bill or against it, saw that they were fighting about 'some of the fundamental principles of Indian policy'.[3]

Consequently, when a year of ferocious agitation by the bill's opponents and of a 'deplorable state of weakness, and alarm'[4] among Ripon's councillors forced him to accept a compromise that sacrificed everything but the bare bones of a principle, it was clear what conclusion to draw. Ripon might feebly claim that the concordat was a victory for the powers of light, but even his friend Hughes could see that 'the battle had been fought in vain'.[5] Whitehall too regretted that the Viceroy had bowed before the storm. It was one thing for the home authorities to check and restrain an eager proconsul, but quite another for the government of India to be dictated to by the settlers.[6] 'No Government can be safe, much less such a Government as that of India, which is at the mercy of a handful of its subjects', the Secretary of State warned his Viceroy.[7] But when it came to the crisis, Ripon's protestations of liberal virtue had not been able to conceal his weakness; and before the opposition of some of these subjects he had backed down. As for his other subjects, the lesson went deep. When Dufferin arrived in India, it was to find the 'whites and blacks [divided] into two hostile and vociferating camps'.[8] The Indian mood after the Ilbert bill affair was summed up by Allan Octavian Hume, the 'father of the Congress':

the prevailing idea is this, if with such a Viceroy things are to be thus, what hope is there for the future? We have never yet had a Viceroy

---

[1] See Aitchison to Ripon, 28 December 1883, RP (B.M. I.S. 290/8), and Ripon to Kimberley, 1 January 1884, RP (B.M. I.S. 290/5).

[2] Ripon to Kimberley, 6 August 1883, RP (B.M. I.S. 290/5). See also V. N. Mandlik to Ripon, 29 December 1883, RP (B.M. I.S. 290/8), where Mandlik wrote: 'we want to raise ourselves to our proper status as sanctioned by law and recognized by Parliament...and this is what you are trying to secure for us'.

[3] Ripon to Kimberley, 18 March 1883, RP (B.M. I.S. 290/5).

[4] Kimberley to Ripon, 10 January 1884, RP (B.M. I.S. 290/5).

[5] Hughes to Ripon, 2 January 1884, RP, Add. MSS 43549.

[6] Kimberley to Ripon, 3 January 1884 and 10 January 1884, RP (B.M. I.S. 290/5).

[7] Kimberley to Ripon, 15 February 1884, RP (B.M. I.S. 290/5).

[8] Dufferin to Kimberley, 15 December 1884, DP, 18 (Reel 517).

more honestly and earnestly desirous of doing us justice and yet he appears as absolutely impotent to correct crying and wicked evils as a man like Lord Lytton...The Govt. seems to be a great, cruel, blundering machine, running on by its own weight...even the driver being incapable of directing its course.[1]

The fact was that Ripon had been the wrong driver for such a juggernaut. Time and again he had proclaimed his liberalism; all his actions had been heralded with what Dufferin termed 'the tremendous flourish of trumpets with which he has paraded his good intentions'.[2] But he was too weak a man to carry them out. He had had the wit to see that the spread of Indian education would force the Raj to make a political choice; and in the light of his mid-Victorian principles, he was clear that it must not choose simply to maintain autocracy. But in working for his policies, he forgot, as his more dexterous successor never forgot, that 'The Colony is easily frightened',[3] and in the event most of his plans had to be abandoned or watered down. Whatever his intentions, his government continued to function in much the same way as Lytton's; and his solutions for the dilemma of the Raj failed as unmistakably as Lytton's. The repressive measures of the 1870s had begun to push educated Indians towards politics; the impotence of Ripon's good intentions could only drive them further along that path.

In their different ways, both Lytton and Ripon had striven to solve the fundamental problem of empire in India. Dufferin had been an ambassador and Governor-General of Canada, and in each capacity had learnt to steer clear of fundamentals. Sent to Cairo to advise the British government about its Egyptian commitments, he had produced an elegant and unrealistic scheme which minimised all the difficulties and told the Gladstone government precisely what he knew it wanted to hear. Now that he was Viceroy, he hoped 'to escape out of India...without any very deep scratches on my credit and reputation'.[4] For a man with his urbanity and his desire to please, it was clear that the upheavals of the Ripon regime had to be avoided at all

[1] Hume to Ripon, 4 March 1884, RP, Add. MSS 43616.
[2] Dufferin to Hardinge, 29 December 1884, DP, 47 (Reel 528).
[3] Dufferin to Kimberley, 15 December 1884, DP, 18 (Reel 528).
[4] Dufferin to Cross, 3 December 1888, DP, 21 (Reel 518).

costs, and soon after reaching India he was writing: '...our holiday is over, we must go to school again, and my sole ambition is to become as commonplace and humdrum as possible'.[1] He agreed with the governor of Madras that 'the undisturbed untalked of ascendancy' of the British in India was desirable from every point of view; he too was 'all for a soothing, cautious, nay even dull policy of peace and public works'.[2] With soporifics such as these, Dufferin hoped for a quiet time in India, so that he could 'keep his head above the rising inundation of business'.[3] In the harsh judgement of a more vigorous administrator, Dufferin 'never did a stroke of work he could avoid'.[4] To Alfred Lyall, who himself achieved high office under the Raj without the bustling diligence of a Temple, this was forgivable; when he came to Simla in the summer of 1885 he noted, in no spirit of reproof, that Dufferin's way was to 'rely altogether for the ordinary working of the great administrative machine upon his councillors and secretaries'.[5] Others might have dreamt of throwing back the forces of unrest; Dufferin's ambition was to lull them to sleep.

But no sooner had the new Viceroy reached Calcutta than there were signs that the passions of the previous viceroyalty were about to be revived. Now the issue was the Native Volunteer movement. Early in 1885, the Russian threat on the north-west frontier had made government so anxious that it set about reorganising the European volunteer corps, at the same time allowing Indian Christians to enrol. Indians in the three Presidency capitals immediately raised the cry that they too should be allowed to volunteer in defence of the Raj, a subtle move sure to embarrass the government.[6] To allow Indians

[1] Dufferin to Hardinge, 29 December 1884, DP, 47 (Reel 528).
[2] Grant Duff to Dufferin, 3 January 1885, DP, 47 (Reel 528).
[3] Dufferin to Granville [n.d.? December 1884/January 1885] cited in A. C. Lyall, *The Life of the Marquis of Dufferin and Ava* (London, 1905), II, 75.
[4] Curzon to Hamilton, 28 June 1899, Curzon Papers, MSS Eur. F. 111 (158). But the Viceroy complained that his job was 'the greatest grind I have ever experienced'. Dufferin to Churchill, 14 August 1885, DP, 18 (Reel 517).
[5] Durand, *Life of Lyall*, p. 306.
[6] Summing up, Dufferin wrote: 'As an outcome of the Russian scare, a pretty general agitation was set on foot for the establishment of Native Volunteers from one end of the country to the other. I have no doubt that the original idea was a genuine expression of a...loyal feeling,

to form volunteer regiments would be to give them the same privilege as the Anglo-Indians; it would enable them to by-pass some of the restrictions of the Arms Act; it would call attention to their exclusion from substantive commissions in the regular army; it would put into practice the principle of equality which had created such a crisis when essayed in Ilbert's bill.[1] So Indians threw themselves vigorously into this new movement. Their press rhapsodised about their loyalty and their desire to join in saving the Raj, and their associations co-operated in stirring up a nation-wide agitation.[2]

Innocently impressed by such an effusion of loyal sentiment, Dufferin began by stating that he was in favour of the idea.[3] He was soon to change his mind when he consulted his local governors. Grant Duff took the opportunity to deliver a serious lecture on first principles. There were, he explained, two opposite schools of thought about Britain's role in India. One argued: '"You are here to educate the natives to govern themselves. That done, you have only to go about your business"'; the other: '..."you must act as if Great Britain were to govern India for all time, doing nothing which...has any tendency to undermine the foundations of British Power"'. Grant Duff had no doubt about the school to which he belonged: Britain's role in India 'is founded on the most absolute negation' of liberal principles, which are 'principles...found to work best in the government of a people by itself'. 'Our task here is a much more difficult one than to apply Liberal principles...It is to create and uphold an enlightened and beneficent despotism'. These views were incompatible 'with allowing any material power or any political power...to pass out of our hands'. The time would come, he admitted, when educated Indians 'will grow stronger; for however well we may rule... the nationality cry will be heard very loudly some day here as

though it was subsequently made use of...as a means of...embarrassing the Government.' Dufferin to Kimberley, 21 March 1886, DP, 19 (Reel 517).

[1] See Lyall to Dufferin, 13 May 1885, DP, 47 (Reel 528); J. G. Cordery to Dufferin, 3 July 1885, DP, 48 (Reel 528); Rivers Thompson to Dufferin, 15 July 1885, DP, 48 (Reel 528), where these points are made.

[2] Hume was in the van; and the newly formed 'National Party', with its inner circle, directed the movement on an all-India scale. Hume to Dufferin, 31 May 1885, DP, 47 (Reel 528).

[3] Dufferin to Hume, 5 May 1885, DP, 47 (Reel 528).

elsewhere'.[1] But here and now the governor of Madras was against recruiting Indians as volunteers.[2]

With the exception of Bombay, all the local governments were emphatically against allowing Indians to volunteer. Ward of Assam thought that the policy of a 'more liberal treatment of the natives' had run wild under Ripon and that now the 'time had come when the Government should draw in its reins and decide for the present it has gone far enough'. Indeed, the *reductio ad absurdum* of this scheme would be the abolition of the British army in India.[3] Lepel Griffin, the hammer of the babus, denounced the scheme as 'impolitic and dangerous' and quite unsuited to India where the government must never let go a jot or tittle of its material power. 'The union between the English and Native races', he reminded the Viceroy, 'is like those mediæval marriages in which the bride and bridegroom were separated by a naked sword.' He scoffed at the proposal as a political ramp by the Bengali, 'notoriously and self-confessedly a coward... What is this grotesque creature to defend?'[4] To the lieutenant-governor of Bengal, the agitation in his province was the work of the Indian Association, which was run by a class of young radicals, landless, and socially inferior to their more conservative countrymen in the staid British Indian Association. The movement was 'an utter sham'. Its chief object was 'the abrogation of the Arms Act', and its members had theories as advanced as they were extravagant. But there was a tone of healthy respect in Rivers Thompson's comments. 'The modern party...', he had to admit, 'are extremely successful adepts at organisation.' They had learnt with astonishing success the uses of the political platform. It would be foolish and dangerous to allow such men to form Volunteer Corps.[5]

[1] Memorandum, 24 June 1885 enclosed in Grant Duff to Dufferin, 24 June 1885, DP 47 (Reel 528). Here we have an excellent example of the thesis developed by Fitzjames Stephen and John Strachey.

[2] In a previous letter, Grant Duff had gone further: 'I am not at all persuaded that all our beneficent rule will be strong enough, when the day of trial comes, to overpower the nationality cry—which will ring...over all the India which we are for the first time in history making into a country and a nation.' Nonetheless he was against any talk of giving Indians a share in 'political affairs an hour before it is inevitable'. Grant Duff to Dufferin, 3 January 1885, DP 47 (Reel 528).

[3] W. E. Ward, to Dufferin, n.d. (received 30 June 1885), DP 47 (Reel 528).

[4] Memorandum, 21 June 1885, enclosed in Lepel Griffin to Dufferin, 21 June 1885, DP 47 (Reel 528).

[5] Rivers Thompson to Dufferin, 15 July 1885 and enclosure, DP 48 (Reel 528).

Lyall, in the North-western Provinces, was anxious to divert people 'from any idea of general disciplined organization', and thought that 'a more liberal working of the Arms Act' might perhaps achieve this.[1] Even the mild approval of Bombay hardly went further than toying with schemes for giving the loyal Parsis the right to volunteer;[2] General Hardinge, the commander-in-chief, loftily conceded that this demand was the 'offshoot of the educational tree of British citizenship', and felt that 'Much might be gained, in consistency of principle, by flattering the well-disposed, into the illusion that they had become defenders of the State'.[3] But Lieutenant-General Phayre thought differently. Since the time when the ruler of Baroda had tried to poison him, he was not prepared to swallow Indian proposals of any sort. Among the elements of danger he classed high on his list:

The educated Hindoo classes throughout India (Brahmins particularly)—men whose violent advocacy in the Native press of national freedom, self-government, native advancement to the highest offices of the State as a matter of right...exercises an incessantly unsettling effect upon...native society generally. These are the men who are loudest in advocating the extension of the Volunteer movement... in order that when the time comes they may have an armed, drilled, and organised force to back them up in advancing their insolent demands.[4]

In London too the scheme was badly received. Although Randolph Churchill, the new Secretary of State, was not averse to it 'tried cautiously on a small scale',[5] all the members of Dufferin's Council, except Ilbert and Colvin, were hostile. In the face of these pressures it was useless for Hume to urge upon the Viceroy that the volunteer question was a test case all over again.[6] Dufferin did not want a test case, and he dropped the scheme, replacing it with vague suggestions for helping the right sort of Indians in the army, instead of giving arms to 'Univer-

---

[1] A. C. Lyall to Dufferin, 4 June 1885, DP 47 (Reel 528).
[2] Memorandum by M. Melvill and J. B. Peile, 18 June 1885, enclosed in Reay to Dufferin, 22 June 1885, DP 47 (Reel 528).
[3] Memorandum by General Sir A. E. Hardinge, 18 June 1885, *ibid.*
[4] Memorandum by Phayre, 17 June 1885, *ibid.*
[5] Churchill to Dufferin, 7 August 1885, DP 18 (Reel 517).
[6] Hume to Dufferin, 31 May 1885, DP 47 (Reel 528). Hume recommended to the Viceroy a pamphlet by 'Trust and Fear not' which argued that the educated classes could either be won by equity or alienated by injustice.

sity students and people of that class'.[1] Nothing came of this. So ended a matter which another member of the Council described to Dufferin as 'perhaps, the most important question of *internal* administration which the Council has had before it since that unlucky day in September 1882 when the "Ilbert Bill" was so light-heartedly accepted'.[2]

While he was still grappling with the volunteer issue, Dufferin had his first taste of a still more portentous problem. 'I never saw such a country as this. One is no sooner out of one kettle of boiling water', Dufferin complained, 'than one is up to the neck in another.'[3] When Ripon left India, he had been given a send-off so rousing that it aroused a great deal of comment. One widely-read pamphlet had argued that these demonstrations were a symptom of a profound change. The British would have to get on, or, in the not too distant future, get out. 'The task of the present generation', the pamphlet maintained, 'is unquestionably far more delicate and far more difficult than that which awaited their predecessors... The problem has been unmistakably formulated in Lord Ripon's time; the solving of it... cannot be deferred... a reactionary policy has now from the force of circumstances become, if persisted in, by far the greatest political danger to which our rule in India can possibly be exposed.'[4] What made the Ripon demonstrations impressive was that Indians from all over the sub-continent had taken a part in them. Now Hume and his Indian collaborators planned to drive forward the 'engine that set the late Ripon demonstrations going'.[5] What they had in mind was no less than a political convention of all India. From Lord Reay, the governor of Bombay, came reports of Hume's political crusades: projects for national conventions, plans for agitation in England, and an alliance with sympathetic politicians there.[6] Reay himself was to be asked to come with official blessing for the convention. Hume approached the Viceroy for permission; it was refused.

In September, several of the Indian political associations sent

[1] Dufferin to Churchill, 28 August 1885, DP 18 (Reel 517).
[2] Hope to Dufferin, 14 May 1885, DP 47 (Reel 528).
[3] Dufferin to Sir Ashley Eden, 24 April 1886, quoted in S. Gopal, *British Policy in India 1858–1905* (Cambridge, 1965), p. 178.
[4] 'If it be real what does it mean?', *Pioneer*, 17 December 1884.
[5] Reay to Dufferin, 4 June 1885, DP 47 (Reel 528).
[6] Reay to Dufferin, 24 May 1885, DP 47 (Reel 528).

joint delegates to argue India's case at the general election in England. When they came back in December, the sub-continent appeared to have suffered a sea-change. Whereas previously political associations had seemed hedged in by provincial boundaries, now they had succeeded in jumping over them. All India seemed to have met together in national confabulation, whether in a National Congress at Bombay, a National Conference at Calcutta or a convention at Madras. Dufferin was forced to take note. Indians standing for parliament, and appearing on political platforms in England were, he realised, 'a new feature in the relations between Great Britain and the Indian Empire'. He called for information. Who were these politicians? Whom did they represent? How much influence did they have in Indian society? He also wanted to know more about the Calcutta National Conference and the associations which had attended it. How far, he asked, do 'they influence public opinion, or command the support of any portion of the community'.[1]

The Home Department reduced all these new activities to neat conclusions, and their findings were sent to London.[2] With them went the viceregal commentary on a subject that 'may or may not hereafter prove of considerable importance... Associations and sub-associations are being formed all over the country, which is also being furnished with a net-work of caucuses, who of course work the telegraphic wire in the orthodox manner'.[3] As Birmingham had done yesterday, so India was doing today. The Indian Association had organised mass meetings of peasants—a 'new development of this popular machinery'—while the local Bengal associations had combined into a National League to agitate for the reform of the Legislative Councils. Cheering on these efforts was the native press of the three Presidencies, unmuzzled once more and led by the Calcutta papers in which 'day after day, hundreds of sharp-witted Babus pour forth their indignation against their English

---

[1] Minute by Dufferin, Home Department, 31 December 1885, DP 27 (Reel 521).

[2] Mackenzie Wallace, Viceroy's Private Secretary, to Permanent Under-Secretary, 23 March 1886, DP 37 (Reel 525). At the same time Wallace sent Maine this information 'about the nature, extent and force of the present political agitation which aims at introducing into India an entirely new order of things'. Wallace to Maine, 23 March 1886, DP 37 (Reel 525).

[3] Dufferin to Kimberley, 21 March 1886, DP 19 (Reel 517).

oppressors in very pungent and effective diatribes'.[1] Dufferin's peace was being shattered, for daily 'an organised system of popular agitation...is assuming more distinct and definite proportions'.[2] Sensing the Viceroy's incipient alarm, his private secretary summed up the new trend as an attempt 'to get up and organize and direct a great political agitation throughout all parts of India'.[3]

Since his professional pride required that there should be tranquillity in India during his time, Dufferin strove to belittle the significance of these events. Computations in the Home Department of the total number of graduates in India had done something to reassure the Viceroy. He found them 'both amusing and instructive'.[4] With Sir Henry Maine, Dufferin could see the incongruity of some 4,500 'of the dominant Baboo caste' claiming to 'give the law to 180 millions of souls'.[5] No doubt Hume, 'cleverish, a little cracked, vain, unscrupulous', was fussing in the press and on the platform as 'one of the chief stimulators of the Indian Home Rule movement', but the Viceroy was confident that 'For the present, and for a long time to come, neither his nor anybody else's efforts in that direction will do us much mischief'.[6] Similarly in Bengal, where there had been a burst of activity following the Calcutta National Conference of December 1885, Dufferin found the organisers of the National League 'sober and respectable men' with 'no desire to embarrass the administration'. Admittedly, Surendranath Banerjea's party seemed 'more violent and less respectable', with an ominous tendency 'to ape the tactics and organisation of the Irish Revolutionaries', but even it 'need not be regarded as very serious', provided that its influence did not spread outside Bengal.[7]

Judging the general trends of the time, Dufferin still viewed them with a bland mixture of satisfaction about the present and doubt about the distant future. The 'Indian Caucus' was a trifle, he told a former Viceroy, but 'what is now in the germ'

---

[1] Dufferin to Kimberley, 21 March 1886, DP 19 (Reel 517).
[2] Dufferin to Kimberley, 26 April 1886, DP 19 (Reel 517).
[3] Wallace to Permanent Under-Secretary of State, 26 April 1886, DP 37 (Reel 525).
[4] Dufferin to Maine, 9 May 1886, DP 37 (Reel 525).
[5] Maine to Dufferin, 15 April 1886, DP 37 (Reel 525).
[6] Dufferin to Maine, 9 May 1886, DP 37 (Reel 525).
[7] Dufferin to Kimberley, 26 April 1886, DP 19 (Reel 517).

could 'some years hence...grow into a very formidable product'.[1] One Secretary of State was advised not to worry about
the peasants' meetings in Bengal; there was 'neither danger nor
inconvenience in them at present', although these bucolic
gatherings might one day turn into 'an anti-rent and an anti-
revenue movement'.[2] Another learned that they were 'childish
and innocuous', although 'they might of course grow into very
inconvenient performances',[3] and that 'to political agitation in
India we can afford to be more or less indifferent at present',
although it was 'by no means certain that this will continue to
be the case'.[4] The Viceroy's argument balanced on his qualifying clauses as though on a tight-rope, but its direction was plain:
for the time being all was well, although after someone there
was likely to be a deluge. But how much time was left in which
to avert it? And how could this be done? Unwilling to alarm
and reluctant to prescribe, Dufferin took refuge in his sonorous
and hollow prose.

He was too intelligent a man, however, not to see the shape of
the dilemma. Grant Duff had put to him the thesis of Stephen
and the conservative civilians, that Britain must choose the
path of autocracy, 'as if Great Britain were to govern India for
all time'.[5] Yet Dufferin could glimpse a state of affairs in which
policy would not possess the freedom to make this choice, and
there would not be unlimited time to act as though it did.
Under the nominal autocracy, the Raj was harassed by the
Indian press, that 'foul torrent of abuse' and 'great river of
calumny'.[6] The days when it could be 'loftily ignored' were
over and done with, because 'the press...does undoubtedly
express the ideas of the educated class'.[7] By doing so, the newspapers had encouraged the political moves which the Indians
had launched in 1885 and 1886. So the central question was
this: '...how long an autocratic Government like that of India
—and a Government which every one will admit for many a
long year to come must in its main features remain autocratic—

[1] Dufferin to Northbrook, 23 June 1886, DP 37 (Reel 525).
[2] Dufferin to Kimberley, 11 June 1886, DP 19 (Reel 517).
[3] Dufferin to Cross, 9 May 1887, DP 20 (Reel 518).
[4] Dufferin to Cross, 4 January 1887, DP 20 (Reel 518).
[5] Memorandum, 24 June 1885, enclosed in Grant Duff to Dufferin, 24
June 1885, DP 47 (Reel 528).
[6] Dufferin to Kimberley, 17 May 1886, DP 19 (Reel 517).
[7] Dufferin to Cross, 18 January 1887, DP 20 (Reel 518).

will be able to stand...the importation *en bloc* from England, or rather from Ireland, of the perfected machinery of modern democratic agitation.'[1] Outside India the problems were still more alarming. The autocracy might hold hard inside the country, but the autocrats were now hampered by a democratic parliament, the final arbiter of Indian policy. It was perturbing to speculate about what would happen if the British Radicals moved behind the Indian 'Home Rule party'.[2] The phrase indicates how far the thinking of Dufferin, the Ulster peer, was influenced by the Irish crisis which dominated British politics and which had brought the whole imperial question to the fore.

Since by his own analysis the future might be so gloomy, Dufferin had no choice except to take some action in the present. The problem was to find a policy which would not lead to an uproar like those of Ripon's time. All those at the head of affairs during the last decade had concurred in the belief that the new educated were the centre of the Indian problem, but there was still no agreement about how to handle them. Kimberley favoured cautious conciliation because the graduates expressed the grievances of the masses; Cross was opposed to it because they did not.[3] In India one school of thought, appalled by the 'luxuriant growth of Colleges', and 'the artificial growth of a caste of semi-seditious critics', thought it could be stunted by reducing state aid;[4] but when the aid was removed, the colleges continued to flourish by drawing on voluntary subscriptions.[5] In London there were optimists who thought that the educational problem was a purely Bengali affair; Dufferin had to shatter their illusions by pointing out that the movement was general throughout the country.[6]

[1] Dufferin to Kimberley, 21 March 1886, DP 19 (Reel 517).
[2] Dufferin to Cross, 4 January 1887, DP 20 (Reel 518).
[3] Kimberley had a Whiggish respect for moral and material progress and the importance of educated men who, 'though few in number, are evidently quite sufficient' to voice the wishes of Indian society; Kimberley to Dufferin, 22 April 1886, DP 19 (Reel 517). Cross on the other hand thought that the 'Babu classes' represented chiefly themselves. His ignorance of Indian society was monumental. 'I suppose that most of the educated so-called natives do not speak these Vernacular tongues', Cross to Dufferin, 8 September 1886, DP 19 (Reels 517–18).
[4] Note by Governor of Bombay, received through Governor of Madras, September 1885, DP 48 (Reel 528); also see Reay to Dufferin, 16 September 1885, DP 48 (Reel 528); Resolution of Government of India, 18 June 1888, *P.P.* 1888, LXXVII, 375–86.   [5] See chapter 1 above, pp. 21–3.
[6] Dufferin to Cross, 20 March 1887, DP 20 (Reel 518).

It was by pondering over its demands that the Viceroy thought he saw the way forward. Leaving aside the extremists' call for an India where the British element in the army and the civil service had been spirited away, and where an Indian parliament had somehow taken shape, Dufferin thought there was a rough identity of demands between the moderates and 'the more advanced party'. 'What they chiefly have in their eye', he reported, 'is a larger share of the loaves and fishes.'[1] A little generosity could separate them from the real extremists, and it could be balanced by a sterner attitude towards these irreconcilables. Government should 'announce that these concessions must be accepted as a final settlement of the Indian system for the next ten or fifteen years, and...forbid mass meetings and incendiary speechifying'.[2] In this way, the two most important interests would be satisfied: curbing the extremists would please the British authoritarians, and conciliating the educated would rally the Indian moderates. The formula was elegant enough; but from where could the loaves and fishes be obtained? After a good deal of consideration, Dufferin decided that they should come from the civil service and the Councils.

Kimberley's rejection of Ripon's proposals for civil service reform had not closed the matter. The statutory service was not a success; and the controversy over the age-limit for the covenanted service examination had not died down. So when in June 1886 a Public Service Commission was set up to review matters, it was optimistically planned to be one of Dufferin's final settlements. The Commission was instructed to produce a scheme 'which may reasonably be hoped to possess the necessary elements of finality, and to do full justice to the claims of natives of India to higher and more extensive employment in the public service'.[3]

The Viceroy's Council had initially opposed its appointment; only the larger threat of a general parliamentary commission of enquiry had persuaded them to change their minds.[4] To have Sir Charles Aitchison as president, and six Indians as members

[1] Dufferin to Kimberley, 26 April 1886, DP 19 (Reel 517).
[2] *Ibid.*
[3] Resolution in the Home Department, 4 October 1886, quoted in H. L. Singh, *Problems and Policies of the British in India 1885–1898* (Bombay, 1963) p. 42.
[4] Dufferin to Cross, 10 August 1888, DP 21 (Reel 518).

of the Commission, was in itself a considerable triumph. The officials, fearful for the future of their service, strongly urged caution upon Dufferin. A Viceroy who depended so whole-heartedly on his officials was bound to be impressed by their arguments. 'Certainly the Civil Service of India', wrote Dufferin to Cross, 'is one of the finest services any country has ever established...and it will be a matter of the most vital moment to avoid doing anything to injure either its efficiency or its prestige.'[1] In London and Calcutta it was axiomatic that the Raj depended on European control over the administration. The only open question was the minimum number of posts necessary for such control. In distributing the remainder to Indians, the Viceroy and Secretary of State were agreed that the interests of the 'non-Babu classes' would have to be considered. Recruitment by competition alone would mean the dominance of the educated Bengali, and the Brahmins from Bombay and Madras. Aristocrats and the martial races of northern and central India, Muslims and other groups backward in education would find no place if academic attainment was the qualification for office. Yet would they tolerate being ruled by the westernised? Therefore competition would have to be tempered by nomination, and to contain the graduates provincial barriers might have to be raised.

Apart from these political considerations, the Commission had to review a complex administrative structure, which now existed on three different levels. At the top was the covenanted service; beneath it was the statutory service, where the annual recruitment could not exceed one-fifth of those entering the covenanted service in that year. Below the covenanted and statutory services lay the third level, the much larger uncovenanted service. What the Commission finally recommended was the creation of two distinct services, both open to Indians. One was to be the covenanted service, with its numbers reduced, recruited exclusively by open competition in England; the other, a provincial service, recruited in India, to which would be given the posts ultimately to be withdrawn from the covenanted service, as well as the higher judicial and executive appointments in the existing uncovenanted service. The statutory service would be abolished, and its members absorbed

---

[1] Dufferin to Cross, 4 March 1888, DP 21 (Reel 518).

into the new provincial service. The covenanted service would thus become more than ever a *corps d'élite*. While the Commission came down firmly against holding any of its entrance examinations in India, it conceded that the maximum age of entry should be raised to twenty-three, and that a few more marks should be given for Arabic and Sanskrit. As for the provincial service, local circumstance would dictate the method of recruitment.[1]

Dispatching the Commission's report to London, Dufferin professed to believe that in 'the chief matter the Natives have at heart, namely, the placing of more important and lucrative civil posts at their disposal, we have done all that their own friends and champions have desired'.[2] This was sanguine. In fact, the Congress leaders were dismayed by 'the really reactionary character of the recommendations'.[3] What the Commission was proposing was the transfer from the covenanted to the provincial service of an ultimate total of 108 posts, ranging from under-secretaries to one member of the Boards of Revenue in Madras, Bengal and the North-western Provinces. These would go to Indians. But ninety-two of these posts were in any case scheduled for Indians under the statutory service programme. So a mere sixteen posts were to be the sum of the benefit. In the event only ninety-three posts were listed. The total gain was thus one post.

Even the proposal to abolish the statutory service was not considered an unmixed blessing. Admittedly it had been disliked by Indians, but that was because of its unequal status with the covenanted service. Yet the new provincial services were to be more markedly the inferior of the covenanted service, without its prestige, prospects, pay or pensions,[4] and by no means all the places in them were intended for the educated classes. Moreover, the Commission had left the method of recruitment to be settled according to local requirements,[5] and all the local governments but one turned out to be against open competition. The Central Provinces feared it would flood their service with

[1] *PSC*, pp. 48–67.
[2] Dufferin to Cross, 30 August 1888, DP 21 (Reel 518).
[3] Wacha to Naoroji, 31 July 1888, NP.
[4] Of course, Indians could still aspire to the covenanted service, now stripped of its minor posts. But the Commission had suggested little to better their chances of entering it.
[5] *PSC*, p. 68.

Maratha Brahmins.[1] Without a system of 'responsible' nomination rather than 'mechanical' competition, Bombay felt it could not safeguard the interests of the different communities in the Presidency.[2] Colvin was in favour of nomination 'pure and simple' for the North-western Provinces,[3] while Sir James Lyall in the Punjab was convinced that competition would be unwise, since it would fill the Punjab service with men ' not from amongst the classes who would naturally take the lead, but from amongst the men who obtain degrees in the Universities'.[4] Madras too had no place for competition-wallahs. Only Sir Stuart Bayley of Bengal was prepared to recruit the greater part of the service by competition.[5]

Even so, it was not the moderation of the report which astounded some of its critics. The India Council was against raising the age limit for the entrance examination for the covenanted service and had to be overruled by the Secretary of State.[6] Some of the younger civilians, led by Macdonnell, disliked the proposals to end the statutory service.[7] When his Council accepted the main recommendations of the Commission, Dufferin felt relieved, 'for it would have been most deplorable had any difference of opinion arisen, as the majority would then have been compelled to point out with unnecessary and undesirable insistence how very moderate are the concessions which have been made to the claims of the educated natives... '[8] Although the government of India accepted most of the Commission's report, it rejected the suggestion that membership of the Boards of Revenue should be transferred from the

---

[1] Minute, 31 March 1888, *P.P.* 1890, LIV, 385.

[2] Government of Bombay to Government of India, 7 June 1888, *ibid.* 338–9. Bombay pointed out that, already, 211 out of a total of 328 Hindu government officers were Brahmins.

[3] Minute, 17 May 1888, *ibid.* 356.

[4] Government of Punjab to Government of India, 25 June 1888, *ibid.* 367. Lyall in fact would have liked to man his service with Europeans domiciled in the Punjab.   [5] Minute, 4 May 1888, *ibid.* 348.

[6] Singh, *Problems and Policies*, p. 55, n. 201.

[7] Dufferin to Cross, 10 August 1888, DP 21 (Reel 518). Sir Antony Macdonnell stuck to this opinion. In 1900 when Curzon was complaining that an increasing number of the higher posts were being 'filched away' by Indians, he quoted Macdonnell, 'who says that it is all due to Lord Dufferin, who might have insisted upon the racial qualification without exciting a murmur, whereas now there would probably be a storm', Curzon to Hamilton, 23 April 1900, Curzon Papers, MSS Eur. F. 111 (159).   [8] Dufferin to Cross, 10 August 1888, DP 21 (Reel 518).

covenanted to the provincial service. There was to be more in this spirit, and by the time the Commission's proposals were finally put into effect some four years later, they had become even more moderate.[1]

Reform of the Legislative Councils was the other concession which Dufferin envisaged in his final settlement. Apart from its political advantages, he thought it would also bring administrative gains to government. Wood's Councils Act, by now a quarter of a century old, had been a cautious measure emerging hesitantly from the shadows of the Mutiny. By this Act a few Indians had been associated by nomination with the business of law-making; but the anxiety after the Mutiny not to tamper with executive authority had kept the Councils both weak and small, free of any suggestion of being miniature parliaments or representative assemblies in embryo. With so small a body of non-official members, who were without the right to discuss the budget, to initiate legislation or to discuss administrative measures, the Councils lacked vitality,[2] and the government was left without a platform from which to explain and defend its policies. All it could do was to consult informally the various political associations about who should be nominated to the Legislative Councils. In Dufferin's opinion, this system had the disadvantage of giving official cognizance to these associations without the advantage of giving the nominees the representative standing which they would gain from being elected.[3] Consequently intelligent political debate was left to the newspapers.

By the spring of 1886 Dufferin was sounding London on the possibility of reform.[4] What he had in mind was a more extensive consultative system along the lines of the ill-starred scheme he had put up for Egypt three years earlier. 'Personally', the Viceroy argued,

---

[1] See *Papers relating to the Provincial Service from 1886–96.* Selections from the Records of the Government of India, Home Department. No. CCCLIII (Calcutta, 1898), pp. 1–29.

[2] According to the Viceroy's private secretary, the Imperial Legislative Council 'rather resembles an extremely well-conducted but moribund jelly-fish', Wallace to Godley, 8 January 1889, Lansdowne Papers, quoted in Gopal, *British Policy in India*, p. 182.

[3] See Lyall, *Dufferin*, II, 42–8.

[4] See Dufferin to Kimberley, 21 March 1886, DP 19 (Reel 517), where the Viceroy described 'the re-construction of the Supreme Legislative and the Provincial Councils' as 'one of the chief planks in the native liberal platform'.

I should feel it both a relief and an assistance if in the settlement of many Indian administrative questions affecting the interests of millions of Her Majesty's subjects, I could rely to a larger extent than at present upon the experience and counsels of Indian coadjutors. Amongst the natives I have met there are a considerable number who are both able and sensible, and upon whose loyal co-operation one could undoubtedly rely. The fact of their supporting the Government would popularize many of its acts which now have the appearance of being driven through the Legislature by brute force, and if they in their turn had a native party behind them, the Government of India would cease to stand up, as it does now, an isolated rock in the middle of a tempestuous sea, around whose base the breakers dash themselves simultaneously from all the four quarters of the heavens.[1]

But before the Viceroy could elaborate his proposals he met with a cold response from London. Kimberley was firmly against allowing interpellations in the Councils, although he conceded that 'Some very cautious step' in the direction of electing members might be desirable.[2] Rather than tamper with India's constitution, he preferred efforts to improve its administration.[3] Sir Henry Maine could see no place in India for representative institutions.

...the ideal at which the educated natives of India are aiming is absolutely unattainable. How can 180 millions of souls govern themselves? Responsible and representative Government are terms without meaning when they are applied to such a multitude. Societies of that magnitude have seldom held together at all under the same political institutions, but, when they have, the institutions have been sternly despotic.[4]

Until Cross took over from Kimberley the Viceroy made no further move.

Early in 1887 Cross was presented with the arguments for reform. The time had come to admit Indians in larger numbers to the Councils. The aim was to get 'really representative men'.[5] To get them, some form of election was necessary, but it should be indirect. To begin with, the provincial Councils should be reshaped.[6] Municipalities in the Presidency towns, the universities, Muslim corporations, 'and other recognized bodies of

---

[1] Dufferin to Kimberley, 26 April 1886, DP 19 (Reel 517).
[2] Kimberley to Dufferin, 22 April 1886, DP 19 (Reel 517).
[3] Kimberley to Reay, 30 July 1886, Kimberley Papers, D/26a, cited in Gopal, *British Policy in India*, p. 166.
[4] Maine to Dufferin, 2 June 1886, DP 37 (Reel 525).
[5] Dufferin to Cross, 1 February 1887, DP 20 (Reel 518).
[6] Dufferin to Cross, 4 January 1887, DP 20 (Reel 518).

the same description' would send a few names from whom the government would select its nominees.[1] This concession would take the wind out of the sails of the agitation; it would also have 'a conservative tendency and provide us with that kind of strength amongst the Natives which we most need'.[2] The municipalities were 'more cautious, conservative and sober-minded than the Associations', who were informally consulted about nominees. The executive would of course 'retain its right of overriding all opposition either by keeping a majority of official votes' in the Council, or by keeping a veto.[3] But Cross was very dubious about the scheme, and in particular about any notion of election in any form. He warned the Viceroy against being misled by the noisy and educated few: 'the masses of the people do not want to be ruled by Baboos, and it is our duty, as well as our interest, and still more the interest of the people, that there is to be English rule and English justice and English consideration for the wants, the prejudices, and the habits, religious as well as social, of all classes.'[4] Moreover, Muslim interests would have to be protected in any reform that was undertaken.[5]

In the last months of his viceroyalty, Dufferin attacked the problem once again with a new vigour. By a last-minute reform of the Councils he hoped both to regain popularity in India and 'to settle satisfactorily all the questions and difficulties raised by the native Home Rulers'.[6] On 20 September 1888 he put his views to his Executive Council and obtained a committee consisting of Sir George Chesney, Sir Charles Aitchison and James Westland to report on the matter. Three weeks later the committee submitted proposals that the provincial Councils of Bengal, Madras and Bombay should be enlarged and given wider functions. To secure the representation of important interests, the Councils were to be split into two divisions. To the first division 'the hereditary nobility' and 'the superior and influential landed classes' would elect their representatives; to the second, the trading, professional and agricultural classes

[1] Dufferin to Cross, 20 March 1887, DP 20 (Reel 518).
[2] Dufferin to Cross, 15 March 1887, DP 20 (Reel 518).
[3] Dufferin to Cross, 20 March 1887, DP 20 (Reel 518).
[4] Cross to Dufferin, 25 February 1887, DP 20 (Reel 518).
[5] Cross to Dufferin, 14 April 1887, DP 20 (Reel 518).
[6] Dufferin to Lord Arthur Russell, 5 November 1888, quoted in Lyall, *Dufferin*, II, 196.

would send representatives by indirect election. Government would retain the right of nominating directly a number of non-officials to ensure that no special interests, such as the Parsis or the European planting and commercial community, were unrepresented. Muslims were to be given representation in proportion to their population. Not less than two-fifths in each division were to be elected, but there would still be a nominated element 'sufficiently large to retain the supremacy of Government in the hands of the Executive'.

The legislative functions of these provincial Councils were not to be enlarged. But their advisory functions would be strengthened. On local matters of internal administration, the Councils would be permitted to originate advice and suggestions; they would be given the right of interpellation and the right to call for papers. Provincial finance would be divided into two parts, general and local. The budgets for both would be laid before the Councils for discussion, and over local financial matters they would be given 'a real control and a real responsibility'. In this way, 'the educated and influential classes' would be associated 'more largely...in the management of local and Provincial affairs', and the Councils would be given 'great opportunities for remonstrance and criticism, as well as considerable consultative faculty'.[1] When he forwarded this plan to London, Dufferin gingerly suggested change at the centre as well: in the Viceroy's Council, besides granting a carefully restricted right of interpellation, there should be 'an annual debate on the Budget' since 'As the law now stands, the Budget can only be discussed when a new tax is introduced'.[2] Dufferin had been forced into the unlikely role of beseeching the India Office to believe there was nothing dangerous in his plans, and of trying to prove it by trimming them at every step. He tried to placate his masters by agreeing that 'You cannot apply constitutional principles to a conquered country', and he was careful not to suggest any change in the composition of the Viceroy's Council.[3] But once again, London received his plan without enthusiasm and he left India without implementing it. Although

[1] See Report on the Subject of Provincial Councils by Chesney, Aitchison, and Westland, 1888, and Summary of Conclusions, Enclosures no. 1 and no. 2, Dufferin to Cross, 20 October 1888, DP 21 (Reel 518).
[2] Dufferin to Cross, 29 October 1888, DP 21 (Reel 518).
[3] Dufferin to Cross, 20 October 1888, DP 21 (Reel 518).

it enjoyed the goodwill of his successor, it was not to find its way on to the statute book until 20 June 1892, and then only in a revised and modest form.[1]

With the Indians, no less than with the India Office, Dufferin tried to hedge his bets. If it was desirable to square the moderates among the western educated, it was no less prudent to placate 'the non-Baboo classes'.[2] This meant trying to keep an uneasy balance between the needs of the peasants and the wishes of the landlords and traditional notables. In the Bengal Tenancy Act Dufferin made larger concessions to the zemindars than Ripon would have done. In the same way the tenancy law in Oudh was revised so as to make it acceptable to the talukdars. One of his reasons for encouraging Lyall's proposal for a Legislative Council in the North-western Provinces was because it would please the landholders; and an attractive part of his own second conciliar scheme was that it would associate the aristocracy more closely with the deliberations of government, while leaving the government with power to legislate in the interests of the masses.

Dufferin could also see that it would be shrewd policy to acquire the reputation of being 'the benevolent protector of the Moslim', without being 'unjust to the Hindoos'.[3] Since Mayo's time, government had realised the importance of winning the Muslims over, recognising that unless they were conciliated, they would remain the 'most dangerous class' in the Raj.[4] But while Mayo resolved that government should do what it could to remove the obstacles keeping Muslims out of its educational system,[5] it could do little. None of his proposed measures

---

[1] See Singh, *Problems and Policies*, pp. 91–124.

[2] '...all the non-Baboo classes are taking the alarm, and are beginning to see that under the ideal Baboo régime they would be completely left out in the cold', Dufferin to Cross, 1 February 1887, DP 20 (Reel 518).

[3] Mackenzie Wallace to Birdwood, 30 March 1887, DP 38 (Reel 526).

[4] Northbrook to Argyll, 28 March 1873, Northbrook Papers, MSS Eur. C. 144 (9). In part, this danger seemed to arise from the international connections of Indian Islam, particularly at a time when the Ottoman empire seemed to be crumbling. See Lytton to Salisbury, 23 July 1877, LP (3/2).

[5] 'we have failed to attract the mass of the Mahomedan people to our system of education, and have moreover created a cause for dissatisfaction, inasmuch as they...are unable to participate in the material advantage which Government education has conferred on the Hindoo...' Note by Mayo, 26 June 1871, Mayo Papers, Add. 7490 (12); also see Resolution of Government of India, Home Department (Education), 7 August 1871 and Resolution, 13 June 1873, *Muslim Selections*, part 2, pp. 152, 226–9.

implied steering a new course or budging from government's provision of an education that was both secular and western. The Education Commission, in spite of Hunter's sympathies for Muslim interests, did not propose any fundamental revision of the system under which these interests were suffering.[1] In the field of public employment, the National Mahommedan Association had asked for a protected quota, but government refused to exempt Muslim candidates from competitive tests. All that Dufferin was prepared to concede was that where local authorities had patronage free of examination, they should lend a kindly ear to Muslim claims in order to 'redress the inequality as opportunity offers'.[2] The Public Service Commission also recommended a certain local latitude in this matter, but this was not much of a sop to the Muslims.

Once Congress had been founded, and once some of the Muslim leaders had decided to oppose it, both London and Calcutta could not fail to see that 'This division of religious feeling is greatly to our advantage...'[3] Dufferin's plans for council reform seemed to be exploiting this advantage. 'In any step that may be taken', the Secretary of State insisted, 'the interests of the Mahomedans must be considered quite as much as the interests of the noisy Bengalee Baboo.'[4] But when Dufferin finally proposed proportional representation for Muslims in the Councils, this was little more than the expression of the principle that it was interests, not heads, which should be counted. Congress itself, as early as 1889, agreed that minorities should receive seats in council in proportion to their population. None of this gives any grounds for supposing that Dufferin was planning a new departure.

The diversity of races in India and the presence of a powerful Mahomedan community, are undoubtedly circumstances favourable to the maintenance of our rule; but these circumstances we found and did not create, nor, had they been non-existent, would we have been justified in establishing them by artificial means. It would be a diabolical policy on the part of any Government to endeavour to emphasize or exacerbate race hatreds among the Queen's Indian subjects for a political object...[5]

[1] *EC*, pp. 480–520.
[2] Resolution of the Government of India, Home Department (Education), 15 July 1885, *Muslim Selections*, part 3, pp. 375–90.
[3] Cross to Dufferin, 14 January 1887, DP 20 (Reel 518).
[4] Cross to Dufferin, 14 April 1887, DP 20 (Reel 518).
[5] Dufferin to G. Allen, editor, *Pioneer*, 1 January 1887, DP 51 (Reel 531).

Moreover, his attitude towards the educated Indians remained a complex mixture of concession and restriction. He wanted another press law, although neither the Liberal nor the Conservative government would support him on that, after the fate of Lytton's measure.[1] He formed a police intelligence department to keep an eye on the new politicians.[2] He authorised the provinces to forbid government servants to assist Congress. He warned the princes against subscribing to Congress funds.[3] At first this sternness was simply the tough attitude towards the extremists which was to balance the tender attitude towards the moderates in Dufferin's final settlement. The existence of these moderates was an essential part of his analysis, and he strove hard to believe in it. But as time went on, he came to think that wherever they might be, they were not in Congress, which seemed to be in the hands of extremists. Thus at the end of his term of office, he decided to show openly that government disliked the new body. On 5 November 1888 Hume confided to Tyabji 'another secret which I learned only this week: Lord Dufferin is *now* against us'.[4] It was not to remain a secret for long. At his farewell speech at the Saint Andrew's Dinner in Calcutta on 30 November, the Viceroy referred contemptuously to Congress as an organisation representing 'a microscopic minority'.[5] But in private his disillusion went still deeper, for it now extended to the educated classes in general:

The chief concern of the Government of India is to protect and foster the interests of the people of India, and the people of India are not the seven or eight thousand students who have graduated at the Universities, or the Pleaders recruited from their numbers who are practising in our Courts of Justice, or the newspaper writers, or the Europeanized Zemindars, or the wealthy traders, but the voiceless millions whom neither education, nor civilisation, nor the influence of European ideas or modern thought, have in the slightest degree

[1] Cross to Dufferin, 8 September 1886, DP 19 (Reel 517), and 25 February 1887, DP 20 (Reel 518).

[2] Dufferin to Cross, 17 October 1887, DP 20 (Reel 518); Dufferin to Cross, 3 October 1887, DP 20 (Reel 518); Dufferin to Cross, 6 July 1888, DP 21 (Reel 518).

[3] Dufferin to Cross, 8 October 1888, and enclosure no. 7, Wallace to Cunningham, 26 January 1888, DP 21 (Reel 518).

[4] Hume to Tyabji, 5 November 1888, Tyabji Papers.

[5] Marquis of Dufferin and Ava, *Speeches Delivered in India, 1884–8* (London, 1890), p. 239.

transfigured or transformed from what their forefathers were a thousand years ago.[1]

※

Lytton, Ripon and Dufferin could all see that what was afoot in India was not simply discontent of the old sort but political change of a quite new kind. Yet the official mind among their advisers on the whole rejected the suggestion that these were changes inside an Indian Nation. In general, the Victorians worked from a particular historiography of nationalism, derived from the recent experience of Europe itself. They defined it in the light of such uprisings as those of the Greeks, the Italians and the Southern Slavs, with their demands for freedom which seemed to unite all groups and classes within the subject people.[2] These criteria they were prepared to apply outside Europe as far as communities of white settlers were concerned. But when the challenge came not only outside Europe but also from groups of non-Europeans, then the response was likely to be different. In Egypt, as in India, activities inconvenient to the British were judged to be self-interested machinations rather than genuine nationalisms. The Gladstone government saw Arabi's revolt in Egypt as a few army officers on the make, abetted by some Egyptian intellectuals who had taken to reading the works of Lamartine—a comforting conclusion, for it justified the Gladstonians in negating their own principles. After all, there were no Garibaldis in Cairo. And neither were there any in Calcutta or Bombay.

In the vastly greater arena of India it was tempting to argue that Surendranath, Pherozeshah and the like represented nobody but themselves; that they were but a small group of wanton men, greedy for a pull at the pagoda tree. To their claims to speak for the Indian Nation, the rulers of India could reply that such a nation did not exist; and in any case, the needs of the peasantry would be better met by the Guardian who knew them

---

[1] Minute by Dufferin on the Congress, November 1888, India Public Letters, vol. 9 (1888), pp. 1195–1200, quoted in C. H. Philips (ed.), *The Evolution of India and Pakistan 1858 to 1947. Select Documents* (London, 1962), p. 144.

[2] For reasons of strategy, by distrust of its leaders, and because of the constitutional device of forming the United Kingdom, Ireland was seen as a special case. The Unionists had to abolish the Irish sea, while claiming that the inhabitants of Western Britain were Hottentots.

than by the Indian lawyer who did not. More and more the civilians were coming to feel that prattle about political experiments was besides the point. The size of their empire haunted them. Across loose talk about the people fell the shadow of the census returns; references to national unity were blotted out by the hundreds of volumes of the *District Gazetteer*. The country teemed with problems of irrigation and cultivation. Fuller bellies not freer presses ought to be the first aim of government. These were the issues with which the Guardians had to grapple, and what they called for were not political but administrative solutions. Take care of the peasants and the politics would take care of themselves. To the charge that year by year the peasant's debts were growing higher, and his children more numerous, they could retort that while money-lenders remained unchastened and the crop blights remained unchecked there was no case for tinkering with the constitution. Working from the luxury of a leisurely timetable, the civilians estimated that they could postpone the political question until a time of their own choosing.[1]

But for the Viceroys it was not so easy to swallow this convenient view in its entirety. As their critics reminded them, they came to India as Griffins. But this gave them the advantage of a fresh eye. They were men with more experience of the world of politics, unlikely to forget that the edifice of Padishah-i-Hind hung on the acquiescence of an electorate in England; and in their differing ways Lytton, Ripon and Dufferin recognised that the problems confronting them in India needed political solutions. Common to their thinking was a growing awareness of the political potential of the Indians they had educated. Yet the aspirations of these Indians were hard to satisfy without clashing with the interests of other clients of the Raj. Faced with these rival claims, each Viceroy took a different view of the political balance he had to strike. While each of them came to favour a policy which would begin to associate Indians more closely with the working of government, Lytton thought the traditional notables should be the associates, Ripon preferred the educated, and Dufferin as usual tried to straddle both positions. In practice, however, the predilections of the Vice-

[1] Curzon was the last great exponent of this particular view. For intelligent and benevolent autocrats it was an understandable judgement. Yet Curzon's own failures suggest one last comment upon it: it was wrong.

roys could affect the logic of political development only on the margin. None of them had much luck with his policies. Lytton's statutory service was scrapped after a decade, his press law in half that time. Ripon's hopes of reforming the Councils and the civil service came to nothing, and his measures for local self-government were watered down. Dufferin's reforms were post-dated cheques. To a government ruling an empire wider than the Romans had ever governed, these temporary hesitations might have seemed insignificant. The Raj appeared much stronger than its subjects, divided as they were. Its collaborators were drawn from many groups and from many parts of the country. Its critics and their programmes depended on the existence of that very imperialism of which they were both the inveterate castigators and the conspicuous beneficiaries. Literary gentlemen could not turn the British out of India. The pitiless lucidity of Salisbury saw this very well:

Whether the aristocracy themselves are very powerful may be doubted, and any popularity we may achieve with them is not much to lean upon in a moment of trial. But it is good as far as it goes; their good-will, and co-operation, if we can obtain it, will at all events serve to hide to the eyes of our own people and perhaps, of the growing literary class in India the nakedness of the sword on which we really rely.[1]

Yet these hesitations of policy helped on a movement which the sword could not cut down.

[1] Salisbury to Disraeli, 7 June 1876, Salisbury Papers (Beaconsfield).

5

The Politics of the Associations

Associations brought nineteenth-century India across the threshold of modern politics. Sometimes religious zeal, sometimes caste solidarity encouraged the propensity towards associations, but during the course of the century more of the associations in India were brought into being by groups of men united by secular interests. What now held them together were common skills and functions, a common education, and common aspirations and resentments against the policies of the Raj, not simply the bonds of joint family, caste and district. There was a time when these would have been the only points of union; but now that this was no longer so, Indians were converging on modern politics.

There are some qualifications to the starkness of this formulation. Associations were not new in India. From one point of view, were not all castes forms of associations? Functionally they were; but the rigidities of endogamous caste systems set them apart from the new unions based on successful adaptation to the demands of a new regime, with its very different viewpoints and novel pressures. A second qualification is that extended patriotisms were not unknown in India, as the history of the Sikhs or the Marathas shows. Thirdly, the new associations of professional men did not at once liquidate the old unities of caste, joint family and district.[1] Indeed, they are still of profound importance today. Some of the associations did, however, provide a method of going beyond them. They may be defined in Hobbesian terms as corporations, whose function

[1] Many of these old unities themselves adopted the new techniques of association once it became necessary for the defence of their caste interests in the competitive circumstances of the nineteenth century. Examples of such groupings which sometimes transcended the boundaries of locality were the Kayasth associations of north India and the Prabhu Association of Bombay.

was to keep themselves as independent entities under the cover of the regime. In British India, independence meant that they could gradually assume postures of continuous and coherent criticism of the state. Loyal to the state many of them might be, but their criticism was likely to go further, and their demands to drive deeper, once the changes in Indian society began to draw more men into the political process. For their part, the rulers of India might begin by tolerating such associations; but they were to find that they had an *imperium* inside their empire.

The study of associations falls outside the formal limits of constitutional analysis as construed until very recently. Yet of all the symptoms of a society about to move into political activity few are more important.[1] In India the earliest associations were limited by language and interest, and they drew support from students, or professional men, or landlords, or merchants in a limited geographical area. But the unities imposed by British rule allowed more ambitious organisations to extend beyond that. These were the provincial associations which began to search for ways and means of working together in India as a whole, a trend which culminated in the Indian National Congress. Accordingly, to chart the genesis of national organisation is to study two simultaneous processes. The first, the subject of this chapter, is the development of the regional associations, and the second, the subject of the next chapter, is their efforts to work together on an all-India basis.

※

The earliest associations were organised in the Presidency capitals where the commerce and administration of the Company had first unsettled the traditional order. The Indians who joined them were men who owed their changed status to British rule and had learnt the language and the political idioms of their rulers. Some of these bodies were designed to meet the demand

[1] A handful of examples from English history makes the point. The associations of the nineteenth century—the General Unions, the Anti-Corn Law League and the Chartists—were pressure groups casting around for a mass basis. In the previous century, operations were not so open. The Yorkshire Association, the Society for the Defence of the Bill of Rights, and the countless Literary and Debating Clubs were pressure groups, of course, but their crucial importance was that by banding together people with common interests they began to transcend the old regional groupings of English politics.

for the new education and to challenge the missionary initiative in it. Others were launched by the alumni of the new schools, who were encouraged to band together, both by the mystique of the syllabus they shared and by the ostracism they suffered at the hands of orthodox society. Eleven years after the founding of Hindu College in 1817, its pupils formed an Academic Association. These students, Young Bengal as they came to be known, debated subjects of the most general kind—free-will, fate, truth, virtue and the hollowness of idolatry; their heroes were the *philosophes*, and their handbook was Tom Paine's *Age of Reason*. Inspired by such lively and unconventional teachers as Henry Derozio and David Hare, they galvanised Calcutta in the late 1820s,[1] flaunting their renunciation of orthodox Hindu society.[2]

Young Bengal's politics lived on ivory towers. While its members defined the rights of man and demanded free and compulsory education for all, more sober Bengalis began to shape local politics, concentrating on specific grievances and remedies. Another typical student club in Calcutta was the Society for the Acquisition of General Knowledge formed in 1838. By 1843 it had 200 members, including many leaders of early Bengali politics, such as Ram Gopal Ghose, Peary Chandra Mitra, and Debendranath Tagore. With the clubs came the papers; Hindu College students produced more than half a dozen different journals between 1828 and 1843.[3] In all this activity, Rammohan Roy had set a brilliant example. His talent for organisation gave Calcutta its leading school, its first Indian newspapers and the Brahmo Samaj, an organisation for religious reform which played an important part in Bengal's renaissance.

In the city of Bombay developments were slower. In 1827 its

[1] B. B. Majumdar, *History of Political Thought from Rammohun to Dayananda* (1821–1884), vol. 1: *Bengal* (Calcutta, 1934), pp. 81–91; and A. Gupta, (ed.), *Studies in the Bengal Renaissance* (Jadavpur, 1958), pp. 16–31.

[2] It was rumoured that the college boys recited the *Iliad* instead of their mantras. Others refused in court to swear by the holy waters of the Ganges, and met at Derozio's house to eat beef and drink beer. One won notoriety by greeting an image of the goddess Kali, not with the customary bow, but with 'Good morning, Madam'. Rajnarain Bose surprised his agnostic friends by joining the Brahmo Samaj, but kept in step by celebrating the event with 'sherry and biscuits'. (See Rajnarain Bose, *Atmacharit* [Autobiography, in Bengali] (Calcutta, 1909).).)

[3] Majumdar, *History of Political Thought*, pp. 87–91.

inhabitants subscribed to found the Elphinstone Institution, which was consciously modelled on Hindu College, but not until 1834 did the college obtain buildings, professors and students. In 1848 a Students' Literary and Scientific Society was established, which brought Parsis, Gujaratis and Maharashtrians together. Two years earlier, a Native General Library gave evidence of new interests, and in 1851 the fortnightly *Rast Goftar* (Truth Teller) was founded, a paper which was to have great influence on Bombay opinion. It was edited by Dadabhai Naoroji, himself a Parsi and the leader of Elphinstone's students, who describes the ferment in Bombay at this time:

The six or seven years before I eventually came to England in 1855...
were full of all sorts of reforms, social, educational, political, religious,
etc....Female Education, Free Association of Women with Men
at public, social and other gatherings, Infant Schools, Students'
Literary and Scientific Society, Societies for the Diffusion of Useful
Knowledge in the Vernacular, Parsi Reform, Abolition of Child
Marriages, Re-marriage of Widows among Hindus, and Parsi Religious
Reform Society, were some of the problems tackled, movements set
on foot, and institutions inaugurated by a band of young men fresh
from College...Such were the first fruits of the English education
given at Elphinstone College.[1]

In these associations many of the Indian politicians of the 1870s gained their first experience. Yet in Bombay's response to western influence several different strains could already be detected. Parsis, Gujaratis and Maharashtrians moved along different lines, and the Deccan could not impose its stamp upon the ethos of the capital.

Since the Company's charter was due to expire in 1853, this was the obvious time for parliament to take stock of Indian developments. So it was equally the obvious time for Indians to float new political ventures whose petitions to Westminster might influence the legislature in making up their minds. Hence the discussions over the renewal of the charter gave birth to the three associations which were to dominate the politics of Bengal, Bombay and Madras for the next quarter of a century.[2] On 29 October 1851 the British Indian Association

---

[1] 'A Chapter in Autobiography', *Speeches and Writings of Dadabhai Naoroji* (Madras, 1910), p. 656.
[2] Apparently a fourth, the Deccan Association, was formed, perhaps as a branch of the British Indian Association. But it was still-born; it sent

was founded in Calcutta. While it had laid plans to petition parliament before the new charter was granted so as to influence 'the system of Government laid down by Parliament', it also wanted 'improvements in the local administration'.[1]

The Bombay Association was founded on 25 August 1852. Its inaugural meeting showed the varied population of the city. Jews and Portuguese mingled with Hindus, and there was a large Parsi contingent. Jamsetjee Jeejeebhoy, the first Parsi baronet, was elected the honorary president; both vice-presidents were also Parsis, and the resolution founding the Association was proposed and seconded by two Parsi alumni from Elphinstone. Much of the impetus behind the new body came from members of the college. The meeting decided that the Bombay Association should be the representative of the people of the Presidency, and that its members were to pay an annual fee of twenty-five rupees. Thirty thousand rupees were immediately subscribed by donation to launch the Association. Its first task was to petition parliament about the charter.[2] Madras began with the more modest plan of starting a branch of the British Indian Association but later decided to create instead an independent Madras Native Association. This looked a more impressive body for supplicating parliament, to which it in fact sent two petitions. Gazulu Lakshminarasu Chetty, who in 1844 had founded the first Indian-owned paper in Madras, the *Crescent*, and P. Somasundaram Chettiar, the Association's secretary, were the prime movers, and they kept the Association busy squabbling with the Christian missionaries of the south.

While the Bombay and Madras Native Associations were the first specifically political organisations in western and southern India, the Calcutta body had taken over from two existing associations, the Landholders' Society and the Bengal British India Society. The Landholders' Society, or Zemindars' Association as it was first called in 1837, had been primarily a pressure group dressing up self-interest as public concern. A

no petition to parliament, and its records have not survived. See B. B. Majumdar, *Indian Political Associations and Reform of Legislature (1818–1917)* (Calcutta, 1965), pp. 38–9.

[1] First Report of the British Indian Association, from its establishment on 29 October 1851 to the 30 November 1852. BIA.

[2] *Minute of Proceedings of the Bombay Association. Established 26th August 1852* (Bombay, 1852), pp. 1–25.

contemporary account delicately explained that, 'intended to embrace people of all descriptions, without reference to caste, country or complexion, and rejecting all principle of exclusiveness, [it] was to be based on the most universal and liberal principles; the only qualification to become its members, being the possession of interest in the soil of the country'. It had planned to scatter 'branch societies in every district of the British Indian empire',[1] claiming for the people the same rights as Englishmen in England. Quickly learning the first lesson in the political manual of British India, it had approached the British India Society in London in 1839 and in 1843 appointed George Thompson its agent there. When he was brought by Debendranath Tagore to visit his principals in Calcutta, Thompson lectured to Hindu College on the art of agitation, and called for a new political association 'with a view to the expansion of just rights, and the protection of the interests of all classes'.[2] His enthusiasm bore fruit in the Bengal British India Society which dutifully professed a broader purpose than the Landholders' Society; it would encourage 'the friendly co-operation of all persons anxious to promote the good of India...without respect of caste, creed and place of birth or rank in society'. It would be law-abiding and constitutional.[3]

There was some competition between these two bodies, since the Landholders' Society was specifically concerned with protecting the rights of landlords while the Bengal British India Society, and in particular its energetic secretary, Peary Chandra Mitra, thought it progressive to criticise the zemindari system and speak up for the rights of peasants. So the Tagores and Debs, big zemindars and important men in Calcutta into the bargain, shunned the British India Society. Reminiscing in 1870 about these early days, Kissory Chandra Mitra described the members of the Bengal British India Society as 'upper middle class men sympathising strongly with the condition of the ryots'.[4] Still more admiringly Bholanath Chandra saw them as the aristocracy of intelligence. But for all this show of

---

[1] Quoted in Majumdar, *History of Political Thought*, pp. 163–4.
[2] See R. J. Mitter (ed.), *The Speeches of George Thompson* (Calcutta, 1895).
[3] *The Bengal Hurkaru*, 24 April, 1843, quoted in Majumdar, *History of Political Thought*, pp. 172–3.
[4] Eighteenth Annual General Meeting of the British Indian Association, 31 March 1870, pp. 7–8. BIA.

division along the lines of interest and education, the difference between the two bodies was more apparent than real. By 1843 the president of one association was the London agent of the other. Neither association flourished, and the Bengal British India Society attracted ten members in all. When the British Indian Association was set up in 1851, it drew its support from both its predecessors.

Until the 1870s, Indian politics were in the hands of these new associations in the Presidencies. This was a time of considerable administrative change and the associations wanted a say in what came out of it. Their main effort came before the charter was granted; after 1853 they established a harmonious routine of memorials and petitions to London, counterpointed with more frequent representations to the local authorities in India. Since the emphasis was on persuading parliament rather than pressing the provincial governments, the wide differences between the Presidencies did not embarrass the convenience of a common demand. Until the Mutiny the associations repeated their burden in unison.[1] After it the British Indian Association sang more and more a solo part, not because it was especially active but because the other two were hardly active at all. The events of 1857 cast a pall on Bombay politics, and for a decade the Association there was moribund. The Madras Native Association lingered on until Chetty's death in 1868. Then it languished, until V. Bhashyam Iyengar resuscitated it many years later.

The lines of the dialogue with the Raj had already been rehearsed in the petitions of 1852 and 1853 which called for the reform of the Legislative Councils and a greater share of public office for Indians—demands which were to have a great future. Since the 1853 charter made no positive provision 'for the appointment of a single native member of the Legislative Council', the British Indian Association called for 'unceasing efforts...to ensure the removal of this great defect from the new enactment'.[2] Suavely arguing that 'the natives of India, although slow to agitate or make any organized resistance, are deeply sensible of the value of political freedom', it petitioned again in 1856 for the gradual grant of a 'deliberative body

---

[1] Each association sent its petitions independently, but there was some contact between Calcutta and Bombay.

[2] Second Report of the British Indian Association, 13 January 1854, pp. 17–21. BIA.

which shall possess all the requisites of a constitutional legis-lature'.[1] The Mutiny was an ironic footnote to these observa-tions. Undeterred, the Association in 1860 argued the growing need to find a place for the 'voice of the people...their views, their wishes, and their wants',[2] and it was disappointed once more by the 1861 Councils Act.[3]

The other complaint was that Indians, 'however respectable, trustworthy, and qualified they may be', were excluded from the highest grades of the public services.[4] Here again the 1853 charter brought no satisfaction. The Association welcomed open competitive examinations for the covenanted service, but com-plained that as these were held in England Indians were in effect kept out. So 'one of the principal grievances remaining to be redressed' was 'the exclusiveness of the civil and scientific services'.[5] Bombay echoed the complaint.[6] The next fifteen years heard variations on the same theme. In 1854 the British Indian petitioned for the abolition of Haileybury;[7] in 1856 and in 1860 it asked for simultaneous examinations in England and in India. In 1861 the new regulations were bitterly criticised; and in 1865 when the age limit for the examination was lowered to twenty-one, a memorial was sent to the Secretary of State pointing out that such a rule would be 'prohibitory' against overseas candidates. The Association approached the London Indian Society and East India Association for joint agitation, and together they appealed for simultaneous examinations.[8]

[1] Petition of the British Indian Association to Parliament, 8 April 1856, and Fifth Annual Report of the British Indian Association, 1856, p. 5. BIA.
[2] Ninth Annual Report of the British Indian Association, 1860, p. 9. BIA.
[3] Report for 1862, Eleventh Annual General Meeting of the British Indian Association, 31 January 1863, p. 1. BIA.
[4] *Petition to Parliament of the Members of the Bombay Association...* (Bombay, 1853), p. 14.
[5] Second Report of the British Indian Association, 13 January 1854, pp. 17, 21. BIA.
[6] See *Minutes of Proceedings of the First Annual General Meeting of the Bombay Association* (Bombay, 1853), p. 24.
[7] Third Annual Report of the British Indian Association, 1854, pp. 9–12. BIA.
[8] See Fourth Annual Report of the British Indian Association, 1855, p. 19; Ninth Annual Report of the British Indian Association, 1860, p. 10; Monthly General Meeting, British Indian Association, 2 October 1861, p. 4; Fourteenth Annual General Meeting of the British Indian Association, 14 February 1866, pp. 7–9; Seventeenth Annual General Meeting of the British Indian Association, 24 February 1869, pp. 4–5. BIA. On the London Indian Society and the East Indian Association, see below, pp. 246–9.

These demands for a career open to the talents and a voice for Indians in law-making were modest when they were first stated, and they remained modest for a long time. The methods of presenting them did not go beyond petitions, memorials and the occasional public meeting; the claim to represent the people was hardly made good. Only a handful of men belonged to the associations. There were no branches in the mofussil, and links between the Presidencies were tenuous. But the mere existence of their managing committees, paying members and regular meetings was important. Transcending the ties of family, caste, religion and locality, and surviving their random beginnings, these associations were the first overt sign of a social and political revolution in the sub-continent.

By the 1870s there were signs of change inside Indian society. The economic changes which had seemed imminent a few decades before had not taken place, but the social changes were clear. In Bengal, as in Bombay and Madras, higher education was well established and members of the new professions were acquiring status and developing ambitions; modes of connection wider than caste and locality being created. In turn, changes of this sort made a political mutation all the more likely. The growth of this new elite in each of the Presidencies meant that they all contained men whose aspirations and status were roughly comparable. Obviously, this increased the chances of forming a movement with an all-India base. But secondly, the fact that each of the local elites was now striking deeper social roots meant that regional idiosyncrasies were likely to count for more in their local politics. Hence there were profound ambiguities within this impulse towards political unity. In the third place, the growth of these elites increased the risk of internal dissension. As their social origins grew more varied, their geographical coverage more extensive, and their age distribution more scattered, they showed signs of schism.

In Bengal the fate of the British Indian Association is one pointer to these changes. After its foundation in 1851 the Association dominated Indian political life in the Presidency. Most of its members were rich zemindars, and its main purpose was the defence of landed interests. But because the Association also claimed a wider function as a national forum for India and an unofficial opposition for Bengal it tried to enlist a more broadly based membership. Besides the zemindars it included traders and such men as Ram Gopal Ghose, Peary Chandra Mitra, Rajendra Lal Mitra and Harish Chandra Mukherjee, whom Calcutta styled its aristocracy of intellect. Reform of the Councils and the public services were regular items on the agenda. More pragmatically, it criticised the Calcutta Municipal bill of 1854, demanded the end of the salt monopoly in 1855, called for the extension of the Permanent Settlement, and reform of the courts. After the Mutiny it agitated against Wilson's financial proposals, petitioned for a Commission of Inquiry into the Indigo riots, opened a famine relief fund in 1860, took a keen interest in plans for the Calcutta municipality, proposed a Governor-in-Council for Bengal in 1868, and petitioned against the Native Marriage bill in 1869.[1] Its interest in the civil service question[2] and the watching brief it maintained over regulations affecting the legal profession,[3] showed the Association to be the spokesman of the educated as well as of the zemindars. Government House also recognised the Association's role, and its leading men were regularly nominated to the Viceroy's Council and to the Legislative Council of Bengal.[4]

[1] See Third Annual Report of the British Indian Association for the year 1854; Fourth Annual Report of the British Indian Association for the year 1855; Draft Petition to Parliament, 1859; Ninth Annual Report of the British Indian Association for the year 1860; Seventeenth Annual General Meeting of the British Indian Association, 24 February 1869; Petition against the Native Marriage Bill, 23 May 1869. BIA.

[2] Second Report of the British Indian Association, 13 January 1854, p. 21; Meeting of the British Indian Association, 15 September 1876, pp. 13–14; Report of the Committee for 1876, Twenty-fifth Annual General Meeting of the British Indian Association, 12 May 1877, pp. 8–9. BIA.

[3] See the Association's representation about Pleaders' Regulations, Second Report of the British Indian Association, 13 January 1854; about the Mofussil Small Cause Courts bill, Fourth Annual Report of the British Indian Association for the year 1855; its plea for reform of the courts, Ninth Annual Report of the British Indian Association for the year 1860; its petition, 28 March 1865 on the Pleaders' bill, Monthly General Meeting of the British Indian Association, 19 July 1865; and its discussions about the difficulties of the legal profession, Seventeenth Annual General Meeting of the British Indian Association, 24 February 1869. BIA.

[4] Of thirty-six Indians appointed as additional members of the Viceroy's Legislative Council between 1862 and 1888, seventeen were zemindars, and two were secretaries of the Association. Many of the Indians nominated to the Bengal Council, including Prasanna Kumar Tagore, Digambar

Its newspaper, the *Hindoo Patriot*,[1] had the reputation of being 'the leading Indian paper in Bengal'. The Association was thus spokesman of moderate but enlightened native opinion. In 1870 it seemed 'the only political body in the whole of India respected by Government',[2] and even its critics agreed that it had no competitors in Bengal.[3]

Five years later, the monopoly had been challenged. In the later nineteenth century the district townships were developing into administrative and educational centres as a more unified system of administration, law courts and English schools came to be established throughout the Presidency. Consequently towns outside Calcutta began to attract small nuclei of educated and professional men, and with them came the press and the associations. As the bhadralok's incomes from rents grew smaller and their holdings shrank through subdivision, more of them were moving to the towns for education and employment. Though most of them tried to retain close links with their villages, this process began to cut them loose from their rural moorings.[4] More and more it freed them from a complete dependence on rents. As lawyers, government servants and clerks they were unlikely to give priority to the defence of landed interests. Moreover, as competition for employment grew more intense, more Calcutta graduates sought a career up the country. Of 1,700 graduates between 1858 and 1881, more than three-quarters sought their fortunes outside Calcutta, taking with them their new political interests. Table 41 shows how widely they were scattering.

Mitra, Ramnath Tagore, Peary Mohan Mukherjee, and Kristo Das Pal, editor of the *Hindoo Patriot*, were members of the British Indian Association. See Majumdar, *Indian Political Associations*, pp. 333, 339; for details about these men, see biographical notes below, pp. 380–5.

[1] Although the *Hindoo Patriot* was technically not owned by the Association, many of its Trustees were members. Founded in 1853, and edited for a while by Harish Chandra Mukherjee, the *Patriot* took the lead in the indigo agitation. In July 1862 ownership was vested in a Board of Trustees, and the paper was managed and edited by Kristo Das Pal, secretary of the Association, from 1879 until his death in 1884.

[2] *Amrita Bazar Patrika*, 10 November 1870.

[3] *Ibid.* 15 December 1870.

[4] They returned to them on ceremonial occasions, referring to their ancestral homes in the village as 'bari' (or permanent home) and their town residences as 'basha' (or temporary dwelling). See *Calcutta Commission Report*, I, part I, 124–5, and Sinha, *Nineteenth Century Bengal*, chapters III and IV.

TABLE 41. *The place of employment of Calcutta graduates,*
1858–81

Place	Number	Percentage
Calcutta	326	19·2
Bengal Proper	404	23·5
Bihar	104	6·0
Orissa	18	1·0
Lower Provinces (district unspecified)	238	14·1
Total in the Lower Provinces	*1,090*	*63·8*
Assam	29	1·7
North-western Provinces and Oudh	107	6·2
Punjab	22	1·3
Central Provinces	27	1·6
Elsewhere (including England)	60	3·5
Total outside the Lower Provinces	*245*	*14·3*
Not returned or dead	*371*	*21·9*
Grand total	*1,706*	*100·0*

Source: Calculated from a list of graduates of Calcutta University, 1858–81, reprinted as Appendix D, Sinha, *Nineteenth Century Bengal*, pp. 161–99. For the occupations of these graduates, see table 51 below, p. 358.

With them came a rapid outcrop of societies, trivial and often short-lived. These local associations took a wide variety of forms: literary and debating societies, leagues for self-better-ment, clubs for buying newspapers, reading groups, societies for social and religious reform, vakils' and teachers' associations. So strong a passion for self-help might not seem to reflect much political interest, but in 1876 Government House could see that the connection was growing:

Another result of education has been the formation of societies and associations, greater and lesser, in all parts of the country; they are about 60 in number, and they have about 2,000 members in all. Their chief objects are somewhat undefined perhaps, but pertain chiefly to educational and social matters, relating to political affairs only in representing to the British authorities the wishes and interests of the people...they indicate a stir of thought and movement in the national mind.[1]

Most of these societies were in Bengal Proper, where they were bunched in the western districts around Calcutta, and in

[1] Minute by Temple, 14 January 1876, p. 93, *Report on the Administration of Bengal, 1874–5.* For comments by the press on the continued growth of these associations, see Supplement to *Bengalee*, 29 January 1876; *ibid.* 4 January 1879; and *Brahmo Public Opinion*, 6 January 1881.

east Bengal. In 1874–5 there were sixty-six societies of this sort, of which twelve were in Calcutta, fifteen in Presidency division, three in Burdwan division, twenty-four in Dacca division and eight in the two divisions of Bihar.[1] Six years later, the total had risen to eighty-eight, seventeen of which had been set up in Chittagong division.[2] After this date the number of societies increased rapidly.[3]

The Brahmo Samaj, a creed by its nature attractive only to the new intelligentsia, had been mainly a Calcutta affair, although for some years it had been entering some of the larger district towns in a hesitant way. In eastern Bengal the Brahmos first organised a branch at Dacca in 1846, at Nasirabad in 1853, Faridpur in 1857, Barisal in 1861 and at Sylhet in 1863.[4] When some of its Calcutta converts moved into the districts, these local samajes expanded considerably. Wherever his duties as a deputy magistrate took Brajsundar Mitra in eastern Bengal he planted a school and a Brahmo Samaj.[5] By the 1870s three hundred men were said to be attending the Samaj's Sunday services in Dacca; another thousand sympathisers, 'nearly all the English-speaking Hindus of Dacca', subscribed to its upkeep. It ran a newspaper, the *Bangha Bandhu*, which had a circulation of 300. So great was the Brahmo impact on Dacca that it provoked the orthodox into founding a rival society, the Hindu Dharma Rakshini Sabha, and the *Hindu Hitaishini*, a rival newspaper, to keep heresy at bay.[6] In Barisal progress was more modest. Here a mere twenty-two families, all high caste and well-educated, were open adherents of the Samaj. In Faridpur, the congregation had at first been limited to just ten of the faithful; by 1875 it had grown to three or four times that number. In Nasirabad only fifty persons openly admitted that they were Brahmos but in fact the Samaj was

---

[1] Return of Scientific and Literary Societies in Bengal, *Report on the Administration of Bengal, 1874–5*, Statistical Returns, C, 1.
[2] Return of Scientific and Literary Societies in Bengal, *Report on the Administration of Bengal, 1880–81* (Calcutta, 1881), pp. ccviii–ccxii. Of the societies in Chittagong division, thirteen were in Noakhali and they were all 'for the improvement of boys'.
[3] See Return of Scientific and Literary societies in Bengal, *Report on the Administration of Bengal, 1885–86* (Calcutta, 1886), Statistical Returns, C, 1.
[4] S. Sastri, *History of the Brahmo Samaj* (Calcutta, 1912), II, 549.
[5] Sinha, *Nineteenth Century Bengal*, p. 86.
[6] *SAB*, v, 58, 117.

'attended by most of the educated natives of the town', and there were another five branches in the smaller towns of Mymensingh district. To these branches the Samaj regularly sent missionaries from Calcutta.[1] Brahmos in Dacca were generally drawn from 'the most respectable families, such as Brahmans, Baidyas, Kayasths', and the Samaj was 'essentially a town sect'; and 'many students who are, if anything, Brahmas when at College, become good Hindus when they return to their country homes'.[2] 'The chief strength of the Brahmo Samaj', according to the ethnographer of eastern Bengal, lay 'in the ranks of the Kayaths, and every Kayath boy attending the Government College becomes a member of this new sect', but he exaggerated in asserting that 'there is reason for anticipating that the whole caste will soon become Brahmos'.[3]

The progress of the Samaj illustrates the social transformation in the districts of Bengal. It also shows how educated Bengalis who were moving outside their own province took with them their new political and religious interests. By 1872 the Samaj had a branch in Gaya and all its members were Bengalis.[4] In Balasore, a district of Orissa, most of the wealthy landlords and most of the higher government servants were Bengalis. However long these landlords had been settled in Orissa, they still continued to live in Calcutta or frequently to visit it, and the small branch Samaj at Balasore, founded in 1869, drew support mainly from the Bengali officials.[5] Cuttack had two branches, founded in 1858 and 1869, and both were run by Bengalis. The older Samaj made no effort to reach the local people, but the newer Samaj conducted services in Oriya and printed a monthly paper in that language.[6] Again, government officials in Chota Nagpur were mainly Bengalis, and the two Samajes there were manned by them.[7]

The British Indian Association had its headquarters in Calcutta, where many of the wealthiest zemindars lived as absentees. At first it showed some interest in forging links with the mofussil; by 1854 it was connected with the Rangpur Landlords' Association and the Indigo Planters' Association.[8] In

[1] *SAB*, v, 197–8, 289, 409–10. [2] *Ibid.* v, 58.
[3] Wise, 'Notes on...Eastern Bengal', pp. 315–16. [4] *SAB*, xii, 41.
[5] *SAB*, xviii, 268, 278. [6] *Ibid.* xviii, 78–9. [7] *Ibid.* xvi, 65.
[8] Third Annual Report of the British Indian Association for the year 1854, p. 17. BIA.

1860 a branch was set up in Sibpur, a suburb of Howrah; in 1862 another at Hooghly and another at Barasat.[1] But by 1870, of the Association's five branches Mymensingh alone showed any life.[2] Yet there was plenty of vitality which the Association could have tapped. In the same year there was a spontaneous outburst of feeling in the districts against the government resolution to cut down state aid to English education. Seventeen Bengal districts sent delegates to the protest meeting in Calcutta organised by the British Indian Association. Forty-seven local meetings were held in support. Rajnarain Bose, once a Hindu College radical, but now more conservative both in religion and politics, urged the Association to seize the chance of building up a body of political workers in the mofussil and to establish district associations under its wing.[3] A circular was issued to this effect,[4] and two years later five district associations were in existence. But they did not make contact with Calcutta.

The British Indian Association had failed to take its opportunity. Furthermore it was losing its appeal. In its early days Hindu College boys had played a leading part in the Association, and after the Mutiny it was still able to attract some of the first graduates of Calcutta University, lawyers and other professional men. Grish Chandra Ghosh, a pioneer journalist, Womesh Chandra Bonnerjee, the first president of the Indian National Congress, Sambhu Chandra Mukherjee, Romesh Chandra Dutt, and Bankim Chandra Chatterjee had become members between 1857 and 1863.[5] In 1867 Manmohan Ghose on his return from England joined the Association to urge it to take a more forceful

---

[1] Ninth Annual Report of the British Indian Association for the year 1860, p. 28; Report for 1862, Eleventh Annual General Meeting of the British Indian Association, 31 January 1863, p. 7; Half-yearly General Meeting of the British Indian Association, 31 December 1862. BIA.

[2] Eighteenth Annual General Meeting of the British Indian Association, 31 March 1870. BIA.

[3] General Meeting of the British Indian Association, 22 September 1870, pp. 5–7. BIA.

[4] See Jotendra Mohan Tagore, Honorary Secretary, British Indian Association to Organisers of District Meetings, circular letter, 1 August 1870, *ibid.* p. 20. BIA.

[5] See Monthly General Meeting of the British Indian Association, 31 December 1859; Monthly General Meeting of the British Indian Association, 26 July 1861; Monthly General Meeting of the British Indian Association, 2 October 1861; Half-yearly General Meeting of the British Indian Association, 29 July 1863; Half-yearly General Meeting of the British Indian Association, 27 July 1864. BIA.

line on the civil service question.[1] But by the 1870s it was becoming clear that Calcutta's new intelligentsia had little time for this unenterprising association. Its membership had always been small. Between 1851 and 1879 about 170 new members had been recruited.[2] After 1879 the trickle ran dry. The Association was an old man's affair. It was controlled by oligarchs, the Debs, the Tagores and the Laws. Digambar Mitra, Raja Narendra Krishna Deb, Joykissen Mukherjee and Ramnath Tagore —young men in the 1830s—had lost any radicalism they ever had under the weight of honours and titles. Young graduates were discouraged by the fifty rupees annual subscription.

When Sisir Kumar Ghose called for reform,[3] he spoke for the many persons in Bengal, both in Calcutta and up country, who found no outlet in the Association for their growing political energies. A correspondent from Dacca suggested reducing the subscription to five or ten rupees to win a larger membership. People in Dacca, he reported, would gladly join, and the British Indian Association should organise a branch there and in every other large town of Bengal.[4] Since Dacca contained few large estates, it had few absentee zemindars in Calcutta to represent the district in the British Indian Association. The higher castes were very numerous, and their need to supplement incomes from the land had encouraged a remarkable growth of English education. In the district capital, a town of about 70,000 persons in 1870, there were a government college, a high school, and aided English schools with more than 2,400 pupils. Besides large numbers of teachers, there were over a hundred pleaders at the local bar, and the town of Dacca also had an active Brahmo Samaj and eight newspapers with a combined circulation of more than 2,300.[5] Here was a vigorous locus of political interest, but being remote from Calcutta it needed an effective lead from the metropolis. The British Indian Association did not provide it.

Although they attacked it for many reasons,[6] the critics of

---

[1] General Meeting of the British Indian Association, 18 September 1867. BIA.

[2] See appendix 4 on Membership of the British Indian Association, below, pp. 364–5.

[3] *Amrita Bazar Patrika*, 6 July 1870.

[4] Letter to editor from unnamed Dacca correspondent, *ibid.* 25 December 1870.   [5] *SAB*, v, 74, 98, 106, 117–18, 136–7.

[6] *Amrita Bazar Patrika*, 6 and 28 July 1870.

the Association could as yet see no satisfactory alternative to supporting it. Any effective political organisation had to have headquarters in Calcutta. Money was needed for politics and the zemindars controlled the purse strings.[1] So in 1870 when the Association had finally nerved itself to approach the districts, Sisir Kumar Ghose felt he must support this uncharacteristic initiative. 'Notwithstanding the ill-feelings that even some of our intelligent countrymen bear to that body, the best we can do at present', he told his readers, 'is to give it our best support.' The patriotic thing to do was to join the Association, 'and try and control and improve it'. By affiliating district bodies to the British Indian Association, Ghose hoped to make it 'the paramount power in the state', and to control its present leaders who 'wish to lead their countrymen by the nose'.[2] The branch associations would inject educated men from the districts into the central committee of the Association; 'this done, the zemindars will be a minority and the Association, by a simple natural process, shall be popularised'.[3]

But these plans came to nothing. The British Indian Association would not reform itself, and its critics did not succeed in capturing its central committee. By this time, the members of the Association were more anxious than ever to concentrate upon the struggle to protect landed interests, in particular their own. It was hardly the moment to admit men who might think there was something to be said on the other side. Their rent rolls were no longer keeping abreast of their numbers; and in eastern Bengal where the cultivation of jute had increased the raiyats' prosperity, the peasantry were showing a new spirit. In some districts they combined to refuse payment of rents. In 1873 they rioted against the zemindars in Pabna.[4] In Chittagong, for example, the commissioner warned that 'A great change has of late years passed over the peasantry in this division as well as over those in other parts of Lower Bengal: increased prosperity among members of the agricultural classes has brought with it a sense of their importance, and a wish to throw off all old feelings of feudal attachment and set up their

---

[1] *Amrita Bazar Patrika*, 15 December 1870.
[2] *Ibid.* 10 November 1870.   [3] *Ibid.* 15 December 1870.
[4] *Report of the Land Revenue Commission Bengal*, 1, 20–6. Pabna district contained a far larger concentration of bhadralok than any other district in Rajshahi.

own interests in opposition to those of their landlords, a course
in which they believe they have the support and sympathy of
Government.'[1] 'The ryots have learnt', another Bengal civilian
reported in 1879, 'how great is their power and are ready at the
slightest pretext to form a combination.'[2]

Far from planning to assist the zemindars in disciplining the
tenantry, the government was at last waking up to its responsi-
bilities. The 1859 Tenancy Act attempted to clarify the relations
between landlords and tenants. It recognised the rights of
occupancy raiyats and defined the right of occupancy as twelve
years' continuous possession of the land. While laying down
that rent must be fair and equitable, it also accepted the
zemindar's right to enhance it in certain circumstances. The
Act proved to be unworkable. There had never been a detailed
survey of the land under permanent settlement in Bengal, and
in the absence of village records the raiyats had great difficulty
in proving possession, and the landlords in justifying enhance-
ments. These efforts to curb their powers alarmed the zemindars. While their share of rents was being crimped, their
prescriptive rights were being sapped. There was worse to come
in 1870, when Argyll ruled that they could be obliged to pay
land cesses for local improvements. Hitherto incomes from land
had been immune from tax; it now seemed as though the uncovenanted mercies of the Permanent Settlement were being
revoked.

The British Indian Association devoted what energies it
possessed to denouncing these outrages. In 1871 Joykissen
Mukherjee, zemindar of Uttarpara, declared that these cesses
violated the Permanent Settlement. Reminding the Association
that 'nothing important in this age can be achieved without
agitation' he urged it to 'agitate! Agitate!! Agitate!!!'.[3] Other
zemindars tried to persuade the world that in their grinding
poverty they could ill-afford the new cesses.[4] The public meet-

---

[1] Annual General Report, 1874–5, dated 21 July 1875, Chittagong Division,
Bengal General and Miscellaneous Proceedings, August 1875, vol. 159.

[2] Annual General Report 1877–8, dated 1 July 1879, Rajshahi and Cooch
Behar Division, *ibid.* September 1879, vol. 1306.

[3] Nineteenth Annual General Meeting of the British Indian Association,
24 February 1871, pp. 12–13. BIA.

[4] See speeches of Digambar Mitra, who, while admitting that some zemindars had handsome incomes, somehow calculated that the average from
each permanently settled estate in Bengal was just Rs 35, and of Rajendra Lal

ing of landholders summoned by the Association on 3 April 1871 did not make these pleas more plausible. About one hundred and sixty of the leading zemindars of Bengal in person or by proxy met amid much pomp and circumstance to protest their indigence.[1] The Association petitioned both houses of parliament about its troubles;[2] failing to find satisfaction there, it tried the Secretary of State again in 1872.[3] The Pabna riots were another bad blow. Government immediately rushed through an Agrarian Disputes Act and set up a Commission of Inquiry which the zemindars feared would lead to another dose of tenancy legislation. On behalf of the Association, Raja Narendra Krishna Deb and Joykissen Mukherjee accused the Bengal authorities of having fomented the disturbances, and they spoke gloomily about the impending agrarian catastrophe.[4] For the next few years the Association was to spend its time in discussing ways and means of bolstering the zemindars' powers of collecting rents and of persuading government to help them.[5] Its preoccupation with landed interests endangered its public position, forcing it to try and refute the insinuation that it 'represented only the interests of the zemindars or landholders and not of the entire community'.[6] But the history of the next five years showed how implausible this refutation really was.

The glaring self-interest of the British Indian Association helped to bring a number of rival associations into being in Calcutta. Plans for a more dynamic body were commonplace among those who had studied in England. There they had

Mitra who said that not more than 5,000 of the zemindaris were really valuable. *Ibid.* pp. 13–14. BIA.

[1] Report of the Native Meeting on the Permanent Settlement Question, 3 April 1871. BIA.

[2] Quarterly General Meeting of the British Indian Association, 7 June 1871, p. 4. BIA.

[3] Quarterly General Meeting of the British Indian Association, 30 September 1872, p. 1. BIA.

[4] Half-yearly Meeting of the British Indian Association, 20 September 1873. BIA. Some of their fears were coming true. In 1879 the Commission of Inquiry recommended a complete revision of tenancy law; and from this recommendation came the Bengal Tenancy Act of 1885. For a brief retrospective survey of Bengal tenancy legislation, see *Report of the Land Revenue Commission Bengal*, I, 17–30.

[5] See Twenty-second Annual General Meeting of the British Indian Association, 7 April 1874; Twenty-third Annual General Meeting of the British Indian Association, 30 April 1875. BIA.

[6] Speech by Uday Chand Dutt, Twenty-fourth Annual General Meeting of the British Indian Association, 29 April 1876, p. 16. BIA.

watched the development of political organisation. Manmohan Ghose and Womesh Chandra Bonnerjee had experimented with politics in the London Indian Society and in the East India Association, and they had heard Dadabhai lecture about the duties of local associations in India.[1] In Bengal also there were various projects in the air. In 1860 Vidyasagar was thinking of a Bengal association,[2] and Sisir, with his brother Hementa Kumar Ghose, in 1872 formed district organisations which palpably needed a Calcutta headquarters to direct them.[3] In Calcutta two groups were maturing plans for a new association with countrywide branches. One was led by Sisir Kumar Ghose, and the other by Ananda Mohan Bose and Surendranath Banerjea.[4] Sisir acted first. He formed the Indian League while the others were still talking over their plans.[5]

The Indian League was intended as a deliberate challenge to the British Indian Association. 'Let these two associations vie with each other to do good to the country', Ghose urged in the columns of the *Amrita Bazar Patrika*.[6] The League's low annual subscription of five rupees was intended to attract a new kind of member,[7] since it hoped to represent not only 'the middle classes' but the masses also;[8] to 'stimulate the sense of nationalism among the people'; and to encourage political education.[9] In the past, religion had been the only bond of unity in India, but now 'another sort of unity is just becoming possible, and

---

[1] See chapter 6, below, pp. 246–7.
[2] Banerjea, *A Nation in Making*, p. 41; *Amrita Bazar Patrika*, 15 December 1870.
[3] 'Wayfarer' (pseud.), *Life of Shishir Kumar Ghosh* (Calcutta, n.d. ?1946), pp. 44–6.
[4] H. C. Sarkar, *A Life of Ananda Mohan Bose* (Calcutta, 1910), pp. 54–5; S. Sastri, *Men I have Seen. Being the Author's Personal Reminiscences of Seven Great Bengalis* (Calcutta, 1919), p. 70.
[5] Sisir admitted the League had been formed by a sort of coup. (*Amrita Bazar Patrika*, 30 September 1875.)
[6] *Amrita Bazar Patrika*, 30 September 1875. The League came out against the British Indian Association in support of Temple's proposal to give Calcutta municipality an elective system. The League hoped the scheme would open the municipality to the intelligentsia. Rival meetings were held, one in the rooms of the British Indian Association, where a mere 200 to 300 attended, consisting mainly of 'richer classes and Europeans'. The other, convened by the League at the Town Hall, attracted more than 2000 people. (*Ibid.* 17 February 1876.)
[7] *Ibid.* 4 November 1875.   [8] *Ibid.* 17 February 1876.
[9] *Sadharani*, 17 August 1875, quoted in J. C. Bagal, *History of the Indian Association 1876–1951* (Calcutta, n.d. ?1953), pp. 7–8.

that is national or political unity. The Mohammedans and Hindus, Mahrattas and Bengalees are just learning to sympathise with each other.'[1] Steered by lawyers, journalists and teachers, the League was clearly meant for the English educated—the class in Bengal that was forced to depend on 'keranship, teachership and pleadership' by the fact that the profits of the land went to the zemindars, the profits of government went to the British and 'trade is the business of foreigners and the half-civilised low caste men among our countrymen'.[2] Its president was Sambhu Chandra Mukherjee, editor of *Mooker-jee's Magazine*, and the secretary was Kalimohan Das, a pleader in the Calcutta high court. Sisir Kumar Ghose was the assistant secretary.

Yet within a year of its foundation, the League had been superseded by the Indian Association. This body echoed the argument that there was no political society in Bengal which represented 'the middle classes and the ryots'.[3] It would take in hand 'the education of the masses', but above all the Association would give the younger generation of the 'middle-class community' a political life of their own 'on a more democratic basis'.[4] Its objects were the same as the Indian League's and it charged the same subscription. Indeed, the League sent a heckler, the Reverend Kalicharan Banerjea, to the inaugural meeting to protest that all the objects of the new association 'were answered by the League already in existence'.[5] As so often in the politics of Bengal, personalities not principles lay behind this duplication of societies. Surendranath and Ananda Mohan had understandably been irritated by the way the *Amrita Bazar* group had stolen a march upon them. Three months after the League had been founded, they resigned their membership, taking with them a number of others including Manmohan Ghose and Nobogopal Mitra.[6] One complaint they made was against the high-handed attitude of the League's

[1] *Amrita Bazar Patrika*, 30 September 1875.
[2] *Ibid.* 6 July 1870.
[3] Speech by Surendranath Banerjea at the Inaugural Meeting of the Indian Association, Albert Hall, Calcutta, 26 July 1876, *Bengalee*, 5 August 1876 (Supplement); also see *ibid.* 29 July 1876.
[4] Banerjea, *A Nation in Making*, p. 40.
[5] Supplement to *Bengalee*, 5 August 1876.
[6] See Majumdar, *History of Political Thought*, p. 493, and Majumdar, *Indian Political Associations*, p. 141.

president, Sambhu Chandra Mukherjee, whom Wilfrid Blunt later described as 'a very superior Hindu'.[1] But before they left they drew up an impressive charge-sheet,[2] so effective that the early members of the Indian Association were 'mostly seceders from the Indian League'.[3] 'The intentions are obviously warlike', the *Amrita Bazar Patrika* realised; '...the new Association to live must feed upon the League or die of starvation'.[4] And feed it did. The League collapsed.

The Indian Association was led, as the *Hindoo Patriot* patronisingly noted, 'by our younger, well-educated country-men'.[5] Of the twenty-six members on its first executive committee, ten possessed degrees from Calcutta and one from Cambridge. Two had tried unsuccessfully to enter the covenanted service. Surendranath had succeeded, but had subsequently been dismissed. There were five editors of newspapers,[6] several pleaders, and a number of teachers including the rector of the Calcutta School and the secretary to Seal's Free College.[7] Of the eighty-five men who sat on the executive committee between 1876 and 1888 the occupations of forty-eight are known, and they are set out in table 42 below.

TABLE 42. *Occupation of committee members of the Indian Association, 1876–88*

Legal Profession: Barristers	5	
Attorneys	5	
Pleaders	16	26
Journalists and editors of newspapers		8
Doctors		1
Priests (Christian)		1
Teachers		2
Secretaries of societies		2
Zemindars		6
Merchants		2

Source: Annual Reports of the Indian Association, 1876–88. IA.

[1] Blunt, *India under Ripon*, p. 106.
[2] *Sadharani*, 2 January 1876.
[3] *Hindoo Patriot*, 31 July 1876.
[4] *Amrita Bazar Patrika*, 3 August 1876.
[5] *Hindoo Patriot*, 31 July 1876.
[6] Joy Govind Shome of the *Indian Christian Herald*, Nobogopal Mitra of the *National Paper*, Khetter Nath Sen of the *Saptahik Samachar*, Ahkoy Chandra Sarkar of the *Sadharani*, and Jogendra Nath Vidyabhoosan of the *Arya Darasana*.   [7] Supplement to *Bengalee*, 5 August 1876.

Of these forty-eight, thirty-one held university degrees.[1] No less than 68 per cent were lawyers. Several were journalists who worked in Calcutta's rapidly expanding native press. The members of the Indian Association were described by Rivers Thompson, the lieutenant-governor of Bengal, as 'landless, comparatively poor, and socially inferior to the older institution'.[2] But the distinction was not sharp. A few members of the committee of the British Indian Association also found places on the executive committee of the Indian Association.[3] Moreover, six out of forty-eight committee members of the Indian Association returned their occupations as 'zemindar'.[4] The Indian Association was a pressure group for graduates and professional men, which claimed to represent the 'middle class'. But it is noticeable that traders, industrialists and, on the whole, landowners of substance were not to be found in it. So it will not do to read into this claim an 'economic interpretation' of the emergence of this group.

With the coming of the Indian Association, students shouted their way into the politics of Bengal which they have continued to enliven. The men who founded the Indian Association had already founded the Students' Association in 1875.[5] Deprived of interest in commerce, influence in local government, and the consolations of high society, the bhadralok of Calcutta were masters only in the schoolroom. Surendranath, professor at the largest school in Calcutta, became the uncrowned king of the students and he could always ensure an impressive turn-out of youths at the Indian Association's public meetings. In the

[1] *University Degrees of Committee Members of the Indian Association*

19 M.A.s	} Calcutta University	1 D.L.
12 B.L.s		1 B.A. (Cantab.)
5 B.A.s		

Source: Annual Reports of the Indian Association, 1876–88. IA.

[2] Rivers Thompson to Dufferin, 15 July 1885, DP 48 (Reel 528).

[3] Among them were Raja Rajendra Narain Deb, who was president of the Indian Association in 1886–7, Nawab Mohammed Ali, a Muslim zemindar, Guru Das Banerjee, a pleader and later judge of the high court, Raja Promonath Rai Bahadur, another zemindar, and Norendranath Sen, editor of the *Indian Mirror*.

[4] See Annual Reports of the Indian Association, 1876–88. IA., and the records of the British Indian Association, especially the list of committee members in Twenty-ninth Annual General Meeting of the British Indian Association, 29 April 1881, p. 2. BIA.

[5] H. and U. Mukherjee, *The Growth of Nationalism in India* (*1857–1905*) (Calcutta, 1952), pp. 60–3. Ananda Mohan Bose was its president.

summer of 1883, when the Ilbert bill controversy, the Saligram Idol case, and Surendranath's Contempt case all coincided, the student community went into a frenzy of protest, noisy enough to make the editor of the *Englishman* fear for the Raj.[1] They held protest meetings, threw stones at Europeans, and generally followed Surendranath's injunction that they should agitate if he were sent to prison.[2] Rivers Thompson regretted that a man 'who talks "of shaking India to its foundations", and told the Bailiff... that he would "yet be a Dictator"', should be so popular an instructor of the rising generation in Bengal.'[3] Students were in the van in the mofussil districts as well, which reported that the schoolboys were doing everything that their city cousins had done for their 'patron saint', Surendranath.[4] A year later the collector of Bankura complained that 'the younger class of natives here, and more specially the boys in the schools, evince more interest on political subjects than is good for them...'[5] It was fashionable to deride this student activity, but Henry Cotton, the commissioner of Chittagong, where there was a concentration of high caste Hindus, reminded his fellow officials that 'the current of public opinion among the educated natives of Bengal is in this division, as well as elsewhere, largely swayed by the views held by the student class, and often even by boys still at school'.[6]

The constitution of the Indian Association was more democratic than that of the older organisation. More attention was paid to the election of officers and to majority votes. Although this was little more than a gesture, it did reflect an awareness that oligarchic control was out of place in a supposedly

[1] '...we are on the eve of a crisis which will try the power of the British Government in a way in which it has not been tried since the Mutiny of 1857.' J. Farrell to Rivers Thompson, 12 May 1883, enclosed in Thompson to Ripon, 16 May 1883, RP, Add. MSS 43594.

[2] See Rivers Thompson to Ripon, 10 May 1883, enclosing H. L. Harrison to Thompson, 8 May 1883; also Rivers Thompson to Ripon, 16 May 1883, and 29 May 1883, enclosing Harrison to Thompson, 21 May 1883, RP, Add. MSS 43594.

[3] Rivers Thompson to Ripon, 12 May 1883, RP, Add. MSS 43594.

[4] See Annual General Report, Chittagong, Burdwan, Presidency and Rajshahi Divisions, 1883–4, Bengal General and Miscellaneous Proceedings 1884, vol. 2226.

[5] Annual General Report, Burdwan Division, 1884–5, dated 3 July 1885, *ibid.* September 1885, vol. 2476.

[6] Annual General Report, Chittagong Division, 1883–4, dated 26 June 1884, *ibid.* August 1884, vol. 2226.

popular organisation.[1] Even the British Indian Association was moved by this current of opinion; in 1879 Rajendra Lal Mitra suggested the time had come to give the younger members a chance to lend a hand in running its affairs. Of the founding fathers only Joykissen Mukherjee, Peary Chandra Mitra and he himself now remained. Moving an amendment to the rule about the election of officers,[2] he said that the original intention had been to elect officers annually at the general meeting 'but the practice had come to be different and the incumbents of these offices had been converted into fixtures until they were removed by death'. Indeed the first president had held the office for eighteen years. By electing its officers 'after the manner of similar institutions elsewhere', Mitra hoped to put new life into the Association, recapture the initiative in Bengal politics, and secure 'wider co-operation'. He told its members that broad acres, long purses, and distinguished pedigrees ought not confer a right to office in it.[3] Two years later, as the newly elected president, he returned to the theme. When the Association had been founded, 'a patriarchal system was then best for its welfare'; now the time had come for a change.[4] Members at last agreed, and the principle of election to office was introduced, tacking a veneer of democratic form on to the most conservative society in Bengal.

For all its propaganda about enlisting the people, the Indian Association had few members and little money. Its first annual report proudly announced that, having begun with only seventy 'we now count on our rolls upwards of two hundred members ...[excluding] the members of the different branch associations'.[5] This compared well with the membership of the British Indian Association and included many graduates who

[1] The Sadharan Brahmo Samaj of 1878 had seen the need for a constitution which would prevent a repetition of Keshub Chandra Sen's autocratic regime. Ananda Mohan Bose, who drew up the Samaj's new rules, was also secretary of the Indian Association.

[2] As amended, rule 25 (*d*) laid down that 'No person who has held office of President or Vice-President during the preceding year shall be eligible for re-election until after the lapse of one year'. The Rules of the British Indian Association 1879, p. 5. BIA.

[3] Twenty-seventh Annual General Meeting of the British Indian Association, 7 June 1879, pp. 1–3. BIA.

[4] Speech by the president-elect, Twenty-ninth Annual General Meeting of the British Indian Association, 29 April 1881, p. 15. BIA.

[5] First Annual Report of the Indian Association, 1876–7, p. i. IA.

had found work in Calcutta. But after this initial fanfare the reports lapsed into discreet silence, which suggests that there was no expansion worth reporting.[1] Moreover, the Indian Association had only one-tenth of the income of its rival.[2] The zemindars were naturally reluctant to support their critics,[3] and attempts to raise funds from a wider but poorer field did not have much success. In 1883 the committee reported that 'by the painful experience of nearly eight years...it often found itself powerless to act from want of funds...'[4]

[1] Some idea of the size of the membership can be had from the subscription figures. These were:

Subscriptions to the Indian Association

	Rs				Rs		
1880	1140	4	0	1884	776	10	0
1881	736	8	0	1885	948	0	0
1882	1653	14	6	1886–7	1502	12	0
1883	1282	8	0	1887–8	1142	8	0

Source: Abstract of the Accounts of the General Fund of the Association, Annual Reports of the Indian Association, 1880–8. IA. The membership cost five rupees a year when the Association was formed. By 1883 the minimum subscription was two rupees, and one rupee for *bona fide* 'tillers of the soil'. The subscriptions for 1886–7 are for eighteen months. These figures hint that the membership was never large, even by contemporary standards, and at no time was there a marked rise. There may have been a modest expansion after 1883–4, if it is assumed that most members paid the new *minimum* subscription.

[2] *Receipts of the Indian Association 1880–8*

		General fund			Special fund			Building fund		
1880	Rs	1,645	4	0	4,820	0	0	—		
1881		1,395	1	0	739	0	0	—		
1882		2,749	3	6	831	0	0	2,468	12	0
1883		1,827	13	0	100	0	0	200	0	0
1884		778	10	0	—			—		
1885		missing								
1886–7 (June)		2,650	14	0	822	0	0	759	1	6
1887–8		1,677	8	6	1,193	2	5	15,187	6	4

Source: Abstract of Accounts, Annual Reports of the Indian Association. 1880–8. IA.

[3] Exceptions to this were donations of Rs 15,000 from the Maharaja of Vizianagram (1887–8), Rs 500 from the Maharaja of Dumraon (1886–7) and Rs 2,000 from the Maharani Svarnamayi of Cossimbazar (1882) to the building fund.
[4] Seventh Annual Report of the Indian Association, 1883, p. 5. IA.

The Indian Association did however step outside Calcutta, and brushed against the growing political consciousness of the district towns and expatriate Bengali communities. It planned a network of branches covering all Bengal and even extending to the rest of India. The Association would not 'confine its efforts to Calcutta'; it regarded 'the deputation of delegates to different parts of the country in connection with the objects of the Association as one of the most important features in the programme of its work'.[1] In 1876 Surendranath went on tour, and in 1879 agents were again on their travels around Bengal trying to establish new branches and to affiliate existing associations.[2] In 1881 and 1882 Banerjea, Kali Sunkur Sukul, Krishna Kumar Mitra, Dwarkanath Ganguli and Dwarkanath Ghose continued this work,[3] and a sub-committee to organise the mofussil was formed.[4] In 1883 the heat generated by the excitements in Calcutta warmed the districts into life. From Presidency division came the report that 'the educated classes... are becoming more and more ambitious and have commenced to take a great deal of interest in political questions'. In Burdwan, 'pretentious "People's Associations" and the like...are springing up on all sides'. Even in Rajshahi the educated class, 'infinitesimally small' though it might be, was taking a keen interest in politics. Everywhere the role of emissaries from Calcutta stirring the localities into action and collecting money for the National Fund was noticed and deplored.[5] In 1884, with forty-four branches in being, the Indian Association considered how to achieve 'more systematic action in the matter of establishing Branch and Affiliated Associations'.[6] The following year it announced 'an elaborate scheme of village organisations', and of the twenty-six new branches formed that year, half were

[1] Third Annual Report of the Indian Association, 1878–9, p. 14. IA. Dwarkanath Ganguli and Dwarkanath Ghose went to Bogra and Jalpaiguri, while Surendranath went to Dacca, Berhampore and Krishnagar and again to the North-western Provinces and the Punjab.

[2] See First Annual Report of the Indian Association, 1876–7; Third Annual Report of the Indian Association, 1878–9, pp. 11–14. IA.

[3] Fifth Annual Report of the Indian Association, 1881, pp. 5–11. IA.

[4] Sixth Annual Report of the Indian Association, 1882, pp. 2–6. IA.

[5] Annual General Report, Presidency, Burdwan and Rajshahi Divisions, 1883–4, Bengal General and Miscellaneous Proceedings, October to November 1884, vol. 2226. Also see Seventh Annual Report of the Indian Association, 1883. IA.

[6] Eighth Annual Report of the Indian Association, 1884, p. 5. IA.

village unions under the new scheme.[1] The growth in the number of branches is set out in table 43.

TABLE 43. *Branch associations of the Indian Association, 1876–88*

1876–7	10	1883	39
1878–9	15	1884	44
1879–80	17	1885	80
1880–1	29	1886–7	110
1881–2	30	1887–8	124

Source: Lists of Branch Associations, Annual Reports of the Indian Association, 1876–88. IA.

Within the Presidency, there were by 1888 two branches in Burdwan, one in Bankura, two in Birbhum, twenty-nine in Midnapore, seven in Hooghly, four in Howrah, seven in Twenty-four Parganas, eight in Nadia, four in Jessore, four in Khulna, one in Murshidabad, one in Rajshahi, one in Rangpur, two in Bogra, thirty in Pabna, eight in Faridpur, one in Backergunge, and three in Mymensingh. The large number of branches in Midnapore and Pabna was due to the village unions established in those districts.[2] Outside the Presidency, the Association had branches in Lahore, Ferozepore, Allahabad, and three in Assam. In 1876 and again in 1879, Surendranath had visited the North-western Provinces and the Punjab, and on both occasions he was welcomed by Bengalis eager to be affiliated to a Calcutta organisation.

The Indian Association had a programme to rouse the districts. Until 1879 its main item was the agitation to change the regulations about entry into the civil service, and Surendranath's tours round India were designed to push forward this demand. From 1879 the demand for local self-government was added to the programme. In 1880 a circular was posted to all the district towns inviting them to join the Association in petitioning for an elective system in the municipalities.[3] The

[1] Ninth Annual Report of the Indian Association, 1885, p. 2. IA.
[2] See Twelfth Report of the Indian Association, 1887–8, pp. 7–11. IA. It is curious that neither Dacca nor Chittagong, the two main towns of eastern Bengal, had a branch. In all of eastern Bengal there were only twelve branches.
[3] It is an interesting comment on the rise in standing of the local bars that this circular was sent, in those district towns where the name of the political society was not known, 'to the members of the Bar'. Fourth Annual Report of the Indian Association, 1879–80, pp. 5–6. IA.

following year's tours were aimed primarily at stirring up this demand.[1] In 1882 the Association's emissaries helped to organise a number of local meetings which called for elected district boards and municipalities,[2] and in the following February there was some show of support from the mofussil when the Association again ventilated the question in Calcutta. In 1884, when new local government rules came into force in Bengal, the Indian Association urged the educated community in the districts to take part in the elections and to press, wherever possible, for a non-official chairman.[3]

The third and most daring item in the programme was peasant right, and it was this that caused the breach with the British Indian Association. For a while the two associations had tolerated each other. Preferring Surendranath's organisation to the League started by the *Amrita Bazar Patrika*, the British Indian Association was prepared to stomach it as a junior partner in the agitation against Lytton's measures. But from its inception the Indian Association justified its existence by claiming to be the tribune of the peasants. Of course there was something bizarre in so unmistakably urban a group masquerading as the voice of the raiyats. But once the government began to make a determined effort to do something for the tenant, Indian politicians were open to the most damaging of all arguments—that whereas the Guardians protected the interests of the masses, they protected no one but themselves, particularly since the leading association was fighting tooth and claw against any concessions to the peasantry.[4] By giving their propaganda a populist, even *narodniki*, slant, the Indian Association hoped to disarm such criticism, and win the credentials necessary for a hearing at Government House. At the same time this gave it a handy weapon in the battle for leadership with the British Indian Association. In this way the

[1] Fifth Annual Report of the Indian Association, 1881, pp. 10–11. IA.
[2] Sixth Annual Report of the Indian Association, 1882, p. 2. IA.
[3] Eighth Annual Report of the Indian Association, 1884, pp. 2–5. IA.
[4] A good example of this favourite argument was given when Dufferin came to contemplate the reform of the Legislative Councils: '...a good deal of our legislation is undertaken in the interests of the uneducated and unrepresented masses, to the prejudice of those classes from whom the amplified Council would be recruited. For instance, we should have had to pass the Bengal Rent Bill of last year over the heads of say a dozen instead of three native Members', Dufferin to Kimberley, 26 April 1886, DP 19 (Reel 517).

young politicians of Calcutta could build up a position of great tactical strength in their dealings with the older leaders, who were patricians first and patriots afterwards.

The Association reduced its subscription to attract raiyats, village headmen, and tillers of the soil.[1] It surveyed the effects of the proposed changes in the rent law, and in 1876 it circulated a questionnaire about them to the branch associations. Its first annual report spoke of 'the vast agricultural community of Bengal [as] constituting the basis and foundation of the whole social fabric'.[2] In 1880 it announced that

the zamindars have commenced a systematic agitation in opposition to the Rent Bill...which seeks to confer a substantial boon on the peasantry of the land...The zamindars have influential organs in the press; they have an influential Association to represent their views. The ryots are practically unrepresented and this Association has undertaken the solemn duty of making known their wants and grievances...[3]

But it was easier to pass resolutions than to tramp the villages. The Association had to make the most of meagre resources.[4] In 1881 its agents tried to discover the views of the raiyats on the draft Rent bill; meetings of 'thousands of ryots' were held in spite of opposition by the zemindars. 'In these meetings', the report claimed, 'the ryots freely expressed their grievances and evinced considerable interest in the work of the Association.'[5] A commentary on the draft bill, based on these investigations, was submitted to government. Indeed, so enthusiastic were its efforts on behalf of the peasants that in 1882 the Association felt it had to refute the charge that it was 'sectional in its character, being simply a ryots' association'.[6] In 1884 it

[1] It was reduced from Rs 5 to Rs 1.
[2] Appendix D, First Annual Report of the Indian Association, 1876–7, p. 52. IA.
[3] Fourth Annual Report of the Indian Association, 1879–80, pp. 7–8. IA.
[4] 'Kalisunker Sookhul and Kristo Commar Mitter were deputed as agents of the Association, and they took part...in the great demonstration in favour of the ryots that took place at Kissengunge, and it was the first of its kind.' Rangolal Mukherjee was another volunteer; through his efforts 'a large meeting of representatives was held [in]...Shamnagore, where no less than 1000 ryots were gathered. Another meeting was held at Beerbhoom', Fourth Annual Report of the Indian Association, 1879–80, pp. 7–9. IA.
[5] Fifth Annual Report of the Indian Association, 1881, pp. 1–2. IA.
[6] Seventh Annual Report of the Indian Association, 1883, p. 10. IA.

raised its voice against the revised draft of the bill;[1] in 1885 it held a series of 'mass meetings', sometimes of more than three thousand raiyats,[2] to support the bill in its last stages.

In 1885 the Tenancy bill finally became law, and now the Indian Association decided to try its credit with the peasantry in another sphere. Mass meetings were advertised to support the demand for representative government.[3] By staging entertainments with song and dance, peasants were attracted to these gatherings. Then some Calcutta politician would interrupt the fun to make a speech, perhaps unintelligible to the raiyats, applauding the virtues of an elective system for the Legislative Councils. Resolutions were proposed, seconded and passed. 'They are very successful adepts at organisation', Rivers Thompson had to admit when reporting to the Viceroy on 'the advanced party'.

They have caught very rapidly the idea of the uses of political platforms in England; and meetings on any question of public notoriety, in which they wish to promote their own opinions, are organized by half-a-dozen wire-pullers in Calcutta, and are represented by sensational posters and large-typed telegrams in the newspapers as the unanimous views of the public-spirited and enthusiastic community. They do not even limit the publicity of their operations to Calcutta and India, but carry the game further by extending the publicity to England.[4]

These more dynamic methods of agitation forced the British Indian Association to retaliate in kind. Zemindars were organised into district committees,[5] a sub-committee was set up to watch the progress of the tenancy legislation,[6] an agent was

1 In it the peasantry had lost some of the rights secured in the previous draft of the bill; Eighth Annual Report of the Indian Association, 1884, p. 4. IA.
2 Ninth Annual Report of the Indian Association, 1885, p. 3. IA.
3 The Viceroy described the new technique: 'In order to collect a crowd, various kinds of popular entertainments are organised, and the affair is really what is called here a "tamasha" or jollification; and although I imagine the numbers of these assemblies are not very numerous, the defect is supplied by the invention of bogus reporters, who describe in picturesque language the incidents of meetings which were never held at places which do not exist', Dufferin to Kimberley, 21 March 1886, DP 19 (Reel 517).
4 Memorandum, 14 July 1885, enclosed in Rivers Thompson to Dufferin, 15 July 1885, DP 48 (Reel 528).
5 Report for 1880, Twenty-ninth Annual General Meeting British Indian Association, 29 April 1881, p. 9. BIA.
6 At a General Meeting of the British Indian Association, 22 December 1882, a Central Committee of Landholders was set up to 'watch the

appointed in London,[1] and a fund of more than Rs 50,000 was raised to finance this activity.[2] Men were deputed to the districts to rally support,[3] and the tenants themselves were cajoled into counter-demonstrations against the Tenancy bill.[4] The Indian Association's efforts to rally the peasantry so angered the zemindars that the British Indian Association refused to join the general agitation of 1883,[5] and the *Hindoo Patriot* advised its readers to shun the Indian Association's National Fund and National Conference of 1883.[6] This move lost the zemindars popularity in Calcutta.[7] In 1885 the lieutenant-governor observed the gulf between the associations. The men of the Indian Association, notorious for 'their activity and ability, and the forwardness of their political aspirations, have quite distanced the older and very conservative associations with whom Government has hitherto had to deal...For the present there is no love lost between the older and more modern schools. The Bengal Tenancy Bill strongly marked the line of distinction between them...'[8] This is why the British Indian Association now tried to hold its position by co-operating in the National

progress of the Rent Bill'; at its second meeting, 11 April 1883, a sub-committee was appointed; Manuscript Minute Book, 1882–8, of the Proceedings of the Sub-committee to watch the progress of the Rent bill [subsequently referred to as B.I. MSS Minute Book, 1]. BIA.

[1] Eleventh meeting of the sub-committee, 17 August 1883; Lethbridge was retained as the London agent on £300 per annum, with £100 expenses; B.I. MSS Minute Book, 1. BIA.
[2] The Fund stood at Rs 56,193 on 24 August 1883, B.I. MSS Minute Book, 1. BIA.
[3] See Abstract of proceedings of the Central Committee of Landholders since its formation, 8 September 1883, B.I. MSS Minute Book, 1. BIA.
[4] A letter from Digambar Mullick was received, reporting a 'monster meeting of the ryots of Jessore numbering about 22,000...to protest against the Bengal Tenancy Act', Fiftieth meeting of the sub-committee, 23 June 1885, B.I. MSS Minute Book, 1. BIA.
[5] Describing the excitements that followed Surendranath's imprisonment, the Commissioner of Police reported: '...the British Indian association ostentatiously kept aloof from these meetings altogether; and have deprecated them. They have therefore lost ground with the populace...', Harrison to Rivers Thompson, 21 May 1883, enclosed in Rivers Thompson to Ripon, 29 May 1883, RP, Add. MSS 43594.
[6] *Hindoo Patriot*, 23 July 1883, 13, 20 and 27 August 1883.
[7] They had 'shared the usual fate of moderate parties in times of excitement and have been discredited', Harrison to Rivers Thompson (n.d.), enclosed in Rivers Thompson to Ripon, 17 June 1883, RP, Add. MSS 43594.
[8] Memorandum, 14 July 1885, enclosed in Rivers Thompson to Dufferin, 15 July 1885, DP 48 (Reel 528).

Conference and by helping to stage the Indian National Congress in Calcutta in 1886.[1] But it soon discovered in Congress a new threat. Feeling that the proposed Congress constitution would end its freedom of action,[2] it decided that abstention was preferable to absorption. By 1888 the British Indian Association and the zemindars had been consigned from the van of Bengal politics to the baggage wagons, thus reverting to their role as camp followers of the Raj.[3]

To the rulers of British India, Bombay city seemed a much happier place than Calcutta. 'Really loyal and well-affected' was Northbrook's description of its people,[4] while Lytton's first impression of the Parsis, the leading citizens, was that they were

among the very best of your Majesty's Indian subjects; and I wish that your Majesty had more of them. They are a wonderfully thriving community...I have not yet seen a thin Parsee, and I doubt if I have seen a poor one. They seem to be all fat, rich, and happy. A population engaged in successful industry, and making money rapidly, is always conservative and loyal to the power which protects its purse.[5]

Sir Richard Temple agreed that in western India loyalty was a function of solvency: 'the rapid development of commerce—foreign and domestic—the expansion of industrial activity, the accumulation of capital, all tend to loyalty and goodwill towards Government.'[6] Only in Bombay city would the Guardians allow Indians to volunteer,[7] and when agitators began to fulminate in Calcutta, Dufferin and Cross considered transferring the capital of the Empire to Bombay's more sedate atmosphere. While the Bengalis were a 'malicious and cowardly

[1] See below, chapter 6.
[2] Secretary, British Indian Association, to the General Secretary, National Congress Committee, 6 December 1888. BIA.
[3] Fifteen years later Curzon referred to them as 'most valuable allies'; 'the present territorial aristocracy of this province...in large measure our own creation...is a potent influence on our side', Curzon to Hamilton, 12 February, 1903, Curzon Papers, MSS Eur. F. 111 (162).
[4] Northbrook to Argyll, 29 April and 24 November 1872, Northbrook Papers, MSS Eur. C. 144 (9).
[5] Lytton to the Queen, 14 April 1876, quoted in Balfour, *Personal and Literary Letters*, 11, 7.
[6] Minute by Temple, 31 July 1879, LP (520/3).
[7] And then only the Parsis were proposed for the privilege.

set of people, who do not know what truth means', in Bombay's 'corresponding class, even of the most advanced type' the Viceroy found a 'totally different tone'. Here were 'men of the highest character and intelligence'. Their press was 'moderate, sensible and statesmanlike; an excellent feeling exists between themselves and the English community, as well as the Civil Service'.[1]

One reason for Bombay's apparent political calm was that while the city teemed with societies, most of them were not organised for politics, but were concerned with improving social conditions and reforming religious practices. Rarely crossing religious, caste and linguistic barriers, each of these charities held that reform too, should begin at home. It was among Parsis that associations of this sort were most conspicuous. In 1851 a handful of Parsi graduates, Dadabhai Naoroji, Sorabjee Bengalee, and Naoroji Furdoonjee among them, took the lead in the Rahnumai Mazdayasnan Sabha (Religious Reform Association), to revive 'the social condition of the Parsees and...[to restore] the Zoroastrian religion to its pristine purity'.[2] Challenging the Parsi Panchayet, they reached a wider audience through lectures, public meetings and the columns of the *Rast Goftar*. By providing schools and by raising the age of marriage, they gradually achieved the emancipation of their women.[3] A Parsi Law Association was formed to secure a code of laws appropriate to their community, and its honorary secretaries were Furdoonjee and Bengalee. In 1862 it presented draft codes to a government commission which were embodied in the Parsi Succession Act and the Parsi Marriage and Divorce Act of 1865.[4]

The other important group of graduates amongst whom a

[1] Dufferin to Cross, 23 November 1886, DP 19 (Reel 518). In Calcutta the Ilbert bill strained relations between the races, but in Bombay it created little friction. Even the meeting of the Bombay Chamber of Commerce on the question passed off quietly. (See *Hindoo Patriot*, 7 May 1883 and *Report of the Bombay Chamber of Commerce for the year 1882–83* (Bombay, 1884), pp. 195–6.)
[2] J. N. Farquhar, *Modern Religious Movements in India* (London, 1929), p. 84.
[3] In 1863 Dadabhai organised a society of Parsis who took an oath not to dine without the women of the family at the same table.
[4] Farquhar, *Modern Religious Movements in India*, pp. 81–91; Karaka, *History of the Parsis*, I, 214–79, 300–32; II, 229–37; and R. P. Masani, *Dadabhai Naoroji; the Grand Old Man of India* (London, 1939), pp. 43–51, 61–70, 90–1.

vigorous reform movement developed consisted of Maharashtrian Brahmins who had been attracted into the city. Mahadev Govind Ranade, one of Bombay's first graduates, was among the founders of the Widow Remarriage Association.[1] From 1862 he propagated reforming policies in the English columns of the Anglo-Marathi journal, the *Indu Prakash*, and in 1867 he took the lead in forming the Prarthana Samaj whose members were mainly Maharashtrian Brahmins. Although influenced by the Brahmo Samaj of Bengal, the Prarthana Samaj was not so westernised and always regarded itself as a movement firmly inside Hinduism. K. T. Telang maintained that he was 'first and last a Hindu',[2] and Ranade stressed that 'The peculiar feature of the movement in the Presidency is that we want to work on no single line...and above all not to break with the past and cease all connection with our society. We do not proceed on the religious basis exclusively as in Bengal... We do not desire to give up our hold on the old established institutions.'[3]

Whereas Parsis shared dominance of the city's education with Maharashtrians, they shared its wealth and power with the Gujaratis who were less eager for the new education. With most of them held in firm control by their caste heads, interest in reform among the Gujaratis came from a small body who in 1851 formed the Buddhi Varahak Hindu Sabha (Society for the Advancement of Knowledge). In the early 1860s Karsondas Mulji attacked Gujarati orthodoxy by his exposure of the immoral practices of the Maharajas, the hereditary priests of the Vallabhacharaya sect. But even Mulji opposed radical reform.[4] Of all the communities in the city the Muslim was the

---

1 In 1840 Dadoba Pandurang (1814–82), and his brother Atmaram founded the Paramahans Mandal which advocated widow remarriage and was critical of idolatry and caste. Balshastri Jambhekar (1812–46), one of the first students at Elphinstone Institution, and its first Indian professor, conducted a monthly reform journal, *Digdarshan*, with similar aims, but these movements began to attract support only a quarter of a century later; see A. K. Prioyalkar, *Dadoba Panduranga* [Biography, in Marathi] (Poona, 1947); and G. G. Jambhekar, (ed.), *Memoirs and Writings of Acharya Bal Gangadhar Shastri Jambhekar (1812–1846)* (Poona, 1950), 3 vols.
2 N. V. Naik, 'Telang as a Social Reformer', quoted in C. H. Heimsath, *Indian Nationalism and Hindu Social Reform* (Princeton, New Jersey, 1964), p. 108.
3 R. Ranade (ed.), *The Miscellaneous Writings of the Late Hon'ble Mr Justice M. G. Ranade* (Bombay, 1915), p. 159.
4 Heimsath, *Indian Nationalism and Hindu Social Reform*, pp. 100–5.

most heterogeneous and the slowest to reform. Arabs, Mughals, Konkanis, Memons, Khojas, Cutchis, Deccanis, Bohras and Sulaimanis lived in different mohallas and spoke different languages. Sulaimanis, among whom the Tyabjis were the most prominent, were a well-to-do and adaptable community but they were few in number and despised as Shias by orthodox Muslims. The Anjuman-i-Islam, formed in 1876 by the Tyabjis to remedy the poor educational facilities available for Muslims, represented only 'the educated and thinking portion of the community',[1] and was in no position to establish an exclusive leadership over it. In each community, these reforming societies took the strain, as groups of young educated and professional men began to question the dominance of orthodox religious heads and conservative men of wealth. Despite the relative success of reform among the Parsis, the graduates did not win command of their community. The Maharashtrian graduates did not have the same struggle to control their community in the city, but they faced splits among themselves.

This is not to say that Bombay lacked the rudiments of a political life; but its political alliances tended to cut across communities and were drawn instead along the lines of wealth, education, age and interest. No less than Calcutta, mid-century Bombay possessed wealthy men prepared to dabble in politics and anxious to see their signatures appended to petitions, so long as the proceedings remained respectable. But even the Bombay Association's mild representations to parliament in 1852 and 1853 seemed too outspoken to the more conservative notables, and once it had failed in the cause for which it had been created, the Association was allowed to slump into torpor. The alarms of 1857 did nothing to revive it; during the next decade it showed few signs of life. In 1867 Naoroji Furdoonjee, whose stay in England had shown him the possibilities of political organisation, put it on its feet again.[2] It is characteristic of Bombay that in this work he should have drawn most of his help from Parsis, Gujaratis and Maharashtrians alike. Sorabjee S. Bengalee, another Parsi, had also been a pupil at

[1] Tyabji to Editor, *Times of India*, 8 May 1882.
[2] *Proceedings of a meeting, held on the 14th December 1867...for the purpose of re-establishing the Bombay Association...*(Bombay, 1868). Eighty-seven resident members enrolled.

the Native Education Society's School, and had worked with Furdoonjee on the Parsi Law Association and in the municipality. Nathabhoy Mangaldas was a wealthy seth, with more interest in public affairs than most Gujaratis in the city, while R. G. Bhandarkar, a young Ratnagiri Brahmin graduate, was a brilliant academic example of the immigration from Maharashtra.

But the revived association did not do much. In 1868 it drew up a memorial on the civil service question, and in 1869 a petition demanding simultaneous examinations in India and England. In 1871 it called on Gladstone to reform the Legislative Councils. Twice, in 1871 and in 1873, it sent its secretary, Furdoonjee, to London, raising the money to do so by public subscription. Nearer home, the Association made a stand against some local taxes in 1871; and in 1873 and 1875, it protested against the exemption of European British subjects from the jurisdiction of ordinary criminal courts. Its representations on the Cotton Frauds Act showed that it had ties with the mill-owners, and its modest success in securing amendments to the Bombay Revenue Jurisdiction Act of 1876 lent a pale colour to its claim to be the political spokesman of western India. By the close of 1877, however, the Association had only sixty-six members, and of them only twenty came to the annual general meeting in 1878, held—as the two previous annual meetings had been—in the president's house.[1] In 1879 this languor was strikingly demonstrated. The abolition of the cotton duties was an issue that irked Bombay particularly, but the protest came first from Calcutta. After his efforts to stir 'the people of Bombay into activity' had proved futile, Nanabhoy Byramjee Jeejeebhoy, a Parsi cotton magnate, wrote in disgust to Pherozeshah Mehta: 'Really this undertaking has caused us both considerable vexation...I too was equally annoyed at the apathetic feeling...of our co-operators...I have grown wiser by this fresh experience, and shall take good care before I again join with such whimsical folk to undertake a work of public

[1] See Minutes and Proceedings of the First Annual General Meeting of the Bombay Association together with the report adopted, 26 June 1869; of the Third Annual Meeting, 1871; of the Fourth, 1872; of the Fifth, 1873; and Minutes and Proceedings of the Annual Meetings of the Bombay Association and the Eighth, Ninth and Tenth Annual Reports of the Committee of Management for the years 1875, 1876 and 1877. Also see Majumdar, *Indian Political Associations*, pp. 67–73.

utility.'[1] Calcutta could congratulate itself on having a more active political life than Bombay.

The life of Bombay city was dominated by its commerce, and this set the tone of much of its politics. In Bombay Indians had better business opportunities and more of their energy was engaged in the task of making money.[2] When the Civil War interrupted the flow of American cotton, western India came into its own as a supplier of raw cotton, giving Bombay's commerce a sharp boost. Between 1861 and 1865 'Bombay had a windfall of eighty millions sterling over and above her normal receipts from cotton', and this sparked off a 'gambling saturnalia'.[3] During the boom 'All Bombay and its wife was too busy amassing handsome fortunes...to manage its domestic affairs', wrote Wacha.[4] In the Chamber of Commerce, Indians were much better represented than they were in Calcutta, and after the boom had ended it was this body that did much of the work of the city's specifically political associations. The Chamber agitated against the proposal to abolish the cotton duties and against the Licence Tax.[5] In 1875 when tariff policy and factory legislation seemed to threaten the Bombay textile interests, they formed a Millowners' Association which combined the function of a commercial pressure group with those of a political body.

In Calcutta the expansion of education and the growth of the professions had been important factors in putting life into its political associations. The same impulses began to make themselves felt in Bombay in the decade after the Mutiny when the first graduates left the University. At the same time a thin trickle of students returned from England, and young Indian lawyers, among them Pherozeshah Mehta, Badruddin Tyabji

[1] Jeejeebhoy to Mehta, 26 May 1879. Mehta Papers.
[2] 'Undoubtedly the Bombay natives have a great advantage over those of Calcutta in energy and practical arts. In Calcutta the European is generally predominant in these matters; in Bombay the natives have a much larger share. The mercantile element is very prominent in Bombay, and they supply the energetic traders who push their way all over the coasts of Africa...', Campbell, *Memoirs of My Indian Career*, II, 116.
[3] R. P. Masani, *Evolution of Local Self-Government in Bombay* (London, 1929), p. 172.
[4] D. E. Wacha, *Rise and Growth of Bombay Municipal Government* (Madras, n.d. ?1913), pp. 20–1.
[5] See *Report of the Bombay Chamber of Commerce for the year 1875–76* (Bombay, 1877), pp. 84–5, 183–8; and *Report of the Bombay Chamber of Commerce for the year 1877–78* (Bombay, 1879), pp. 260–303.

and Kashinath Telang began to acquire status and build up practices. But this new intelligentsia was still small enough to enjoy professional opportunities larger than any Bengal could offer; and faced with good options in business, in law, in government service and in native states, they were less ardent in politics. While still a young man, Bal Manghesh Waglé was appointed chief judge in Baroda, and Dadabhai Naoroji, the mentor of the city's graduates, became prime minister of that state in 1874.

Yet their similar education and employment cut across the distinctions of race and community among the new intelligentsia as successfully as wealth had brought the oligarchs of the city together. From the common interests of the new men came the thrust that began to move the city's politics forward. Hitherto, political associations, the municipality and the press had all been controlled by the oligarchs of caste, property and trade, Parsi, Gujarati and Muslim alike. The founding of the Bombay Association had already shown signs of the coming challenge, for among its most active founders were several Elphinstone graduates, including Dadabhai Naoroji. When the Association revived in 1867, it attracted young graduates and lawyers, such as Bhandarkar, Ranade, Mehta, Waglé, Telang and Tyabji, who took their place alongside the notables of wealth and property. They also joined the Bombay branch of the East India Association which Dadabhai organised in 1869. The main target of their assault, however, was the municipality. In 1870 they formed the Ratepayers' Committee and fought energetically to secure a new constitution for the city. The franchise granted in 1872 was heavily weighted in favour of owners of real property and until 1878 was under 4,000, a little over a half per cent of the population. Although such men as Mehta and Tyabji could now stand for election to the Corporation, it was not until the municipal reform Act of 1888 that they got what they wanted. The number of councillors was now increased to seventy-six of whom thirty-six were elected, and the franchise was widened to include ratepayers and the professional classes as well as men of property. The qualifying tax was reduced to thirty rupees a year and all graduates were given the vote at ward elections.[1] This gave Mehta his opportunity. Ever since

[1] See Masani, *Evolution of Local Self-Government in Bombay*; Wacha, *Rise and Growth of Bombay Municipal Government*; H. P. Mody, *Sir Pherozeshah Mehta: A Political Biography* (Bombay, 1921), I, chapters V–XII;

his return from England he had been pressing for changes of this sort; now he could deploy the inter-communal alliance among the intelligentsia as a way of establishing a local predominance.

After 1888 it required a coalition between the politicians of the four communities to win control of the city of Bombay. This meant that a political programme designed around purely communal or sectarian issues was impossible. Successful programmes had to consist of those issues which divided these mixed groups least, they had to be restricted to professional interests, and they had to be moderate. In January 1885, such a coalition had launched the Bombay Presidency Association, which quickly became the spokesman for the interests of the city, a position it owed to the energy of its creators: Mehta, Tyabji and Telang. Through its three sub-committees for revenue, agriculture and finance, for legislation, justice and local self-government, and for politics and administration,[1] the Association was able to scrutinise public affairs in the round. Its leaders ventilated local grievances, advised the Bombay government about municipal affairs and laid before the government of India memorials and telegrams making demands along the familiar lines.[2] The Bombay Presidency Association kept carefully aloof from the people. Its public meetings were infrequent, and they were of a different nature from those in Calcutta, being simply gatherings of more people than could be accommodated in the Association's rooms, mustered to give gentlemanly support to its representations.[3] Most of the Association's members lived in the city, and there were no branches in the mofussil.

So secular and moderate an organisation was unlikely to go deep in its Presidency; but precisely those factors which kept it on the surface of Bombay politics helped to pull it towards similar associations in other Presidency capitals. But for this advantage

H. B. Tyabji, *Badruddin Tyabji* (Bombay, 1952), pp. 37–45, and C. E. Dobbin, 'The Growth of Urban Leadership in Western India, with special reference to Bombay City, 1840–85'. Unpublished D.Phil. thesis, Oxford University, 1967.

[1] Minutes of Council Meeting, 7 April 1885, Bombay Presidency Association, MSS Records I. (MSS Minute Book of Council Meetings.)
[2] See, for example, Minutes of Council Meeting, 9 May 1885, 17 June 1887, and 15 March 1889, Bombay Presidency Association, MSS Records I.
[3] For example, the meeting to ask for a Royal Commission on India. See Minutes of Council Meeting, 7 February 1886, Bombay Presidency Association, MSS Records I.

the politicians of Bombay city had to pay their price. They rejected the option of extending their politics from the municipality to the Presidency as a whole, since to do so would have involved an appeal to one or another of the sectional interests in the districts. Trying to gain influence where they were not well connected would have risked its loss in the city where their connections were promising. In this way the deliberate parochialism of the Bombay leaders was to allow the political initiative in western India to go by default to Poona.

In 1878 Sisir Kumar Ghose exhorted Bengalis to shed their illusions about being India's leaders and to learn about politics from the Bombay Presidency. What he was urging them to follow was less the example of Bombay city than of Poona with its political association, the Sarvajanik Sabha, which had 'succeeded in making itself the organ of the Mahratta community'.[1] When the official telescope swung from Bombay towards the Deccan, it also detected a lively political scene. For the Brahmins of Maharashtra, Bombay was the city of parvenus, time-servers and quill-drivers, the centre of an alien, and with luck a temporary, power. 'Never have I known in India a national and political ambition so continuous, so enduring, so far reaching, so utterly impossible for us to satisfy as that of the Brahmins of western India', the governor of Bombay asserted in 1879; for the Brahmins appeared to believe that 'the Hindoo policy...will one day reassert itself over the white conquest'.[2] Consequently Sir Richard Temple was disturbed by the state of feeling in western India.

Throughout the whole of the Deccan, the mind of the people is... affected by the past associations of Maratha rule, which, so far from being forgotten, are better remembered than would ordinarily be expected, and by the long-retained memory of the Maratha uprising against the Mahomedans...This memory constantly suggests the analogy between the position of the British and that of the Moguls in the Deccan. There is a general tendency also to criticise to an extreme degree, not only the proceedings of Government and its officers, but also the national conduct and policy of the British in respect to India.[3]

A minor revolt in 1879 seemed to justify these trepidations. Wasudeo Balwant Phadke, a petty government clerk in Poona

[1] *Amrita Bazar Patrika*, 26 September 1878.
[2] Temple to Lytton, 9 July 1879, Temple Papers, MSS Eur. F. 86.
[3] Minute by Temple, 31 July 1879, LP (520/3).

for fifteen years, deserted his post and took to the hills, proclaiming himself 'Pradhan to Sivaji II',[1] and preaching revolt against the British. Although his followers were Ramoshis, a semi-aboriginal and criminal tribe who cared only for loot, Phadke and his lieutenants were Chitpavans; and the government saw his motives as clearly 'political, however insane his ideas may have been'.[2] Hoping 'to have a Hindu raj, and to establish the Hindu religion',[3] he had planned

> to send to all sides three or four men a month in advance that small gangs might be raised by them from which great fear would come to the English. The mails would be stopped, and the railway and telegraph interrupted...Then the jails would be opened...How many and where the military were would not be known, and thus thousands of ignorant people would collect. This would be good and my intention carried out.[4]

The rebels had raided villages near the Western Ghats and carried off the plunder to the hills. 'It was', the governor of Bombay noted ominously, 'in imitation of the tactics pursued by Sivaji...against the Mogul Empire, and on exactly the same field of action.'[5] But Phadke was disappointed by the lack of patriotism among his men and by the lack of support from the Brahmin community. When the gang was rounded up, Phadke himself was sentenced to transportation for life.

These dacoities looked like evidence of a new Brahmin conspiracy in Maharashtra against the Raj. The Poona press showed cautious sympathy for a Maratha patriot, misguided perhaps in his actions, but estimable in his intentions. Praising Phadke for 'his disinterestedness and patriotism', the *Shivaji* merely judged that he had not gone 'the right way to work',[6] while the *Deccan Star* took the risk of saying that 'in the eyes of his countrymen, Wasudewa did no wrong'.[7] Consequently Anglo-Indian newspapers openly accused Poona Brahmins of com-

---

[1] *Source Material for a History of the Freedom Movement (1818–1885)*, I, 73–129.
[2] Temple to Lytton, 9 July 1879, Temple Papers, MSS Eur. F. 86.
[3] See Account of Proceedings against Phadke, 1879, *Source Material for a History of the Freedom Movement (1818–1885)*, I, 81–2.
[4] *Ibid.* 85–6.
[5] R. Temple, *The Story of My Life* (London, 1896), II, 29.
[6] *Shivaji*, 21 November 1879, quoted in RNP (Bombay), 29 November 1879.
[7] *Deccan Star*, 23 November 1879, quoted in RNP (Bombay), 6 December 1879.

plicity,[1] and some anti-Brahmin Marathi papers improved the golden hour by suggesting that all Brahmins should be expelled from their posts.[2] So vehement was the attack that the *Indu Prakash* advised the Brahmins of Poona to form an organisation to defend their interests.[3]

But by this time such movements as Phadke's revolt were out of date in Deccan politics. In the old centres of Maratha power, the Brahmins 'instead of adopting a policy of resistance, have adopted a policy of acceptance', and they had become 'the chief native administrators of the system which has superseded their own'.[4] Indeed their insistence had provided most of the drive behind the growing demand for English education. In consequence, the resentments and ambitions embedded in the Maratha tradition were coming to the top in a more ambiguous and possibly more menacing form in constitutional politics and the press.[5] In April 1870 Poona had launched a political association of its own.[6] The Poona Sarvajanik Sabha grew out of two different organisations. One was an association of Poona Brahmins intended to settle the management of the hereditary religious property of the Peshwas upon a sound basis,[7] and the other was the remnants of a local association started in 1867 to act as an intermediary between the district and the government. From the start the rules of the Sabha insisted that members should be representative Indians, with a mandate from at least fifty persons suitably qualified by locality, profession or caste. In this way the ninety-five members enrolled in the first year claimed to represent more than 6,000 persons. Its presidents and vice-presidents were annually elected, and at first they were Maratha Sirdars.[8] But most of the ordinary members were local lawyers, teachers, government servants and journalists. Although it was stigmatised as a Brahmin pressure

---

[1] The *Deccan Herald* and the *Bombay Gazette* led the campaign.
[2] For example, see *Yajdan Parast*, 18 May 1879, quoted in RNP (Bombay), 24 May 1879.
[3] *Indu Prakash*, 19 May 1879.
[4] Hunter, *Bombay*, p. 12.
[5] On the Poona press, see below, appendix 5, pp. 371–2.
[6] *The Quarterly Journal of the Poona Sarvajanik Sabha*, New Series, I, no. 1 (April 1916), 3.
[7] T. V. Parvate, *Mahadev Govind Ranade. A Biography* (London, 1963), p. 75.
[8] See *The Constitution of the Poona Sarvajanik Sabha and its Rules* (Poona, 1870).

group,[1] in fact the Sabha had no caste qualification for membership. Of course, Brahmins controlled it, but this resulted from
their social dominance in the region rather than from any
contrived exclusiveness.

Ranade set the Sabha on its feet and became its guiding
influence. A giant among moderates, he was, in Reay's opinion
'a thoroughly representative man, speaking with authority on
all legal, economic, and social questions...the ugliest man in
the Presidency, and leads a hermit life, inspiring most of the
critics of Government'.[2] Having served his apprenticeship in
Bombay, in 1871 Ranade came as a subordinate judge to Poona.
Here he became leader of the Sabha, which he was to conduct
for twenty-one years with a calculated moderation, winning for
it the reputation of being the most sober and effective political
organisation in western India, and using as his platform the
journal it established in 1878. But at the time when troops were
still hunting for Phadke, government looked so darkly upon
Poona that both Ranade and the Sabha fell under suspicion.
Ranade, at this time a judge at Nasik, happened to be in Poona
during the troubles, and in fact he encouraged the Sabha to help
bring the rebels to book.[3] But now the Bombay government
transferred him to Dhulia, out of an unfounded conviction
that he had sympathised with the conspiracy in the worst
Irish fashion. As a member of the Bombay Council wrote in
1880:

The position...which he [Ranade] holds among his countrymen,
and the views he entertains are those of Mr Parnell in Ireland: and
in short, he is in the Deccan what Mr Parnell is in Ireland. There is

[1] *BG*, XVIII, part 3, 64. In 1885 Lee-Warner, the Officiating Director of
Public Instruction referred to the Sabha as 'an Association which specially
safeguards the interests and claims of the Brahmin caste'; this brought a
fierce refutation from the Sabha. See Correspondence on the new Free
Studentship Rules, 1885, *The Quarterly Journal of the Poona Sarvjanik
Sabha*, VIII, no. 3 (January 1886).
[2] Reay to Dufferin, 24 May 1885, DP 47 (Reel 528).
[3] Before Phadke's arrest the Sabha called for action to restore order (S. H.
Sathe, Secretary, Poona Sarvajanik Sabha, to Chief Secretary, Government of Bombay, 25 April 1879, *The Quarterly Journal of the Poona
Sarvajanik Sabha*, II, no. 1 (July 1879), 68–70); the dacoits who set
fire to some Poona buildings 'were first discovered by the united efforts
of some of the leading members of the Sabha' (Letter of 20 May 1879,
ibid. 74–5); in an address to the governor, 11 July 1879, the Sabha
again showed itself anxious to refute charges of complicity (*ibid.* II, no. 2
(October 1879), 99–102).

not an educated Brahmin in the Deccan who does not know that Mr Ranade's sentiments are those of a strong and impassioned Home Ruler. They all know, moreover, that the government of Sir R. Temple, being convinced of the fact, removed Mr Ranade first from Poona, and then from Nasik to Dhulia, because the first two places swarm with Brahmins on whose minds... Ranade was believed to be exercising a pernicious effect.[1]

Just as the Indian Association stimulated political life in Bengal, so too did the Poona Sarvajanik Sabha in the western Presidency. In 1874 it was demanding Indian representation in parliament. At the Delhi Durbar it appealed to Indian delegates to combine for the discussion of national questions, and later that year it convened a conference of all native editors in Bombay city, in the hope of organising the press of western India on the model of the Calcutta Press Conference. In 1878 it protested publicly in Poona against the Vernacular Press Act, and in the same year it sent a delegation to confer with the associations in Calcutta. Since it joined with the Indian Association in petitioning parliament and appealing to the British electorate in 1880, it supported Lalmohan Ghose, Calcutta's representative in England. To back its petitions in England, the Sarvajanik Sabha circularised 'the leading newspapers and representatives of the local communities in the mofussil towns', and received letters of support from twenty-seven editors. Until the Bombay Presidency Association got under way in 1885, the Poona Sarvajanik Sabha was the leading association in western India and so had to concern itself with a wide range of subjects —agitating against the Bombay forest regulations, the Licence Tax, and the Ilbert bill, and in favour of local self-government. The Sabha was among the first to petition for an extension of Ripon's viceroyalty. In 1884 it pressed for reform of the Legislative Councils and of recruitment to the civil service.[2] By building-up a reputation for moderation and good sense, the Sabha suc-

[1] Minute by E. W. Ravenscroft, 16 June 1880. Government of Bombay; Home Department (Special) File no. 797 (Confidential), J.D. 1880.

[2] On the Calcutta press conference, see *Hindoo Patriot*, 22 January 1878, and for the Bombay session, *Times of India*, 30 March 1878; for a report on the meeting against the Vernacular Press Act, 7 May 1878, see *The Quarterly Journal of the Poona Sarvajanik Sabha*, I, no. 2 (October 1878), 14–28; for the text of the appeal, the decision to join with the Indian Association in backing Lalmohan Ghose and the proceedings of the meeting on 16 May 1880, which resolved to petition Parliament, see *ibid*. II, no. 4 (April 1880), 132–3; *ibid*. III, no. 1 (July 1880), 10–16; on its circular and the replies, *ibid*. III, no. 4 (April 1881), 59; on local self-

ceeded in winning some influence with government which it retained until Tilak took over the Sabha in the 1890s.

Unlike the city politicians of Bombay who kept aloof from the countryside, the Sabha from the start immersed itself in the problems of agrarian society. In 1873 it appointed twelve of its members as a sub-committee to make a statistical inquiry into agrarian problems. During the famine it was very active, conducting field surveys,[1] making detailed representations to government when the bankrupt peasantry of the Deccan rose in hopeless fury against the sowkar,[2] scrutinising government legislation on peasant indebtedness,[3] and investigating the Deccan dacoities.[4] It also set up arbitration courts to settle agrarian disputes.[5] But despite this down-to-earth approach, the Sarvajanik Sabha could no more become the tribune of the raiyats than the Bombay Association or the Indian Association in Bengal. The aim behind its solicitude for the Deccan was to win a permanent settlement of the land revenue over as much as possible of the Bombay Presidency. Such a settlement, the Sabha argued, would give Bombay a version of the great European advantage of forward-looking and prosperous land-lords, recruited from the professional classes and higher castes. Capital would marry land, bringing the able Brahmins of the Deccan more swiftly into an arena they were already entering. In a backward country like India, the Sabha argued,

government, see *ibid.* v, no. 2 (October 1882), 17–34, *ibid.* v, no. 3, (January 1883) 35–52, *ibid.* VI, no. 3 (January 1884), 29–54, *ibid.* VI, no. 4 (April 1884), 55–68; on the Ilbert bill meeting, 19 May 1883, *ibid.* VI, no. 1 (July 1883), 5–10; the address to the Queen on Ripon's viceroyalty, 1 June 1883, *ibid.* VI, no. 1 (July 1883), 1–3. The memorial on the civil service examination, 23 August 1884, is reproduced *ibid.* VII, no. 2 (October 1884), 7–11.

[1] *The Quarterly Journal of the Poona Sarvajanik Sabha*, I, no. 2 (October 1878), 8–13.

[2] 'Letter to the Government reviewing the report of the Deccan Riot Commissioners', 14 April 1877, *ibid.* I, no. 3 (January 1879), 35–43. Here it was stated that 'during the last 4 years the Poona Sarvajanik Sabha has devoted its most anxious thoughts to the consideration of the condition of the agricultural classes in this Presidency'.

[3] For example, see its Representation to Government, 6 September 1879, *ibid.* II, no. 3 (January 1880), 103–19.

[4] *Ibid.* II, no. 1 (July 1879), 68–76; and *ibid.* II, no. 4 (April 1880), 120–6.

[5] Proceedings of a public meeting of the inhabitants of Poona to consider the establishment of panchayets, 4 May 1879, *ibid.* II, no. 1 (July 1879), 78–84.

...only a minority of people...monopolise all the elements of strength. They are socially and religiously in the front ranks, they possess intelligence, wealth, thrifty habits, knowledge and power of combination. The majority...are unlettered, improvident, ignorant, disunited, thriftless, and poor in means. No political manipulation can hold the balance between these two classes...and it is a hopeless struggle to keep up a poverty-stricken peasantry in the possession of the soil, and divorce the natural union of capital and land...Democracy cannot be transplanted into the Indian soil at a start, it will take many generations...to raise the Indian peasant to...equality with the Brahmin and the Bania.[1]

Such an approach was unlikely to bring the Kunbis and Marathas flocking behind the Sabha's banner. It was typical of the Sabha's approach that when they carried out their surveys in the villages, it was to the Brahmin kulkarni, and not to the non-Brahmin headman, that they went. Even less than the Indian Association did the Sabha succeed in organising the peasantry behind its demands. It remained an elite organisation whose approach was academic rather than tactical until it was captured by Tilak in the political upheavals which were breaking the unity of the Deccan at the end of the century.

While the Poona Sarvajanik Sabha was becoming the spokesman of the Deccan Brahmins, a movement of scarcely-veiled hostility was being organised against them. In Maharashtra the Brahmins and non-Brahmins had vied with each other for at least six hundred years,[2] but by the later nineteenth century the most bitter disputes were over the Brahmin grip of education, which now seemed the main avenue to domination. The most influential critic of the social order was a Sudra, Jotirao Govindrao Phule, who had himself been educated at a mission school where he was deeply influenced by Christian teachings on equality.[3] Belonging to the Phul Malis,[4] Jotirao was well placed to voice a general protest against the Brahmins, because

[1] 'The Agrarian Problem and its Solution', *The Quarterly Journal of the Poona Sarvajanik Sabha*, ii, no. i (July 1879), Independent Section, pp. 18–19.
[2] See M. L. P. Patterson, 'A Preliminary Study of the Brahman versus Non-Brahman Conflict in Maharashtra' (Unpublished Master of Arts dissertation, University of Pennsylvania, 1952), p. 1.
[3] V. D. Govande, *Tri Murti Darshan* [in Marathi] (Poona, 1894), pp. 34–5; also see D. Keer, *Mahatma Jotirao Phooley. Father of Our Social Revolution* (Bombay, 1964).
[4] The Phul Malis were florists by occupation; see Enthoven. *Tribes and Castes* ii, 422–6.

his own caste, while standing below the Maratha-Kunbis, could eat and drink with them, and it could also speak for the untouchable Mahars and Mangs. Having completed his own education, he did not seek office but devoted himself to educating the non-Brahmins, organising schools for them in Ahmadnagar and Poona.[1] In 1873 he founded the Satya Shodak Samaj, or Society of Truth Seekers. Its aims were to challenge Brahminical supremacy; to prove from Hindu scriptures the equality of mankind, while denying the need for priestly mediation between man and God; and to dispense with the services of Brahmins at religious rituals.[2] Phule's writings gave

a vivid picture of the mental slavery imposed by the sacerdotal class which began by subjugating the original inhabitants of the country... and then by means of mythological stories, religious teachings, literary fabrications and the rest, strengthened their hold upon the people who now became either Sudras (menials) or Ateesudras (supermenials or the so-called untouchable classes).[3]

British rule, according to Jotirao, was a divine dispensation: 'Christ raised the British people from a very barbarous state, and sent them to India to deliver the crippled Sudras from the cunning Aryan Brahmins.'[4] The Poona Sarvajanik Sabha he denounced as a totally unrepresentative Brahmin affair that should be boycotted.[5] Later, at a Poona public meeting in 1889, he called upon the non-Brahmins to condemn Congress as an engine of Brahminical despotism.[6] 'If the Aryans hold not one but a hundred Congresses', Phule wrote, 'no sensible Sudra or Atisudra would become its members. I can confidently state that if Sudras do join, our beneficent rulers will be disgusted with them.'[7] In 1890 Jotirao died, 'only a pioneer, a

[1] History of the Freedom Movement, Regional Office, Bombay. Records: MSS File no. 3 [Henceforth HFMB, MSS File no. 3]; Keer, *Phooley*, pp. 17–88.
[2] *Memorandum prepared by the Government of Bombay for submission to the Indian Statutory Commission, 1928* (Bombay, 1929), pp. 227–8.
[3] A. B. Latthe, *Memoirs of His Highness Shri Shahu Chhatrapati Maharaja of Kolhapur* (Bombay, 1924), I, 322–3.
[4] J. G. Phule, *Sarvajanik Satyadharma Pustak* [Everybody's Book of True Religion, in Marathi], (Poona, 1891), p. 29.
[5] *Dinbandhu*, 14 October 1888, RNP (Bombay), 20 October 1888. For Phule's campaign against the Sabha and Congress, also see *Dinbandhu*, 30 January and 11 December 1887, RNP (Bombay), 6 February and 17 December 1887.
[6] HFMB MSS File no. 3.
[7] Phule, *Sarvajanik*, p. 89.

solitary beacon light in the darkness of the age, for the guidance of the non-Brahmin reformers who had yet to come'.[1]

Although Brahmin dominance was still unshaken, there were signs that its Poona leadership was not as solid as it had been. Some of the younger Brahmins were becoming restive at the old moderates who controlled the Poona Sarvajanik Sabha. In 1874 Vishnu Krishna Chiplonkar had launched a nationalist journal, the *Nibandhamala*, in which he called upon his compatriots to return with pride to their own country, religion, history and language.[2]

In the last century [he wrote], terms like Hindu people's rule, Hindu people's wealth, and Hindu people's learning, etc., had some meaning. Have they any meaning today? At present our grand and minor kings are almost like pawns in a game of chess—they cannot move, cannot talk, are always under the control of the big Sahibs with troops at their side!...Our wealth is like that of a prostitute. If a strong man comes, and starts beating us on the mouth, we have not the power to protect it.

The cause of this degradation was clear to Chiplonkar; it was 'the loss of our independence'.[3] When in 1879 he quit his government post, he did so not as a sacrifice but a liberation:

No wonder that my throwing up my appointment has called forth many a remark both here (Poona) and there (Ratnagiri). In these days of helplessness and subserviency Government service is looked upon in something of a heavenly light and one deliberately giving it up must be looked upon as little short of a madman or a suicide. But for my own part I have thought differently of the matter. Rather than bend the knee to tyranny I would snap asunder the chain once and forever. I am resolved to try what might be done for the public good with the potent instrumentality of a press establishment worked by a vigorous hand.[4]

Once clear of the bureaucracy, Chiplonkar set up the New English School in Poona, where his efforts were aided by a selfless group of young Brahmins who included Tilak, M. B.

---

[1] Latthe, *Memoirs*, I, 324.
[2] For a life of Chiplonkar (1825–81), see G. T. Madholkar, *Vishnu Krishna Chiplonkar* [in Marathi] (Poona, 1934). Also see V. K. Chiplonkar, *Nibandhamala* [Garland of Essays, in Marathi] (3rd edn, Poona, 1926).
[3] V. K. Chiplonkar, *Amcya Deshaci Stitti* [Our Country's Condition (1881), in Marathi] quoted in S. A. Wolpert, *Tilak and Gokhale: Revolution and Reform in the Making of Modern India* (Berkeley and Los Angeles, 1962), p. 10.
[4] In a letter to his brother, September 1879, quoted in Limaye, *The History of the Deccan Education Society*, part I, p. 2.

Namjoshi and G. G. Agarkar. Spurning the rewards of law or service, they preferred to mould the coming generation of Maharashtrians to their way of thinking. The success of the school encouraged them to form the Deccan Education Society, and in 1885 to make a more ambitious venture into higher education by founding Fergusson College in Poona.[1] Already in 1881 they had started the *Kesari* and *Mahratta* which quickly became the leading papers in Poona.[2]

While these activities instilled new energy into the city, they also laid bare the disagreements among its leaders over tactics. Ranade's programme had shrewdly coupled moderate politics and social reform, so as to give the Maharashtrian leadership an image of enlightenment and responsibility.[3] Obviously this would please Government House; but it would also establish a connection with the non-sectarian politicians in Bombay city. This opening into a wider field was vital to the politicians of the Deccan; and to win it they had to avoid the suspicion that they were merely the Peshwai in Victorian guise. Yet although the reformers of western India held close to tradition and were 'never estranged from popular sympathy to the degree they have done in Bengal',[4] their programme aroused suspicion inside their own country. The orthodox were against it, and it was also unacceptable to those whose interest in social reform was languid, and who thought in any case that it was not the way to add to their support in Maharashtra. Chiplonkar's uncompromising attitudes and the appeal to the past glories of the empire in the columns of the *Mahratta* suggested an alter-

---

[1] Limaye, *The History of the Deccan Education Society*, part 1, pp. 1–5.

[2] The *Kesari* was first published on 4 January 1881; it began with a circulation of 200. By 1888 its circulation had risen to 4,400, the largest of any paper in western India (see RNP (Bombay), 7 February 1881 and 29 December 1888). The *Mahratta*, published in English, had a smaller circulation; this stood at 400 by 1888.

[3] On Ranade's life and work, see K. Deshpande (trans.), *Ranade, His Wife's Reminiscences* (Delhi, 1963); N. R. Phatak, *Nyayamurti Mahadev Govind Ranade. Yance Caritra* [Life of Ranade, in Marathi] (Poona, 1924); G. A. Mankar, *A Sketch of the Life and Works of the late Mr Justice M. G. Ranade...* (Bombay, 1902), 2 vols.; Parvate, *Mahadev Govind Ranade*; Ranade, *The Miscellaneous Writings of the Late Hon'ble Mr Justice M. G. Ranade*; M. G. Ranade, *Religious and Social Reform. A Collection of Essays and Speeches* (Bombay, 1900); Idem, *Essays on Indian Economics. A Collection of Essays and Speeches* (Bombay, 1898); Idem, *Rise of the Maratha Power* (Bombay, 1900).

[4] W. M. Kolhatkar, 'Widow Remarriage', in C. Y. Chintamani (ed.), *India Social Reform* (Madras, 1901), p. 311.

native way of mobilising support.[1] Ostensibly, the battles opened over the issue of social reform, but the clash of personalities, the rivalry for the control of the Deccan Education Society, of the newspapers, and eventually of the Poona Sarvajanik Sabha itself were really a struggle for leadership between these competing attitudes. In 1884 Tilak attacked Agarkar's plans for promoting female education, while he and Ranade took opposite sides in the hotly debated Rakhamabai case. By 1888 the split was open. Losing the *Kesari* and *Mahratta* to Tilak, Agarkar started his own paper, the *Sudharak*; and two years later Tilak was edged out of the Deccan Education Society after his attempt to discredit Agarkar and to capture control of it.[2] With Ranade, Agarkar, and Gokhale—Ranade's political heir and Tilak's main adversary—on one side, and Tilak and his followers on the other, the parties were grouped in readiness for the coming struggles in Maharashtra.

[1] In its very first issue, the *Mahratta* set out to revive the glories of 'the nation of Shivaji', claiming that then 'the instinct of nationality [was] wide awake among us'. Supplement to *Mahratta*, 2 January 1881.

[2] An analysis of these developments in Poona, based upon the private papers of Tilak, Agarkar and Gokhale, and the records of the Deccan Education Society, will be made in the second volume of this work.

6

The Politics of Union

The idea that Indians should take up a common political stance was almost as old as the first stirrings of constitutional politics in India. As soon as the British Indian Association was established in 1851, it made contact with 'the most influential native gentlemen of Madras and Bombay',[1] since it knew that petitions to parliament would carry greater weight 'if they were made simultaneously by the Natives of every part of British India'.[2] Since the three Presidencies would all be affected by the impending changes in the Company's charter, their demands on Westminster should bear 'the impress of unity'.[3] In the event, the associations of Bombay and Madras decided to act independently. Although Bombay admitted the principle of co-operation[4] and all the petitions to London took the same line,[5] the co-ordinating impulse was still weak. All that united the men of Calcutta, Bombay and Madras was the yoke of British administration. Few of these men knew each other, or the first thing about other parts of India. So although the British Indian Association after 1853 urged 'the other Societies of the other Presidencies... [to] continue the united agitation',[6] its larger ambition to represent India came to nothing.[7]

[1] Report of the Committee, para. 17, First Report of the British Indian Association, from its establishment on 29 October 1851 to 30 November 1852. BIA.
[2] Debendranath Tagore, circular letter, 11 December 1852, quoted in C. F. Andrews and G. Mukerji, *The Rise and Growth of the Congress in India* (London, 1938), p. 105.
[3] *Bengal Hurkaru*, 10 May 1852.
[4] Third resolution, Inaugural meeting of the Bombay Association, 26 August 1852, *Minute of Proceedings of the Bombay Association*, p. 8.
[5] Report of the Committee, para. 17, First Report of the British Indian Association, from its establishment on 29 October 1851 to 30 November 1852. BIA.
[6] Second Report of the British Indian Association, 13 January 1854, p. 20. BIA.
[7] During the 1850s and 1860s, there were some exchanges of views and vague promises of co-operation between Calcutta, Bombay and Madras. See Third Annual Report of the British Indian Association for the year

The first Indian organisation to cross provincial boundaries was formed in England by the first generation of Indian students who went there to qualify for the bar or the covenanted civil service.[1] Among these pioneers were four future presidents of the Indian National Congress: Pherozeshah Mehta and Badruddin Tyabji from Bombay, and W. C. Bonnerjee and Manmohan Ghose from Calcutta. In 1865, directed by Dadabhai Naoroji, these students launched the London Indian Society. Among their activities was the ventilation of Indian 'political, social, and literary' subjects. They formulated Indian grievances and countered misrepresentations about India in the English press. Europeans might become honorary members only; they could not vote or hold office in the society. Since many of the students came from Bengal, their first act was to seek the co-operation of the British Indian Association in Calcutta.[2]

The London Indian Society was soon superseded by the more ambitious East India Association, founded in London on 1 October 1866 'for the independent and disinterested advocacy and promotion...of the public interests and welfare of the inhabitants of India generally'.[3] More than any of the political groups in India before the founding of Congress, this London-based association had some claim to be a national body, although many of its members in England were Old India Hands. It had a large Indian membership, drawn from all over the sub-continent. Out of a total of 594 members in 1868, 324 were Indians, most of whom were not resident in England.[4] But the activity of the Indian members hardly went beyond paying a

---

1854, p. 18; and Seventeenth Annual General Meeting of the British Indian Association, 24 February 1869. BIA.

[1] In 1845, the first four students left India. In 1880 there were about 100 Indian students in England; in 1885 there were 160. One unofficial estimate of the number who studied in England between 1865 and 1885 put the total at over 700. Bengalis took the lead. But by 1885 Bombay was close behind. By 1894 there were 308, and in 1907 780, students in the United Kingdom. See F. Leger, *Les Influences Occidentales dans la Révolution de l'Orient* (Paris, 1955), p. 44; Anonymous, 'Indian Students in England', *Journal of the National Indian Association in Aid of Social Progress and Education in India* (January 1885), no. 169, pp. 1–9; and Supplement to *Bengalee*, 29 January 1876.

[2] Fourteenth Annual General Meeting of the British Indian Association, 14 February 1866, p. 22. BIA.

[3] New Rules, *Journal of the East India Association*, I, no. 1 (1867).

[4] Membership lists, *Journal of the East India Association*, II, no. 1 (1868), 5–12.

subscription and receiving the *Journal*. In London, too, few of the members were fiery spirits, and these grew fewer when the first student members sailed home to India and were replaced by newcomers more given to trimming.

However, Dadabhai Naoroji did what he could to make the Association speak for India as a whole. British rule, he told his followers in 1867, had injected a 'new political life' into India; its 'educated classes' were fast becoming 'the natural leaders of the masses'; a common language among them was 'forging strong bonds of nationality'; and all in all, 'the nation is now becoming gradually assimilated for political purposes'.[1] This made two steps necessary. First, the credibility of the new politics in India had to be strengthened by forming new associations and reviving old ones; and secondly all this work in India needed to be directed by a London centre, since local Indian associations, whose 'efforts have a parochialism about them', could not effectively rally British opinion. Their role was to supply London with funds and information, to hold a watching brief over the local governments in India, and to train the people in their political rights so that in time they would be ready 'for that great end, a Parliament of Parliaments in India'.[2]

Making the plan work was not so simple. The new body sent its missionaries to the key Presidencies of Bengal and Bombay.[3] But only in the latter did it make any converts. Thanks to Dadabhai's own efforts, a Bombay branch was set up in 1869.[4] It was meant to be the clearing house between associations in India and the London headquarters, collecting information and remitting funds,[5] as well as working with the existing Bombay Association. In fact, many of the Association's members did join the new branch. An impressive managing committee of Bombay notables was cajoled into office. Sir Jamsetjee Jeejeebhoy was president of the branch, and among the vice-presi-

[1] Meeting, 2 May 1867, *Journal of the East India Association*, I, no. 1 (1867), 26–46.
[2] D. Naoroji, 'On the Duties of Local Indian Associations in connection with the London Association', Appendix to *Journal of the East India Association*, II, no. 1 (1868).
[3] Meeting of the East India Association, 29 October 1868, *Journal of the East India Association*, II, no. 4 (1868), 327–30.
[4] 'Report of a meeting called for the consideration of the Desirability of forming a Bombay Branch of the East India Association, 22 May 1869', *Journal of the East India Association*, III, no. 3 (1869), 71–6.
[5] 'Rules of the Bombay Branch of the East India Association', *ibid.* 76–7.

dents were another two Parsis, Framjee Nusserwanjee Patel, and Dinshaw Manackjee Petit. Sir William Wedderburn, a Bombay civilian, was vice-chairman of the managing committee; Pherozeshah Mehta was one of the honorary secretaries, and the committee members included such leading Maharashtrians as M. G. Ranade, V. N. Mandlik, and R. G. Bhandarkar. Lawyers, doctors, government officials and graduates filled its ranks.[1] The branch made a promising start. By the end of the year it had 628 members, some from the mofussil, and about forty from Calcutta.[2]

Its early promise notwithstanding, Dadabhai's grand design was destined to be frustrated. The East India Association never won effective support in Bengal or Madras, and this only accentuated its Bombay bias, unfortunate in an organisation claiming to represent all India. In 1871 Major Evan Bell, writing from London, upbraided Sambhu Chandra Mukherjee for 'the small amount of support...at Calcutta'. 'I was sorry to hear that it is a common saying..."Oh, it [the East India Association] is quite a Bombay concern!"'[3] But even in Bombay it did not flourish. Sporadically it put out a few petitions against the Vernacular Press Act, the abolition of cotton duties and the expenses of the Afghan war, but this was the sum of its activity.[4] By 1879, most of the subscriptions due to it were unpaid. Two years later its total membership had fallen to seventy-three.[5] Then there followed a new effort to put life into it, but it died. The growing divergence between London and Bombay was responsible for this failure. The branch in Bombay was only a local appendage of a headquarters in London which retired British civilians and army officers had increasingly taken over. In origin, the association had been a development of the Indian Army Committee combined with the London Indian Society, but as the former ousted the latter, so the Indian case went by default. Early in 1883, the *Indian Mirror* declared that the East India Association had 'proved a decided failure'.[6] Its departure from the intentions of Dadabhai

[1] 'Rules of the Bombay Branch of the East India Association', *ibid.* 71–82.
[2] Jotindra Mohan Tagore and Vidyasagar sent the Calcutta names.
[3] Quoted in F. H. Skrine, *An Indian Journalist: being the life, letters and correspondence of Dr Sambhu C. Mookerjee* (Calcutta, 1895), p. 84.
[4] *Journal of the East India Association*, xv, no. 2 (1883), 157–9.
[5] *Ibid.* 157, 161.   [6] *Indian Mirror*, 17 February 1883.

and the students was shown later that year when the Association came out strongly against the Ilbert bill. Robert Elliot now used it as a platform to attack 'Baboo politicians', and to warn the British against the 'danger of losing sight of the material and general interests of those silent masses on whom the stability of the Empire really rests...in our haste to gratify the very natural ambition of the educated classes'.[1] Politicians in Bombay were not prepared to play second fiddle in such an orchestra. Even Dadabhai reluctantly recognised the trend.[2] Between 1881 and 1883 he formulated new rules for the Bombay branch and launched a drive for members,[3] but he could not win over Mehta, Telang and Tyabji. Despite his promise to reform the branch,[4] they pressed on with their own plans for a new and autonomous body,[5] plans which materialised two years later in the Bombay Presidency Association.[6] Now Dadabhai's branch no longer had any 'regular general or local public work to do'.[7] Indian politics could no longer be controlled by *emigrés*.

※

It was not through secular politics, but through quasi-religious societies, that educated Indians first fell into the habit of thinking and organising on a national scale. One of these sects was the Brahmo Samaj, the most conspicuous of the movements in nineteenth-century India which tried to effect a compromise between the ethical and social teachings of western Christianity and the traditional values of Hinduism. Having taken charge of the younger Brahmos in 1857, Keshub Chandra Sen encouraged them to push the Samaj outwards from Calcutta into the districts of Bengal; and in 1861, declaring that 'Brahmo is

[1] Meeting of the Association, 13 June 1883, *Journal of the East India Association*, xv, no. 4 (1883), 246.
[2] Later Dadabhai admitted: 'Times had changed, new forces and influences were at work and a more extended and differently constituted organisation was now necessary.' Naoroji, Diary, 20 April 1886. NP.
[3] *Journal of the East India Association*, xv, no. 2 (1883), 161.
[4] Naoroji to Mehta, 26 January 1883. Mehta Papers.
[5] Telang to Mehta, 26 January 1883. Mehta Papers.
[6] In his inaugural speech, Tyabji stressed the inadequacies of the Bombay branch, and argued the need for 'a truly national association... upon a permanent basis'. 'Establishment of a Native Political Association in Bombay', Report of a public meeting of natives held on Saturday, 31 January 1885, at the Framjee Cawasji Institute. Mehta Papers.
[7] Naoroji to W. M. Wood, 30 January 1885. NP.

destined to become a power in the land',[1] he decided to spread his message beyond Bengal by touring the sub-continent. After the first of these tours, a branch Samaj was formed in Madras and a Prarthana Samaj in Bombay.[2]

Suggestively enough, Keshub called his wing of the movement the Bharatvarshiva Samaj, the Brahmo Samaj of India. Although all India was to be its field of operations, the Samaj did not greatly flourish beyond Bengal, while its outposts in other parts of India made a point of stressing their autonomy. Yet the idea of a national reform movement made a deep impression on Keshub's generation. In Bengal itself, the Brahmos were not numerous, but they were influential, supplying many of the leaders in the Indian Association which was to take the initiative in agitating for a national front.[3]

The other organisation was the Theosophical Society, whose history has been so mysteriously associated with the birth of Congress. It was founded in 1875 by the spiritualist, Madame Blavatsky, a veteran of several shady affairs in Europe and America, and by Colonel Olcott, a veteran of the American Civil War. The Society reached India in 1879 and won many supporters among educated Indians by its demonstrative sympathy for the native, by its enthusiasm for Aryan philosophy, and by its strange dogmas and esoteric beliefs that added piquancy to an already highly-spiced dish. Its professed aims were to form in India the nucleus of a Universal Brotherhood of Humanity, to study Aryan culture and to explore the hidden mysteries of nature and the latent powers of man.[4] 'The natives', wrote an editor of the Anglo-Indian *Pioneer*, who himself became a votary of Occult Science, 'were flattered at the attitude towards them taken up by their new "European" friends...and showed a shallow eagerness to become Theosophists.'[5] Bombay was the first centre, but the Society soon cast a network of branches throughout India, and its journal,

[1] Quoted in Wadud, Kazi Abdul, *Banglar Jagaram* [The Awakening of Bengal, in Bengali] (Visvabharati, 1956), p. 90.
[2] Farquhar, *Modern Religious Movements in India*, p. 41.
[3] They included Sivanath Sastri, Ananda Mohan Bose, Dwarkanath Ganguli, Nagendranath Chatterjee and the Ghose brothers of the *Amrita Bazar Patrika*.
[4] Published rules of the Theosophical Society, quoted in J. Ransom, *A Short History of the Theosophical Society* (Adyar, 1938), p. 155.
[5] A. P. Sinnett, *The Occult World* (6th edn., London, 1892), p. 26.

the *Theosophist*, circulated widely in all three Presidencies.[1] An Anglo-Indian branch at Simla, with Allan Octavian Hume as president, demonstrated some welcome European support for these Indian aspirations, and in December 1881 there was even talk of a National Fund for reviving industry and Sanskrit literature in India. The Society organised an annual convention of delegates from its branches throughout India. The convention was held first at Bombay, and later at Madras, after the Society had moved to its permanent headquarters on the banks of the Adyar.[2] In 1884, it had plans for provincial conferences. The Indians joining the Theosophical Society tended to be lively and important members of the new elite, belonging to every religious community; and the Society gave them valuable experience in national organisation, as well as providing them with a forum at an all-India level.

Although the Indian branch of the Society had no explicitly political aims as yet,[3] it was undoubtedly connected with the formation of Congress, even if not so directly as Theosophical folklore has sometimes claimed. According to the later account of Annie Besant, the decision to convene the first Congress was taken in Madras by seventeen leading Indians after the Theosophical Convention of December 1884.[4] This assertion was echoed, although less specifically, by Bipin Chandra Pal. 'By the beginning of the eighties', he wrote, 'the Theosophical Society had covered the Indian continent with quite a number of branches'; and the success of these annual Theosophical conventions 'encouraged some of the leaders...to make an experiment of an Indian political congress'.[5] It is certainly true that Hume, who had a hand in launching the Congress, also had a long and stormy relationship with the Theosophists.[6] Miracles and Mahatmas were a stimulating diversion from the

---

[1] H. S. Olcott, *Old Diary Leaves. The only authentic history of the Theosophical Society. Second Series, 1878–83* (3rd edn., Adyar, 1954), pp. 92–4.

[2] *Ibid.* and *Third Series, 1883–7* (2nd edn., Adyar, 1929).

[3] The authorities suspected the Society of political aims, which it successfully denied. See *Theosophist*, IV, no. 8 (44) (May 1883), 2–6.

[4] A. Besant, *How India Wrought for Freedom* (Adyar, 1915), pp. 1–2. In 1917 Mrs Besant was to be president both of the Theosophical Society and of the Congress—a striking example of the Gelasian doctrine of the two swords.   [5] Pal, *Memories of My Life and Times*, II, lvii–lviii.

[6] For this little known connection, see Sinnett, *The Occult World*, and A. T. Barker (ed.), *The Mahatma Letters to A. P. Sinnett from the Mahatmas M. and K. H.* (2nd edn., London, 1948), and Hume to Ripon, 11 January 1884, RP, Add MSS 43616.

monotonies of life in a hill station, and moreover the Society gave this supposed expert on Indian opinion a chance to meet some Indians. Having failed to capture the Society,[1] Hume was forced to look elsewhere for opportunities to organise Indians. The man who was rebuffed by the Mahatmas[2] was later to become the first secretary of the Indian National Congress.

While these societies were providing a precedent for all-India work, the political associations newly formed in the 1870s also came to see its value. In Bengal, the older British Indian Association was too preoccupied with the defence of landed incomes to care much about its links with other Presidencies, where the special interests of zemindars found no counterpart. The Indian Association, however, from its inception had plans to go further. They owed something to Surendranath who had returned to India determined to teach the lessons of Italian nationalism and English organisation to young Bengal. The decision to call the new association the Indian, and not the Bengal, Association was significant,[3] and Banerjea found able coadjutors among the Brahmos. Moreover, it is clear from the contemporary Indian press that different parts of India were growing more interested in the affairs of one another. Here the railways helped,[4] and so did the *lingua franca*. Nevertheless, the newspaper readers still had much to learn about their country. It was with surprise that Sisir Kumar Ghose discovered that western India was not as backward politically as he had supposed.[5] The emissaries of the Indian Association made a more painful discovery when, dressed for the mild Bengal winter, they arrived in the bitter cold of the Punjab.

[1] Ransom, *A Short History of the Theosophical Society*, pp. 221–8.
[2] Already in 1881, the mythical Mahatma 'M' called Hume the 'evil genius' of the Society; a letter from Mahatma 'K. H.' received in March 1883 refers to the 'incessant *underground* intrigues of our ex-friend Mr Hume—(now entirely in the hands of the Brothers of the Shadow)', Barker, *The Mahatma Letters to A. P. Sinnett*, pp. 207–44, 337.
[3] Banerjea, *A Nation in Making*, p. 41.
[4] Encouraging Bengalis to discover India, Banerjea informed them that a second class ticket to Lahore only cost Rs 97; it was their patriotic duty to travel and thus 'promote friendly feelings among the Presidencies', 'Special Report on the Civil Service Questions, 17 September 1877', First Annual Report of the Indian Association, 1876–7. IA.
[5] *Amrita Bazar Patrika*, 7 October 1875.

Entry into the civil service was the issue which first launched the Indian Association into political action outside Bengal. When Salisbury reduced the age limit for the service examination, the Association resolved upon 'a national movement'.[1] Lytton's regime helped the trend forward, for the issues which he raised were well fitted to stimulate the habit of co-operation. Entry into the covenanted service was an honour which few could achieve, but to which all could aspire. When government blocked it, Surendranath organised the protest by travelling the length and breadth of the sub-continent. In the North-western Provinces and the Punjab, the response he evoked came mainly from small communities of expatriate Bengalis. In Delhi, he failed to rouse the local leaders from their apathy, and although, on his second tour, he met with greater success in Bombay,[2] in Madras the response was poor.

In any case, these peregrinations were undertaken largely to impress an audience six thousand miles away. Their chief purpose was to strengthen the Association's petition to London by the appearance of unanimous Indian support. The same tactics lay behind the two large Calcutta meetings which the Association organised in 1879, when messages received from all parts of India were solemnly recorded. But support in England could be effectively organised only by agents on the spot; and so in due course the Association sent Lalmohan Ghose to London, scoring a notable achievement by associating the Poona Sabha in this move. Although politicians in India were looking further afield, they remained deeply deferential, concerned far more to canvass their requests in the metropolis than to stir up support for demands in India. When they did attempt to rouse opinion in India, it was chiefly to enhance their credibility in London.

During the term of office of Ripon, whom they were to see as a benevolent Viceroy frustrated by bureaucrats and Anglo-Indians, they continued to look to England. This view was partly based on faith in English justice, and it drew strength from what they remembered about the large hopes of the early

---

[1] 'Special Report on the Civil Service Question, 17 September 1877', First Annual Report of the Indian Association, 1876–7. IA.
[2] In November 1877 Banerjea met Mandlik, Telang, and Mehta; in Poona he was Ranade's guest, Banerjea, *A Nation in Making*, pp. 49–50.

Victorians. Never quite in step with changes in British attitudes
to India, both Dadabhai and his generation, and Surendranath
and his, clung to this belief in Albion the Just. 'We have only
to persevere', Dadabhai argued, 'and I am satisfied that the
English are both willing and desirous to do India justice.'[1]
Decades later, when he could no longer ignore the impatience
of the young,[2] he was less sure about his premise,[3] but bravely
maintained nonetheless that his generation 'had their eyes first
opened to the high character of British institutions and they
became attached to them. They cannot now readily throw aside
their first love'.[4] Surendranath, too, argued that India could
expect fair treatment from the British public.[5] But they both
realised that, to reach parliament and the constituencies, the
political associations in India would have to come together.
How could a medley of discordant voices represent the people?
They must say the same things. This was the oldest and the
best argument for a common political attitude.

From Poona, there came a similar impulse towards co-
operation. In January 1877 the Poona Sarvajanik Sabha, noting
that the leading men of Bengal and Bombay were in Delhi for
the Durbar, urged them to work together.[6] The following year
the Sabha sent a deputation to Bengal, to 'hold a conference
with the representatives of the native press and the political
associations in Calcutta for the interchange of ideas'. The discussions ranged over the civil service question, Lytton's
imminent assault upon the press, the cotton duties, and the
income tax which was about to be imposed—policies which
were equally objectionable to Bombay and Bengal. The Poona
delegates also wanted to work out a common demand for the
reform of the Legislative Councils 'by the admission of more
non-official members', and for extending the franchise in the

---

[1] D. Naoroji, 'On the duties of Local Indian Associations in connection
with the London Association', appendix to *Journal of the East India
Association*, II, no. 1 (1868).

[2] See Naoroji to Wedderburn, 23 September 1904. NP.

[3] In 1905 he actually wrote 'we need to move the masses', Naoroji to Wacha,
27 July 1905. NP.

[4] Naoroji to Wedderburn, 23 September 1904. NP.

[5] See 'Special Report on the Civil Service Question, 17 September 1877',
p. 28, First Annual Report of the Indian Association, 1876–7. IA.

[6] *Source Material for a History of the Freedom Movement in India* (*Collected
from Bombay Government Records*), *1885–1920*, II (Bombay, 1958), 8–
10.

larger municipalities.[1] All these issues came later to be the stock-in-trade of the Indian nationalists.

When Bengal, where there were no cotton mills owned by Indians, took the lead in protesting against the abolition of the cotton duties, this was not so surprising as it seemed. It was not only altruism and national solidarity that stirred the Bengal associations into moving. The Licence Tax of 1878, imposed to meet the deficit caused by the abolition of the cotton duties, affected the professional and trading classes of Bengal as much as those of Bombay. Meanwhile their common dislike of Lytton was so great that both the Poona Sarvajanik Sabha and the Indian Association decided to petition parliament—the usual remedy, but now backed by unusual indignation. In 1880 they cemented their alliance by appealing jointly to the British electorate to support the Liberals, and by again deputing Lalmohan Ghose as their joint agent. By this time there had grown up a political liaison between Lytton's Indian critics and the Liberal party in England.[2] This was something new. Since the parliamentary tradition had been to keep India out of party politics, it had been sound tactics for Indians also to practise non-alignment. Such was their common antipathy towards Lytton, however, that Indians and British Liberals felt drawn together. As one Poona politician put it, Lytton's vice-royalty had taught 'one great political lesson above all others that India must identify herself with one or other of the two great political parties at home...'[3]

When Ripon arrived in 1880, hope triumphed at first over experience. But Indian politicians, eagerly scanning the English political horizon, soon began to suspect that Gladstonian liberalism stopped short of India. Hence the coming of a Liberal Viceroy in no way deadened the impulse towards more active politics. Quickened at first by hopes of his intentions, it was later strengthened by fears that without their aid he might fail. Both the Indian Association and the Poona Sabha

---

[1] 'Conference with the delegates of the Poona Sarvajanik Sabha', Twenty-seventh Annual General Meeting of the British Indian Association, 7 June 1879, p. 14. BIA.

[2] *Annual Register, 1879* (London, 1880), p. 249.

[3] S. H. Chiplonkar's use of the word 'home' is a revealing example of westernisation. See Public meeting, 16 May 1880, Proceedings of the Sabha, *The Quarterly Journal of the Poona Sarvajanik Sabha*, III, no. 1 (July 1880), 13.

had petitioned for the repeal of Lytton's 'repressive measures', for a larger share in the administration, and for the extension of the elective principle in the municipalities as a first stage in the journey towards representative government, 'the great question of the future'.[1] When Ripon announced his local self-government policy, well-informed Indians quickly discovered that official opinion in London and Calcutta was alarmed by these modest proposals. Clearly this set them two tasks: to show that they welcomed Ripon's initiative, and to impress upon their rulers that their support was a factor not to be ignored.

Step by step these developments gradually pushed the hesitant leaders of the associations towards plans for a more concerted action. Already by 1882 they were talking of a national meeting. The Indian Association's plan to hold a National Conference that year at Calcutta came to nothing, but those who conceived the idea were fully conscious that 'such an experiment, if successful, would open a new chapter in the history of this country, and would be the nucleus of new hopes and aspirations'.[2] Early in 1883 Telang went from Bombay to Calcutta to arrange 'more political concert' between the two cities. In Calcutta, he made contact with the Indian Association and with the conservative leader, Kristo Das Pal.[3] Several schemes were now in the air: launching a national newspaper to represent all India, forming a national federation of Indian editors, and setting up an 'Indian Constitutional Reform Association'.[4] All three of these schemes aimed at unifying Indian opinion and political effort.

At Wedderburn's suggestion,[5] the indefatigable Dadabhai established the *Voice of India* in January 1883. It was to be a monthly journal of extracts from the native press all over the subcontinent—political India's answer to the confidential reports on native newspapers drawn up by the local governments. English education, so its prospectus stated, was creating

---

[1] 'Petition of the members of the Poona Sarvajanik Sabha...', *The Quarterly Journal of the Poona Sarvajanik Sabha*, III, no. 1 (July 1880), 1–10; and Fourth Annual Report of the Indian Association, 1879–80, 2–3. IA.

[2] Sixth Annual Report of the Indian Association, 1882, p. 5. IA.

[3] Telang to Mehta, 26 January 1883. Mehta Papers.

[4] *Indian Mirror*, 17 February 1883.

[5] Wedderburn to Editor, *Bombay Gazette*, 2 January 1883.

'a moral unity' in India, 'drawing races and creeds together, once profoundly separated, and filling them with common aspiration and sympathy. It has already created a very definite public opinion which moves freely in one and the same intellectual atmosphere, if with unequal energies, in every province of India.'[1] This new venture was meant to convince the British public that India's expanding press spoke with one voice on most matters of importance. Within a year, Dadabhai and Malabari, who edited the *Voice* in Bombay, were planning an edition in England, where there was a great need for 'instruction in Indian subjects'.[2] Dadabhai's guiding principle was that 'the English middle classes should take a correct view of the Indian position'.[3] Bringing out the *Voice* meant enlisting the aid of editors in all the main cities of India,[4] and this in turn helped to forge links between these centres.

Plans for a 'systematically organised federation of the Native Press in India'[5] had less success. They had first been proposed by the Poona Sarvajanik Sabha at the time of the Delhi Durbar as a means of unifying editorial policy and providing a forum to discuss 'the great political questions' of the day.[6] A Press Conference did meet once in 1878, when it discussed a list of subjects prepared by the Poona Sabha; but it never met again.[7] Attempts to organise the Calcutta press also came to nothing. On the other hand Lytton's threat to the freedom of the press had been a warning to Indian journalists that they must organise in self-defence; while under Ripon, the case for unity rested not on defence but on opportunity, since the Viceroy invited the editors to submit opinions on legislation. When in December 1882 Norendranath Sen, editor of the *Indian Mirror*, who was in Bombay attendingt he annual Theosophical Convention, again raised the question of a press federation,[8] many Indian papers lent their support.[9] The *Bengalee*, edited by Banerjea, was enthusiastic. 'There are great questions of

---

[1] Prospectus, *Voice of India*, I, no. I (January 1883).
[2] Malabari to Naoroji, 7 February 1884. NP.
[3] Prospectus, *Voice of India*, I, no. I (January 1883).
[4] Naoroji to Editor of *Hindoo Patriot* (April 1884). NP
[5] *Indian Mirror*, 2 February 1883.
[6] *Ibid.* 4 January 1878 and 17 June 1883.
[7] *Ibid.* 4, 12, 15 January 1878.
[8] 'A Federation of the native press', editorial, *Indian Mirror*, 28 November 1882.   [9] See *Voice of India*, I, no. 7 (July 1883); and *Tribune*, 30 June 1883.

national importance upon which the country is united', he wrote. '...Our public bodies are known to act in concert. Why should not the Press act in concert too...? The voice of an unified nation, backed by a united press, would be simply irresistible.'[1] But enthusiasm was not enough. Problems of organisation, location, and finance were still too great. The press association did not materialise.

The scheme for a Constitutional Reform Association sprang from the Irish party at Westminster. In 1874 Frank Hugh O'Donnell, who claimed to be the directing brain of Isaac Butt's parliamentary group, and who took it upon himself to represent the unenfranchised Empire, had suggested that Indian political leaders should co-operate with the Irish. In 1883, when the Irish were more militant, these plans were revived. Besides publishing a scheme for a Constitutional Reform Association for India, Davitt toyed with the notion of giving Dadabhai an Irish seat. Parnell, it is said, 'liked the plan very much' but feared it might not be understood in Ireland.[2] However, the suggestion that the Indians should form an association with a central office in London and branches in all the Presidency capitals found a grateful response in the Indian press, and several detailed schemes were put forward.[3] The *Hindu* of Madras came closest in its plans to anticipating the future Congress. Calling for a 'national movement', the paper deplored the lack of an 'organised and central outlet' which could command the ear of government; '...we do not see', the *Hindu* declared, 'why the associations that have been started in several important towns throughout the country cannot arrange to depute delegates to meet in a central place. They can devise a scheme of perpetual constitutional agitation and thereby provide a means of bringing the united Indian public opinion to the notice of Government or Parliament in a manner the force of which it will be impossible for the Anglo-Indian or the English public to mistake.'[4]

---

[1] *Bengalee*, 23 June 1883.

[2] See F. H. O'Donnell, *A History of the Irish Parliamentary Party* (London, 1910), II, 428–31 and C. C. O'Brien, *Parnell and his Party 1880–90* (Oxford, 1957), pp. 22–3.

[3] See *Native Opinion*, Bombay, 4 February 1883, quoted in *Voice of India*, I, no. 2 (February 1883); and *Brahmo Public Opinion*, 18 January 1883, quoted in *Voice of India*, I, no. 1 (January 1883).

[4] *Hindu*, 18 January 1883.

It was at this point that the Ilbert bill was brought forward. The rodomontade it evoked from the Anglo-Indian community surprised not only the Viceroy but also leaders of Indian opinion. They had greeted the bill with mild enthusiasm, as a 'small improvement in the Code'. Ilbert, they were prepared to admit, had moved 'in the right direction...but he does not proceed very far'.[1] 'We fight for the right', the *Kesari* told its readers in the Deccan, 'because it is the first step on the great ladder.'[2] The racial extravaganza conjured up by the embattled defenders of white supremacy at first merely irritated Indians, but it ended by driving their movements closer to national organisation.

No one in India doubted that the compromise over the bill was a defeat for Ripon's liberal policy. Hume summed up the 'sadness and dissatisfaction' among Indians following the affair. '...there is', he wrote, 'a deepseated growing belief that the existing form of Govt. has been weighed in the balance and found wanting...our failure in the Ilbert Bill matter has unquestionably prepared the way for this feeling.'[3] The Indian press drew the same moral. In the old days co-operation and partnership with Anglo-Indians had seemed possible, but now 'friendship between the races has...become utterly impossible'. 'We must agitate', the *Amrita Bazar Patrika* concluded.[4] The organ of the Poona elite drew the same lesson, telling its readers to banish any 'fond day-dream that the Anglo-Indian Community will ever make common cause with them...We can never hope or deserve success if we foolishly rely upon the personal magnanimity of those who rule India'.[5] Moreover, the tactical lesson was drawn. 'Why should we regret that this spirit of union and agitation has ended in success for those who have shown it', asked one Bombay newspaper, on hearing of the concordat, 'when it is possible for us to act likewise when placed in similar circumstances?'[6]

But the Indians saw the advantages of appearing as the

[1] *Amrita Bazar Patrika*, 3 February 1883.
[2] *Kesari*, 6 March 1883, quoted in *Voice of India*, I, no. 3 (March 1883); and see B. Krishna Singh, *Lord Ripon's Policy: observations on the Criminal Jurisdiction Bill* (Bangalore, 1883), p. 8.
[3] Hume to Ripon, 4 March 1884, RP, Add. MSS 43616.
[4] *Amrita Bazar Patrika*, 26 April 1883.
[5] *The Quarterly Journal of the Poona Sarvajanik Sabha*, v, no. 4 (April 1883), Independent Section, pp. 25–6.
[6] *Indu Prakash*, 31 December 1883, quoted in RNP (Bombay), 5 January 1884.

defenders of the British Viceroy against the British community; and so the exigencies of this campaign forced on them another bout of all-India activity. In Bengal and Bombay the politicians decided to forget their local grievances and to 'uphold Ripon in any course he thinks proper to follow'.[1] Calcutta called upon Mehta, Tyabji, Naoroji and Mandlik in Bombay for a memorial to stiffen Ripon's resistance,[2] and the leading men of the Presidency capitals acted in close co-operation to secure as favourable a settlement as possible.[3] Although they were disappointed at the outcome, they stood together behind the Viceroy. Mandlik, the elder statesman of Bombay, successfully urged moderation in Calcutta.[4] 'For the first time in modern history', the *Indian Mirror* stated, 'Hindus, Mohammedans, Sikhs, Rajputs, Bengalis, Madrasis, Bombayites, Punjabis, and Purbiahs have united to join in a constitutional combination to support the policy of...Government.'[5] It was equally striking that this all-India solidarity had been shown over what was chiefly a Bengali issue, for race relations were more acrimonious in Bengal than elsewhere.

While the battle over the bill was being fought out, other lively issues had arisen. One was the Saligram Idol case and the subsequent imprisonment of Surendranath Banerjea for contempt of court. The sufferings of Surendranath for having so strenuously and demonstratively defended the idol elicited Sanskrit verses in his honour from the pandits of Nadia[6] as well as a National Fund from the generosity of Bengal.[7] The

[1] Mandlik to Manmohan Ghose, telegram, 25 December 1883, enclosed in Mandlik to Mehta, 25 December 1883. Mehta Papers.

[2] Ghose to Mehta, 21 December 1883; and Mandlik to Mehta, 24 December 1883. Mehta Papers.

[3] See Mandlik to Mehta, 27 December 1883; Ghose to Malabari, and Amir Ali to Malabari, enclosed in Malabari to Mehta, 8 January 1884; also Malabari to Mehta, 6 January 1884; Furdoonjee to Kristo Das Pal, 12 January 1884, enclosed in Furdoonjee to Mehta, 12 January 1884. Mehta Papers.

[4] 'The situation is no doubt grave', wrote Mandlik in justification of this advice, 'but it is very delicate. The only Viceroy (recently at all events) who has done some real service, shall we drive away?...I am angry too. But let no man act spasmodically and strike a man who has made it possible to speak fearlessly. Hit the rest as hard as you please,' Mandlik to Mehta, 27 December 1883. Mehta Papers.

[5] *Indian Mirror*, 23 May 1883.   [6] *Ibid.* 2 June 1883.

[7] Apparently the National Fund was first suggested by Tarapada Banerjea, a pleader from Krishnagar, Nadia. In 1883 he also proposed a National Assembly, or Congress, for India. See *Indian Mirror*, 4 July 1883.

Idol case illustrates how bad relations between the communities had become in Calcutta. No doubt the cry of religion in danger was factitious, since Mr Justice Norris had the stone idol brought to court after both parties in the dispute had agreed to its production;[1] but it touched off a furore in which orthodox Hindus combined with the western educated to demonstrate vigorously against the court and in favour of Surendranath who had dared to criticise it.[2] Admittedly the total subscriptions to the National Fund were less than ten thousand rupees, whereas the Anglo-Indian Defence Association was reputed to have raised fifteen times that amount.[3] Moreover the Fund was almost wholly a Bengali affair, although the press in other parts of India donated a few lines to it.[4] Even in Bengal, the *Hindoo Patriot* and the zemindars' association, fearing perhaps that their rivals would in this way form a central organisation which would swamp the provincial associations, boycotted the Fund.[5] Nevertheless the National Fund was important, and since its sponsors intended to send delegates to England,[6] they needed the credential of being national representatives. This made a National Conference essential.

During December 1883, the government held an International Exhibition in Calcutta, to which visitors came from all over the country. Seeking to profit from this, the Indian Association had decided to hold its first National Conference in Calcutta at the same time. The organisers hopefully claimed that the meeting would pave the way 'for holding such Confer-

---

[1] 'The history of the case', the lieutenant-governor of Bengal reported, 'is instructive and ludicrous. It was a family quarrel about the idol. The elder brother had stolen it, and when told to produce it said his younger brother had taken it to some temple...Then both parties...agreed to its production, and...brought from the temple...[it] was found to be not the real idol but a sham one!' Rivers Thompson to Ripon, 16 May 1883, RP, Add. MSS 43594.

[2] H. L. Harrison, Commissioner of Police, to Rivers Thompson, 8 May 1883, enclosed in Thompson to Ripon, 10 May 1883; H. J. Wilkins, Deputy Commissioner of Police, to Private Secretary, Lieutenant-Governor, 9 May 1883 enclosed in Thompson to Ripon, 12 May 1883; Wilkins to Private Secretary, 13 May 1883, enclosed in Thompson to Ripon, 16 May 1883, RP, Add. MSS 43594.

[3] Seventh Annual Report of the Indian Association, 1883, pp. 4–7. IA.

[4] See for example, *Native Opinion*, 22 July 1883, quoted in *Voice of India*, I, no. 8 (August 1883); and *Indian Spectator*, 22 July 1883.

[5] *Hindoo Patriot*, 23 July and 13, 20, 27 August 1883.

[6] *Bengalee*, 21 July, and 18 August 1883.

ences from year to year'.[1] According to Ananda Mohan Bose, it would be the first stage towards a National Parliament, and Wilfrid Blunt, premature as usual, saw the Conference as evidence that India was ready for self-government.[2] The reality was in comparison drab, for only a hundred or so delegates turned up; a handful came from Bombay, Ahmadabad, Madras and upper India, but the rest were all local men.[3] The British Indian Association, seeing in the Conference nothing more than their Bengali opponents disguised as all-India figures, boycotted its proceedings. Newspapers in Bengal gave the Conference some space, but elsewhere in India it attracted no attention. Yet in its programme and its proceedings, the Conference was a dress rehearsal. Among the subjects discussed were the employment of Indians, representative government, the separation of judicial and executive functions—much the same as those which were to be brought up at the first Congress. The proceedings of the Conference were conducted in English,[4] as those of Congress were to be.

Early in 1884 another call for experiments like the Calcutta Conference was made by Robert Osborne, an English member of parliament. Osborne sympathised with these aspirations, but he saw that he could not present India's case at Westminster unless it was first presented in India. Serious lobbying in England required an organisation in India with claims to speak for the country as a whole. For this purpose, a London-based group would not do.[5] He explained this to leading Indians in the three Presidencies.

If you succeed in establishing a permanent organisation, the first thing you ought to do is to draw up a programme of political reform, and if possible, obtain for this programme the approval of the educated classes in all three Presidencies. This, I apprehend, might be easily done through the various associations. Nothing would more strengthen the hands of your friends in this country than to have some authoritative statement which should show to all the world exactly what the people of India want...to set the constituencies in motion will not

[1] Seventh Annual Report of the Indian Association, 1883, p. 12. IA.
[2] Blunt, *India Under Ripon*, pp. 114–18.
[3] *Bengalee*, 5 January 1884.
[4] Banerjea, *A Nation in Making*, p. 85; and *Bengalee*, 5 January 1884.
[5] What he had in mind was the National Representative Committee, formed by Indian students and businessmen in 1883. It had aims similar to Dadabhai's East India Association. But it did not survive long. See Majumdar, *Indian Political Associations*, pp. 103–4, 180–1.

be difficult, as soon as they know for certain what the people of India wish for.[1]

By now there were more and more political activities to be co-ordinated in the way Osborne was suggesting. In 1884 the Indian Union, an organisation consisting mainly of Hindu lawyers but containing a few Muslims, was formed in Calcutta with the specific aim of drawing together the various strands in Bengal's politics. At the same time the Indian Association was expanding, so that by 1885 it controlled some eighty branches.[2] When the second National Conference met in December 1885 (simultaneously with the National Congress in Bombay), it was convened through the joint efforts of the Indian, the British Indian and the National Mahommedan Associations, together with the Indian Union.[3] The Conference of 1885 claimed to be 'National' in scope,[4] although it was still primarily a Bengali affair.

In the other Presidencies there were similar trends. In Madras there had been a remarkable expansion of small local associations during Ripon's viceroyalty. Almost fifty had appeared in 1882;[5] three years later there were nearly a hundred.[6] In May 1884 the Madras Mahajana Sabha was founded to co-ordinate them and so to 'provide a focus for the non-official intelligence spreading through the Presidency'. By holding an annual convention in Madras, and smaller district conferences in the mofussil towns, it would play its part 'in developing into a national feeling what has been, till quite recently, an essentially local feeling, with the prospect...of further enlargement, when Calcutta, Bombay, and other capital cities hold similar Conferences and step forward to fraternise with us'.[7] At its first conference for the Madras Presidency,

---

[1] Osborne to Mehta, 18 April 1884. Mehta Papers.
[2] Ninth Annual Report of the Indian Association, 1885, pp. 9–11. IA.
[3] According to its organisers, 'This instance of united action on the part of the different sections of the Calcutta community' was 'the first of its kind in the history of this metropolis', Ninth Annual Report of the Indian Association, 1885, p. 5. IA.   [4] Banerjea, *A Nation in Making*, p. 98.
[5] G. Subramania Iyer, quoted in *Indian Mirror*, 2 June 1883.
[6] *Report of the Administration of the Madras Presidency during the year 1885–6* (Madras, 1886), part III, appendix, pp. cliv–clvii.
[7] *First Conference of Native Gentlemen from the different parts of the Presidency of Madras held under the auspices of the Madras Mahajana Sabha... on 29th and 30th December 1884 and 1st and 2nd January 1885.* (Madras, 1885), p. vi.

convened in December 1884, the Sabha lived up to these hopes by putting forward a programme similar to the proposals of the National Conference of 1883. Thus in Madras, as in Calcutta, a centre had been formed for the political experiments of the whole region. At the same time Madras was moving out of the traditional isolation of south India, and was considering liaisons with the rest of the country.

Since 1883, Telang, Mehta, and Tyabji had been striving to rally support for a new association in Bombay. In January 1885 they succeeded in establishing the Bombay Presidency Association. 'The desire of the promoters of this movement', said Sir Jamsetjee Jeejeebhoy, that old name in Bombay politics, 'is to concentrate existing forces';[1] Tyabji proclaimed that 'a city like Bombay, the capital I may say of Western India ...ought to possess a well-organised and truly national organisation'.[2] Not only did it quickly prove itself the champion of local interests,[3] it also became a pioneer of new methods in national politics. By April, the Bombay Presidency Association had taken up the project for a National Telegraph Union: and it had resolved to approach 'the leading recognised associations in Calcutta, Madras, the Punjab, Poona and elsewhere', and to collect accurate information concerning the 'public interests of the Country'.[4] In September, working together with the Poona Sabha, the Indian Association and the Madras Mahajana Sabha, the Bombay Presidency Association made a joint appeal to the British electorate, sending three delegates to England, N. G. Chandavarkar from Bombay, Manmohan Ghose from Calcutta, and S. Ramaswami Mudaliyar from Madras.[5] In

---

[1] Report of a public meeting of natives held on Saturday, 31 January 1885, at the Framjee Cawasji Institute. Mehta Papers.

[2] *Ibid.* By the end of 1885 the new body possessed 385 members. (Proceedings of the First Annual General Meeting, 7 April 1886, para. 2.) *Bombay Presidency Association. First Annual Report, 1885* (Bombay, 1886), p. 9.

[3] The Bombay Presidency Association had welcomed Lord Reay, the new Governor, on behalf of the Bombay Presidency; representations were made to government on the Forest grievances of the people of Thana and Kolaba; also on Abkari grievances (including passing on the petition of the owners of toddy-trees, again in Thana and Kolaba). *Ibid.* pp. 25–32, 177–88.

[4] Minutes of Council Meeting, 25 April 1885, Bombay Presidency Association, MSS Records, 1.

[5] *Report of a General Meeting of the Bombay Presidency Association, 29 September 1885*; also see *Bombay Presidency Association. First Annual Report, 1885*, pp. 61–9.

December it was to do better still. It was to play host to the first National Congress.

Throughout the sub-continent there were signs of preparation for action which would rise above the merely local level. In 1884, following the first National Conference, Banerjea went on a propaganda tour in upper India.[1] The most impressive effort at co-operative planning came later that year—the 'spontaneous' demonstration in November and December 1884 to mark Ripon's departure from India, which showed 'a spirit of organisation which India has never known before'.[2] Meetings, processions, and a flood of appreciative addresses were arranged, not just in Bengal, but all over India. 'From Madras, from Mysore, from the Punjab and Gujerat they came as an organised voice, from the communities, where caste and race had merged their differences, in order to express their appreciation of the new principles of government.' As the Bombay crowds wished the Viceroy on his way, 'waving their banners, rushing along with the carriages, crowding the roofs, and even filling the trees, and cheering their hero to the very echo',[3] Malabari was moved to verse. Addressing Ripon, he wrote: 'Thou foundest us a weak, incoherent mass but leav'st us now one compact nation strong.'[4]

This enthusiasm had still to be given permanent institutional form. In a series of letters and editorial articles published between 20 December 1884 and March 1885, the *Indian Mirror* called for a 'national assembly' for India.[5] Indian leaders, assembled in Bombay to bid farewell to Ripon, made plans for a congress.[6] In the spring of 1885 the volunteer movement attracted the attention of educated Indians, with Surendranath's *Bengalee* again in the van.[7] In April, a project to keep the English press informed about India resulted in a National Telegraph Union, yet another instance of co-operation between the Presidencies, and a testimonial to Hume's energy. Next

[1] See *Bengalee*, 10, 17 May 1884, and 7, 14 June 1884; and Banerjea, *A Nation in Making*, p. 87.
[2] S. [Justice Scott] to editor, *Times of India*, 22 December 1884.
[3] *Ibid.*
[4] *Indian Spectator*, 21 December 1884.
[5] *Indian Mirror*, 20, 30 December 1884, 13, 15, 20, 21, 28 January, 13 February, 12 March 1885.
[6] See below, p. 274.
[7] *Bengalee*, 16 May, 20 June, 11 July 1885.

month, with a British election on its way, the politicians in Bombay and Calcutta saw that the 'crisis was at hand', and that 'an Indian reform party earnest and hard-working, well-coached, must be formed mainly from the Liberals in that Parliament'.[1] By June the feeling was general that 'now is the time to act'.[2] In July the associations agreed to send their delegates on a joint mission to England. By that December, 'a time of exceptional political activity in India',[3] everyone seemed to be going to meetings. In the south, the Madras Mahajana Sabha and the Theosophical Society were assembling. At Jubbulpore, the Eurasian and Anglo-Indian Conference met for the first time.[4] At Calcutta, there was the second National Conference, and at Bombay the first Indian National Congress. Banerjea, speaking at the Calcutta Conference, noticed this new vogue for national confabulations. 'Indeed all India',—he said, after listing the various conferences—'seem at the present moment to have met in solemn conclave to think out the great problem of national advancement.'[5]

The National Congress and the National Conference were organised 'on almost the same lines'.[6] Both passed resolutions on the need to reconstitute the Legislative Councils, both demanded simultaneous examinations for the civil service, with a change in the age limit, both called for cuts in civil expenditure and condemned the proposed increase in military charges. Moreover their plans for their own future were much the same: an annual convention meeting in the main cities of India in rotation.[7] Where there was so much in common, the obvious outcome was union, and in fact in December 1886 the National Conference was to merge with the Congress when the latter

[1] Summary of letter from Telang, in Wacha to Naoroji, 13 May 1885. NP. In April William Digby had offered his services in parliament as 'member for India' (Digby to Mehta, 24 April 1885. Mehta Papers).
[2] Malabari to Naoroji, 10 June 1885. NP.
[3] *Bombay Gazette*, 17 December 1885.
[4] A Eurasian Association had been formed in Calcutta in 1876; since then another half dozen branches had been formed in Madras, Bombay, Simla, Mysore, and Burma, modelled on the Calcutta association, and operating under its aegis, *Bombay Gazette*, 30 December 1885.
[5] Proceedings of the National Conference, Calcutta, 25–27 December 1885. IA.
[6] *Bombay Gazette*, 17 December 1885.
[7] Compare *I.N.C.* 1885, with Proceedings of the National Conference, Calcutta, 25–27 December 1885. IA.

met in Calcutta.[1] Neither body was conspicuously stronger than the other, and it was merely the play of personalities and circumstances which decided that the Indian National Congress rather than the National Conference should become the matrix of the later national movement.

It seems surprising that Surendranath Banerjea and the Indian Association, who organised the Calcutta National Conference, were not apprised earlier of the plans for the Bombay Congress; and there is reason to believe that some of the organisers of the National Congress disliked Surendranath and conspired to exclude him. Many resented his showmanship in politics, and considered a civilian dismissed from the service to be an unsuitable leader of the new organisation.[2] As it was, only three men from Calcutta attended the Bombay Congress.[3] In contrast, Madras was certainly informed in good time to send a powerful contingent to Bombay.[4] If Congress wanted to appear moderate, the co-operation of Madras was its best advertisement. In pushing the claims of the Congress, much was made of the fact that the National Conference was backed by the Calcutta associations alone, while the Congress had two Presidencies solidly behind it. Yet there could not be an all-India organisation which excluded the Bengal politicians. The decision to hold the second Congress session in Calcutta resolved the issue, and gave Surendranath a place inside the Congress pandal which he jealously guarded for more than thirty years.

※

[1] As Surendranath wrote, 'The two Conferences met about the same time, discussed similar views and voiced the same grievances and aspirations... Henceforth those who worked with us joined the Congress and heartily co-operated with it', Banerjea, *A Nation in Making* p. 99.
[2] B. C. Pal, *Character Sketches* (Calcutta, 1957), p. 29.
[3] Besides these three, the three delegates representing Lahore, Allahabad and Benares were also Bengalis.
[4] Madras resolved to give the Bombay Congress its full support; see *The Madras Mahajana Sabha: Annual Report for 1885–86* (Madras, 1886), pp. iv, 6; twenty-one delegates came from Madras presidency, of whom eight were from Madras itself. The delegates included the president and the secretary of the Mahajana Sabha, the editor of the *Hindu*, and the president of the Tanjore People's Association. At least ten were lawyers. (*I.N.C.* 1885, pp. 7–11.)

India's organisation for freedom was established by a Briton. His role in promoting it is both legendary and obscure. Allan Octavian Hume had come to India before the Mutiny, with a bias in favour of its natives inherited from his Radical father. During the crisis he had, like others, shown courage: what was not so common, after it, he showed moderation.[1] But he was never to forget the lessons of the revolt. His abiding fear was that the Raj was on the brink of destruction. 'You are driving a coach', Hume wrote to Northbrook in 1872, 'that however grand it looks, is utterly top heavy, that the slightest jolt, a single stone under a single wheel will probably upset [it].'[2] Acutely sensitive to the changing climate of opinion in India in the decades after 1857, Hume came to feel that even the dark days of the Mutiny had been better than the grey neutrality of these later years. Then many of the princes and people of India had rallied behind the British to crush the rising; who would rally now? 'I doubt whether one vestige could now be found', Hume declared, 'of those old loyal feelings that 20 years ago animated so many of the best and most influential of our subjects.'[3]

An able if an eccentric civilian, Hume's official career was distinguished by his propensity to give the Viceroys his unsolicited advice. Step by step, this specialist in agriculture and expert on ornithology came to think of himself as the great authority on Indian opinion. 'I know it is a strange thing to say', he told the Viceroy in 1872, 'but I have lived much among Natives, and know more of their language, habits of thought, and feelings, than most officials.'[4] This was his qualification for reminding the Viceroys of the fatal defects in their empire. His theme was that things had changed for the worse since the Mutiny:

A studied and invariable disregard, if not actually contempt for the opinions and feelings of our subjects, is at the present day the leading characteristic of our Government in every branch of the administration. We know, or believe we know, what is right and what is best for the people, and on this, strong in the consciousness of the best of

[1] W. Wedderburn, *Allan Octavian Hume, C.B.* (London, 1913), pp. 9–15.
[2] Hume to Northbrook, 1 August 1872, Northbrook Papers, MSS Eur. C. 144 (13).
[3] *Ibid.*
[4] *Ibid.*

motives, and heedless that these are wholly misunderstood by and cruelly misrepresented to the millions who are affected by our acts, we insist. Restless north men utterly incapable of appreciating or realizing in any practical manner the *dolce far niente* philosophy of our southern subjects, we hurry on from change to change, seeking to force in a life time that to be healthy must be the product of ages[1] [*sic*].

Even when public opinion was 'ostensibly represented', it was 'utterly disregarded'. He asked 'whether something more real in the shape of a Native element cannot be introduced into the Government of the country; and whether...it is really too late to expect ever to regain the confidence and (so far as such *can* be given to Foreign rulers) the affection of our subjects... I am strongly impressed with the conviction that the fate of the Empire is trembling in the balance'.[2]

Such apprehensions constantly haunted him, although his grounds for them kept changing. In the early 1870s, Hume's contacts were not in the main with educated and politically-minded Indians, which may explain why it was not from that direction that he then feared catastrophe. On the contrary, he looked to education, as the Utilitarians had done before him, to reconcile India to British rule. 'It is possible...', Hume conceded, 'that...the evil days will be tided over, and the people weaned from their anger with us, and as education spreads taught somewhat to appreciate our measures.'[3] Later, it was as the spokesman of the educated Indians that Hume saw himself. To this role he brought all his prognostications of the sudden and awful dissolution of the Raj. These fears help to explain the story, encouraged by him and still in vogue, that the Congress was conceived as a 'safety valve' for pressures which might otherwise destroy the Raj.[4]

[1] Hume to Northbrook, 1 August 1872, Northbrook Papers, MSS Eur. C. 144 (13). When he protested against the Masters and Servants bill, Hume returned to this argument. 'Nations, states, communities, are...the evolved results of the conflict or co-operation of an interminable series of internal and external activities; neither they nor their laws nor institutions are any one man's, or any one time's creations—they are growths.' Hume to Lytton, 11 January 1878 [incorrectly dated 1877], LP (519/7).
[2] Hume to Northbrook, 1 August 1872, Northbrook Papers, MSS Eur. C. 144 (13).   [3] *Ibid.*
[4] Hume (and Baring) had indeed referred to Ripon's local self-government schemes as a safety valve (Hume to Ripon, 30 December 1882, RP, Add. MSS 43616), and the Congress was described by Hume in the same terms in his Allahabad speech in 1888. But the undocumented (and

After his retirement in 1882 Hume let it be known that he had turned down high office—a place on the Viceroy's Council, or the lieutenant-governorship of the Punjab—so as to devote himself to the Indian cause. This story deeply impressed the Indians, who, after all, had no experience of high government posts. Like so many stories of sacrifice for the Indian National Congress, it was to become enshrined in mythology; the truth is less romantic. Late in 1877 when a vacancy on the Council had occurred, John Strachey grudgingly admitted that Hume, 'notwithstanding his obvious faults', was the likeliest man for the place.[1] Conspicuous among these faults was his habit of castigating the 'clique of civilians (of which Strachey was the head)' as 'uncompromising despots, who wanted to keep the people for ever in the cradle'.[2] In the event, Strachey came down against the appointment,[3] and this decision hit Hume hard, for he had been passed over for a man younger and not obviously abler. '...I suppose that I have more ill-wishers than any man in India', he complained to Lytton. Hume who 'never knowingly did a single soul an injury' was at a loss to understand this 'final and irretrievable failure, which closes my public career'.[4] In 1879 Hume suffered a further humiliation: he was deprived of his post as secretary to government,[5] and three years later he retired. Self-esteem, not self-denial, took him out of the service. The same self-esteem kept him in India.

This reverse explains in part why Hume now turned his back on his old colleagues in the bureaucracy and became one of their fiercest critics. It also throws some light on that hunger for recognition and influence that characterised the rest of his time in India. As Ripon's trusted adviser, apportioning praise and blame to senior officials,[6] as self-elected spokesman of the Indians, and later as organiser and secretary of the Indian National Congress, Hume consoled himself for his humiliation in Lytton's time. Dufferin's private secretary noticed this:

improbable) story that Hume had knowledge of some vast conspiracy to overthrow the Raj, and that he used Congress to head it off is what has kept this theory alive.

[1] Strachey to Lytton, 13 October 1877, LP (519/6).
[2] Hume to Ripon, n.d. (received 23 January 1883), RP, Add. MSS 43616.
[3] Strachey to Lytton, 25 January 1878, LP (519/7).
[4] Hume to Lytton, 8 February 1878, LP (519/7).
[5] See *Englishman*, 27 June 1879.
[6] See Hume's correspondence with Ripon, 1882–4, RP, Add. MSS 43616.

'Hume...aspires, I think, to become the Indian Parnell, and already dreams of a House of Representatives in which he would be a leader of the Opposition.'[1] But Hume's motives were more complex than that; respect played as large a part as revenge. His sympathy for India was as real as that of William Wedderburn, William Wordsworth, Henry Beveridge and Henry Cotton, men who still retained their faith in collaboration with educated Indians. Such men were the true heirs of mid-Victorian liberalism, but in British India they were coming by this time to sound like voices from the past.

In retirement Hume was valuable to Ripon who wanted to go some way towards meeting Indian aspirations and who thought Hume was the man who could tell him what they were. On their side, Indians esteemed Hume as the man who could tell them what Viceregal Lodge was thinking. Hume's account of his popular connections lost nothing in the telling. When he wrote a letter supporting the new local self-government policy, he forecast to Ripon that it would be reproduced 'in every native paper in India'.[2] At the same time, he was willing to give Ripon the benefit of his popularity, proposing that the Viceroy's views should be distributed among Indians under Hume's name[3]—a dexterous way of showing the Indians that he was the Viceroy's spokesman, while showing the Viceroy that he was the Indians' spokesman. This particular proposal was turned down by Ripon, but Hume strove to maintain this role of post office for the hopes and fears of New India. Through him the politicians sent their promises of support;[4] through him they mailed their fears that the district officers would not work the local self-government scheme.[5] As the spokesman of political India he turned even his errors to good account. In 1884 he warned Ripon that the Indians would not accept the compromise on the Ilbert bill. They did accept it. So Hume changed from

[1] Mackenzie Wallace to A. Mackenzie, 11 May 1886, DP 37 (Reel 525).
[2] Hume to Ripon, 6 November 1882, RP, Add. MSS 43616. In fact it did appear in a hundred newspapers.
[3] Hume to Ripon, 18 December 1882, RP, Add. MSS 43616.
[4] For example, Sisir Kumar Ghose, the editor and proprietor of the *Amrita Bazar Patrika*, (described by Hume as 'one of the dearest, best and purest of men') wrote saying that Ripon's self-government scheme 'has unnerved me a good deal...and taken away from me the "ferocity"...that I feel for your officials', Ghose to Hume, 24 May 1882, enclosed in Hume to Ripon, 28 May 1882, RP, Add. MSS 43616.
[5] Hume to Ripon, 30 December 1882, RP, Add. MSS 43616.

prophet to penitent. He had only conveyed what he thought to be 'native opinion'; he had been wrong in thinking that 'the opposite party were irreconcilable and too strong for the moderate party'. He made much of his limitations. 'Personally I have no power, and very little influence or knowledge', Hume wrote:

> ...by myself I should be a broken reed on which to lean...I generally can learn what will be the outcome of cogitations of the native mind, but not from any superior acumen or knowledge of my own, but simply because for their own and their country's sake a body of men, mostly of Asiatic origin, who for a variety of causes are deeply and especially interested in the welfare and progress of India and who possess facilities which no other man or body of men living do, for gauging the feelings of the natives, have seen fit...to give me their confidence to a *certain limited* extent... And it is the same (let me make a clean breast of it) in the many cases in which I may have appeared to have supported your policy and aided you...the action was in most cases initiated through me, and I have worked like a slave at it, but the success, such as it has been that has attended the various movements—whether petitioning the Queen for your reappointment, tranquillising the native press, reconciling them to any modifications you found necessary in your policy, or preparing counterdemonstrations of goodwill to rebut those in a contrary sense of the Europeans— have been due solely to those who have allowed me to work for, and practically with, them...I borrow no plumes, but others choose to invest me at times with an appearance of what I do not possess.[1]

These then are some of the qualifications that must be borne in mind when assessing the role of Hume in the founding of the Indian National Congress. By the early 1880s the idea of a national representative body was being discussed in every Presidency of India, and there had already been a number of attempts to bring it into being. The 1885 Congress itself was one of several such attempts, and its organisation owed something to men in Bombay, Poona, Madras and Calcutta. It was not the work of Hume alone, although he had a hand in it. During Ripon's viceroyalty, Hume had made himself very useful as a sub-editor of Indian opinion and as an agent of Indian action. As such he was admirably suited to be one of the organisers of the Congress. His visit to England in the summer of 1885 was a further inducement to accept his services, because the new body which was coming into existence felt the old need to appeal to London.

[1] Hume to Ripon, 25 December 1883, RP, Add. MSS 43616.

Another myth about the origin of Congress must be dispelled. Years later its first president, W. C. Bonnerjee, who should have known better, put about the story that the idea of Congress was Dufferin's. He recalled Hume's saying that in 1884 he had the notion of bringing together leading Indian politicians once a year to discuss social reforms, that he consulted Dufferin early in 1885, and that the Viceroy suggested instead a specifically political annual convention, which would give the government a useful idea of what was being felt in 'native circles'.[1] *A priori*, the story that the Indian National Congress was conceived by the Viceroy of India is unlikely, and Hume's testimony is always suspect.[2] A better witness is Hume's biographer, Sir William Wedderburn, who was a judge of the Bombay high court, and in close touch with Indian opinion both in the city and in Poona where he had previously served. Wedderburn's version of the founding of Congress states that in 1883 Hume issued an appeal to the young men of Bengal to form an 'Indian National Union'. It was set up, apparently, but there is little evidence of its activities. It is supposed to have set up a number of local committees, and on the strength of their support the organisers decided to hold a conference at Poona, where all those who were interested in the Union could 'exchange opinions'. The meeting was later switched to Bombay where it became the first session of the Indian National Congress. In all this organising, Hume, so his biographer implies, had taken a leading part.[3] But when exactly did it all happen? Wedderburn is silent; nothing conclusive about Hume's role can be deduced from his evidence. The Bombay Congress gave an account of its own origins. According to its report, the decision to hold a conference 'of the Indian National Union' was taken in March 1885. Poona was settled upon as the venue, and a circular announced that the conference would be held between 25 and 31 December 1885. The delegates would be 'leading politicians well acquainted with the English language'; they would be drawn 'from all parts of the Bengal, Bombay and Madras Presidencies'. Besides enabling 'all the

[1] Bonnerjee in his introduction to G. A. Natesan (ed.), *Indian Politics* (Madras, 1898), pp. vii–viii.
[2] 'Hume was said in my time to be the greatest liar who ever came to India,' Maine to Dufferin, 2 June 1886, DP 37 (Reel 525).
[3] Wedderburn, *Hume*, pp. 47–57.

most earnest labourers in the cause of national progress to become personally known to each other', the conference would 'decide upon the political operations to be undertaken during the ensuing year'.[1] Obviously, this version is inadequate.

But it is possible to get closer to the facts. From October 1884 Hume had been active in organising the Ripon memorial; after Ripon's departure in December he stayed on in Bombay, busily stirring up the local leaders as well as representatives from other provinces who had come to see the Viceroy off. By March he was in Calcutta, working hard to launch the National Telegraphic Agency.[2] In May, Hume saw Dufferin to discuss the volunteer movement,[3] and afterwards he issued a circular, marked 'Private and Confidential. For the information of the Inner circle or Select Committee', urging the 'National Party' to be patient.[4] By July, Hume, in Bombay *en route* to England where he intended to raise support for these various schemes, met the members of the Bombay Presidency Association.[5] While he was in England, doing the rounds of the Liberal leaders,[6] the associations in Calcutta, Madras, Poona and Bombay were preoccupied with their scheme for sending three delegates to England, where they would put India's case before the electorate.[7] Throughout September and October, they were busy drafting leaflets and instructions for this mission.[8] In November the British general election failed to produce the conclusive Liberal majority which Hume had hoped for, and

[1] *I.N.C.* 1885, p. 5.
[2] See Bose's Diary, 22 March 1885 quoted in Sarkar, *A Life of Ananda Mohan Bose*, p. 85.
[3] Granting Hume an interview on 5 May 'to discuss the volunteering question', Dufferin told him that 'Personally, I am rather favourable than the reverse to the idea', Dufferin to Hume, 5 May 1885, DP 47 (Reel 528).
[4] See enclosed circular, Hume to Dufferin, 12 June 1885, and Reay to Dufferin, 24 May 1885, DP 47 (Reel 528), quoted below, p. 276.
[5] Minutes of Council Meeting, 11 July 1885, Bombay Presidency Association, MSS Records 1.
[6] For Hume's visit to England, see *Indian Spectator*, 29 November 1885; Wedderburn, *Hume*, p. 54; G. L. Chandavarkar, *A Wrestling Soul: story of the life of Sir Narayan Chandavarkar* (Bombay, 1955), pp. 48–56, and R. A. J. Walling (ed.), *The Diaries of John Bright* (London, 1930), pp. 530–1.
[7] The decision was taken in June 1885 (see Minutes of Council Meeting, 20 June 1885, Bombay Presidency Association, MSS Records 1); the decision was formally announced at a General Meeting on 29 September 1885.
[8] See *Indian Leaflets*, nos. 1–14. (India Office Tracts, 658.)

the following month he was back in India. But as late as the middle of the month the Bombay Presidency Association still knew little about the projected conference at Poona. On 15 December the secretaries of the Association found it necessary to explain the objects of the Poona meeting and to ask the Council to support the Sarvajanik Sabha in holding it. Four days later, Bombay formally gave its backing and nominated its delegates.[1] At this point cholera broke out in Poona, and so the conference was moved to Bombay,[2] where the Presidency Association now acted as host. The decision was taken as late as 24 December;[3] Hume, Wedderburn,[4] Mehta, Telang and Dadabhai took the initiative in making the necessary arrangements.[5] Before the session of what was now called the Indian National Congress came to a close, the three delegates returned from England to report on their mission.

All the evidence suggests that none of this was Dufferin's handiwork. In May he had already informed the governor of Bombay that:

There is here a gentleman of the name of Hume...He was at one time employed by Government, but was got rid of on account of his impracticability. Since then he has become a resident in the country, and a disciple of Madame Blavatsky. He is clever and gentleman-like, but seems to have got a bee in his bonnet. Ripon told me that he knew a good deal of the Natives, and advised me to see him from time to time, which I have done with both pleasure and profit. At his last interview he told me that he and his friends were going to assemble a Political convention of delegates, as far as I understood, on the lines adopted by O'Connell previous to Catholic emancipation, and he said that they propose to ask you to act as Chairman. I took it upon myself to say that it would be impossible for anyone in your situation to accept such an offer. The functions of such an assembly must of necessity consist in criticizing the acts or policy of the Government, in formulating demands which probably it would be impossible to grant, and in adopting generally the procedure of all reform associations. The idea of wishing to associate the head of the Executive Government of a Province with such a programme I told him was absurd.[6]

[1] Minutes of Council Meeting, 15 December, and 19 December 1885, Bombay Presidency Association, MSS Records 1.
[2] *I.N.C.* 1885, p. 6.
[3] See Naoroji to Javerilal Umiashankar, 24 December 1885. NP.
[4] Before and during the first Congress, Wedderburn's house was the rendezvous of the organisers.
[5] Naoroji to Malabari, 24 December 1885. NP.
[6] Dufferin to Reay, 17 May 1885, DP 47 (Reel 528).

In his reply Lord Reay commented that Dufferin's letter confirmed what he 'had suspected about Hume';

With reference to Mr Hume, I was able to discover in the *most* confidential manner that he is the head-centre of an organisation from which emanated all the Ripon demonstrations, which has spread, and is spreading, all over India, and has for its object to bring native opinion into a focus. For that purpose the native press and the telegraph wires to the English papers are set in motion. I saw a printed slip which had been issued by Mr Hume to urge on his allies not to be hasty in the Volunteer movement, as his interviews with you had been very satisfactory.[1]

From these documents two conclusions seem to follow. In the first place, the organisation which produced the Congress had come into existence at the time of the Ripon demonstrations in the winter of 1884. Reporting on the progress of the 'Hume Crusade', Reay mentioned a memorandum that was being circulated in Bombay by the 'National party'. It urged that 'the engine which set the late Ripon demonstrations going must not be stopped!'[2] Secondly, there must be doubt about Bonnerjee's tale that Hume had in mind a social conference which he converted into a political organisation at the prompting of a sympathetic Viceroy. Long before he saw Dufferin, Hume had already declared to Malabari, who was trying to enlist his support for a programme of social reform, that a national organisation would have to leave such matters strictly alone.[3] Dufferin, on the other hand, always regretted that Congress had neglected 'social topics'.[4] From the time it was projected, the Congress was a specifically political convention.

Whatever its chroniclers may later have asserted, the founding of Congress did not mean that some great new force had been born in a twinkling. Such a romantic view does violence to the facts, and raises problems which no amount of ingenuity can solve. What matters is the trend towards national political organisation, and not the minutiae which accompanied it. To linger over the details of the formation of Congress would be to bring the history of the national movement down to the level of a detective story. Many of the riddles dissolve when the

---

[1] Reay to Dufferin, 24 May 1885, DP 47 (Reel 528).
[2] Reay to Dufferin, 4 June 1885, DP 47 (Reel 528).
[3] Hume to Malabari, *Indian Spectator*, 1 February 1885.
[4] Speech at St Andrew's Dinner, 30 November 1885, Dufferin and Ava, *Speeches delivered in India, 1884–8*, pp. 240–3.

genesis of Congress is examined in a more historical way, and put back into the framework of trial and error out of which the modern party was slowly to emerge. It should be obvious that before the delegates assembled at Bombay, there was already a tendency to raise its activities to the all-India level. The repeated efforts in the early 1880s to form a united organisation show that this tendency was growing stronger and stronger, and that the odds on one or other of these efforts succeeding were getting shorter. Congress was the experiment which, for reasons partly adventitious, was to survive.

Large claims have been made for this meeting of seventy-two men at Bombay in December 1885. Indeed, the claims began almost at once. The Bombay Presidency Association declared that the Congress marked 'an epoch in the political history of our countrymen';[1] the thought was echoed by the Indian press which promptly announced 'the birth of their national unity',[2] 'an era in the history of Indian political unity',[3] and 'an event of the highest significance'.[4] At the second Congress in 1886 there were 434 delegates, and at the third in 1887 there were 607. 'Indeed, what in 1885 was little more than an experiment', the Madras Congress announced, 'in 1887 bore every appearance of becoming a permanent National Institution'. In 1888 despite opposition from Government House and Muslims, the Congress at Allahabad attracted more than twice as many delegates as had gone to Madras in 1887.[5] To its supporters, in moments of euphoria, Congress might have seemed to be India's national party, but during its early years it was hardly that. It was more of a ramshackle set of local linkages whose task was to organise an annual tamasha. There were no paying members, no permanent organisation, no officials other than a

---

[1] 'It was the most visible outcome of that revolution in the political life of the Indians which has been slowly transforming their thoughts and intellects for the last 28 years, and which has evoked the national spirit...' *Bombay Presidency Association. First Annual Report, 1885*, p. 15.

[2] *Hindu*, 7 January 1886.

[3] *Indian Nation*, 4 January 1886, quoted in *Voice of India*, IV, no. 1 (January 1886).

[4] *Indu Prakash*, 4 January 1886.

[5] See *I.N.C.* 1885, p. 8; *I.N.C.* 1886, p. 3 and appendix I, pp. 113–40; *I.N.C.* 1887, p. 2 and appendix I, pp. 168–98; *I.N.C.* 1888, p. iii and appendix I, pp. 97–157.

general secretary, no central offices and no funds. Each year the annual conference was held in a different city, where a Reception Committee locally recruited and locally financed collected funds, hired lodgings and generally prepared for the winter's meeting. When the session was over, this committee remained in being for a few weeks to arrange the printing and distribution of the Congress reports. Then there was an interregnum for some months until another Reception Committee was organised in the city where the next Congress was to be held. As far as its organisation and finances were concerned, each session was thus a separate and independent undertaking.

The leaders and the rank and file of Congress were drawn from those quasi-political groups which had been active before it was formed. Since delegates came as representatives of local associations, naturally the old names appear in the new leading roles—Mehta, Telang and Tyabji from Bombay, Banerjea, Ghose and Bose from Bengal, and Ananda Charlu and Subramania Iyer from Madras. One delegate in four was a graduate. Over half the delegates at the first Congress were lawyers, and for decades to come more than a third of the delegates at every Congress belonged to that profession.[1] Journalists, doctors and teachers[2] mingled with the lawyers. Government servants, who were discouraged and later formally prohibited from taking an active part in politics, came to the Congress only as '*amici*

TABLE 44. *The professions and Congress, 1885–8*

	1885	1886	1887	1888
Total number of delegates	72	434	607	1248
Lawyers	39	166	206	455
Doctors	1	16	8	42
Journalists	14	40	43	73

Source: *I.N.C.* 1885, 1886, 1887, and 1888.

[1] Of a total of 13,839 delegates who attended the Congress sessions between 1892 and 1909, 5,442 (or over 39 per cent) were lawyers. See P. C. Ghosh, *The Development of the Indian National Congress 1892–1909* (Calcutta, 1960), p. 24.

[2] There were only two teachers at the first Congress, and fifty-nine at the fourth. But many more teachers sympathised with the movement. As the second report noted, 'the great bulk of those engaged in the work of higher education are Government servants, and hence did not appear as delegates' (*I.N.C.* 1886, p. 7).

curiae'.[1] Table 44 sets out the professions of some of the delegates at the first four sessions.[2] Quite clearly the Indian National Congress was an affair of the educated and it conducted its proceedings in English.

There was an 'entire absence of the old aristocracy'; the report of the second Congress explained that 'the policy of the Government has excluded these gentlemen persistently from all positions worthy of their rank, whether in the army or in the civil administration of the country, and they have consequently...entirely lost the desire, if not the capacity...for any direct active interest in public affairs'.[3] But the fact was that in its attitude towards the traditional notables Congress was as equivocal as the associations had been. It knew that support from the princes and aristocrats was worth having. Besides demonstrating the solidarity of all India, Native and British, it would impress the conservatives in Britain, and, above all, it would help to finance the movement. Dadabhai, who had been 'helped handsomely' in the past by the Maratha chiefs,[4] felt that, so far as money was concerned, 'the Princes seem the only quarter where we can expect to get it to any large extent'. But it was not clear that the princes welcomed Congress, and it was certain that the Residents would soon discipline them 'if they were to have anything to do with us'.[6] So Wacha doubted whether they would subscribe 'to any fund that may be started to place the Congress on a permanent basis',[7] and Congress came round to his view. After the Viceroy in 1888 had formally warned some of the native states not to support Congress, the Bombay committee, collecting money for the 1889 session, decided to leave the local chiefs and princes alone because 'it would be prejudicial to them and to our cause if the hostile officials try to make out that these chiefs are in league with us'.[8]

Local associations had joined together in a Congress so as to

[1] Thus men such as Ranade and R. C. Dutt had to work from behind the scenes.
[2] These figures are not complete since the occupation of some of the delegates was not given; they should be compared with those collated in B. B. Majumdar and B. P. Mazumdar, *Congress and Congressmen in the Pre-Gandhian Era 1885–1917* (Calcutta, 1967), p. 18.
[3] *I.N.C.* 1886, p. 5.
[4] Naoroji to Mansuhkram, 7 November 1885. NP.
[5] Naoroji to Hume, 5 January 1888. NP.   [6] *Ibid.*
[7] Wacha to Naoroji, 23 March 1888 N.P.
[8] Wacha to Naoroji, 9 July 1889. NP.

acquire a national platform for their demands. Not only did Congress borrow its leaders from the associations, it also served as an amplifier for their policies. None of the resolutions passed by the early Congresses was new. They demanded the reform of the Legislative Councils, simultaneous examinations in India, a royal commission of enquiry into Indian affairs, and the abolition of the India Council. They called for the right to volunteer and the abolition of the Arms Act, for the reduction of military expenditure and for raising the taxable minimum on incomes, for reforms in the legal system and police administration, for the separation of judicial and executive functions, and for the permanent settlement of the land revenue. All these demands had been made by the various associations in the years before the first Congress.[1]

Early in 1885 Dadabhai had already defined India's aims: 'Simultaneous examinations for *all* the services should be held both in India and in England...In India also they must adopt the system for the Uncovenanted Services...achieve this, and next representation in the Legislative Councils, and India will have nothing or little to complain [of].'[2] Congress was equally moderate. There was nothing in its programme about Home Rule, in spite of Dufferin's fears that Britain would find another Ireland in India. 'With regard to Home Rule', Dadabhai explained in London, '...I am a warm Home Ruler for Ireland, but neither myself nor any other Indian is asking for any such Home Rule for India. You must have seen from the Report of the Congress that our demands are far more moderate, in fact only a further development of existing institutions (the Legislative Councils).'[3] In another letter, drafted for him by Sir William Hunter, Dadabhai denied the allegation of *The Times* that Congress had radical aims. 'We are proceeding upon cautious and conservative lines to obtain definite developments of existing institutions in the changed state of things that British rule and British education has brought about in India.'[4] Even the demand for the reform of the Legislative Councils was hedged with qualifications.[5] And Tilak himself, when he

---

[1] See appendix 6, below, p. 373.   [2] Naoroji to Wood, 12 February 1885. NP.
[3] Naoroji to Wilson, 23 September 1888. NP.
[4] Hunter to Naoroji, 26 May 1888. NP.
[5] See Resolution III, *I.N.C.* 1885; Resolutions III and IV, *I.N.C.* 1886, pp. 41–3; Resolution II, *I.N.C.* 1887, p. 63; and Resolution I, *I.N.C.* 1888, p. lix.

appeared before the Public Service Commission, agreed that most of the top posts in the civil service must be kept for Englishmen.[1]

There was no popular programme here to rally the peasantry. To be sure, the poverty of India gave rise to some academic speculation inside Congress. For many years the politicians, and Dadabhai in particular, had spoken of the economic 'drain' from India, and their political demands were designed to stem the flow of money to England.[2] But when Congress came to discuss the condition of the people, it resolved that the first step to improvement was the grant of representative institutions.[3] By voting in this sense the delegates were no more seeking the Political Kingdom for themselves than they were trying to bring the levers of power within the reach of the downtrodden. The reformed Councils would simply confine themselves to 'everyday legislation', as Naoroji had put it.[4] If this needed any confirmation, the moderation of the new councillors would be assured by the moderation of their constituents; for Congress resolved that the voters should be men of education and property.[5] There was no place for the agricultural population in Hume's plan for an electoral college. None of these schemes was likely to unleash the Condition of India Question. When Congress passed a resolution on this subject, the delegates were impatient with the arguments of the odd man out who suggested that there were perhaps other causes, not necessarily political, behind India's poverty, and other remedies besides conciliar reform.[6] When another delegate suggested that they should encourage Indian-owned industries by a policy of swadeshi, he struck no responsive chord among Congress leaders.[7] But to explain the moderation of Congress in terms of the self-seeking of its members would

---

[1] *PSC (Bombay)*, IV, section 2, 324.
[2] See B. Chandra, *The Rise and Growth of Economic Nationalism in India. Economic Policies of Indian National Leaders (1880–1905)* (New Delhi, 1966), pp. 636–708; and D. Naoroji, *Poverty and Un-British Rule in India* (London, 1901).   [3] Resolution II, *I.N.C.* 1886, p. 41.
[4] Naoroji to Wood, 12 February 1885. NP.
[5] Resolution IV, *I.N.C.* 1886, pp. 41–2.
[6] See speech by A. Sabapathy Mudaliyar of Madras, *ibid.* p. 65.
[7] 'We should try and compete with England by establishing institutions which would support our own artisans...', Lala Hukm Chand told the Congress; 'I think it is possible...to take measures to support the artisans of the country quite independently of any representation,' *ibid.*

be simple-minded. When framing their policies the leaders of the movement were faced with a number of complications which set limits to their freedom of choice. They were governed by foreigners stronger than themselves; this foreign regime was itself under the control of a government and an electorate thousands of miles away; and the unevenness of Indian development constantly threatened disunity inside their own movement.

From the outset, Congress was anxious to make the right impression in England; propaganda there was its first concern. Tactically, therefore, Congress politicians wanted to show by their moderation that India was fit for representative government. Other factors made it easier for them to take this view: it was not British rule, but its machinery, that educated Indians wanted to change; their faith in England's willingness to do justice to India was still strong; and they had to say so, whether it was or not.[1] This made it respectable for them to attack the bureaucracy in India and to appeal from them to the electorate in Britain. All that was needed was 'to reach the ears and touch the hearts of the great English people'.[2] A decade later the Secretary of State could still write 'I look upon the Congress movement as an uprising of Indian Native opinion against, not British rule, but Anglo-Indian bureaucracy'.[3]

This was why Dadabhai returned to England in 1886 with plans to stand for parliament.[4] He was not the only Congress representative there, since many Congress leaders contrived to come to the West, and in England itself they could be sure of allies. But for the next twenty years the mainstay of the Committee and the most fervent advocate of the thesis that the real work of Congress lay in England was to be Naoroji. In 1886 he tried without success to find a constituency.[5] His failure

---

[1] 'All of us', said Subramania Iyer, at the first Congress, 'have the utmost faith and confidence in the justice and fairness of the English people, and we only have to solicit an enquiry into the facts, being content to leave the issue in the hands of their great political leaders,' *I.N.C.* 1885, p. 24.

[2] Eardley Norton, *I.N.C.* 1887, p. 92.

[3] Hamilton to Curzon, 20 October 1899, Curzon Papers, MSS Eur. F. 111 (158).

[4] Two years before, Martin Wood, once editor of the *Times of India*, had suggested that Dadabhai do this. See Wood to Naoroji, 12 September 1884. NP.

[5] Among the forty-one persons and organisations Dadabhai interviewed in his quest for a constituency were Sir George Birdwood, John Bright, Florence Nightingale, Kimberley, Sir George Campbell, H. M. Hyndman,

only strengthened his conviction that his place was 'here, and more so because there is nobody else here, European or Indian, to do this work'. Brushing aside the plea that Congress needed him in India, he insisted that the labours of the Bombay 'or of any other similar Congress' were bound to be fruitless 'unless there is somebody here to work for and support them'.[1] The main achievement of Congress lay 'in creating a permanent and effective interest in this country'.[2] So he took rooms in the National Liberal Club, hurried around England addressing temperance workers and other philanthropists, and urged Congress to appoint a committee to assist him. Even so modest a mission needed money, and money was hard to find. The previous year Bengal had raised Rs 11,000 for Lalmohan Ghose's pioneering but abortive candidature at Deptford, and it was unlikely to contribute to the election fund of someone from Bombay.[3] By 1887 Dadabhai's funds were low, and he looked to Bombay for help. 'My intention', he wrote to Malabari, 'is to devote my whole time and energy for India's work in England', whether in parliament or out of it. 'My wants, therefore, are not only the expense for one or two elections, but also the means to enable me to live in England in suitable style.'[4] But Bombay did not rush to the rescue; six months later Malabari had collected only Rs 15,000 for Dadabhai.[5] A few rich Parsis in the city subscribed,[6] but both Telang and Pherozeshah Mehta were sceptical about the enterprise and donated Rs 500 with reluctance. 'Telang has no belief in your mission to England', Malabari reported, 'You are wanted here, he says.' Pherozeshah, who was surprised in his bath by the fundraiser, 'showed himself even more firm in his conviction'.[7]

Sir Harry Verney, W. S. Blunt, Milner, Ripon, the president and committee of the East India Association, W. Digby, Hodgson Pratt, T. B. Potter of the Cobden Club, and several newspapermen. See Naoroji's Diary in London, 26 April 1886 to 3 July 1886. NP.

[1] Naoroji to Wedderburn, 20 August 1886. NP.
[2] Naoroji to Malabari, 30 January 1887. NP.
[3] Malabari to Naoroji, 12 October 1886. NP.
[4] Naoroji to Malabari, 1 March 1887. NP.
[5] Malabari to Naoroji, 29 August 1887. NP.
[6] See Naoroji to Malabari, 27 May 1887. NP. The Parsis in Poona and the mofussil, however, refused to subscribe for Dadabhai and Congress. They 'not only do not appreciate the work but say it is a sin for Parsis to risk all on Hindus and Mohammedans', Malabari to Naoroji, 15 August 1887. NP.
[7] Malabari to Naoroji, 7 March 1887. NP. Dadabhai was not the only man whose dreams of a comfortable political pension were disappointed. When

Despite the misgivings and the shortage of funds, in 1887 Dadabhai took the first steps towards a more permanent Congress organisation in London.[1] He wanted the Congress at Madras to organise a mass petition stating 'the reforms we want from Parliament in a practical shape, and signed by hundreds of thousands'.[2] Since such a petition proved to be far beyond the resources of Congress, Dadabhai pressed instead for a properly constituted political agency in London.[3] As the official mind in India seemed to be closing, the case for keeping it open in London grew more cogent.[4] When a move was made in London 'to get up an Anglo-Indian Society or Committee in connection with Sir Sayyed Ahmed's Association against the National Congress', Dadabhai pounced on this as another proof that 'the chief fight will have to be carried out here'.[5]

Meanwhile he was trying to organise a group in parliament. Bradlaugh and Caine showed some interest, and there seemed a chance of striking a bargain with the Irish. Warned that such an alliance was an uncertain asset, that 'Dadabhai and Davitt will become synonymous, one for fomenting Indian and the other for Irish rebellion',[6] he resisted the temptations of an Irish ticket. Another of his plans was to invite members of parliament to the Allahabad Congress so that they could see for themselves just how loyal, moderate and representative the movement was. Dinshaw Wacha, Dadabhai's regular correspondent in Bombay agreed that this would be 'the boldest and most strategic step we can take at this juncture'; it would show

we are so fearless as regards our sure attachment to the British Raj that we have not the slightest hesitation in inviting England's aristo-

---

in due course William Digby became the paid agent of Congress, he had to be content with a honorarium more modest than he had originally demanded. Bombay would only contribute £100 annually to his Political Agency, thus throwing a 'cold damper over the whole project' (Wacha to Naoroji, 21 September 1888. NP.); even this meagre sum it was slow in sending. (See Wacha to Naoroji, 22 February 1889. NP.)

[1] See Naoroji to Telang, 21 February 1887. NP.
[2] Naoroji to Hume, 8 December 1887. NP. Also see Naoroji to Hume, 30 December 1887. NP.
[3] See Wacha to Naoroji, 26 June, 1 July and 8 August 1888. NP. In these letters the financing of the London Agency is discussed in detail. Also see Naoroji to Malabari, 31 August 1888. NP.
[4] Wedderburn, *Hume*, p. 85.   [5] Naoroji to Malabari, 12 October 1888. NP.
[6] Wacha to Naoroji, 26 June 1888. NP.

cracy and democracy to come down and see for themselves...they will see whether we are the hollow sedition-mongers that our enemies have painted us...or whether we are real patriots yearning for the good of the country and trying by *parliamentary* procedure and methods (without having a regular Parliament or the rudest semblance of it) to *inform* Government of our lifetime's aspirations, and that in temperate language.[1]

A formal invitation was sent out, and this was a triumph of sorts for Dadabhai. In July 1889, he enjoyed another, when the British Committee of the Indian National Congress was at last formed in London.[2] In the following December, the Congress, presided over by Wedderburn, voted an annual sum of Rs 45,000 for its support, and Rs 63,000 was subscribed on the spot for this purpose.[3] This was more than the combined annual income of all the leading associations in India and twice what it had cost to hold the third Congress at Madras. Solvent at last, the British Committee was able to launch its journal, *India*, to make Congress known in England. In England Congress was spending more money than it did in India; and in England it had a journal, which was more than it had in India. What Congress had done was to shift the centre of Indian politics still further towards London.

Nevertheless in India Congress was producing genuine changes in the structure of politics. The annual session was already becoming the high point of the political year, as well as an outstanding social event. Attending it might be a mark of a man's political stature in his district; to propose or second a resolution or serve on a Congress committee became honours keenly sought by Indian politicians. Of course, it was true that without the local associations, Congress was nothing. But they came increasingly under its central direction. Their political demands were amplified by Congress, and it was quickly accepted that their first task was to reiterate these demands while Congress was not in session. Many of the associations merged into the local standing committees of Congress, and from now on their initiative became more and more restricted to purely

[1] Wacha to Naoroji, 31 July 1888. NP.
[2] Among the men on this Committee were Wedderburn, Naoroji and W. S. Caine. These were later joined by Bonnerjee. See M. Cumpston, 'Some early Indian Nationalists and their allies in the British Parliament, 1851–1906', *English Historical Review*, LXXVI (April 1961), 294–5.
[3] See Wacha to Naoroji, 3 January 1890. NP.

provincial matters. In 1888 provincial conferences, another new feature that Congress brought in its train, were held at Poona, Calcutta and Madras. Their aim was to discuss local matters outside the ken of the all-India body, and at the same time to 'strengthen the hands of the great National Congress'.[1]

This was all the more necessary because the Congress sessions at the end of December lasted for a few days only, and once the delegates returned home, the tempo of politics slowed down. There were frequent complaints about apathy when it came to working in the districts. 'Unity of interest is lacking', Wacha told Naoroji. 'It breaks out sporadically at a Congress, but soon, the occasion being over, it subsides—to be restored again for a time on another occasion. The spirit of persistent disinterested agitation *all over* the country is not visible. There may be here and there a few seized of the spirit, but they have not the strength and influence to cohere round a central point.'[2]

Bombay was a flagrant example of these weaknesses. By 1888 Wacha complained that 'Bombay is...cutting a very sorry figure in every way. The spirit of political activity which was so visible and strong three years ago is nowhere. A sort of languor has intervened.'[3] There was no one in the city willing to devote all his time to political work. Telang, although a busy lawyer, was a 'most energetic' and 'really good leader', but his appointment to the bench in 1889 removed him from 'the sphere of active public life'.[3] Pherozeshah's success at the mofussil bar kept him out of the city during much of the time, and for him every political meeting was measured by the loss of fees. In Wacha's opinion he lacked 'the energy and promptitude of despatch that are such marked characteristics of Mr Telang's public life. With Pherozeshah it would be impossible in case of emergency to get out any work until the time is past.'[4] Tyabji, the Muslim member of the trio, was in Telang's opinion a 'slippery fellow',[5] who perhaps thought that 'a

---

[1] Proceedings of the Bombay Provincial Conference, 2 November 1888, *The Quarterly Journal of the Poona Sarvajanik Sabha*, XI, no. 3 and 4, (January and April 1889). For the Bengal Provincial Conference, 25–27 October 1888, see Bagal, *History of the Indian Association*, pp. 105–7.

[2] Wacha to Naoroji, 16 August 1887. NP.

[3] Wacha to Naoroji, 5 October 1888. Also see Wacha to Naoroji, 9 February, 29 May 1888, and 8 July 1889. NP.

[4] Wacha to Naoroji, 11 October 1889. NP

[5] *Ibid.*

complete alliance and sympathy with the objects of the Congress may make him unpopular among his own people—that large but ignorant majority which glories in calling itself backward'.[1] Bombay's apathy was reflected in the falling membership of the Presidency Association.[2] In Poona there were men with more time for politics, but Bombay city was unwilling to let Poona take the lead.[3]

Hume worked untiringly for Congress and did something to keep it alive between annual sessions. Once the local committees were set up, he co-ordinated their efforts.[4] In 1886 Ananda Mohan Bose praised 'all the precious work he is doing for us; more I suppose, than all of us put together',[5] and Dadabhai told Hume that he often wondered 'what would become of the Congresses if you did not keep them up'.[6] Hume himself thought it wise to be more modest about his role. 'The whole principle of our movement', he told Tyabji who had been recently elected president of the Madras Congress, 'is not that I should do this or that off my own bat, but that I, having leisure, should watch your case and at each step get those of you whom common consent declared to be most competent to deal with that particular branch, to do the needful—leaving, of course, yourselves to decide what exactly the needful is.'[7] But in practice Hume, formally recognised as general secretary at the second Congress, took total charge of all Congress affairs. At the Madras session some of the delegates from Bengal and Poona complained about the 'hole and corner way' the general secretary and his henchmen managed every Congress session, making 'all the arrangements for it, including the settlement of the programme of the public session', and they pressed 'for the adoption of more democratic methods'. Hume, however, treated their complaints 'with ill concealed contempt'; and only Ranade's tactful intervention prevented an open conflict.[8] After the 1888 Congress Hume, in another show of authority,

[1] Wacha to Naoroji, 18 November 1887. NP.
[2] Wacha to Naoroji, 11 November 1887. NP.
[3] Wacha to Naoroji, 7 August 1888. NP.
[4] See for instance, Malabari to Naoroji, 3 August 1886, and Wacha to Naoroji, 2 November 1888. NP.
[5] Diary, 7 April 1886, quoted in Sarkar, *Life of Ananda Mohan Bose*, p. 82.
[6] Naoroji to Hume, 25 August 1887. NP.
[7] Hume to Tyabji, 22 January 1888. Tyabji Papers.
[8] Pal, *Memories of My Life and Times* II, 33-4.

decided to discipline Bombay for its failure to contribute towards the Political Agency by cutting off its supply of Congress reports; this drew a protest from Wacha that 'because he is indispensable...[Hume] ought not to behave as a tyrant ...He thinks in all matters he must have the upper hand.'[1] Despite their growing doubts about Hume's good judgment,[2] Indians continued to depend on this strenuous Scotsman. 'On broad grounds I would rather not have his assistance,' Wacha told Naoroji. 'We ought to be energetic and patriotic enough to make an advance in our political progress without such aid. We cannot expect a perennial crop of Allan Humes to assist us.'[3] Yet Wacha himself reported that Hume had been the life and soul of the 1888 Congress,[4] and the following year, when the session was to be in Bombay, he looked forward to Hume's arrival because 'he is the man to give us steam'.[5]

What ensured Hume's dominance over the early Congress was the feeble nature of its organisation. The vagueness of the Congress constitution was very marked at the first and second sessions. At Calcutta in 1886 the chairman of the Reception Committee, Rajendralal Mitra, had insisted on Bengalis being given a proper share in its direction; 'we cannot join the Congress to play the role of the bearer of the hubble bubble (*Hukka bardar*) of anybody else', he is reported to have told the assembled delegates from Bengal.[6] At this session the need for local activity was admitted by the decision to form 'Standing Congress Committees...at all important centres'.[7] By March 1887, the Bombay Presidency Association had named its local committee,[8] but Calcutta was the only other centre to act promptly. Both the Calcutta and Bombay committees sent round circulars about the need for better organisation before

---

[1] Wacha to Naoroji 23 July 1889. NP.
[2] See Wacha to Naoroji, 21 September 1888. NP. On two occasions in 1888 and 1892, Congress had publicly to dissociate itself from Hume's views.
[3] Wacha to Naoroji, 9 March 1888. NP.
[4] Wacha to Naoroji, 2 January 1889. NP.
[5] Wacha to Naoroji, 1 November 1889. NP. However in 1889 Wacha, seeing himself the man for the job, unsuccessfully proposed that there should be a Political Agent in India to co-ordinate the activity of the provincial political associations, to supply 'a central active force', and be for the associations 'what Hume is for the Congress', Wacha to Naoroji, 13 August 1889. NP.
[6] Pal, *Memories of My Life and Times*, II, 16.
[7] Resolution XIII, *I.N.C.* 1886, p. 45.
[8] See Naoroji to Hume, n.d. March 1887. NP.

the 1887 session,[1] but when Congress met at Madras its working was still palpably deficient. No one was told what the agenda was,[2] or how it should be settled. There was still no constitution to lay down rules for electing delegates or conducting the sessions. The arrangements for publicity were also bad.[3] This was the occasion for protests by Bipin Chandra Pal and Nam-joshi of Poona at the way 'half a dozen leading men' settled the programme without reference to the delegates. Even Wacha, himself no mean purveyor of bombast, could see that without 'a settled constitution', the Congress would become hampered by 'frothy and unsubstantial speeches' and a 'crop of minor personal grievances'. 'We are already being unreasonably taunted as a set of inflated talkers.'[4] These weaknesses were so glaring that the Madras Congress set up a representative committee to draft the new rules.[5] These were intended to give the Congress a definite institutional form, which would keep it alive between its annual meetings. Its local standing committees were to meet regularly, and they were to be composed of all the delegates who had attended the previous Congress. Under their auspices sub-committees would be formed to meet once a week at important centres. There was to be a change in the central organisation as well. Hitherto the general secretary had held office at the pleasure of the several Congress committees;[6] from now on, he was to be elected by each Congress for the ensuing year.

To the British Indian Association, already disturbed by the direction in which Congress was moving,[7] the implications of these proposals seemed all too clear:

In all these details we have the constitution of a distinct political body perfectly independent of the existing political institutions, and no-where and in no respect showing any subordination to them...If the Congress be constituted as a permanent institution, and not a perio-dical conference of the representatives of the political associations of the country...all the existing associations would virtually lose their

[1] Wacha to Naoroji, 23 September 1887. NP.
[2] Wacha to Naoroji, 13 September 1887. NP.
[3] Wacha to Naoroji, 30 December 1887. NP.
[4] Wacha to Naoroji, 27 January 1888. NP.
[5] Pal, *Memories of My Life and Times*, II, 31–5; and Resolution I, *I.N.C.* 1887, p. 63.
[6] *I.N.C.* 1885, pp. 94–5. At the fourth Congress Hume was reappointed according to the new procedure.
[7] See Wacha to Naoroji, 9 March 1888. NP.

autonomy, and simply become branches of the Congress or sub-Committees of the Standing Congress Committees...[and] the distinctive character of the existing political associations will be entirely lost.

When differences of opinion arose, the local associations would always have to give way to Congress. Behind these complaints lay the Association's fear that Congress would become 'a rival association—whose mode of action, whose methods and measures might be diametrically opposite to its own'. Accordingly, the Association wanted to peg Congress down at the level of a 'casual gathering which came together for the discussion of some specified subjects, and which separated when the consideration was over'.[1]

By the late 1880s this was already an old-fashioned view, and it found little support from the other associations. But neither was there much support for the clear-cut and rationalising proposals in the draft rules.[2] They were never adopted, and Congress was to remain as shapeless and flaccid as ever until it agreed on a constitution in 1899.[3] The reason for this lay in the uneven development of the country which gave rise to considerable disparity in political sophistication between the various regions of India which the Congress claimed to represent. Consequently the movement was difficult to hold together. Hard and fast rules which would have worked in Bombay, Bengal and Madras would not have suited the more backward provinces. A sophisticated procedure would have advertised the ascendancy of the three Presidencies; rules suited to the primitive political conditions of the other provinces would have lowered the level for the whole Congress.[4] Not only would the

[1] Secretary, British Indian Association to the General Secretary, National Congress Committee, 6 December 1888. BIA.
[2] The Bombay Provincial Conference, which was held at Poona on 2 November 1888, did, however, accept the rules with minor amendments. See Proceedings of the Bombay Provincial Conference, 1888, *The Quarterly Journal of the Poona Sarvajanik Sabha*, XI, no. 3 and 4 (January and April 1889), 1–12.
[3] N. V. Rajkumar, *Development of the Congress Constitution* (New Delhi, 1949), pp. 1–5; also see Majumdar and Mazumdar, *Congress and Congressmen*, chapter II.
[4] In the first Congress constitution, of the forty elected members of the managing Indian Congress Committee, eight each were allocated to Bombay, Bengal and Madras, six to the North-western Provinces, four to the Punjab, and three each to Berar and the Central Provinces (Rajkumar, *Development of the Congress Constitution*, p. 7). Behind this façade of all-

new rules have sharpened rivalries between the provinces, but they would also have dragged into the open rivalries inside each province—between the cities and mofussil, between one local association and another, and between the communities. Whatever the merits of a settled constitution might have been, its drawbacks seemed greater.

This can be seen most clearly in the problem of how Congress delegates were to be chosen. Congress hoped that the way it organised itself would be an argument for the reform of the Legislative Councils. 'Indirectly this Conference will form the germ of a Native Parliament', the circular convening the first Congress had prophesied, 'and if properly conducted will constitute in a few years an unanswerable reply to the assertion that India is still wholly unfit for any form of representative institutions.'[1] If the delegates to Congress were duly elected, this would both refute the criticism that it was unrepresentative and suggest that the same system of election could bring Indians to the Council chamber. Hume's scheme for elections to the second Congress envisaged in each province an electoral college representing various interests: graduates, municipalities, income tax payers, political associations, bar associations, journalists and Chambers of Commerce were to enjoy the franchise. This college would then elect representatives to the provincial Council, and these representatives would also be its delegates at Congress.[2] In the winter of 1886 there had been some desultory electioneering of a sort, and so the Congress report announced that whereas 'volunteers' had come to the first session 'delegates' had come to the second.[3] It was a hollow claim. Working such a scheme was quite beyond the resources of Congress. In any case there was a more fundamental objection to a regular system of electing delegates which Wacha noted: 'Uniformity in method cannot be obtained at present as all the provinces have not the same degree of education and progress. The backward provinces may fight shy of elective members for the Congress; and there will always be found astute people behind, who would dissuade the people

India coverage, the Committee merely partitioned India into spheres of influence, each dominated by the educated of one or other Presidency.
[1] *I.N.C.* 1885, p. 5.
[2] Subjects for the National Congress, 5 November 1886, *I.N.C.* 1886, appendix III, pp. 153–4.　　　　[3] *Ibid.* p. 1.

from doing anything of the kind...'[1] For the sake of appearances, there had to be places in the Congress pandal for delegates from the less advanced regions; but an electoral system that would suit them would not suit the more advanced regions; and so the need for unity was the rock on which all electoral systems would founder.

Nevertheless the question of electing delegates was repeatedly raised. While Hume kept 'exhorting every local Standing Committee to adopt some form, however rudimentary, of representative election', Ranade's advice was more specific: in the districts, the electors should be members of the rural boards and municipalities, while in the cities, 'we can invite each sectional society and association to elect a few among their own'.[2] As systems of representation, these remained mere blueprints; but as an aid to political awakening they had some importance. Any pretence at forms of election entailed a more systematic appeal to societies and associations outside the Presidency cities, for they had to hold meetings to pick their men. In this way Congress was forced to cast its net wider and deeper. In Bombay for example, the newly instituted Intelligence Branch of the Police was flooded in 1888 with reports about meetings throughout the province, at which Congress propaganda was preached and delegates for the coming session were 'elected'.[3]

Another weakness of Congress lay in its finances. Although the work in England was the main call on its resources, something had to be found for activities in India. Holding the first Congress cost Rs 3,000, the second, Rs 16,000[4] and for the third Madras raised Rs 25,000.[5] Double this amount was spent on the fifth Congress at Bombay.[6] These sums were raised locally and spent entirely on the one session, leaving nothing over to pay for political workers and propaganda in India. In 1888 Hume came to Bombay to investigate the chances of raising 'a permanent fund for future Congresses'. He wanted

[1] Wacha to Naoroji, 23 September 1887. NP.
[2] Wacha to Naoroji, 31 July 1888. NP.
[3] Confidential Abstracts, I, 1888, nos. 15–38, 46–92, Police Records, Intelligence Branch, Government of Bombay.
[4] Majumdar, *Indian Political Associations*, p. 207.
[5] Wacha to Naoroji, 9 February 1888. NP.
[6] 'Congress expenses will reach fully Rs 50,000', Wacha to Naoroji, 13 December 1889. NP.

a capital of Rs 400,000 but he was alone in thinking he could get it.[1] In Bombay, the most likely source of large contributions was the Parsi community, but by 1888, the Parsis were having second thoughts about supporting Congress, and the *Rast Goftar*, Bombay's leading Parsi paper, advised them to refrain from attending the fourth session.[2] When in April Sir Dinshaw Petit threatened to resign as president of the Bombay Presidency Association, Wacha saw the need to 'take a new departure and cut ourselves adrift from the illiterate and unsympathetic aristocracy of wealth'.[3] In 1889 the idea of a Parsi 'anti-Congress' movement was mooted,[4] and Malabari wrote to Naoroji that 'our Parsi friends are unreasonable in organising opposition to Congress', but they 'have good reason at times to be away from the contagion, as they call it, of Hindu politics'.[5] In the end only thirty-six Parsis attended the 1889 Congress session,[6] which indeed was almost moved to Poona because Parsi and Muslim propaganda in Bombay against it had been so virulent.[7] This Parsi breakaway affected the city's capacity to raise funds for the Congress. 'It is a pity', Wacha wrote, 'our leading Parsis are indifferent or waverers. Some are positively dead against the Congress, such as Sir D. M. Petit. And you know that the largest funds are always subscribed by the Parsis.'[8] Similarly in Bengal, the British Indian Association's defection was another blow to the accounts, for the prospect of zemindar donations was as important to Congress finances in Bengal as Parsi donations were in Bombay.[9] Not surprisingly, nothing came of Hume's plan to raise a large fund.

These weaknesses in organisation and finance had much to do with confirming Congress in its moderation. Even when

[1] Wacha to Naoroji, 23 March 1888. NP.
[2] Wacha to Naoroji, 23 November 1888. NP.
[3] Wacha to Naoroji, 6 April 1888. NP.
[4] Wacha to Naoroji, 10 May 1889. NP.
[5] Malabari to Naoroji, 8 November 1889. NP.
[6] Wacha to Naoroji, 24 January 1890. NP.
[7] Wacha to Naoroji, 18 June 1889. NP.
[8] Wacha to Naoroji, 25 June 1889. NP.
[9] Some of the wealthy zemindars helped the Congress cause. The Maharaja of Darbhanga was reputed to have given Rs 10,000 annually for many years, and the Maharaja of Vizianagram, who had once given the Indian Association Rs 15,000 for their Calcutta headquarters, continued to give money to the Congress. See Majumdar, *Indian Political Association*, pp. 205–6, and Misra, *The Indian Middle Classes*, p. 354–5.

plans were made for wider or rasher agitations, the forces of restraint always reasserted themselves. Having pioneered the device of 'mass meetings' during the Tenancy bill debate, the Indian Association now tried to give an appearance of mass support for the Congress demand for reforming the legislative councils. Its meetings calling for this reform gave the Viceroy visions of an Irish type of movement against paying rents, and he was not persuaded by the Association's retort that it was wrong 'to suppose that the Bengal peasant is really so simple as not to understand what benefit he will derive from such a boon as the reconstruction of the legislative council'.[1] Hume too had his plans. In 1887 a catechism in the vernacular was drawn up, explaining Congress demands in simple language. These outspoken tracts, which were scattered in tens of thousands across the country, set the tone of a more active campaign of publicity in the early months of 1888. It was this that finally convinced both Colvin and Dufferin that the Congress was getting out of hand and ought no longer to be countenanced. 'It is not...the periodical meetings of the Congress which gives me concern', Colvin wrote to Dufferin. 'It is the esoteric doctrine daily preached to the people by a great variety of agents of unknown character and antecedents during the year which precedes that meeting.'[2] His fears seemed justified when Hume, with his usual exaggeration, announced that many of the sepoys had been won to the Congress cause.[3] But Congress leaders repudiated the indiscretions of their general secretary.[4] In their eagerness to reassure government, they passed a resolution at Allahabad disclaiming all responsibility for what their officers and members did or said outside the pandal. Congress was responsible 'for the formal resolutions passed at its sittings and for nothing else'.[5] Over the issue of political tactics the moderates got their

[1] Eleventh Annual Report of the India Association, 1886–7, pp. 3–4. IA.
[2] Colvin to Dufferin, 10 June 1888, enclosed in Dufferin to Cross, 29 June 1888, DP 21 (Reel 518).
[3] 'Nor is the silly threat of one of the chief officers—the principal secretary, I believe—of the Congress that he and his Congress friends hold in their hands the keys not only of a popular insurrection but of a military revolt, calculated to restore our confidence in their discretion,' Dufferin, *Speeches delivered in India, 1884–8*, p. 244.
[4] At least one, Sambhu Chandra Mukherjee, now declared against Congress. See Skrine, *An Indian Journalist*, pp. 283–4.
[5] *I.N.C.* 1888, p. lviii.

way. There were no more mass meetings in Bengal, and no more vernacular catechisms. When in 1892 the incorrigible Hume spoke ominously about a revolution brewing among the people, the moderates were quick to say he was talking moonshine, and repudiated him once again.

Some aspects of this moderation were designed to reassure the British; others were intended to hold the Indians together. Since it was vital not to damage their credit in London, and since it was also vital not to split the fragile alliance among the all-India elite, the movement had to remain not only ill-organised but highly restrained. Hence the leadership chose to limit the range of subjects with which Congress could deal. The decision to keep questions of social reform out of Congress was carefully calculated, since this was above all the type of issue likely to divide Indians. 'We cannot afford to alienate a single coadjutor', Hume had announced in 1885, explaining why the new National party would have nothing to do with Malabari's crusade for social reform.[1] At Calcutta and at Madras, Congress leaders reaffirmed that their objects were political.[2] Malabari, the editor of the *Voice of India* and an enthusiast for widow remarriage and raising the age of consent, was urged by Dadabhai to keep such subjects out of the paper.[3] Hence social reform was scrupulously excluded from the Congress programme, and the social reformers had to be content with a separate organisation, the Social Conference, which met simultaneously but separately. Another self-denial for tactical reasons was the decision not to discuss anything that related to one region but not to the country as a whole. Even before the first Congress, Hume had instructed the National party that 'One rule...should...be everywhere observed. Only those matters should be brought forward in which we are ...at one *versus* the administration. Questions like the Bengal Tenancy Bill, in which we, natives, are at variance amongst ourselves, should be studiously excluded from discussion at these meetings.'[4] As a result, regional issues however important

[1] Hume to Malabari, *Indian Spectator*, 1 February 1885.
[2] See *I.N.C.* 1887, pp. 6–7.
[3] Naoroji to Malabari, 27 May 1887. NP. One reason why Malabari left the Congress was its reluctance to take up social reform. (See Malabari to Naoroji, 9 November 1888. NP.)
[4] Memorandum of the 'National Party', quoted in Reay to Dufferin, 4 June 1885, DP 47 (Reel 528).

were kept out of Congress. Since Digby's Political Agency in London was subsidised by Congress, Wacha objected to its putting the case for an extension of the Bengal Permanent Settlement;[1] and likewise the Allahabad Congress refused to discuss the grievances of the Assam coolies, since these were a matter for one province only.[2]

Just as the uneven level of political organisation in the different provinces weakened the Congress machinery, so also their uneven level of educational attainment hampered the forming of common demands. This was most clearly seen over the question of simultaneous examinations. Here was one of the main demands of Congress, for which Indians had been 'well nigh crying out for the last quarter of a century'.[3] But when the Public Services Commission called for evidence, most of the witnesses from northern India rejected the whole principle of examinations, fearing their men would fail and Bengalis would succeed.[5] The claim of Congress to represent the nation could hardly have been more stingingly refuted. 'These are the backward folk', Wacha lamented, 'whom we have all said in our evidence that we should make some special provision for till they were equally advanced with those already considered as advanced.'[6] The backward folk had chosen not to believe them.

A more serious threat was the prospect of a split between the communities of India when first the Muslim associations of Calcutta refused to join the 1886 session and then, the following year, Syed Ahmed launched his crusade against Congress. This 'alienation of the Mohammedans, at least a not inconsiderable majority of them', Congress leaders realised, 'has more or less thrown obstacles in our path of reform',[7] doing incalculable harm to 'the idea of unity'.[8] As Malabari pointed

---

[1] Wacha to Naoroji, 18 January 1889. NP.
[2] Pal, *Memoirs of My Life and Times*, II, 54–5. On the fourth day of the second Congress, when Surendranath tried to raise the question of the Assam Emigration Act, Dadabhai persuaded him to drop it since it was 'rather a subject for the discussion of the Bengal Provincial Congress' (*I.N.C.* 1886, p. 95.)
[3] Wacha to Naoroji, 2 August 1887. NP.
[4] See Wacha to Naoroji, 9 March 1888. NP.
[5] See below, chapter 7, pp. 320–4.
[6] Wacha to Naoroji, 31 July 1888. NP.
[7] Wacha to Naoroji, 2 August 1887. NP.
[8] Malabari to Naoroji, 20 January 1888. NP.

out, 'it is impossible to have a National Assembly without good Mohammedans included'.[1] The effects on English public opinion of this Muslim breakaway were particularly serious for Congress. Muslims had joined the Hindus of upper India in rejecting the Congress demand for simultaneous examinations; now their leaders had declared against Congress itself. 'The result of the Commission', Dadabhai wrote from London, 'and the split of the Mahomedans, has for the present paralysed me in my work here. Anywhere an Anglo-Indian can shut me up with these two facts.'[2]

[1] Malabari to Naoroji, 20 January 1888. N.P.
[2] Naoroji to Hume, 5 April 1888. NP.

7

The Muslim Breakaway

The Muslims in India differed from the Hindus in being part of an oecumenical community stretching from Morocco to Chinese Turkestan. Since the end of the eighteenth century Islam had been hammered by the blows of European expansion, and at its very heart and centre, the Sultan of Turkey had become the Sick Man of Europe, his bed surrounded by quack doctors and hopeful heirs. Throughout the world the community had been thrust into a crisis that was both political and religious. Wherever Muslim rule had been overthrown, the Faithful lived uneasily under the foreign yoke.[1] Doctrinally it was difficult for them to combine their faith with obedience to infidel masters, as the Dutch, the Russians and the French discovered in the course of the century.[2] At the same time the shock of deprivation had thrown Islam into a religious crisis. On the one hand it provoked the spread of a powerful reformation which claimed that decline had followed from the corrup-

[1] 'Dans le territoire de l'Islam même, le souverain non musulman est une anomalie: on ne peut le supporter qu' aussi longtemps qu'on est impuissant à réagir', C. Snouck Hurgronje, Politique Musulmane de la Hollande, Verspreide Geschriften, IV², p. 233, quoted in J. M. S. Baljon (Jr.), The Reforms and Religious Ideas of Sir Sayyid Ahmad Khan (3rd edn, Lahore, 1964), p. 29 n. 2.

[2] In Central Asia the Russians would gladly have limited themselves to informal control over the Emirates of Khiva and Bokhara, but these Islamic rulers spurned the role of satellite, and drove the Russian to outright annexation. See R. A. Pierce, Russian Central Asia 1867–1917. A Study in Colonial Rule (Berkeley and Los Angeles, 1960), p. 20. In Indonesia, the population clung to Islam as its only identification against white man's rule, and its culture grew drabber as it failed to adapt to the demands of the new age (G. M. Kahin, Nationalism and Revolution in Indonesia (Ithaca, N.Y., 1952), pp. 30–51). In 1871 the Algerians tried to promote an uprising in the Maghreb—so little had French imperialism been able to fit its own purposes into the aspirations of the most progressive Muslims in North Africa (A. Bernard, Histoire des Colonies Françaises, II, l'Algérie (Paris, 1930), 385–92).

tion of priests and other academics. In Africa and Arabia, Muslim dissenters called the community to arms, preaching the need to return to the pristine purity of scripture and to rescue Islam from its enemies.[1] On the other hand there were those who saw the need for coming to terms with the west and adapting its technical skills to their own purposes.[2] In this move towards western education they faced formidable difficulties, since they would have to unsettle both the content and the control of traditional education.

Although Islam in India was in many ways isolated from the community as a whole, it did not escape these deep trends. The collapse of the Mughals had been one of the most conspicuous catastrophes afflicting Islam.[3] After the deposition of the Nawab-Wazir in 1856, Hyderabad alone remained as a centre of Muslim supremacy. In the reactions of Indian Islam there were echoes of Islamic movements elsewhere—those who called for resistance, and those who preached the need for reconciliation and adaptation, the harsh militancy of Waliullah and Syed Ahmed of Bareilly, the Farazis of Bengal and the Deoband school of north India and the suaver moderation of the Aligarh school. But there were also ambiguities specific to India. In

TABLE 45. *Distribution of Muslims in British India, 1881, as a percentage of the total population*

	Muslims	Hindus
Bengal	31·2	65·4
Bombay	18·4	74·8
Madras	6·2	91·4
North-western Provinces and Oudh	13·4	86·3
Punjab	51·4	40·7
Central Provinces	2·5	75·4
Assam	27·0	62·7

Source: Table 4, above, p. 26.

[1] For many of them—the Wahhabis and some of the Muslim brotherhoods—the enemy was as likely to be the Sultan of Turkey, the Commander of the Faithful, who had betrayed them, as the Frank who was attacking them.
[2] Perhaps the only societies of nineteenth-century Islam which managed to adapt successfully to the age of liberalism were those of the eastern Mediterranean. See G. Antonius, *The Arab Awakening* (London, 1938), pp. 35–60, 79–100; E. Lamy, *La France du Levant* (Paris, 1900), pp. 63–162.
[3] Although of course the Marathas and the Afghans did as much as the conquistadors of the Company to pull it down.

part this was the result of the isolation of Indian Islam, in part too of the position of its Muslims as a minority population under foreign rule, but above all it resulted from the differences inside the community itself.

Table 45 recapitulates the inequalities of Muslim distribution between the provinces of British India. In terms of provinces as a whole, only the Punjab contained a majority of Muslims, but inside the Presidencies of Bengal and Bombay, Muslims were a decided majority in the eastern districts of Bengal and in Sind respectively. Elsewhere they were small minorities.

Yet the community was not homogeneous. Language, caste and economic standing worked together to divide Muslim from Muslim no less than Hindu from Hindu. Some Muslims were descended from foreign invaders, but many came from families of native Indian converts. The invaders, who were held by popular myth to be a band of brothers, in fact came from different stocks which had settled in different parts of the sub-continent at different times. The converts continued to display much the same variety of languages, races and customs as their Hindu neighbours. At the doctrinal level also there were divisions between the Sunni Muslims and the minority sects of Shias, Bohras and others. There were furthermore divisions at a social level: town-dwellers and rural dwellers, landlords and tenants, majority and minority were all divided. Above all, the Muslims were by no means a subordinate community everywhere in India. They might have lost their empire, but their status in a locality depended on the land, patronage and education they continued to enjoy. In some places they enjoyed a good deal. To state that Muslims were backward throughout India is meaningless; indeed, over the whole country, it would be as hard to find a generally accepted ranking of religious communities as it would be to find a generally accepted ranking of Hindu castes.

More than half the Muslims in India lived in Bengal, and they differed profoundly from Muslims in other parts of the country. Nearly all of them were descended from indigenous converts, while 'the descendants of the conquerors...count perhaps their hundreds'. At the time of the legendary conquest of Bengal by a handful of Muslims, those Bengali peasants who were to embrace Islam 'were already in an inferior social position. Their masters at that time were the ancestors of the present Hindus, who, possessing more culture and a more highly-organised society, were able to withstand the influences which brought about the conversion of the rural masses... The Hindu element of the population, therefore, by its constitution, represents a higher social stratum, the Muhammadan element a lower one'.[1] Even in the heyday of Muslim rule most of the well-to-do and literate inhabitants of east Bengal were not Muslims, but Hindus of the higher castes; the imposition of British rule strengthened, and did not create, their hold upon administration and the land. For the old Muslim aristocracy, always thin on the ground, the conquests of Clive and the settlements of Cornwallis meant the loss of privileges of all sorts: the levy of tolls, the monopoly of posts in the army and in some few branches of civil employ. The working of the Permanent Settlement step by step expropriated most of the Muslim landlords; the Resumption proceedings after 1828 accelerated their decay: 'Hundreds of ancient families were ruined, and the educational system of the Musalmans, which was almost entirely maintained by rent-free grants, received its death-blow.'[2]

By the later nineteenth century most of the land was owned by Hindus. In the eastern districts, where Muslims were most numerous, this was particularly evident. In Backergunge district, for example, Muslims were 64·8 per cent of the population but owned less than 10 per cent of the estates and paid less than 9 per cent of the total land revenue. In Mymensingh, just under 16 per cent of the proprietors were Muslims, paying just over 10 per cent of the district's land revenue.[3] Indeed most Muslims

[1] Note by C. J. Lyall, Secretary to the Chief Commissioner, Assam, 24 September 1882, *Muslim Selections*, part 3, p. 336.

[2] W.W. Hunter, *The Indian Musalmans* (reprint of 3rd edition, London, 1876, Calcutta, 1945), p. 177; The Resumption proceedings 'impoverished... many families...But a larger number of families became poor by the substitution of English for Persian. It was not merely that the Muhammadans lost the monopoly of the courts and several branches of the Executive Service; the old system of education was also rendered useless, and this proved disastrous from a pecuniary point of view. (H. Blochmann to J. Sutcliffe, Principal, Calcutta Madrassa, 9 October 1871, *RDPI (Bengal) 1871–2*, p. 73.)

[3] *SAB*, v, 194, 214, 226, 458, 465.

were simple cultivators, artisans and fishermen who, in social standing, appearance, language and customs, closely resembled the lowest Hindu castes.[1] In other parts of India, Muslims tended to be more numerous in the towns than in the country-side, but in east Bengal they did not 'evince any tendency towards city life'.[2]

By sweeping away the old structure of administration, Cornwallis and his successors had edged Muslims out of the revenue-collecting system. For a time Muslims continued to hold their own in the judicial service and the law, so long as Persian and Urdu, around which their traditional education had been built, continued to be the language of British admin-istration in Bengal. But when English was needed in the public services and the high courts,[3] they began to be squeezed out. In 1867 Muslims held 11·7 per cent of government jobs in Bengal staffed by Indians; twenty years later they had less than 7 per cent.[4] In 1871 they had about 12 per cent of the gazetted appointments; a decade later their share had dropped to just over 8 per cent.[5] In 1886–7, there were only fifty-three Muslim officers in the uncovenanted judicial and executive service of

[1] 'Wherever the Muhammadans form the bulk of the population in Bengal ...they are the cultivating classes of the people, while the upper and mercantile classes are Hindus' (*HIG*, II, 294). Earlier in the century 'the masses of the rural Musalmans had relapsed into something little better than a mongrel breed of circumcised low-caste Hindus', and were 'less widely separated from the lower orders of the Hindus than the latter were from the Kulin Brahmans'. But the Muslim revival in Bengal had the effect of purging Islam of its Hindu practices and widening the gulf between Hindus and Muslims (*ibid.* II, 288–90).

[2] *SAB*, V, 60.

[3] In 1837 the government of Bengal decided to conduct its business either in English or in the local vernacular. In 1844 the Council of Education began examining candidates for official employment. From 1859 a quarter of the posts of deputy magistrate and deputy collector in the Lower Provinces were reserved for those who knew English. In 1863 it was ruled that half the posts as munsifs, darogas and pleaders would be reserved for those who had passed the university entrance or higher examinations. In 1864 the high court ruled that all law examinations would henceforth be in English; in 1866 it was laid down that only Bachelors of Law would be eligible to become munsifs. See L. Khatoon, 'Some Aspects of the Social History of Bengal, with special reference to the Muslims, 1854–84' (Unpublished Ph.D. Thesis, University of London, 1955), pp. 180–201.

[4] See below, appendix 3, table 57, p. 362.

[5] Calculated from Hunter, *Musalmans*, p. 161, and from Memorial of the National Mahommedan Association, 6 February 1882, *Muslim Selections*, part 3, p. 240.

Bengal, or one in twelve among Indians.[1] In the law, 'the only secular profession open to well-born Muhammadans',[2] Muslims had been in a relatively strong position during the first half of the century. Until 1851 there had been more Muslim pleaders in Calcutta than Hindus and Christians combined. Between 1852 and 1868, however, not one of the pleaders admitted to the rolls of the high court in Calcutta was a Muslim. In 1869 among the attorneys, proctors and solicitors there were twenty-seven Hindus, but there were no Muslims.[3] In both administration and the professions Muslims were being forced out. Educational qualifications were growing more and more important in occupations of this sort: by 1887, for example, almost all the uncovenanted officers in the judicial and executive service of Bengal had passed some university examination, and one-third had degrees.[4] Therefore the small Muslim share in higher education goes far to account for the small Muslim share in higher employment.[5]

In upper India the Muslims were in a strikingly different position. The North-western Provinces and Oudh had been a centre of Muslim power since the end of the twelfth century. Here the community was a minority of some 13 per cent,[6] but as a whole it was more influential, more prosperous and better educated than its co-religionists in any other province of British India. In Agra and Oudh, the Muslim notables—the Pathans, Mughals and Saiyids who claimed descent from the conquerors —were far more numerous than in the outlying province of Bengal. A far larger proportion of the community lived in towns,[7] and of the rural Muslims many were landlords, whereas in Bengal the typical Muslim was a poor peasant.

[1] *PSC*, p. 36.　　[2] Hunter, *Musalmans*, p. 163.　　[3] *Ibid.* pp. 163-4.
[4] *PSC*, pp. 34-5; see above, table 38, p. 118.
[5] In 1870, only two Muslims sat for the B.A. examination in Calcutta, and neither passed; in the same year, 151 Hindus took the examination, and fifty-six received degrees (*Muslim Selections*, part 2, p. 179). Between 1876-7 and 1885-6, fifty-one Muslims and 1,338 Hindus took the B.A. degree at Calcutta. Calculated from *PSC*, appendix M, pp. 78-9.
[6] In 1881, there were just under six million Muslims in the province, of whom more than half lived in the Rohilkhand, Benares and Meerut divisions. In Allahabad and in Agra divisions, Muslims were 10·5 and 9·6 per cent of the population. *HIG*, x, 371-2.
[7] In the province as a whole, 9·7 per cent of the population was urban; the Muslims, however, were 34·6 per cent of the total urban population. Twenty-five per cent of the Muslims lived in towns; only 7 per cent of

In much of upper India the Muslim notables had survived the rigours of British rule as landholders, administrators and professional men. Here the revenue settlements had done less to upset the old patterns of landownership. In the North-western Provinces where Thomason's policies were intended to preserve the *status quo*, the settlements had mainly been made with the village zemindars or headmen.[1] In the permanently settled regions of Benares, much land had indeed changed hands, but many of the new owners were Muslims.[2] In Oudh the taluk-dars, or owners of large estates, had their ups and downs during the 1850s, but after the Mutiny they were able to consolidate their rights as masters of their tenants. Two out of three villages in Oudh were held by talukdars, of whom there were 337 in 1883. Of these, seventy-eight, or almost a quarter, were Muslims.[3]

The overhaul of the administration in upper India had been much less drastic than in Bengal. There was less insistence on educational attainment. Urdu, the medium of Muslim educa-tion, remained the language of administration. Consequently, the Muslims retained their important place in the public services. In 1850 they still filled three-quarters of the judicial

the Hindus. (*1881 Census, North-western Provinces and Oudh*, pp. 57, 60, 98). On the other hand, only 3·5 per cent of Bengali Muslims were town-dwellers.

[1] Baden-Powell, *Land-systems of British India*, II, 3–194; also see *HIG*, x, 382–6.
[2] In the districts of Benares, Ballia, Ghazipur and Jaunpur, there were 134 persons in 1885 paying land revenue above Rs 1,000 per year; of these about a third are estimated to have been 'new men', whose fortunes had been made under the British, mainly as administrative officers. Of twenty-nine large revenue payers whose careers had been in government service, fifteen were Muslims—which shows the results of the British policy of keeping Persian and then Urdu as the language of administration, and of recruiting its subordinates from the traditional Muslim bureaucratic elites of Persian origin. For this information I am indebted to Professor B. Cohn, whose article 'What Happened to the "Dispossessed"?' in the forthcoming R. E. Frykenberg (ed.), *Land Control in India* should be consulted.
[3] Two-thirds of all the villages in Oudh were held by these talukdars, who on average paid land revenue between Rs 17,000 and 18,000 per year. Thirty-eight talukdars paid more than Rs 50,000 a year. In Oudh, Brah-mins were very numerous—about one-eighth of the population—but only six of them were talukdars. Among the Hindu talukdars, Rajputs or Kshattriyas were the largest group. They shared with the Muslim talukdars both a local dominance and a common culture. One of the reasons why this culture had flourished was because some Muslim talukdars had once been Hindus. *HIG*, x, 384, 497–8.

posts held by Indians in the North-western Provinces.[1] Despite growing Hindu competition, Muslims in the 1880s continued to hold more than 45 per cent of all the uncovenanted executive and judicial posts in the provinces.[2] In the second half of the nineteenth century the Hindus were making efforts to increase their share of official posts but, as table 46 shows, the Muslims held their own.

TABLE 46. *Indians holding appointments at Rs 75 per month and above in the government of the North-western Provinces and Oudh, 1867, 1877, and 1887*

	1867	1877	1887
Hindus	692	936	933
Muslims	333	354	393
Muslim percentage	32·5	27·4	29·6

Source: Government of India, Home Department (Establishment) A, Proceedings, June 1904, no. 103, p. 134.

In addition to these perquisites at home, Muslims from the North-western Provinces and Oudh were public servants in other parts of upper India, in the Punjab, and in Hyderabad state.[3] They were well placed in the professions too. In Lucknow the bar was composed almost wholly of their men. In Allahabad, where the high court had been established, Bengalis and some local Hindus had forced an entrance, but even at the end of the century some of the most eminent lawyers were still Muslims.[4] As C. J. Lyall noted in 1882, 'In the North-Western Provinces we have a complete reversal of the state of things in Bengal. There the Muhammadans are vastly outnumbered by the Hindus; but, inasmuch as the unlettered multitudes are mainly Hindu, while the Muhammadans as a class belong to the middle and higher strata, the latter possess much more than the share

[1] *P.P.* 1852, x, 597–617, cited in Metcalf, *The Aftermath of Revolt*, p. 301; also see Misra, *The Indian Middle Classes*, pp. 189–91.

[2] *PSC*, p. 35-8.

[3] Just as Maharashtrians held many of the best jobs in the Central Provinces, and Bengalis in Bihar and in upper India itself, so too Muslims from the North-western Provinces and Oudh had their sphere of influence.

[4] *HIG*, x, 497; Misra, *The Indian Middle Classes*, p. 329. In 1886, of a total of nine Indians who were advocates of the high court, five were Muslims and three were Bengalis. (*The India List, Civil and Military, January 1886*, p. 85.)

of Government employment which their mere numbers would give them, and are comparatively a thriving and energetic element in society.' In so far as there was a Muslim 'depression' in India, 'religious causes' by themselves had little to do with it. 'I believe it is almost entirely a question of social position.'[1]

One of the determinants of this social position was education. In absolute terms there was far less English education in the North-western Provinces and Oudh than in the coastal Presidencies. Western schooling here was estimated as being at least a quarter of a century behind Bengal, and 'almost in its infancy'.[2] Between 1860 and 1870, only about 500 persons matriculated; the total for the following decade was still a mere 1,600 or so, while the number of Bachelors of Arts increased from twenty-six to 130.[3] But in relative terms the Muslims held more than their share. In 1871 18 per cent of all those under instruction were Muslims. Ten years later they were 20 per cent of the high and middle school pupils, and 13 per cent of the college students.[4] Since many of the college students were Bengalis,[5] at this level too Muslims were more than holding their own among the indigenous communities of the province. In the growing competition for education in the second half of the century, these Muslims of upper India had shown themselves at least as alert as the Hindus. Here there was no question of their being 'prejudiced against State education'. In fact, as one Director of Public Instruction in Oudh noticed, Muslims were more ready to avail themselves of its benefits than the Hindus were. As for Muslims being averse to English education, 'whatever may be the case in Bengal or elsewhere, it is not so in Oudh'.[6]

Pondering on the Muslim resentment which had led to the Wahhabi conspiracy, Sir William Hunter explained this by

[1] Note, 24 September 1882, *Muslim Selections*, part 3, p. 337.
[2] Evidence by A. C. Bannerjee, Additional Sub-Judge, Agra, *EC* (*North-western Provinces and Oudh*), pp. 158, 162.
[3] *EC* (*North-western Provinces and Oudh*), pp. 22, 24, 47, 57.
[4] See Resolution, Government of India, Home Department (Education), 15 July 1885, *Muslim Selections*, part 3, p. 381.
[5] This was particularly the case at Canning College, Lucknow, *EC* (*North-western Provinces and Oudh*), p. 48.
[6] *RDPI* (*Oudh*), *1875*, pp. 7–9. English schools in fact flourished more easily in Muslim towns such as Kakori, Bilgram and Jais than in conservative Hindu towns such as Ajodhya. So 'In Oudh itself the political danger, if there is one, lies in there being too many educated Mahomedans to find employment in the public service' (*ibid.* p. 10).

their despair at being the chief victims of the British occupation. Yet most of the evidence for the Muslim decline cited in his influential work, *The Indian Musalmans*,[1] applied 'only to Lower Bengal, the Provinces with which I am best acquainted, and in which...the Muhammadans have suffered most severely under British Rule'.[2] When the National Mahommedan Association complained in 1882 about 'the present impoverished condition of the Muhammadans of India, as compared with their past prosperity',[3] and when in 1888 its secretary again deplored 'the state of utter disintegration into which Musalman society has fallen within the last century',[4] it was the Muslims of Bengal they had particularly in mind, although by *suggestio falsi*, it was the Muslims of India of whom they appeared to be speaking. None of these interpretations paid due heed to the unevenness of development of the community throughout India. It was true that in Bengal, a generally forward region in terms of education and economic change, the Muslims were generally backward.[5] But in upper India, a generally backward region in terms of education and economic change, they were, if anything, generally forward. So great were the differences between the position of Muslims in one part of India and another that their standing relative to other communities can be defined only at a local level. Assertions that Muslims and Hindus were

[1] *The Indian Musalmans* has had a curious history. Compiled in three weeks on Mayo's orders, it has been the source of many of the polemics launched on behalf of the two-nation theory; the statistics which Hunter culled from the context of Bengal, and his conclusions about British discrimination and Muslim backwardness, have been made to march and counter-march across the sub-continent as a whole according to the interests or prejudices of those who, with or without acknowledgement, have borrowed them. In addition to its long term influence, the work had an immediate success, since its publication coincided so closely with the death of its patron at the hands of one of the Wahhabis whose grievances it had sought to explain. See F. H. Skrine, *Life of Sir William Wilson Hunter* (London, 1901), pp. 198–200.

[2] Hunter, *Musalmans*, p. 149.

[3] Memorial of the National Mahommedan Association, 6 February 1882, *Muslim Selections*, part 3, p. 237.

[4] Amir Ali to Tyabji, 5 January 1888. Tyabji Papers.

[5] So, of course, they were too in Bombay and Madras. In Bombay between 1876–7 and 1885–6, 392 Hindus had become B.A.s; in Madras, 1,060; but in Bombay only ten, and in Madras twelve, Muslims had achieved this degree (*PSC*, appendix M, pp. 78–9). But in these two Presidencies, there were too few Muslims for their position to be comparable with that in Bengal or in the North-western Provinces.

competing against each other have to be broken down. How keen was their competition in one region as compared with their competition in another? How keen was their competition with each other in the same region? Not only might Muslim be set against Hindu, but Muslim might be set against Muslim, Hindu against Hindu.

In none of the three most westernised provinces was there a large elite of educated Muslims who could be drawn into the politics of the associations or later of Congress. Only in regions where Hindus and Muslims alike were backward in the new education and where interest in the new politics was small, were Muslims in fact influential and well-placed. So it is not difficult to see why they played so inconspicuous a part in politics of this type, and why initially Congress gave them so little thought. But Congress soon discovered the tactical importance of being able to show that it had Muslim support, while the government found it useful to deny the existence of any such common front. It was only at this stage that Muslim attitudes towards an all-India movement began to take shape. Until then their politics had been dictated primarily by the local and sectional needs of the several branches of their community.

In Bengal the Muslim zemindars had interests no different from those of their Hindu peers, and both joined in the British Indian Association to defend the Settlement and the rights of landlords. Hindus led the Association, but this was not surprising since most zemindars were Hindus and few Muslim zemindars lived in Calcutta.[1] In eastern Bengal, where the peasantry was predominantly Muslim, the issue of tenant right might have become a Muslim cause, if it had not been so unattractive to Muslim landlords. Again, Hindus and Muslims with similar social backgrounds shared a similar enthusiasm for the new education. For ashraf, or respectable, Muslims in the towns, traditionally employed by government or in the professions—a class described with some exaggeration by the

[1] There were no Muslims on the committees of the Landholders' Society, the British India Society and the British Indian Association in its early years. But on the deputation of the British Indian Association to Lytton in 1879, for example, there were three: Nawabs Amir Ali, Ahmed Ali and Mir Mohamed Ali.

National Mahommedan Association as 'totally extinct'[1]—
education took a high priority. The traditional Islamic education
taught at the madrassas at Calcutta, Hooghly and Dacca did not
qualify their students to compete with Hindus for the jobs on
which their livelihood depended.[2] By the mid-century, Calcutta's 'higher and more respectable' Muslims were already
showing 'a growing desire for sound English education',[3] and
it became increasingly clear that what held them back from the
new learning was poverty rather than religious prejudice.[4]

In 1863 Abdul Latif, a leading public servant and one of the
first Bengali Muslims proficient in English, organised the
Muhammadan Literary and Scientific Society of Calcutta, to
represent those 'Bengal Mussulmans who wish to adopt English
education and European customs...without contravening the
essential principles of Islam, or ruffling the traditional prejudices
of their Mohamedan fellow-countrymen'.[5] Its purpose was
primarily educational and social. Meeting once a month in
Latif's house, it tried by lectures and discussions to 'impart
useful information to the higher and educated classes of the
Mahomedan Community',[6] and its annual soirée in the Town
Hall became an event in the Calcutta calendar.[7] One of Latif's
moves was to offer a prize of Rs 100 for an essay discussing:
'How far would the inculcation of European Sciences through
the medium of the English language, benefit the Muhammedan
students in the present circumstances of India, and what are
the most practicable and unobjectionable means of imparting
such instruction.'[8] By 1865 the Society had about 200 members;

[1] Memorial of the National Mahommedan Association to Ripon, 6 February
1882, *Muslim Selections*, part 3, p. 241.
[2] On madrassa education, see A. R. Mallick, *British Policy and the Muslims
in Bengal 1757–1856* (Dacca, 1961), pp. 231–82; and Hunter, *Musalmans*,
pp. 190–9.
[3] *Report of the Council of Education, 1852–5*, quoted in Khatoon, 'Some
Aspects of the Social History of Bengal', p. 84.
[4] See for example, *RDPI (Bengal) 1871–2*, p. 73; Blochmann argued that
Muslims 'whenever they can afford it, do send their children to school',
explaining 'the "backwardness" of the Bengali Muhammadans...[by] the
small number of such Muhammadan families as can afford to send their
children to our schools'.
[5] Private Secretary, Viceroy, to Private Secretary, Secretary of State, 28
December 1886, DP 37 (Reel 525).
[6] *Thacker's Directory for Bengal...for 1865* (Calcutta, 1865), p. 214.
[7] Temple, *Men and Events of My Time in India*, p. 426.
[8] Quoted in Gupta, *Studies in the Bengal Renaissance*, p. 473.

twelve years later it had more than 500.[1] As the leader of one
section of Calcutta's small community of educated Muslims,
Latif was regularly consulted by the government, and the
Literary Society intentionally avoided any adventurousness
in its politics. Its members were keen to shake off the suspicion of disloyalty which the activities of the Farazis had
aroused;[2] fatwas in favour of the Raj were energetically elicited
from the ulema, and in 1870 Maulvi Karamat Ali lectured to
the Society on the duty to refrain from waging war upon the
British.[3]

Amir Ali's National Mahommedan Association, launched in
1878, was an organisation of a different sort. It too spoke of
loyalty to the Raj and of western education.[4] But around Amir
Ali, a Calcutta graduate and barrister-at-law, gathered those
Muslims who found Latif too conservative and his programme
of self-help ineffective. Educated in government colleges,
affecting English dress and manners, knowing little Persian or
Arabic, 'the language of good Society' among Calcutta Muslims,
Amir Ali and his coterie were regarded as unsound by the men

[1] *Thacker's Directory for Bengal...for 1865*, p. 214; Majumdar, *Indian Political Associations*, p. 222.

[2] In the early nineteenth century a brand of Wahhabism had taken hold in Bengal, particularly in its eastern districts. Under Shariatullah and his son Dudhu Miyan, a sect known as the Farazis sounded the call for a return to primitive Islam shorn of Hindu excrescences. Large numbers of the peasantry were won to the Farazi cause, and since they were mainly Muslim and their landlords and moneylenders mainly Hindu, the movement to resist the exactions of the latter took on a communal tone and brought Muslims into conflict with government. There is little evidence that the Farazis had political aims. Dudhu Miyan was arrested during the Mutiny, but the peasantry of eastern Bengal did not rise. Only after the Wahhabi trials of the 1860s had shown that the conspiracy had supporters in Bengal were the Farazis suspected of having systematically planned the overthrow of the Company's Raj. See Chaudhuri, *Civil Disturbances during the British Rule in India (1765–1857)*, pp. 112–14; Mallick, *British Policy and the Muslims in Bengal*, p. 87, and Hunter, *Musalmans*, pp. 124, 126, and appendix III, p. 210.

[3] See W. C. Smith, *Modern Islam in India* (Lahore, 1963; reprinted from revised London edition, 1943), p. 6; and Hunter, *Musalmans*, p. 108 n. 2; compare Shah Abdul Aziz's fatwa in 1803 declaring India to be Dar-ul-Harb, Faruqi, *The Deoband School and the Demand for Pakistan*, pp. 2–3.

[4] The Association was grounded 'essentially upon the principle of strict and loyal adherence to the British Crown'; it too 'proposes to work in harmony with Western culture and the progressive tendencies of the age', Prospectus, *Report of the Committee of the Central National Mahommedan Association for the Past 5 Years* (Calcutta, 1885).

of the Literary Society. In their educational schemes they ignored religion, and their leader was a Shia.[1]

Amir Ali held that Muslim fortunes would not revive by Muslim efforts alone. Government help was essential, and if it was to be won Muslims needed a political organisation of their own. So when he was invited by Surendranath to join the Indian Association, his refusal was logical enough. In the first place, simultaneous examinations, the apple of Surendranath's eye, could only handicap Bengali Muslims still further. Moreover, local boards, municipalities and Legislative Councils elected on a franchise of property, wealth and education, would give Muslims small say in their proceedings. Ripon's local self-government schemes gave point to these fears. They led Yusuf Ali, the Muslim spokesman in the Bengal Legislative Council, to demand separate representation for his community.[2] According to Rivers Thompson, so 'insuperable' were 'religious animosities' that, if Hindus replaced the district officer as the power in the localities, local government would come to a halt.[3] The lieutenant-governor was able to use this spectre to deny Ripon's experiment a fair trial in Bengal. Similarly, the Muslim leaders were cool about reforming municipal government at the centre. In the Calcutta Corporation they had only five out of forty-eight seats in 1883.[4] This meant, as one Muslim councillor told Blunt, that 'as more power was given to the natives the Mahomedan position would get worse and worse'. Government service, he explained, was the only possible avenue of advance for the small Muslim intelligentsia, but most of them could not afford the necessary education. 'In the struggle for existence' they were left behind; as 'the weakest community' they were going 'to the wall', and were 'all in despair'; 'it was impossible for them to combine with the Hindus who were so selfish, they wanted every post for themselves'.[5]

[1] Blunt, *India under Ripon*, pp. 86, 97–8, 104. Shias were a small minority among the Muslims of Calcutta. In 1881, there were 7,667 of them, while the Sunnis numbered 213,334. (*1881 Census, Calcutta*, p. xxxii.)
[2] Proceedings of the Bengal Legislative Council, 3 May 1883, quoted in Majumdar, *History of Political Thought*, p. 399.
[3] Rivers Thompson to Ripon, 1 May 1883, RP, Add. MSS 43594.
[4] Secretary, National Mahommedan Association, to Secretary, Government of Bengal, February 1884, enclosed in Amir Ali to Private Secretary, Viceroy, 12 March 1884. RP (B.M. I.S. 290/8).
[5] Blunt, *India under Ripon*, pp. 110–16.

Amir Ali's solution for this dilemma was a pressure group run by Muslims specifically for Muslims. Its programme would be based squarely upon the demand for preferential treatment.[1] Hunter's *Musalmans* had conveniently argued that government was largely to blame for the Muslim decline; now the state would be called upon to redress the balance. The size of the Muslim community, together with its present 'decadence and ruin', were powerful arguments for giving Muslims a definite share of patronage. In its memorial of 1882, the National Mahommedan Association listed its demands: a proportion of jobs to be reserved for the Muslims,[2] less emphasis to be placed on university education as a qualification for office, no simultaneous examinations for the covenanted service and no competitive examinations for the uncovenanted, and provision for the special educational requirements of the Muslim community.[3] To associate Muslims in other parts of India with their demands, this Bengal pressure group tried to extend its field of action. Calcutta was to be the headquarters for branches 'spreading from Madras to the Punjab, from Chittagong to Karachi'.[4] To advertise its new role, the Association changed its name, and Amir Ali travelled around India visiting other Muslim centres and busying himself with their problems.[5] By

[1] In its 1882 memorial the Association argued that 'no measure of reform adopted *within* the community would have any appreciable effect in arresting the progress of decay... it is therefore that your memorialists look to Government for those steps which the necessities of the case require', Memorial of the National Mahommedan Association, 6 February 1882, *Muslim Selections*, part 3, p. 237.

[2] In 1884, Amir Ali again insisted that 'the unequal distribution of State patronage is the most important question of all; it has given rise to the greatest discontent and bitterness of feeling, and will continue to do so unless Government emphatically lay down the principle that in Bengal at least one-third of the State employment should be reserved for the Mahommedans', Amir Ali to Private Secretary, Viceroy, 10 March 1884, RP (B.M. I.S. 290/8).

[3] Muslim Selections, part 3, pp. 242–4. Also see *PSC (Bengal)*, VI, 193–202, 262–9.

[4] *Islamic Culture*, January 1932, pp. 9–10, quoted in Majumdar, *Indian Political Associations*, pp. 223–4.

[5] In 1883 the word 'Central' was added to the Association's title; the following year Amir Ali claimed branch associations 'in almost every important station in Northern India and in Bombay and Madras' (Amir Ali to Private Secretary, Viceroy, 10 March 1884. RP (B.M. I.S. 290/8)) and made representations on behalf of the Bombay Muslims for a reserved proportion of seats on municipalities (Amir Ali to Private Secretary, Viceroy, 12 April 1884. RP (B.M. I.S. 290/8)). Early in 1885 he was soliciting aid

1888 more than fifty branches had been affiliated, including twelve in Bengal, eleven in Bihar, seven in the North-western Provinces and Oudh, eight in the Punjab and five in Madras.[1] In 1884 the Association proposed an annual conference of Muslims from all over India.[2] Thus almost two years before the first Indian National Congress was convened a separate Muslim political conference had been suggested.

Even before the Congress was launched, the Muslims of Bengal had begun to go their own way in organisation and in policy. For a time there was talk about co-operation with the Hindus. In its prospectus the National Mahommedan Association piously announced that 'the welfare of the Mahommedans is intimately connected with the well-being of the other races of India', expressing its benevolence towards the 'advocacy and furtherance of the public interests of the...country at large'.[3] Hindus were allowed to become honorary members.[4] On occasion the Muslims worked with the other associations: for example, on the Imperial Legislative Council Amir Ali joined with Hindu members to support the Ilbert bill, although Surendranath complained that Calcutta Muslims showed little enthusiasm for the cause.[5] 'Neither Amir Ali nor Abd-el-Latif could afford to come forward as champion', Blunt reported, 'as all their prospects depended on the Government.'[6] In December 1885, in its last overt act of co-operation, the National Mahommedan Association helped to stage the second National Conference.[7]

for a special college for the Muslims in Sind (Amir Ali to Tyabji, 19 February 1885, Tyabji Papers) and by 1886 it was clear to Government House that 'the Mohamedan National Association (representing the most advanced section of the Indian Mussalmans)...aims at serving as a bond of union for all Mussalmans throughout India' (Wallace to Maitland, 28 December 1886, DP 37 (Reel 525)).

[1] Majumdar, *Indian Political Associations*, p. 225; R. Gopal, *Indian Muslims. A Political History (1858–1947)* (Bombay, 1959), p. 329.
[2] *Report of the Committee of the Central National Mahommedan Association for the Year 1883–84* (Calcutta, 1885), pp. 82–3.
[3] *The Rules and Objects of the National Mahommedan Association with a list of the members,* (Calcutta, 1882), p. 5.
[4] *Ibid*, pp. 6, 23–4.
[5] P. Sharan, *The Imperial Legislative Council of India* (Delhi, 1961), pp. 73–4; Blunt, *India under Ripon*, p. 109.
[6] Blunt, *India under Ripon*, p. 110.
[7] The leading Muslim newspaper encouraged members of the community to attend as delegates. *Mahomedan Observer*, 19 December 1885, quoted in *Voice of India*, IV, no. 1, (January 1886).

The following year, when the Congress came to Calcutta, both the Muhammadan Literary Society and the Central National Mahommedan Association decided not to send delegates.[1] Already that April they had steered clear of the Bengal National League which had been formed specifically to agitate for elected councils, fearing that since few Muslims would get the vote under the proposed franchise evidently the 'unqualified adoption of the programme of the Congress will lead to the political extinction of the Mohammedans'.[2] Nomination, in one form or another, was essential for the protection of Muslim interests.[3]

The employment question decided the Muslim leaders. In 1883 the Education Commission, accepting Hunter's theories, had recommended measures to combat Muslim backwardness.[4] In July 1885, after an exhaustive enquiry, the government of India resolved that wherever Muslims failed to get 'their full share of State employment'—and nowhere was this so conspicuous as in Bengal—the local authorities would try to distribute its patronage so as to 'redress this inequality'.[5] The Resolution gave less than the Central National Mahommedan Association had demanded, but at least it conceded that in some parts of the country Muslims needed government help and ought to have it. In 1886 a Public Services Commission was appointed to review the whole question. Educated Hindus had already set out their demands at the first Congress. It was clear to Amir Ali that if these were accepted, Muslims in Bengal would be 'utterly swamped in every department of state', and that 'the unequal political development of the two communities, coupled with the comparatively recent growth of English education among the Mohammedans', left them unready for the rigours of competitive coexistence.[6] It was better to keep clear of Congress.

---

[1] Amir Ali to Secretaries, Indian National Congress, 12 December 1886 and Abdul Latif to same, 22 December 1886, enclosed in Private Secretary, Viceroy, to Private Secretary, Secretary of State, 21 and 28 December 1886, DP 37 (Reel 525).

[2] *Report of the Committee of the Central National Mahommedan Association, for 1885–8*, pp. 21–2, quoted in Gopal, *Indian Muslims*, p. 76.

[3] It was by nomination that Amir Ali himself had found a place first on the Bengal, and then on the Imperial Legislative Council.

[4] *EC*, pp. 480–520.

[5] Resolution of Government of India, Home Department (Education), 15 July 1885, *Muslim Selections*, part 3, p. 389.

[6] *Report of the Committee of the Central National Mahommedan Association, for 1885–8*, pp. 21–2, quoted in Gopal, *Indian Muslims*, p. 77.

'So far as the Mussulmans are concerned,' the *Liberal* commented on this decision, 'we admit that the Government is doing much for them...and the concessions made in their interest are of a really substantial nature. We have noticed with pleasure this change of policy towards a neglected portion of the population...It will not do for the Mahomedans to take part in public agitation, for the simple reason that clamour may lead to the loss of what they have gained from the good graces of the rulers.'[1] Abdul Latif told the Congress secretaries that he did not think 'the moment is opportune for forcing the hand of Government'.[2] The reasons behind the decision were summed up by the *Mahomedan Observer* of Calcutta:

To insist upon open competition as the only mode of selection for State employments means the absolute exclusion of the Mahomedans from the public service. To ask for representative institutions, without sufficient guarantees for the representation of the minority means the swamping of the minority by the majority. From almost every part of Bengal, where Local Self-Government has been introduced, comes the cry that the minority is tyrannised over by the majority; from every part of Bengal comes the cry that the organisation of the majority is more solid and stronger than that of the minority. Even in places where the Mahomedans outnumber the Hindus, the representation is entirely in the hands of the latter. What guarantees have the so-called Mahomedan delegates extorted from this irresponsible Congress for the protection of Mahomedan interests? If their political foresight had been keener, they would have seen that though the influence of the majority is predominant even at present in the Councils of the State, which shows at times too great a subserviency to their intelligence, wealth and power of combination, yet there is more hope of a fair equilibrium being maintained from the political wisdom of a neutral Government than from the generous instincts of a majority looking primarily, but naturally, to the interests of its own bulk. The minority have a right to see their interests safeguarded. And we say advisedly that until our people have come abreast with the Hindus in education and political intelligence, political concessions to the majority, without sufficient guarantees for the protection of the interests of the minority, would be destructive to the latter.[3]

Opposition to Congress of a sterner sort came from Muslims in the North-western Provinces and Oudh, where it was led by

---

[1] *Liberal*, 26 December 1886, quoted in *Voice of India*, v, no. 1, (January 1887).

[2] Abdul Latif to Secretaries, Indian National Congress, 22 December 1886. See above, p. 314, n. 1.

[3] *Mahomedan Observer*, 1 January 1887, quoted in *Voice of India*, v, no. 1 (January 1887).

315

Syed Ahmed Khan. Until this time upper India's political attitudes had mainly been voiced by small groups of educated Bengalis, whether they were representative or not. These expatriates from the Lower Provinces founded branches of the Indian Association, organised meetings for Surendranath on his political tours, and ensured that the political response of upper India echoed that of Calcutta. Faithfully they sent delegates to the two National Conferences, and they could be relied upon to attend Congress in the name of upper India.

But in upper India Muslims, not Bengalis, were traditionally the dominant community. After the Mutiny, there were two main threats to their position. One was the conviction in official circles that Muslims had been responsible for the revolt.[1] The other was the growing competition both from Bengalis and from local Hindus. Syed Ahmed Khan was the first to look synoptically at these problems. Unless Muslims could be persuaded to come to terms with their Christian rulers and the new learning, they would continue to fall behind 'in the race for position among the magnates of the world'.[2] They would remain inflexibly orthodox; their rulers would discriminate against them, and more adaptable groups would usurp their offices.

Syed now tried to restore the good name of his community by denying that the Mutiny had been a Muslim conspiracy. After all, Bahadur Shah's cause had been self-evidently hopeless, and since 'the English Government does not interfere with the Mahommedans in the practice of their religion', Muslims had had no reason to launch a jehad.[3] Most of them, according to Syed, had in fact stood by the Raj.[4] In 1871 when Hunter wrote that the Muslim volcano was not extinct but dormant, Syed hurried to deny it.[5] But together with these political vindications went Syed's new orientations in religion,

---

[1] See Metcalf, *The Aftermath of Revolt*, pp. 298–304.
[2] Speech by Syed Ahmed, 8 January 1864, at opening of Scientific Society, Ghazipur, G. F. I. Graham, *The Life and Work of Sir Syed Ahmed Khan, K.C.S.I.* (New and revised edition, London, 1909), p. 52.
[3] Syed Ahmed Khan, *The Causes of the Indian Revolt. Written...in Urdoo in the year 1858, and translated into English by his two European friends* (Benares, 1873), pp. 3–10.
[4] Syed Ahmed Khan, *An Account of the Loyal Mahomedans of India*, part I (Meerut, 1860), pp. 40–2.
[5] See Syed Ahmed Khan, *Review of Dr Hunter's Indian Musalmans: are they bound in conscience to rebel against the Queen?* (Benares, 1872).

without which his educational projects could not have succeeded. He had to show that western learning was compatible
with the faith. On the assumption that the Koran was the only
reliable guide to Islam, Syed set himself to formulate traditional
Koranic teachings anew, so as to extirpate all that was irrational
in Islam. This brought him into conflict with the ulemas and all
their orthodox followers in upper India. They branded Syed
and his supporters as Necharis;[1] at Deoband they combined to
defend the old faith together with the old politics of resistance.[2]

Education was the heart of Syed's policy of reconciliation
and his panacea for the community. 'If the Muslims do not
take to the system of education introduced by the British,' he
warned, 'they will not only remain a backward community,
but will sink lower and lower until there will be no hope of
recovery left to them...The adoption of the new system of
education does not mean the renunciation of Islam. It means its
protection...How can we remain true Muslims, or serve
Islam, if we sink into ignorance?'[3] In 1864 he put his ideas into
practice by forming the Translation Society, later known as the
Scientific Society of Aligarh, and his visit to England in 1869
strengthened his convictions.[4] In an excess of enthusiasm he
wrote from England that 'All good things, spiritual and
worldly...have been bestowed by the Almighty on Europe,
and especially on England', and he contrasted this with 'the
fatal shroud of complacent self-esteem...wrapt around the
Mohammedan community'.[5] Unless Muslims 'assimilate these
[European] arts and sciences into our own language, we shall
remain in this wretched state'. Syed returned to India more
conscious than ever of the importance of persuading Muslims
that 'independence of mind and political liberation' were not
'symptoms of heterodoxy'.[6]

---

[1] Baljon, *The Reforms and Religious Ideas of Sir Sayyid Ahmad Khan*; and
B. A. Dar, *Religious Thought of Sayyid Ahmad Khan* (Lahore, 1957). One
of Syed's aunts 'maintained throughout the rest of her life her refusal to
see him only on account of his taking too kindly to the culture of the
foreigner and the infidel', Mohamed Ali, *My Life: a Fragment* (ed. A.
Iqbal) (Lahore, 1942), p. 7.

[2] Faruqi, *The Deoband School and the Demand for Pakistan*, pp. 22–46.

[3] Syed Ahmed Khan to Maulvi Tassaduq Husain, quoted in W. T. de
Bary (ed.), *Sources of Indian Tradition* (New York, 1958), pp. 744–5.

[4] He was one of the first Indian Muslims to send his son to Cambridge.

[5] Letter from London 1869, quoted in Graham, *Syed Ahmed Khan*, pp. 127,
129.   [6] *Ibid.* p. 138.

At first Syed had argued that the best way of bringing western learning to the people of his province was through the vernacular, but later he became convinced that English must be the medium. His most notable educational achievement was to found the Anglo-Oriental College at Aligarh.[1] When he broached the subject, a committee to investigate the difficulties was set up. Dismissing the Muslim schools of the old sort at Deoband, Cawnpore, Delhi, Jaunpur and Aligarh as 'altogether useless', Syed told the committee that their syllabus and books

deceive and teach men to veil their meaning, to embellish their speech with fine words, to describe things wrongly and in irrelevant terms... to live in a state of bondage, to puff themselves up with pride, haughtiness, vanity and self-conceit, to hate their fellow creatures, to have no sympathy with them, to speak with exaggeration, to leave the history of the past uncertain, and to relate facts like tales and stories. All these things are quite unsuited to the present age and to the spirit of the time, and thus instead of doing good they do much harm to the Muhammadans.[2]

Naturally the committee reacted 'with abhorrence',[3] but in 1872 a fund was started. Although the lieutenant-governor, aware that Syed was 'unfortunately *not* a favourite generally with his own people', feared that 'the project will never go beyond the embryonic stages',[4] it did succeed. In June 1875 the school was opened with twenty-five students. By 1878 the school had classes for the First Arts examination, and by 1881 it had 300 pupils and was giving degree courses.[5] 'In respectable families the study of English, with the object of obtaining a post in Government service' had once been 'highly discreditable'; the proverb ran that '*angrezi parhi, admiyat jati rahi*' ('He has read English, his *human nature* has left him'); but Syed congratulated himself that 'the prejudice has now... much slackened'.[6] In Aligarh Muslims had a college of their

---

[1] See T. Morison, *The History of the M.A.-O. College, Aligarh* (Allahabad, 1903).
[2] Report of the members of the Select Committee for the Better Diffusion and Advancement of the learning among the Muhammadans of India (translated), 1872, quoted in Philips, *The Evolution of India and Pakistan*, p. 179.   [3] *Ibid.* p. 180.
[4] Muir to Northbrook, 25 June 1872, Northbrook Papers, MSS Eur. C. 144 (13).
[5] Syed Ahmed Khan to Director of Public Instruction, June 1881, quoted in EC (*North-western Provinces and Oudh*), pp. 51–5.
[6] Syed Ahmed's evidence, *ibid.* pp. 88, 298.

own where they could study the new learning without jeopardising their souls.[1]

By 1883 the local government suspected that Aligarh 'bids fair to be of the greatest importance from a political as well as an educational point of view',[2] but there was little in Syed's early political attitudes to suggest that he wanted separate and favoured treatment for Muslims. He himself had been the first to argue that the Mutiny had been in part caused by the failure to grant Indians a modest say in the Councils.[3] When he moved to Aligarh, he helped to found a branch of the British Indian Association, urging both the Hindus and Muslims of the North-western Provinces to take a greater interest in their affairs and to speak up for their rights, while assuring them that this was compatible with perfect loyalty to the Raj.[4] Far from hinting that Muslims should stand aloof, his argument implied that it was by joining a moderate association that they could show they were no longer irreconcilable. As for recruiting more Indians into the services by examination, Syed would not condemn this demand simply because some Muslims were not ready for it. Indeed Syed often held up the Bengalis as an example to be admired and imitated;[5] and the future author of the two-nation theory dwelt in glowing terms upon Hindu–Muslim unity.[6]

[1] This however meant that Aligarh had to give religious instruction of a rather vague and unspecific kind. See Mohamed Ali, *My Life: a Fragment*, pp. 21–4.

[2] *EC (North-western Provinces and Oudh)*, p. 52.

[3] Syed Ahmed Khan, *The Causes of the Indian Revolt*, pp. 11–15.

[4] Syed Ahmed Khan, *A Speech on the Institution of the British Indian Association, N.W. Provinces* (Aligarh, 1867), pp. 3–7. On the British Indian Association of Oudh, which became the spokesman of the talukdars, see Metcalf, *The Aftermath of Revolt*, pp. 160–2.

[5] See Syed Aethmed Khan to Secretary, Scientific Society of Aligarh, 15 October 1869, cited in Graham, *Syed Ahmed Khan*, p. 129; and Syed's speech to the Indian Association, Lahore, 1884, where he said: 'Bengalees are the only people in our country whom we can properly be proud of and it is only due to them that knowledge, liberty and patriotism have progressed in our country', quoted in G. A. Natesan (ed.), *Eminent Mussalmans* (1st edition Madras, n.d.), p. 33.

[6] The M.A.-O. college was originally meant for Muslims alone, but according to Syed the Hindu nobility and gentry showed so much goodwill, sympathy and generosity to the college that a few Hindus were given places, (*EC (North-western Provinces and Oudh)*, p. 51). On 27 January 1884 Syed told an audience at Gurdaspur 'Remember that the words Hindu and Mahomedan are only meant for religious distinction—other-

This was why Congress was so surprised by Syed Ahmed's opposition. But it ought not to have been. While Syed and the Bengal Muslims had different reasons for their action, both were against joining Congress when the time came for them to decide. Congress wanted representative Legislative Councils. It hinted at a parliament for India in the future. But in any such parliament, Syed Ahmed Khan realised, Muslims would be 'in a permanent minority', and they would always be outvoted as the Irish were at Westminster.[1] When in January 1883 the Imperial Legislative Council was debating a local self-government bill for the Central Provinces, where Muslims were a small minority, Syed spoke against introducing the elective principle into India:

> The system of representation by election means the representation of the views and interests of the majority of the population...in a country like India, where caste distinctions still flourish, where there is no fusion of the various races, where religious distinctions are still violent, where education in its modern sense has not made an equal or proportionate progress among all the sections of the population, I am convinced that the introduction of the principle of election, pure and simple, for representation of various interests on the Local Boards and District Councils would be attended with evils of greater significance than purely economic considerations. So long as differences of race and creed, and the distinctions of caste form an important element in the socio-political life of India, and influence her inhabitants in matters connected with the administration and welfare of the country at large, the system of election pure and simple cannot safely be adopted. The larger community would totally override the interests of the smaller community, and the ignorant public would hold Government responsible for introducing measures which might make the differences of race and creed more violent than ever.[2]

In November 1886, before the second Congress met, Syed Ahmed Khan publicly declared India unready for representative or popular government, and condemned Congress as 'seditious'.[3]

In upper India, Congress demands about employment did

wise all persons, whether Hindu or Mahomedan or even Christians who reside in this country, are all in this particular respect belonging to one and the same nation'. (Quoted in Natesan, *Eminent Mussalmans*, p. 32.)

[1] *Aligarh Institute Gazette*, 23 November 1886.
[2] Proceedings of the Council of the Governor-General, 1883, quoted in R. Coupland, *India, A Restatement* (London, 1945), p. 93, and Natesan, *Eminent Mussalmans*, p. 30.
[3] *Aligarh Institute Gazette*, 23 November 1886.

as much to bring the Muslims into opposition as they did in Bengal; but not for the same reasons. In the North-western Provinces and Oudh, which were backward in the new education, the most coveted and best-paid posts in the public service did not go to those schooled in English.[1] By 1886 only 18 per cent of the executive and judicial officers in the uncovenanted services had passed the university entrance examinations.[2] If competitive examinations and university degrees were to be the pass to office, as Congress demanded, then the local population, Muslim and Hindu alike, would be hard hit. Graduates, whether from Aligarh, Muir or Canning Colleges, were not numerous and men from outside the province—Bengalis in particular—would get the jobs. So with one voice the witnesses from the North-western Provinces denounced the Congress line before the Public Services Commission. One of Aligarh's first products, Syed Habibullah, who had gone to Balliol and the Inner Temple before becoming a barrister at Allahabad, criticised simultaneous examinations because 'neither Mahomedans nor Hindus would succeed, but only Bengalis would get all'.[3] Ajudhia Nath, a Kashmiri Brahmin, the leading Hindu pleader at Allahabad and a member of the local Legislative Council, felt that the services ought not to be recruited by examination unless this was done on a strictly provincial basis. The 'difference...in the education of the different Provinces', made this necessary, particularly since opinion in upper India held strongly that 'it is better to be ruled by gentlemen who belong to the same Province'.[4] Witness after witness took the stand simply to state that 'Bengalis should not hold executive appointments in these Provinces'; and the Raja of Benares, Shiva Prasad, a government servant and landowner with a term's experience on the Imperial Legislative Council, fulminated to the Commission against Bengalis, describing them as 'bred in chicanery', 'naturally timid and slothful', and declaring that 'never, never' should there be simultaneous examinations in India.[5] A year later this Hindu joined Syed in his assault upon the Congress.

---

[1] *EC (North-western Provinces and Oudh)*, p. 164.
[2] *PSC*, p. 35.
[3] *PSC (North-western Provinces and Oudh)*, II, section 2, p. 2.
[4] *Ibid.* section 2, p. 18.   [5] *Ibid.* section 3 (B), p. 44.

What the principal of Aligarh College had to tell the Commission was interesting. Theodore Beck, 'a pretty young man with pink cheeks and blue eyes, certainly not an average Englishman',[1] was a Quaker who had come to Aligarh in 1883 as principal at the age of twenty-four after having been a scholar at Trinity and president of the Cambridge Union. He has been seen as the *éminence grise* behind Syed Ahmed Khan, the agent of an official policy to 'divide and rule', and the first of the notorious Aligarh principals who were the alleged architects of Muslim separatism.[2] Yet his evidence on 30 December 1886, three years after his arrival in India, simply repeated the commonplaces of the province. Competitive examinations were repugnant to him because they would give 'a very unjust advantage to Bengalis; unjust, because the British Government has been educating Bengalis for a much longer time...'. 'Already employed largely in the North-western Provinces', Bengalis were 'much disliked by the people.' By flooding the service with men from the Lower Provinces, competitive examinations would dispossess 'Mahomedans and the upper classes in general, such as the Rajput aristocracy.' This would have 'a very bad political effect'.[3]

When the Commission, with the Bengal Muslims in mind, asked Beck whether he would welcome a rule 'that the proportion of Hindus and Muslims appointed be related to the population proportion in the Province', his answer showed that the Muslims in the North-western Provinces were a special case. Since they already had a share of office far larger than their population proportion, such a rule would harm rather than benefit them. With scant regard for the interests of Muslims in Bengal, Punjab or Sind, he announced:

The principle of proportionate representation of different classes in high Government posts is unworkable in India and is accepted by nobody... It is necessary to see what classes of men have been in the

[1] Blunt, *India under Ripon*, p. 156.
[2] For this argument in an extreme form see A. Mehta and A. Patwardhan, *The Communal Triangle in India* (2nd revised edn., Allahabad, 1942), pp. 24, 57–61.
[3] *PSC (North-western Provinces and Oudh)*, II, section 2, pp. 35–8. In its official return of the nationality and caste of executive and judicial officers in the subordinate service, the Provincial government reported that there were eighteen Bengalis. This figure probably did not include Bengalis domiciled in the province (*Ibid.* section 1, pp. 43–4).

habit of acquiring, and have grown dependent on, official employment. These are the educated classes, and among them we shall find a very large number of Mahomedans and men belonging to only a few of the superior castes of Hindus. If the system of numerical representation were adopted, there would be five Hindus to every one Mahomedan in the North-Western Provinces. The result would be the enormous political preponderance of Hindus and the practical extinction of Mahomedan influence in civil affairs. It must be remembered that Mahomedans ruled this part of India for five centuries, and are not prepared to accept a position of political insignificance.[1]

Then came the scarcely veiled threat which made the most of the Muslim equivocation between loyalty and hostility to the Raj. 'If the Government shut to them the door by which they may hope to gain legitimate influence, it will give a dangerous impetus to those with whom the idea of the *jehad* is not yet dead, and will discourage those who by their efforts to introduce English education are trying to extinguish that idea.'[2] So if there had to be a rule about appointments then Beck would have a rule giving the two communities absolutely equal shares.[3]

What was to become political orthodoxy for Muslim and civilian alike was solemnly enunciated by a Muslim district judge from Rae Bareli:

India is not a country but a continent with as many varieties of race, religion and language as the whole of Europe...Moreover, not only the various provinces but also the various sections of the population in each province have reached varying educational standards, and it does not follow that the classes most adapted to pass educational tests of the English competitive type are best fitted for administration... there is not sufficient homogeneity of the Indian population to render an open competitive examination desirable.[4]

The root of the difficulty, Syed Mahmud explained, was 'the fact that the standard of education of the English type attained in the various parts of India and among the various sections of the population is far from equal'.[5] Thus these witnesses sketched out the argument that Syed Ahmed Khan was now to propagate with such enthusiasm. A few months later he announced that 'our country is not fit for the competitive examinations: there is marked disparity in the educational

[1] *PSC (North-western Provinces and Oudh)*, II, section 2, pp. 38–9.
[2] *Ibid.* section 2, p. 39.   [3] *Ibid.*
[4] *Ibid.* section 2, p. 132.   [5] *Ibid.* section 2, p. 134.

attainments of various people—Muslims are educationally backward; the Hindus of this province are backward compared to the Bengalis'.[1] Therefore the statutory service, which had given Muslims fifteen out of forty-eight places, ought to stay; so should nomination as a method of selecting men.

In December 1887, with Syed in the van, the Muslims became more openly hostile to Congress. Beck fired the opening shots in the campaign, but his arguments were so similar to Syed's that it is difficult to tell whether it was he who followed Syed's lead or Syed his.[2] In a series of articles in the *Pioneer* and the *Aligarh Institute Gazette* Beck pronounced that a parliamentary system of government made no sense in 'a country containing two or more nations tending to oppress the numerically weaker'.[3] To bring into India liberal institutions designed for England's homogeneous population would do violence to 'all historical continuity', and to all 'the traditions of autocratic rule'. It was an idea 'so preposterous as to need no refutation'.[4] Syed himself now bluntly attacked Congress and what it stood for. If the Imperial Legislative Council became an elected body, Hindus would have at least four times as many members as the Muslims. If examinations became the rule, Hindu graduates from Calcutta would bundle Muslims out of office. So Syed urged them to stand aloof from Congress, which was a movement run by Bengalis for Bengalis. 'If you accept that the country should groan under the yoke of Bengali rule and its people lick the Bengali shoes, then in the name of God jump into the train, sit down and be off to Madras, be off to Madras.'[5]

In this onslaught upon Congress Syed Ahmed might have won more support from the Hindus of upper India by driving home the differences between their interests and those of the maritime provinces. But in stressing the divisions between Hindus and Muslims, he lessened the chances of a local inter-communal alliance. One reason for this new note in

---

[1] Syed Ahmed's speech before the second Muslim Educational Conference, Lucknow, quoted in Gopal, *Indian Muslims*, p. 66.
[2] See T. Beck, *Essays on Indian Topics* (Allahabad, 1888), pp. 39–87, 93–127.
[3] *Pioneer*, 2 and 3 November 1887.
[4] *Aligarh Institute Gazette*, 5 and 12 November 1887.
[5] Speech at Lucknow, 28 December 1887, Syed Ahmed Khan, *On the Present State of Indian Politics* (Allahabad, 1888), pp. 11–12.

his propaganda lay in the growing competition between the two communities for education and employment. Between 1867 and 1887 Hindus had increased their share of government patronage,[1] and in particular the determination of the Kayasths to improve their condition was beginning to threaten the Muslim preserve. By their own admission, they were 'exclusively a literary class'; their principal occupation was public service, and they had always 'considered it a disgrace to follow any occupation unconnected with letters'.[2] In a pattern closely resembling Syed Ahmed's, their leaders argued in their own special pleading that the Kayasths had 'developed habits and customs that considerably handicapped them in the race for life under the altered conditions introduced into the country by the constitutional Government of England', and Munshi Kali Prasad of Lucknow 'preached to them that their salvation lay in their applying themselves to the study of Western arts and sciences and availing themselves of the means of education placed by our kind and benign Government within the reach of everyone'.[3] In 1886, the same year that Syed held the first Muslim Educational Conference, a Kayastha Conference was organised to take 'decisive measures for the amelioration of the condition of their race';[4] they planned to turn it into a pressure group to ensure that Kayasths would not be 'beaten back in the competition of nations by any unjust means'.[5] Two Lucknow pleaders, Munshi Har Govind Dayal and Sri Ram, both graduates, were the founders of this new body which held annual meetings from November 1887. It also organised a number of local branches and controlled its own newspapers.[6]

Among their demands was that Urdu should be replaced as the language of administration in the North-western Provinces by Hindi in the Devanagari script. This agitation had begun in Benares in 1867 when Fateh Chand organised committees

[1] See above, table 46, p. 305.
[2] *A Short Account of the aims, objects, achievements and Proceedings of the Kayastha Conference and Letters of Sympathy from eminent rulers and High Government Officers* (Allahabad, 1893), p. ii.   [3] *Ibid.* pp. ii, iv.
[4] *Ibid.* p. 1.
[5] *Kayastha, Quarterly Organ of the Kayastha Clubs Association* (Agra), I, no. 1, (October 1895), 1. It is interesting to find a caste association using the language of international politics.
[6] *A Short Account...of the Kayastha Conference*, part I, pp. 1–16.

to press for Hindi.[1] Syed Ahmed's Translation Society, which at first had some Hindu support, split when Shiva Prasad, a champion of Hindi, proposed that Devanagari should be used in their translations. By 1870 Hindus and Muslims were hardening in their attitudes to this issue. According to the Department of Education, most Hindu pupils 'spontaneously chose to be taught Hindi in preference to Urdu'. Hindus argued that Urdu was the language of a small minority in the towns, unintelligible to the Hindi educated, and that its status as the official language gave Muslims unfair advantages in gaining government employment. In 1881 the decision in the neighbouring districts of Bihar to make the change to Devanagari for all official work sharpened the controversy, and the following year both sides marshalled their arguments before the Education Commission. Although the government of the North-western Provinces did not decide in favour of Hindi until 1898, the controversy was already helping to divide the communities.[2]

In September 1888, the second Kayastha Conference was held at Allahabad, and 626 of its delegates were local men, thus pointing to possible sources of support for the coming session of the National Congress. When Colvin reviewed this Congress, he pointed out that the literary class in the North-western Provinces and Oudh was

drawn mainly from the writer or Kayeth caste, a caste which is near the bottom of the social scale, and which, except in virtue of its clerical attainments, commands little respect among other classes. There is a sprinkling, at the same time, of men of the trading class and of Brahmans. These,...like the Muhammadans, are in a large minority. The impact on the Government is not that of a class which combines with education social weight or practical knowledge of affairs; but of a section whose duty has hitherto been to perform the clerical part of public business; whose qualities for higher employment or whose aptitudes for dealing with affairs upon a large scale have, until very recent

---

[1] Hindus in Bihar had succeeded in getting Urdu replaced by Hindi in the law courts, and in 1873 the Central Provinces made the change in subordinate government offices. The agitation for Hindi in Bihar had in part come from Bengalis who found it easier to master a language in the Nagari script, A. K. Majumdar, *Advent of Independence* (Bombay, 1963), pp. 41–2, 57 n.5.

[2] See *EC (North-western Provinces and Oudh)*, pp. 416–91; J. H. Garcin de Tassy, *La Langue et la littérature Hindoustanies en 1870* (Paris, 1871), pp. 13–24, 40–1; Ahmad, *Studies in Islamic Culture in the Indian Environment*, pp. 260–1; Gopal, *Indian Muslims*, pp. 30–43.

years, neither been asserted by themselves nor admitted by others; and who, if they attract attention at the present date from the fact of their being able to handle literary weapons, are none the less regarded by more masterful sections of the community with indifference and contempt.

Assessing the strength of Congress in upper India, the lieutenant-governor stated that 'to any one who is conversant with these provinces there is abundant evidence that the immense majority of the people is at present either indifferent to the new ideas or is actively hostile to them'. Referring to the strong Muslim opposition to Congress, he confirmed that the community had begun to realise the threat of being subjected to 'the influence of classes whom they despise'; they were 'hurt in their sentiment of family pride and their dignity of landlords by the prominence given to a class of men whose slender stock of acquirements, whose hereditary occupations, and whose obscure antecedents, unfit them, in their eyes, for the position they are encouraged to assume under British rule'. Of the 587 delegates from the North-western Provinces and Oudh at the 1888 Congress, only sixty-three, in Colvin's opinion, could be described as 'men of note'; 217 were pleaders; twelve were editors, and the rest were 'miscellaneous'. Almost half the delegates came from Allahabad, Benares and Lucknow;

From the powerful districts of the Rohilkand division there were 30 only; and putting aside Aligarh, where there is active Hindu antagonism to the strong Muhammadan party which owes its existence there to the presence of Sir Syed Ahmed and his College, from the populous and important Meerut division, there were only 37. The Muhammadans came mainly from Allahabad and Lucknow; 79 that is to say out of 161. The great Muhammadan districts returned few or none. From Agra, for instance, there were 3; from Bareilly and Jaunpur, none. Reference to the Allahabad district return will show from what class of men Muhammadans were recruited. Unscrupulous efforts were evidently made to sweep Muhammadans of any kind into the net, in order to be able to reply to the unanswerable criticisms that the movement is resisted by Muhammadans...I am aware that, with scarcely any exception, no Muhammadan of character, standing, or fortune would for a moment consent to be returned as a delegate, or would in any way associate himself with the ideas and aims put forward by the literary party.

Upper India was more conservative than maritime India. Not only the Muslims but the most powerful Hindu influences were against the Congress.

The North West was the central seat of recent Muhammadan rule, of which the tradition and memory are still fresh and powerful in the minds of the present generation. In Oudh the priestly forces of Hinduism, and the religious basis of life and conduct, survive in far greater degree than in the neighbouring province; while the landed influence exercised by the talukdars is paramount.

These groups had no interest in the demand for the reform of the Legislative Councils.

We are, in the true sense of the word, provincial. Whatever, therefore, may be contended for in the case of Calcutta, Madras, or Bombay, finds little support in our circumstances. To establish changes in the Council here would gratify a few young graduates, a few pleaders, a Bengali judge or two, and their immediate followers, but would vex and disgust the whole of Oudh, the whole of the Muhammadan community whether in Oudh or the North West, and while proving a source of annoyance and discontent to the vast majority of the Hindu community in the North West would seem to them an innovation introduced at the demand of a small section whose inexplicable influence over the Government must furnish growing ground for alarm.[1]

Thus local support for the Congress at Allahabad came mainly from the Kayasths, and although the caste Conference claimed to be interested only in social and educational matters, having 'nothing to do with politics or religion', it was soon having to refute the charge that it was 'the agent of the Indian National Congress to disseminate political theories and to further its aims'.[2]

The decision to hold the fourth Congress at Allahabad in 1888 forced Hindus and Muslims alike into open positions drawn along lines of local interests. On the one hand the social and administrative elites of the province found themselves at one; Muslim landowner and administrator sided with Hindu talukdar, and together they joined the United Patriotic Association, Syed Ahmed's answer to the challenge of the Congress. On the other hand, the Kayasths, who in the North-west were of relatively low social standing, were eager to use the Congress as a vehicle for their aspirations and as an opportunity to gain allies outside their own province, particularly to associate themselves with the Bengal Kayasths who were of considerably

[1] Note by A. Colvin, 11 June 1889, Notes, Home Public A, August 1892, nos. 237–52.
[2] *A Short Account...of the Kayastha Conference*, p. v.

higher status. Orthodox Muslims, hating Syed and the British alike, made Congress the beneficiary of their resentments.[1] Congress made strange bedfellows at Allahabad. The Muslim delegates had little interest in Councils and simultaneous examinations, while Kayasths were as keen as the local Muslim elite to stave off employment competition from outside. Thus the first loyalty of many local delegates lay not with India but with their sectional interests. In support of its claim to represent all regions and communities, Congress had deliberately pitched its tents at Allahabad. It had come to a province where many of its demands made little sense to most of the inhabitants. Yet by providing a convenient forum for local grievances it helped to shape competing aspirations and alliances within the region. This signified that the wider the area from which Congress attempted to draw its following, the less unanimous a voice it could win in the politics of India, and the less solidarity it could possess as a national pressure group.

At the first Congress there were two Muslim delegates, at the second thirty-three, at the third seventy-nine and at Allahabad, in 1888, two hundred and twenty-two.[2] They came from every province, but the most prominent among them was Badruddin Tyabji of Bombay who presided over the third Congress at Madras. Moving easily in Bombay's cosmopolitan society and earning a handsome salary at the bar, he had been at the fore of Bombay politics for more than a decade.[3] He was one of the leaders of the city's young intelligentsia, working closely with his Hindu and Parsi colleagues in municipality and association. But the Muslims of Bombay, a much divided body, could not easily be led and represented by one man.

[1] On the United Patriotic Association and orthodox Muslim opposition to Syed, see below, pp. 336–7.

[2] The percentage of the Muslim delegates to the total in each of these years was 2·7, 7·6, 13·0 and 17·7 at Allahabad in 1888. The percentage of Muslim delegates was never again to be as large as it was at Allahabad except at Lucknow in 1899. See B. B. Majumdar, 'The Congress and the Moslems', *The Quarterly Review of Historical Studies*, v, no. 2 (1965–6). Colvin had a different estimate of the number of Muslims at Allahabad (see above, p. 327).

[3] The Tyabjis, Sulaimani Bohras, were pioneers in adaptation. Badruddin was the first Muslim to qualify at the London bar; his brother, Camruddin, was the first Muslim to train as a solicitor in England; Badruddin's son was the first Muslim to pass the covenanted civil service examination; yet another member of the family was the first Muslim civil surgeon. See Tyabji, *Badruddin Tyabji*, p. 105.

As Shias, the Bohras were looked upon as heretics by the majority, and the Anjuman-i-Islam which Badruddin founded in 1876 was by his own admission a society to represent only 'the educated and thinking portion of the community'.[1] Its main work was to set up an English school,[2] and to act as a pressure group for Muslims who wanted government employment.[3] Besides the Anjuman-i-Islam, there was another association in the city representing the orthodox Muslims, the Anjuman-i-Ahab, and over the Anjuman-i-Islam itself Tyabji and his friends had only an uncertain control. A determined body of opponents tried first to oust Tyabji, and after they failed to do so, in 1882 formed a rival association, the Bombay National Mahommedan Association, claiming that the Anjuman-i-Islam was simply a scientific and literary society, unrepresentative of the political interests of Bombay Muslims.[4] Tyabji's response to this charge made his position clear:

The Anjuman has as a rule abstained from discussing political questions because the majority of such questions affect not merely the Mahomedans but the whole population of India in general, and therefore it is better that they should be discussed by the general political bodies composed of all classes of Her Majesty's subjects, and not merely by a body of Mahomedans as the Anjuman is.[5]

The nature of city politics in Bombay, and Tyabji's own place in them, explain both this stand and his later support for the Indian National Congress. Politics here tended to be a compromise between the different communities and were not vulnerable to the rebuke that they were simply Hindu. In Bombay, Muslims had a smaller voice in the municipality than they had in Calcutta.[6] Moreover, Badruddin discovered that co-operation with his educated Parsi and Hindu colleagues paid dividends. They both came to his support when the

[1] Tyabji to Editor, *Times of India*, 8 May 1882.
[2] The school was set up in 1880. Its success, as one influential Muslim told Badruddin, was entirely owing to 'the small party of which you are so active a member', Kazi Shabuddin to Tyabji, 21 May 1881. Tyabji Papers.
[3] On the activities of the Anjuman, see Tyabji, *Badruddin Tyabji*, pp. 88–107.
[4] *Ibid.* pp. 92–101.
[5] Tyabji to Editor, *Times of India*, 8 May 1882.
[6] In the first election in 1873 for the Corporation under the new Act, Muslims, 21·4 per cent of the city's population, had 896 votes, or 23 per cent, in an electoral roll of 3,918. For this information, I am indebted to Miss C. Dobbin.

Anjuman's school was attacked by Tyabji's Muslim opponents.[1] In 1882 he was given a place on the Legislative Council to represent graduates and lawyers and not simply the Muslims.[2] In municipal affairs, the educated worked together;[3] a Parsi nominated Badruddin in the municipal elections of 1883,[4] and in 1884 the Parsi and Hindu press supported the candidature as sheriff of Bombay of another Muslim. This was Rahmatulla Sayani, who later served as president of the Indian National Congress. In 1885 Tyabji was one of the founders of the Bombay Presidency Association which that December played host to the first Congress.

Although he had not attended this Congress, Tyabji assured his friends in the Presidency Association that 'when a political question was involved', the Muslims 'were one with their Parsee and Hindoo brethren'.[5] Three weeks before the Calcutta session, W. C. Bonnerjee, an old friend from student days in England, suggested Tyabji should take the presidential chair at the second Congress.[6] Ill health prevented Tyabji from going to Calcutta, but the following year, when Syed's outburst made a show of Muslim support for the Congress imperative, the Congress leaders decided to choose a Muslim president. Their choice again fell on Badruddin. All the Congress Standing Committees, Hume told him in November 1887, are 'unanimous in their desire that you should preside over the coming Congress'; Tyabji was 'not only the best, but the only possible man for the post', and he was called to it 'by the unanimous voice of your fellow-countrymen'.[7]

Since Tyabji was to be the symbol of Muslim support for Congress, Amir Ali tried to head him off with an invitation to attend a Muslim conference that the Central National Mahommedan Association was now planning as a supplement to the

[1] Eight of Bombay's leading men, including Mandlik, Mehta, Telang and Waglé, reported on Tyabji's school and refuted the criticism that its teaching was worthless. Tyabji, *Badruddin Tyabji*, pp. 99–100.
[2] See Atmaram Pandurang to Tyabji, 25 August 1882. Tyabji Papers.
[3] See Kabraji to Tyabji, 10 December 1882; Byramji Jeejeebhoy to Tyabji, 21 December 1882; Dosabhoy Framji to Tyabji, 27 December 1882, Tyabji Papers.
[4] See report on the municipal elections, *Times of India*, 10 February 1883.
[5] Proceedings of the Annual General Meeting, 7 April 1886, *Bombay Presidency Association. First Annual Report, 1885*, p. 21.
[6] Bonnerjee to Tyabji, 1 December 1886. Tyabji Papers.
[7] Hume to Tyabji, 3 December 1887. Tyabji Papers.

Muhammadan Educational Congress launched by Syed in 1886. It would work for the 'material and political advancement' of Muslims, and give 'a double impetus to their political development'.[1] Although the Conference was intended for Muslims only, the proposal was not actuated 'by any spirit of rivalry towards our Hindoo compatriots'.

> Our main object [Amir Ali assured Tyabji] is to bring about some degree of solidarity among the disintegrated masses of Mahomedan society; to reconcile in some measure the conflicting aims and objects of different sections and parties; to introduce some amount of harmony into the discordant and jarring elements of which the Mussulman educated classes are composed; to devise some means of self-help for Mahomedan advancement and lean less upon Government patronage; to give a real impetus to the process of self-development going on among our community; to safeguard our legitimate and constitutional interests under the British Government; to become the exponent of the views and aspirations of educated Mahomedan India; and to serve as the means of reconciliation between our Hindoo fellow subjects and our own community.[2]

In fact the programme of the Conference would be 'extremely moderate and suited to our own progress'; it would not discuss 'high politics'.[3] Amir Ali wanted the power which would flow from a communal demand without the responsibility attaching to political activity.

But Tyabji was not persuaded. If Amir Ali's Muslim conference was simply to be a rival to Congress, he was against it. He now stated the thesis which the uncompromising hostility of Syed Ahmed and Amir Ali forced him to develop during his one year of hectic association with Congress. Its major premise was that there were certain questions which affected all Indians alike, whether Hindu, Parsi or Muslim. For Muslims the 'proper course is to join the Congress and take part in its deliberations from our own peculiar stand-point'.[4] In his presidential address to the third Congress Tyabji elaborated the argument. No doubt the Muslim community had 'its own peculiar social, moral and educational and even political difficulties to surmount', and he admitted that India was in no sense one nation. Yet there were some 'general questions

[1] Amir Ali to Tyabji, 27 November 1887. Tyabji Papers.
[2] Amir Ali to Tyabji, 5 January 1888. Tyabji Papers.
[3] *Ibid.*
[4] Tyabji to Amir Ali, 3 December 1887. Tyabji Papers.

affecting the whole of India'. Many Muslims, Badruddin claimed, recognised this and supported Congress. There were seventy-nine Muslim delegates at the Madras session to prove his point. Certainly some Muslims had held aloof, but this, he sanguinely hoped, was due simply to 'certain special and local temporary causes' and applied 'only to a particular part of India'.[1]

Bold words; but privately Tyabji had his doubts. Many of his co-religionists had told him of their fears that the Hindus might pass a resolution in Congress directly hostile to Muslim interests. So Hume and Tyabji together drafted a rule intended to effect 'a complete reconciliation with all those sections of our Mahomedan brethren which have hitherto held aloof from us'. It laid down that no subject to which all the delegates of any community, as a body, were opposed should be brought before Congress, 'without reference to whether the opposers constitute the majority or minority'.[2] This draft was circulated to the Standing Congress Committees for their approval. While there were obvious tactical advantages in such a rule, some of the Congress leaders disliked its wider implications, for it might be made to mean that the Muslims could prevent Congress from adopting the very programme for which it had been founded. So they insisted upon adding that subjects upon which the Congress had already passed resolutions were excluded from the operation of the rule. With this important qualification the Allahabad Congress accepted the rule.[3]

Armed with this proposal, Tyabji approached the Muslim leaders who opposed the Congress. Its aims, he told them, 'are and must be, for the *benefits of all communities*, and any proposition that is disliked by the Mahomedans as a body must be excluded from it'. To ensure the latter a rule had been framed 'to the effect that no proposition to which the Mussulmans generally object shall be considered by the Congress. This rule

[1] *I.N.C.* 1887, p. 72.
[2] See Hume to Secretaries, Standing Committees of Congress, Circular Letter, 5 January 1888. Tyabji Papers.
[3] 'Resolved—That no subject shall be passed for discussion by the Subject Committee, or allowed to be discussed at any Congress...to the introduction of which the Hindu or Mahomedan Delegates as a body object... provided that this rule shall refer only to subjects in regard to which the Congress has not already definitely pronounced an opinion,' Resolution XIII, *I.N.C.* 1888, p. lxii.

will be formally embodied in the constitution of the Congress.'[1]
Writing to Syed in February 1888, Badruddin stated:

We can as little stop the Congress as we can stop the progress of
education. But it is in our power by firm and resolute action to direct
the course the Congress shall take and my strong conviction is that
the Mussulmans can by united action confine the Congress to such
topics only as they may deem desirable or safe for discussion. Take for
instance the question of the Legislative Councils. If the Mussulmans
as a body do not like that the member should be elected, they could
easily modify the proposition so as to suit their own interests. My
policy, therefore, would be to act from *within* rather than from *without*.
I would say to all Mussulmans 'act with your Hindu fellow-subjects
in all matters in which you are agreed but oppose them as strongly
as you can if they bring forward any proposition that you may deem
prejudicial to yourselves'. We should thus advance the general
progress of India, and at the same time safeguard our own interests.[2]

It was in vain. From Syed all he evoked was a blunt statement about the political facts of life. Muslims who opposed
Congress, Syed told him, 'do not mean to retard the national
progress of India' or 'to prevent other people from enjoying
rights for which they are qualified; and even if we try we cannot
hope to succeed; but at the same time it is not obligatory on our
part to run a race with persons with whom we have no chance
of success'.[3] It was all very well for Tyabji to exhort Muslims
to 'raise ourselves in the scale of progress', but he ought to
recall 'the saying of the old Philosopher that "before we get
the antidote from Irak, the snake-bitten person will die"'. It
was impossible for the different castes and creeds living in India
to become one nation; there could be no such thing as a
National Congress equally beneficial to all the different peoples
of India. 'The doings of the misnamed National Congress',
Syed asserted, were 'injurious not only to our community
but also to India at large.' 'I object to every Congress in any
shape or form which regards India as one nation...'[4]

Tyabji's efforts galvanised his Muslim opponents into a
counter-attack where the first casualty was the Congress claim
'that the whole Muhammadan community had joined them'.
On 14 March 1888 Syed declared that, Tyabji excepted, there

[1] Tyabji to Amir Ali, 13 January 1888. Tyabji Papers. Similar letters were
   sent by him to Abdul Latif and to Syed Ahmed.
[2] Tyabji to Syed Ahmed, 18 February 1888. Tyabji Papers.
[3] Syed Ahmed to Tyabji, 24 January 1888. Tyabji Papers.
[4] *Ibid.*

had been no 'eminent' Muslims at Madras. He gave Tyabji credit for honestly trying to discover which subjects the Muslims wanted kept out of the Congress programme, but castigated him for failing to realise that 'in fact all the subjects of the Congress are unsuitable to our community'.[1] When Hunter, an authority on the Muslims, suggested that Bengali Muslims alone had been absent from Madras, he too came under heavy fire from Syed's men. The Muslim delegates at Madras were contemptuously described by Mohammed Shafi, later a president of the Muslim League, as men of no substance, unrepresentative and 'self-elected'.[2] All over India, Muslim associations, including the two Calcutta organisations, two in Madras, and one in the Punjab, denounced the Congress. At Allahabad, Lucknow, Meerut and Lahore, Muslims met to condemn the Congress, and their newspapers took up the cry.[3]

Meanwhile Aligarh exhorted Muslims to reaffirm their loyalty to the British, who were described as Khalifatullah, or the representatives of God on earth. The Koran was cited to show that the Faithful could consort with Christians since they too were People of the Book.[4] Muslims were reminded that if they came to terms with their rulers they would be rewarded by the Raj. By August Syed had decided to push the campaign further. Envoys went to persuade Muslims in other parts of India to repudiate Congress.[5] In Hyderabad, Syed had natural allies: Muslim officials from the North-western Provinces, such as Salar Jung,[6] Mushtaq Husain, Nawab Vignam-ul-Mulk, and the Nizam himself.[7] In Bombay, the Anjuman-i-Ahab was 'rabidly Mahomedan and Syed to a man'[8] and refused to have anything to do with Congress.[9] Syed's emissaries even entered Tyabji's preserve, and scored a telling blow by persuading his own organisation, the Anjuman-i-Islam, to

[1] Syed Ahmed Khan, *On the Present State of Indian Politics*, p. 34.
[2] Mohammed Shafi to Editor, *Pioneer*, 13 July 1888.
[3] *Aligarh Institute Gazette*, 21 July 1888.   [4] *Ibid.*
[5] In Bombay, for example, a meeting of 'all sections of the Mahommedan community' was called on 4 August to dissuade Muslims from joining Congress. Confidential Abstracts I, no. 25 of 1888, paras. 2, 65, Police Records, Intelligence Branch, Government of Bombay.
[6] See Lal Bahadur, *The Muslim League* (Agra, 1954), p. 8.
[7] Wacha to Naoroji, 14 August 1888. NP.
[8] Wacha to Naoroji, 7 August 1888. NP.
[9] Confidential Abstracts I, no. 25 of 1888, paras. 5 and 67, Police Records, Intelligence Branch, Government of Bombay.

declare against Congress. Only by excluding Syed's converts from the Anjuman was Tyabji able to reverse this decision.[1] Even so he felt that he now lacked a sufficiently clear mandate from the association to represent it at the next Congress.[2]

When the Congress planned to take its next session into Syed's own territory, he waged open war against it by establishing the United Patriotic Association.[3] Founded in August 1888, the Association denounced the claims of Congress to be representative and set out to refute its propaganda in England.[4] In the main it was confined to the North-western Provinces and Oudh, where its protestations of loyalty attracted some of the leading Hindu talukdars and chiefs of upper India besides the Muslims for whom it had been primarily intended. But more durable and important was the Muhammadan Educational Congress which Syed had already launched. Its aims were to bring western knowledge to the community in India as a whole, so that it could better combat the inroads of their rivals. From its inaugural meeting at Aligarh in 1886 when forty-six members attended, it gradually expanded to 120 at Lucknow in 1887, and 251 at Lahore in December 1888. By now it was becoming a regular event. In the course of a two-hour lecture, Maulvi Nazim Ahmed of Delhi proclaimed the need to 'stimulate the Muhammadans to SELF-HELP in education and to encourage in them friendly sentiments towards the British Government'; and Syed Ahmed and his party stressed the need for setting up standing committees in every district in British India, so as to spur on the community.[5] In a sense the Muhammadan Educational Congress was already a mirror image of the Indian National Congress. The one had been formed from the nuclei of educated men in the coastal provinces; the other was spreading outwards from its base in upper India. Once again the advanced sections of a community were seeking to redress the balance by purporting to speak on behalf of their more backward members in other regions. The irony of these rival

[1] See Tyabji, *Badruddin Tyabji*, pp. 232-3.
[2] Tyabji to Hume, 27 October 1888. Tyabji Papers.
[3] See Wacha to Naoroji, 14 August 1888. NP.
[4] See *Pioneer*, 10 August 1888; and *Aligarh Institute Gazette*, 28 August 1888.
[5] Khair-ud-din Shaikh, *A Brief Report of the Third Muhammadan Educational Congress held at Lahore on the 27th, 28th, 29th, and 30th December 1888* (Lahore, 1889), pp. 1-41.

Congresses meeting in upper India at the same time was not lost upon the *Pioneer*, that gruff spokesman of Anglo-Indian feelings:

the one flying the banner of magnificent political projects...the other bent on education, on setting right affairs within the house, lamenting the falling off of their people and learning and elaborating schemes for self-sacrifice and self-help. From the Muhammadan standpoint the contrast is far more striking. The one proposed to represent the Muhammadan community; the other represented it...The Muhammadans at Lahore subordinated Politics to Education, and no speeches of a political character were made.[1]

By the end of 1888 the breach was clear. 'The prime object of the Congress was to unite the different communities and provinces into one and thus promote harmony', Tyabji reminded Hume. 'As it is, however, not only have the Mahomedans been divided from the Hindus in a manner they have never been before, but the Mahomedans themselves have been split into two factions, the gulf between whom is becoming wider every day.'[2] In Calcutta the brittle alliance between Hindus and Muslims achieved during the National Conference of 1885 had been broken. In the North-western Provinces Syed had come out fiercely against the Congress, and his breakaway had exacerbated a whole range of differences. Hindus had been set against Muslims, upper India against Bengal, and the superior classes of Hindustan against the Kayasths. To meet Syed's crusade, Congress in turn had tried hard to rally Muslims, and in upper India this meant an appeal to the orthodox. Even the diehards of Deoband had become improbable recruits in the battle against Aligarh, firing off fatwas condemning Syed and showing some sympathy for a Congress which unwillingly found itself portrayed as an enemy of the Raj.[3] Even in the Muslim backwater of Bombay, Tyabji saw that 'we are not able to act in the same way as we did before'.[4] The split between the Anjuman-i-Ahab and the Anjuman-i-Islam had become wider, and the Anjuman-i-Islam had broken into two.[5] Moreover on the all-India stage itself, Tyabji could

[1] *Pioneer*, 4 January 1889.
[2] Tyabji to Hume, 27 October 1888. Tyabji Papers.
[3] See Faruqi, *The Deoband School and the Demand for Pakistan*, pp. 43–5.
[4] Tyabji to Hume, 27 October 1888. Tyabji Papers.
[5] See Wacha to Naoroji, 7 August 1888. NP. Confidential Abstracts I, no. 26 of 1888, paras. 5, 67, Police Records, Intelligence Branch, Government of Bombay.

see that 'the Nizam, and all the principal men of the state such as Munirul Mulk, Fateh Nawab Jung, and above all Syed Husain Belgrami, have joined the opposition led by such well-known men as Syed Ahmed, Ameer Ali and Abdul Latif'. So it was 'useless saying that the intelligent and educated Mahomedans are in favour of the Congress'. From now on the Congress would have to take account of 'the fact that the overwhelming majority of Muslims are against us'; it followed that 'the movement ipso facto ceases to be a general or national Congress'.[1]

❦

The growing rift between the politics of the two communities has been explained in a number of ways. One school of thought which derives from Hunter's magisterial simplifications has insisted that in the race for education, employment and other less tangible benefits of western influence, the Muslims fell far behind the more adaptable Hindus. Whether handicapped by the prejudice of the ulemas against secular education, by the peculiar obscurantism of Indian Islam, or by government's suspicion of their intentions, they became a backward community. Retarded by this time lag, they were wary of attaching themselves to the politics of a Congress dominated by the more successful community and preferred to ask the Raj to discriminate in their favour. Those whom study or desire has persuaded that all the troubles of India have come as gifts from abroad, have emphasised the role of imperialism in putting asunder two communities which history had joined. At the simpler levels of discussion, those holding this view see the alien government throwing its weight first behind one community and then behind the other, so as to hold them in perpetual deadlock and to prevent them from ever uniting against it. At a more interesting level, this view has become an argument that so long as there was British rule there was bound to be Indian division, since each of the two rivals would be tempted to make its own terms with the third party rather than to search for a solution between themselves. Finally there came the highly charged and polemical doctrine that these two communities

[1] Tyabji to Hume, 27 October 1888. Tyabji Papers. Tyabji added that in his opinion 'it is time to cease holding the Congress every year'.

were in fact two nations, distinguishable ever since the time of the Muslim invasions and separable at the time of the British retreat.

All these theories begin from the common assumptions that the Islamic community in India can be referred to as a bloc of peoples whose conditions were generally equal, whose interests were generally the same and whose solidarity was generally firm. None of these assumptions is true. Unevenness of development in India produced disparities between Muslims in different provinces and between Muslims in the same province, just as it was doing between Hindus. In the face of these disparities it is easy to see why some Muslims shunned Congress from its earliest days. But it is also easy to see why common interests between Muslims at this time were so unreal, even where they were extolled for tactical reasons. As competitiveness in upper India spread between Muslim and Hindu, it forced the Muslims to concentrate on defending their own dominant position there, while the case of their less fortunate brethren in other provinces went by default. In eastern India, where the interests of one Bengali Muslim conspicuously clashed with those of another, there was not much in common between Muslim zemindars and Muslim tenants; and for the ashraf of Calcutta, the poor peasants of east Bengal were merely so many statistics computed to point out their own plight. Consequently, when Syed Ahmed Khan and Amir Ali purported to act as spokesmen of all Muslims in India, their claim was as hollow as that of the Congress leaders to represent all Indians or as that of the government to be the trustee of all Indians. In so shapeless, so jumbled a bundle of societies, there were not two nations, there was not one nation, there was no nation at all. What was India?—a graveyard of old nationalities and the mother of new nationalisms struggling to be born.

As yet it was too early to divine what form these would take. Among the masses of Hindus, with interests so varied and opposed, the only political form any all-India aspiration could take at this time was an organisation of educated men. It might be desultory, it might be skin-deep, but it provided a central structure towards which groups with more limited horizons might turn. Other regions, other organisations and other castes might take up this option and make their way into the all-India body; and so why not other communities? But here another option was opening as well. Besides the linkages of the educated, only one other form of all-India political organisation could be visualised at this time: a linkage of Muslims uniting the community from all corners of the sub-continent. This was not practical politics at the end of the nineteenth century. But the decision of some of their leaders to hold aloof from Congress was of great potential importance. It gave them an incentive not to hold aloof from each other but to move towards genuine inter-regional alliances; and on certain assumptions it could justify them in working to find a solution for themselves alone. Many factors were to influence their choices after the end of the 1880s. Another sixty years were to pass before the final decision.

8

Perspectives

Indian nationalism seems the most impressive of the movements which have led to the emancipation of Asia and Africa from colonial control. The long struggle inside this vast country, together with the stature of the men who led it, encouraged the progress of similar movements elsewhere; while the dramatic events of 1947 had much to do with the dismantling of imperialism in the old sense of the term. Yet whatever its importance in inspiring other seekers after the Political Kingdom, the history of the Indian movement has too many special features to be characteristic of these nationalisms as a whole. Consequently it is best to begin a definition by stating what the movement was not. The political arithmetic of India during the 1870s and 1880s, when the movement was taking shape, shows that it was not formed through the promptings of any class demand or as the consequence of any sharp changes in the structure of the economy. India had been little developed, and efforts at development had brought about a new unevenness in the social and economic structure of the country. There were keen internal rivalries, but these were between caste and caste, community and community, not between class and class. Moreover, those groups which felt a similarity of interest were themselves more the product of bureaucratic initiative than of economic change. Since these groups can be largely identified with the men educated in western styles, and since it was these men whose hopes and fears went into the building of the new associations that emerged as the Indian National Congress, a conceptual system based on elites, rather than on classes, would seem more promising.[1] Yet educated men had many roles to play and

[1] Certainly Pareto's doctrines about the circulation of elites have a possible application to Indian conditions, but the peculiarities of Indian society make this a special application at best.

341

several loyalties to preserve. As they moved into secular organisations, they remained riddled with allegiances to caste or community, and what from a distance appear as their political strivings were often, on closer examination, their efforts to conserve or improve the position of their own prescriptive group. Since these groups were usually castes, and since caste is unknown outside South Asia, this was obviously an elite of a special kind.

Since the movement contained so many features peculiar to itself, the apologists for British rule were hardly mistaken in asserting that it did not square with what they had been schooled to regard as the genuine nationalisms of nineteenth-century Europe. Plainly too, the movement had general differences from the nationalisms of China, Japan and Islam, as well as from its successors in Africa. At first sight this seems to dismiss the possibility of making any statements of high generality about all these movements. But it would be a spirit-less historiography which clung to the particular and eschewed the general. By looking more deeply at the emergence of Indian nationalism it is possible to relate it to these other large movements which have marched across Asia and Africa during the last three-quarters of a century.

At their deeper levels the political mobilisations of India were related to a growing rate of social change which bore unevenly on different parts of the country and which sharpened the rivalries between its inhabitants. It is misleading to view these native mobilisations as directed chiefly against foreign overlordship. Much attention has been paid to the apparent conflicts between imperialism and nationalism; it would be at least equally profitable to study their real partnerships. Both British rule and Indian enterprise had a hand in bringing these mobilisations about. By swinging the power bases of the country away from Hindustan to the coastal regions, British rule had redefined the unevennesses of India. By shifting its internal alliances from time to time, the Raj re-emphasised the rivalries which furrowed the empire. It was not contrivance but its own lack of strength which brought this about. During the last century of its existence, the weakness of British rule in India broadened down from precedent to precedent. Like most other empires, its efficient spheres of action had always been determined in part by the pre-colonial system it replaced. It might draft whatever plans for change that it pleased; but they would work best when they fitted predilections for change that were already there. In any case, the Indian commitment was too large and too unrewarding for the British to maintain an administrative system close enough for them to be sure what the people were thinking; so it was safer to do too little than too much. Once the trappings of its power are peeled away, British rule is exposed as soft in the centre. Notables might quake at the sonorities of imperial prose, but words could no more transform India than the system could govern it at the level where raiyats doled out handfuls of grain to their labourers. But the fact that the regime was superficial did not mean that it was labile: the British could not be pushed into the sea, for there were always some Indians ready to repel the attacks of others. But it did mean that so large an empire could be comfortably governed only so long as its politics remained of the traditional sort. With the coming of new political methods, with their extension from one region to another, and with their employment by one group after another in these regions, the Raj began to lose some of its options. Step by step its freedom of action vanished in a maze of calculations about how a concession to one group might alter the attitude of another. The imposition of colonial rule had meant a shuffling of the elites in British India; its continuance meant that they had to be continually reshuffled. Collaborators came and went; new allies and new enemies envenomed the rivalries inside the country.

Trends inside Indian society worked to strengthen these processes. As in most Asian countries, the eagerness with which western learning was received by the more adaptable Indians had little to do with the charms of this knowledge itself. Both the old term 'westernisation' and its younger synonyms have been too generously construed to imply a series of vast dualisms between the West on the one side and India, China or Islam on the other. But everything turns on who was westernising whom and why the latter acquiesced. Just as there are many Wests, there are many Asias. At one level, it is true, there has been a common motive behind the reception of western knowledge. It has lain in the desire to defend by new methods the old essences of the society under pressure. When Liang Ch'i-Ch'ao announced that: 'If we wish to promote nationalism in China, there is no other means of doing it except through the renovation of the people', he was arguing much the same case as Mohammed Abduh in Egypt and Bankim Chandra Chatterjee in India. The translations of Yen Fu placed a stress upon social discipline which might have been approved by the Young Turks or by Ranade. In his calls for new energies to mobilise, al Afghani seems to anticipate the slogans of Sun Yat-Sen and the insistence of Tilak upon the doctrines of shakti.[1]

But to another audience these clarion calls sound more ambiguous. Plans for the saving of Muslim, Confucian or Hindu societies turn out to have been hopes of a more selective salvation. Their chief aim has been to conserve or to achieve a special position for those enlightened enough to see both the dangers and the opportunities in the situation, whether they were those learned in Islam or the scholar-gentry of China or the learned castes of India. The process was particularly clear in India because of the colonial status of the country. Here the British presence had altered the rules of the game, so that accepting western learning from British hands was a necessary price the learned castes had to pay for following their traditional occupation of working for government. Indeed, a mastery over these new idioms might do more than merely conserve their status. The successful scholars from Bengal and Madras might fan out to win a new pre-eminence in upper and central India, while those from Bombay moved to restore an old pre-eminence in the provinces of the lost Maratha Confederacy. The British had done much to increase the unevenness and competition which formed the national movements. The Indians did as much again.

In large part the answer to the question why modern Indian politics began when they did, depends on defining the period

[1] The quotation from Liang Ch'i-Ch'ao is translated in Ssu-Yu Teng and J. K. Fairbank, *China's Response to the West* (Cambridge, Mass., 1954), p. 222. His thought has been generally surveyed in J. R. Levenson, *Liang Ch'i-Ch'ao and the Mind of Modern China* (Cambridge, Mass., 1953). The translations of Yen Fu are studied in B. Schwarz, *In Search of Wealth and Power* (Cambridge, Mass., 1964). For Muslim developments see A. Hourani, *Arabic Thought in the Liberal Age, 1798–1939* (London, 1962). The doctrines of Tilak will be studied in the second volume of the present work.

when the regime was no longer able to satisfy enough of these conflicting aspirations. In its earlier days the Raj had been able to shed its more primitive collaborators as simply as changing walking-sticks; but the western educated could not be discarded so easily. Once they took to the technique of secular association, they possessed a type of organisation which could be generalised to the all-India level, while they were precisely the sections of the population whose interests could be most plausibly unified at this level. During the last quarter of the nineteenth century none of them cut themselves off from the Raj. With varying degrees of enthusiasm they were all still backing the British horse, although some were now hedging their bets by joining the new associations. By cajoling the Sarkar they could still enter its offices and then bang the doors in the faces of aspirants from circles other than their own.

The growth of their numbers, together with the increase in the number of their competitors whether from their own or other regions, made it harder to meet their wishes. But the calculations and the subjective assessments of government also worked to disappoint them. On the face of it, a decision to give them the positions they hoped for might not have worked against British interests. If some powers were slowly being devolved from the centre to the provinces, why should a few of them not be devolved upon Indians? But everything depended on what sort of Indians these would be. At a time when the rulers had less elbow room for distributing their favours, it did not seem practical politics to govern their provinces through squadrons of nimble scholars. There were other voices to be listened to. In the event, the Raj, like some of the western educated, preferred to hedge its bets. The favourites of yesterday found they had to reckon with the upstarts of today. In this way the realignment of allegiances began.

The first overt sign of this slow redeployment can be observed in the period when the romantic conservatism of Lytton drove him to provoke the educated men, when Ripon's ineffectual liberalism was thwarted in its plans to conciliate them, and when Dufferin was trying to plaster over the cracks. They still seemed as thin as hairlines. The educated were few, and most had been absorbed into the public service and the professions. Their associations were cautious bids to pre-empt positions of standing or profit. They were highly selective bodies of high caste men, living in the towns, although claiming to represent the villages. As so often in Indian history, the scholars and the town-dwellers were claiming to speak for those who had not spoken. The national organisation they founded in Congress was as little effective as the Raj.

But in the background a host of lesser groups were being marshalled. Castes were beginning to organise associations of their own. The dissident Hindu sects of Jains and Lingayats were linking their members on an all-India scale. So too were the Muslims, the only force whose claims could rival those of Congress, and it was characteristic of the themes of the period that their linkage should have taken the form of an Educational Congress. Behind these bodies again stood the forces of the old India: the power of the local notable, the prestige of pandit and pir, the immemorial authority of headman and panchayat. A history of nationalist origins has little to do with these men at this time. With the intricacies of association they as yet had little to do. Silently they stood in the wings, awaiting their cue. Today it has come.

This analysis of its origins suggests some fresh approaches to the history of Indian nationalism after 1888. Naturally, such a superficial alliance of chosen men from the Presidencies followed moderate ends. This policy it has become orthodox to stigmatise as 'political mendicancy', but inside the context of their long-term aims the educated chose their methods well. Moderation seemed the most persuasive way of bringing the Raj to bargain with them, particularly when it was expressed in the idioms of British politics. More important, the alternatives to moderation threatened to endanger the position which these men already enjoyed. To hustle the Raj into giving way would require a campaign of deliberate incitement. This would produce a wider opposition, spreading the movement beyond its original bases, and a deeper opposition, driving it down to levels hitherto avoided. Either course would entail great risks for the leadership. In the restricted form in which the movement had worked, their authority was sure enough, but extending it would alert other groups, less instructed, less easy to control and with less to lose. On the other hand, what seemed baleful risks to the leadership impressed their opponents as opportunities which beckoned. Estranged by issues of principle or clashes of personality, certain of defeat in the narrow circles where votes were cast, these dissidents had everything to gain from upsetting comfortable arrangements and from extending the movement to levels less concerned with the susceptibilities of the India Office. In their efforts to sap the leadership, they organised district and provincial conferences, designed to prove that while the twice-born were calm the people were angry. As the leaders in turn were compelled to canvass this widened audience, they began to search for causes likely to appeal to it.

These considerations suggest that many of the developments inside Congress between 1888 and 1907 should be reinterpreted in terms of unevenness and competition. The disputes between the leaders of the educated still turned on the issue of how best to conserve their own position; the innovation of the period was that these disputes now drove the movement into regions whose backwardness would otherwise have still left them politically inert. For all the disputes over tactics or over the principle of social reform, 'Extremism' was less an ideology than a technique. Its most conspicuous form was an all-India coalition of dissidents, who having been outmanœuvred in their own provinces, tried to reverse at the top the defeats they had suffered in the localities. Their organisation was another skin-deep affair. After Tilak was transported to Mandalay, it fell to pieces.

Much of the drive which was ultimately to bring new provinces into the political process came from those regions whose language and tradition had been submerged or pushed aside. In Bihar, a movement demanding separation from Bengal had taken shape at the end of the nineteenth century; after it had its way in 1911, it went on agitating against Bengali dominance in the new province. During the first years of the new century, the demands of the Oriyas for separation both from Bengal and Madras were being framed, while Telegu leaders inveighed against the Tamils and called for an Andhra desh of their own. It is an indication of the speed of political change in the country during the first world war that these demands increased so much in depth and extent. The stirrings of Kanarese-speakers in the Karnatak, hitherto confined to sentimental allusions to Vijayanagar, now swelled into a full-blown demand to be rid of the domination of Maharashtra. Hindi-speakers in the Central Provinces, based on Jubbulpore, now called for severance from the Marathi-speakers, based on Nagpur. In the same way, regions where one language and one people were dominant, pressed for separate recognition: in the far south, Malayalam-speakers; in Bombay Presidency, Gujaratis and Sindis. These new surges of competitiveness were sweeping over castes and communities as well. The Muslim League, no less than the Congress, had become an arena where old leaders were shouldered aside and their successors swung against the British. In the Punjab, the Akali Dal began to wrest control of Sikhism from the Khalsa Darbar. After their long concentration upon private affairs, caste associations now marched on to the political stage: the Justice party in Madras, the non-Brahmins in Bombay.

These developments led to large changes in political alignments. They gave the Home Rule Leagues the support they needed to shake Congress leadership in the Presidencies. Again, the influx of new regions into Congress politics helped to bring about a revolution in the national leadership of the movement. Gandhi's rise to power was assisted by the support he won from Gujarat, the United Provinces, and the urban Hindus of the Punjab whose hopes for power in their province were otherwise small. His influence was greatly increased by the reorganisation of Congress on the basis of linguistic provinces, which canalised into the movement men from regions hitherto dormant. Above all it was supercharged by the Khilafat movement, which swung much of Muslim India against the Raj, and by the peasant risings in the United Provinces. These changes brought many casualties to the old leadership: Surendranath was ejected into knighthood, Srinivas Sastri into membership of the Privy Council. They also began to transfer the control of Congress from its old headquarters in the Presidencies towards Gujarat and the United Provinces. Regions newly recruited into the political process were easily attracted into Gandhian politics. Since these were much more candidly hostile to the Raj than those of any other leader, they met a wary and sceptical reception in the Presidencies, where the educated were still concentrated; up country they found an army of enthusiasts, even if few of them had been to Cambridge. From this time began the political decline and fall of the Presidencies, and the more or less polite dislike of many Chitpavans and bhadralok for the leadership of the Mahatma. But in the south the alignments were different. Here, where dyarchy brought the non-Brahmins to power, many Brahmins now espoused Congress with a new enthusiasm. Congress on any terms was better than the Justice party.

Already during the war, the trends of Indian politics had worried the British government. The Montagu–Chelmsford reforms, which had begun as an administrative overhaul, had to be broadened into a large political measure, conceding dyarchy in the provinces. But if the widening of political activity wrecked Montagu's plans for strengthening the old collaborators, it also threw up new allies for the Raj. The larger electorates conceded by the reforms gave the non-Brahmins a political opportunity at last, and they readily worked the new constitution. At the bottom of the caste hierarchies, the new organisations of such groups as the Mahars also held aloof from the Congress, which now paid for its earlier lassitude over social reform. This divisiveness of caste in Madras and Bombay was matched by the divisiveness of community in Bengal and upper India. Montagu's hopes of rallying the moderates had failed, for during the political transformations between 1917 and 1920 many of the men he had had in mind dropped through the trap-door of history. But in a larger sense, the Raj had now found new moderates with whom to deal, men whose caste and communal rivalries with other Indians inclined them to work with the British. This hardly required any contrivance on the part of the rulers. Like a croupier, the Raj made contracts with one player after another; but as the one turned aside, the next always made his way to the table.

Just as Gandhi had been helped to the leadership of Congress by the widening and deepening of political activity, so the revival of these processes in the later 1920s might have ejected him. By now there was a growing demand, especially in the United Provinces and the North-west Frontier Province, to try conclusions with the British. By going with the current into Civil Disobedience, Gandhi saved himself from going the way of Surendranath. After the constitutional reforms of 1935 granted almost full self-government in the provinces, Indian politicians had prizes worth fighting for; by extending the franchise to more than thirty million voters, the Act drove them into efforts of organisation more elaborate than ever before. The rivalry between government and its allies on the one hand and Congress and its allies on the other now became a competition for the sympathies of these new voters. The rulers who had once spoken scornfully about microscopic minorities now found themselves striving on almost equal terms with Congress in a propaganda battle for the support of the uncommitted in ten provinces, of which six returned Congress majorities.

This strange rivalry was to continue in inconclusive fashion until 1947: two sides willing to wound, and yet afraid to strike. Characteristically, a greater rivalry was now coming to poison the relations between groups of competing Indians themselves than any which divided the Indians from the British; equally characteristically, both these forms of rivalry were more severe in some regions of the sub-continent than in others.

Why had these struggles between British rulers and their Indian subjects been so tentative, so limited and so inconclusive? Apologists for the Raj have found some inherent liberalism in the imperial system; but this is the talk of men whose heads have never been cracked with a lathi. Some critics of the Raj have pointed to a general magnanimity on the part of Indians; but those who believe they can usefully draw up an encomium in favour of a whole people will believe anything. Others have declaimed against the Indian leaders for having held back their followers from a general onslaught against government; but it would be more profitable to inquire whether such onslaughts could ever have been launched. Government, Congress, and that late arrival the League, were all riddled with internal weaknesses. The clients of the Raj had grown so numerous and their demands so various that grievances sprouted from every concession. Many of the inflexibilities of Delhi came from the impossibility of pleasing all of the clients all of the time. The stultification of government was matched by the stultification of Congress, and of the League. If it was a ramshackle sub-continental authority, they were ramshackle sub-continental coalitions. The choices of all three were crimped by fears of the reaction in their fragile alliances.

Many of the battles which the Raj and the Congress waged were mere feints between two sides each held back by the unreliable troops in its own front line. Non-co-operation, Civil Disobedience, the new constitution, the clashes of 1942 were all parts of this strange struggle between impotent rivals, a Dasehra duel between two hollow statues, locked in motionless and simulated combat. Towards the end, when they had come to control their own allies, the Muslim League broke up this mimic warfare, and at once a real ferocity appeared— between Indian and Indian.

It seems bizarre that the largest exemplar of struggle against colonial rule should have been fought with such limited liability. But there is a certain justice about this. If imperialism and nationalism have striven so tepidly against each other, part of the reason is that the aims for which they have worked have had much in common. Each, with its own type of incertitude, each with grave limitations on its power, has set about modernising the societies under its control; nationalism has sought to conserve the standing of some of those elites which imperialism had earlier raised up or confirmed; at various times both have worked to win the support of the same allies. In India they have sometimes achieved similar results as well: each in its own fashion sharpened the rivalries that were already stirring in the country; each grappled with the countervailing forces thrown up by the unevennesses of Indian society, and by the mobilisation of further ranges of its population.

If imperialism summed up a period in western history, nationalism symbolised a new phase in the history of the East. But by the side of the vast swell of aspiration and rivalry which has hurled it forward, the political readjustments of independence seem of small account. These nationalisms have been merely the swirling surface of the waters; below them pulse the tides of social change, pulling Asia no man knows where.

APPENDICES

GLOSSARY

BIOGRAPHICAL NOTES

BIBLIOGRAPHY

INDEX

Growth of Education at the Universities of Calcutta, Bombay and Madras, 1857–88

TABLE 47. *Calcutta University, 1857–88*

	Entrance	First Arts	B.A.	M.A.	Law	Medi-cine	Engin-eering
Until 1863	2,063	N.A.	N.A.	N.A.	N.A.	N.A.	N.A.
1864–8	3,345	521*	238*	52*	114*	91*	8*
1869–73	4,513	1,078	485	121	443	285	20
1874–8	5,173	1,277	467	133	313	426	34
1879–83	5,027	1,513	569	148	196*	214*	19*
1884–8	6,741*	2,428	1,273	191*	587*	163*	21*
Total*	26,862	6,817	3,032	645	1,653	1,179	102

Source: Statistical Abstract relating to British India, 1858–67...Third Number, *P.P.* 1868–9, LXIII, 39; Tenth Number, *P.P.* 1876, LXXVII, 344; Twentieth Number, *P.P.* 1886, LXVIII, 566; Twenty-fourth Number, *P.P.* 1890, LXXVIII, 425.

* The figures exclude the following returns which are not available in this source: 1864, 1865; First Arts, B.A., M.A., Law, Medicine, Engineering. 1883, 1884; Law, Medicine, Engineering. 1885; Entrance, M.A.

TABLE 48. *Bombay University, 1857–88*

	Entrance	First Arts	B.A.	M.A.	Law	Medi-cine	Engin-eering
Until 1863	77	27	7	—	—	22	—
1864–8	499	99	69	20	7	23	2
1869–73	1,139	174	76	14	23	51	58
1874–8	1,471	281	141	14	17	164	127
1879–83	2,086	473	315	20	62	216	172
1884–8	3,626	732	854	21	83	487	131
Total	8,898	1,786	1,462	89	192	963	490

Source: Tabulated from same source as table 47 and *RDPI (Bombay) 1878–9*, p. 21.

TABLE 49. *Madras University, 1857–88*

	Entrance	First Arts	B.A.	M.A.	Law	Medi-cine	Engin-eering
Until 1863	342	—	34	—	10	1	—
1864–8	1,239	382	55	—	27	1	5
1869–73	2,252	643	202	8	42	5	3
1874–8	4,129	817	294	6	47	21	11
1879–83	5,586	1,336	602	16	56	70	7
1884–8	9,365	2,411	1,443	26	150	226	26
Total	22,913	5,589	2,630	56	332	324	52

Source: Tabulated from same source as table 47, and *RDPI* (*Madras*) *1876–7*, p. 5.

The Employment of Graduates

The tables below give some details about the careers of Indian graduates.

TABLE 50. *Employment of graduates: all-India review by region until 1882*

Province	Number of graduates	Public services (British India and Native States)	Law	Medi-cine	Civil engineer-ing
Bengal*	1,696	534	471	131	19
Bombay	625	324	49	76	28
Madras	808	296	126	18	—
N.-W.P. and Oudh	130	61	33	—	—
Punjab	38	21	5	—	—
Central Provinces	14	8	—	—	—
Total	3,311	1,244	684	225	47

Source: *EC*, p. 281.
* Compare the Bengal figures with table 51 and with the details given by the Bengal Provincial Committee, which are set out below:

Employment of Graduates in Bengal, 1857–82

		Public services	Private service	Law	Medi-cine	Civil engin-eering
Bachelors of Arts 1,589 Masters of Arts 389	} 1,978	526	180	581	12	—

Source: *EC* (*Bengal*), p. 103.

TABLE 51. *Employment of Calcutta graduates, 1858–81**

	Number	Percentage
Government Service		
Judicial		
Judge, High Court	1	
District Judge	1	
Sub-Judge	34	
Munsif	163	
Executive		
Joint Magistrate	2	
Assistant Magistrate	1	
Deputy Collector	53	
Extra Assistant Commissioner	15	
Education	168	
Medical	2	
Engineer	8	
Assistant Comptroller of Accounts	2	
Registrar of Deeds	1	
Police Inspector	1	
Postal Department	6	
Translator and Interpreter	13	
Librarian	2	
Clerk	45	
Nazir	2	
Tahsildar	1	
Chaplain	1	
Government Pensioner	3	
Total Government Service	525	30·6
Education		
Teacher	158	9·2
Law		
Barrister	4	
Pleader	466	
Attorney	14	
Articled Clerk	29	
Law Student	100	
Total Law	613	35·8
Service in Native States	19	
Medical Practitioner	7	
Editor and author	5	
Zemindar	5	
Planter	2	
Merchant	1	
In England	5	
Others (clerk, Brahmo missionary, etc.)	5	
Dead	33	
Not returned	334	
Grand total	1,712	

Source: *Hindoo Patriot*, 23 October 1882.

* This table should be compared with the list of graduates, with their names and occupations, in Sinha, *Nineteenth Century Bengal*, appendix D, pp. 161–99. Calculations based on Sinha's list do not differ substantially from the results above.

TABLE 52. *Employment of Bombay graduates, 1870–82*

	Arts	Law	Medi-cine	Civil engin-eering	Total
Government Service					
Revenue or Education	134	—	—	12	
Judicial	2	21	—	—	250
Medical	—	—	47	—	
Public Works Department	—	—	—	34	
Service, Native States					
Revenue or Education	33	—	—	—	
Judicial	—	7	—	—	74
Medical	—	—	19	—	
Public Works Department	—	—	—	15	
Independent					
Legal	3	46	—	—	
Medical	—	—	76	—	
Engineering	—	—	—	28	231
Miscellaneous (Teaching, Commerce)	78	—	—	—	
Not traced or dead	41	3	6	20	70
Grand total	291	77	148	109	625

Source: *EC (Bombay)*, I, 143–4.

TABLE 53. *Employment of Madras graduates, 1871–82*

Number of Bachelors of Arts until 31 March 1882	971
Government Service	
Judicial	118
Revenue	36
Education	90
Engineering	4
Indian Medical Service	3
Clerical	1
Clerks under Rs 100 per month	96
(Government Service total)	348
Service in Native States	68
Professions	
Vakils*	92
Teachers	118
Students at professional colleges	103
Others	
Merchants	4
Independent	55
Mirasidars	4
Pensioners	4
Occupation unknown	175
Total	971

Source: *EC (Madras)*, p. 119.

*According to the registrar of the high court, between 1872 and 1881, 126 graduates became legal practitioners, seventy-seven in the Madras high court, and forty-nine in district courts. Many of these had become district munsifs, and therefore were entered under 'Government Service' in the table.

TABLE 54. *Employment of graduates from Presidency College, Madras, 1871–82*

Government service	151	
Service in Native States	24	
Professions		
Vakils	54	
Teachers in private schools	27	
Professional training		
Law	49	
Medicine	3	55
Engineering	3	
Merchants	5	
Mirasidars	1	
Independent means	10	
Not known	27	
Dead	33	
Total	387	

Source: *EC (Madras)*, p. 120.

Opportunities in the Public Service

The tables set out the numbers employed in government posts with salaries of Rs 75 per month and over; they show the size of the Hindu and Muslim share in this group and to what extent the better paid (and more responsible) posts were held by Europeans.

TABLE 55. *Number and distribution, by race and religion, of government appointments in British India at Rs 75 per month and over, 1867, 1877, and 1887*

	1867	1877	1887
Europeans			
Number	4,760	5,701	6,154
Percentage	35	32	29
Eurasians			
Number	2,633	3,448	4,164
Percentage	20	19	19
Hindus			
Number	5,090	7,450	9,757
Percentage	38	42	45
Muslims			
Number	918	1,176	1,391
Percentage	7	7	7
Totals	13,431	17,775	21,466

Source: Government of India, Home Department (Establishment), A, Proceedings, June 1904, no. 103, pp. 118–19.

TABLE 56. *Number and distribution, by race and religion, of appointments directly under the government of India (imperial) at Rs 75 per month and over, 1867, 1877, and 1887*

	1867	1877	1887
Europeans			
Number	563	1,070	1,828
Percentage	27	29	30
Eurasians			
Number	1,047	1,513	2,296
Percentage	50	41	38
Hindus			
Number	462	1,012	1,750
Percentage	22	28	29
Muslims			
Number	22	90	185
Percentage	1	2	3
Totals	2,094	3,685	6,059

Source: Government of India, Home Department (Establishment), A, Proceedings, June 1904, no. 103, pp. 122–3.

TABLE 57. *Number and distribution, by race and religion, of government appointments in Bengal at Rs 75 per month and over, 1867, 1877, and 1887*

	1867	1877	1887
Europeans			
Number	1,080	1,212	968
Percentage	35	33	25
Eurasians			
Number	457	449	387
Percentage	15	12	10
Hindus			
Number	1,334	1,868	2,286
Percentage	44	50	60
Muslims			
Number	177	183	166
Percentage	6	5	5
Totals	3,048	3,712	3,807

Source: Government of India, Home Department (Establishment), A, Proceedings, June 1904, no. 103, pp. 131–2.

TABLE 58. *Number and distribution, by race and religion, of government appointments in Bombay at Rs 75 per month and over, 1867, 1877, and 1887*

	1867	1877	1887
Europeans			
Number	762	917	960
Percentage	38	37	34
Eurasians			
Number	101	151	157
Percentage	5	6	6
Hindus (including Parsis)			
Number	1,056	1,330	1,557
Percentage	53	54	55
Muslims			
Number	68	93	129
Percentage	4	3	5
Totals	1,987	2,491	2,803

Source: Government of India, Home Department (Establishment), A, Proceedings, June 1904, no. 103, pp. 128–9.

TABLE 59. *Number and distribution, by race and religion, of government appointments in Madras at Rs 75 per month and over, 1867, 1877, and 1887*

	1867	1877	1887
Europeans			
Number	412	594	601
Percentage	25	28	23
Eurasians			
Number	440	543	565
Percentage	27	25	22
Hindus			
Number	756	960	1,315
Percentage	46	45	51
Muslims			
Number	41	45	91
Percentage	2	2	4
Totals	1,649	2,142	2,572

Source: Government of India, Home Department (Establishment), A, Proceedings, June 1904, no. 103, pp. 125–6.

Membership of the British Indian Association

There are no membership lists of the Association, but one indication of its size is the annual subscriptions, which are set out in table 60. The annual subscription was Rs 50; but a simple division of the total receipts by 50 does not give an accurate figure for the membership: in the first place the heading 'subscriptions' in the accounts includes 'other receipts'; in the second, Rs 50 was the *minimum* subscription—the Rs 8,479.12.6½ in 1856 were subscribed by only thirty-two members. Even so, the table indicates that the membership at its largest could never have been more than 300 and that by the end of the period it was hardly 100.

Another indication of the size of membership can be gained from the monthly and annual reports which list the names of new members. Between 1851 and 1879 approximately 170 men were recruited—an average of six a year. From these reports it is also apparent that by the 1870s the Association was finding new members hard to come by.

TABLE 60. *British Indian Association, subscriptions and receipts,*
1851–89

	Subscriptions and receipts		
	Rs.	a.	p.
October 1851–November 1852	18,601	0	0*
1853	21,500	0	0
1854	10,900	0	0
1855	9,900	0	0
1856	8,479	12	6½
1857–61	Missing		
1862	10,781	12	7
1863	Missing		
1864	8,606	7	6
1865	6,787	1	9
1866	Missing		
1867	8,383	10	3
1868	8,847	4	9
1869	15,358	11	3
1870	12,692	0	0
1871	14,606	7	4
1872	14,134	0	0
1873	12,936	6	0
1874	13,606	12	0
1875	13,574	7	11
1876	10,253	0	0
1877	12,744	0	0
1878	13,012	4	0
1879–80	Missing		
1881	12,558	2	3
1882–7	Missing		
1888	6,201	0	0
1889	5,086	0	0

Source: Tabulated from the First to Thirty-eighth Annual Reports, British
Indian Association, 1851–89. BIA.

* Total receipts from all sources.

Growth of the Press in Bengal and Bombay, 1878–88

The following tables give details about the number of Indian-owned newspapers in Bengal and Bombay, their circulation, the languages in which they were published and their place of publication. During the decade, the number of vernacular newspapers in Bengal increased from thirty-nine to sixty-two, but more significant was their rise in circulation, particularly after 1883 (table 61).[1] In addition to these newspapers there was a large English-language press, based almost entirely in Calcutta, which in 1881 consisted of sixteen newspapers—some of them owned by Indians—with a total circulation of about 15,000.[2] Tables 62 and 64 show that, as the press expanded, the extraordinary predominance of Calcutta was increasing. In 1878, out of a total circulation of 23,893 in the Presidency, Calcutta newspapers accounted for 14,242; in 1888 of a total circulation of 77,190, Calcutta newspapers accounted for 67,070. This vividly demonstrates the dominance of the metropolis and shows how much the mofussil depended on it for its political lead. Tables 62 and 64 also show that there was an increasingly large number of newspapers published from the districts but that they had a restricted readership. An indication

[1] 'The influence of the Native Press in Bengal is not, however, to be measured by the number of Native newspapers published, but by the circulation possessed by the leading ones. During the last five years this circulation has been steadily increasing. In 1882–83 there were only two papers, namely the *Bangabasi* and the *Sulabha Samachar*, which possessed a circulation of 4,000 copies, and that was the highest at that time, but at present there are no less than four native papers having a circulation of 4,000 copies and upwards. The highest (said to be 20,000 copies) is now possessed by the *Bangabasi*. The *Dainik*, a Bengal daily newspaper, comes after it with a circulation of 7,000 copies; while in 1882–83 that of the leading daily newspaper in Bengali was only 700,' Grierson, *The Administration of the Lower Provinces of Bengal from 1882–83 to 1886–87*, p. 63.
[2] *HIG*, II, 321.

of the limitations on up-country journalism is that the *Amrita Bazar Patrika*, successfully launched in Jessore, then became irresistibly drawn to the city.

In Bombay on the other hand, there was no equivalent concentration of papers in the capital. In 1878 more than half the total circulation in western India had been captured by the newspapers of Bombay city; by 1888 they possessed considerably less than half, and Poona in particular had developed a lively press of its own. Elsewhere in the Deccan and in Gujarat, the press was smaller, but it also was growing (tables 67 and 68). The expansion of the press in western India was steadier than in Bengal, but the figures in table 64 and table 66 are not wholly comparable, since the Bombay figures include newspapers published entirely in English, while the Bengal figures do not.

As tables 63 and 65 show, Bengali virtually monopolised the vernacular press of Bengal. By 1888 however, there was evidence of some growth in the Hindi press and there were signs of a nascent Oriya press. In Bombay the picture was different. Gujarati and Marathi between them shared the field, and they were about equally balanced in their numbers of readers. But the vitality of the Gujarati-language press owed

TABLE 61. *Growth in number and circulation of vernacular newspapers, Bengal, 1878–88*

Year	Number of papers	Number for which circulation is given	Circulation
1878	39	23	23,893
1879	44	22	17,826
1880	40	35	22,187
1881	37	29	19,110
1882	48	27	19,079
1883	55	28	18,889
1884	64	36	25,680
1885	52	41	38,894
1886	63	45	72,823
1887	62	43	64,102
1888	62	37	77,190

Source: Calculated from RNP (Bengal), 5 January 1878; 4 January 1879; 3 January 1880; 1 January 1881; 7 January 1882; 6 January 1883; 5 January 1884; 3 January 1885; 2 January 1886; 1 January 1887; 7 January 1888.

most to the Parsis; in 1881, of thirty-eight Gujarati and Anglo-Gujarati newspapers then in existence, nineteen were edited by Parsis. On the other hand, of forty-five Marathi and Anglo-Marathi papers, forty-one were edited by Deccani Hindus.[1]

TABLE 62. *Distribution of vernacular newspapers in Bengal, 1878*

Division	Number of papers	Number for which circulation is given	Circulation
Burdwan	5	4	2,149
Presidency	22	12	18,877
Calcutta	*16*	*8*	*14,242*
Twenty-four Parganas	*1*	*1*	*4,000*
Nadia	*2*	*2*	*400*
Murshidabad	*3*	*1*	*235*
Rajshahi	3	1	250
Dacca	5	5	2,108
Chittagong	—	—	—
Total Bengal Proper	35	22	23,384
Patna	2	1	509
Bhagalpur	2	—	—
Orissa	—	—	—
Total All Bengal	39	23	23,893

Source: Calculated from RNP (Bengal), 5 January 1878.

TABLE 63. *Distribution of vernacular newspapers in Bengal by language, 1878*

Language	Number of papers	Number for which circulation is given	Circulation
Bengali	31	17	19,917
English/Bengali	4	3	2,817
English/Urdu	1	1	400
Urdu	1	—	—
Hindi	1	1	509
Persian	1	1	250
Totals	39	23	23,893

Source: Calculated from RNP (Bengal), 5 January 1878.

[1] *Report on the Administration of the Bombay Presidency for the year 1881–82* (Bombay, 1882), p. 292.

TABLE 64. *Distribution of vernacular newspapers in Bengal, 1888*

Division	Number of papers	Number for which circulation is given	Circulation
Burdwan	5	3	2,122
Presidency	29	21	70,058
Calcutta	24	20	67,070
Rajshahi	3	2	405
Dacca	7	3	1,350
Chittagong	4	3	1,500
Total Bengal Proper	48	32	75,535
Patna	4	1	150
Bhagalpur	2	1	1,000
Orissa	8	3	605
Total All Bengal	62	37	77,190

Source: Calculated from RNP (Bengal), 7 January 1888.

TABLE 65. *Distribution of vernacular newspapers in Bengal by language, 1888*

Language	Number of papers	Number for which circulation is given	Circulation
Bengali	38	25	67,937
English/Bengali	1	—	—
Hindi	7	4	7,500
Urdu	7	4	898
Persian	1	1	250
Oriya	8	3	605
Totals	62	37	77,190

Source: Calculated from RNP (Bengal), 7 January 1888.

TABLE 66. *Growth in number and circulation of Indian-owned newspapers in Bombay, 1878–88/89*

Year	Number of papers	Number for which circulation is given	Circulation
1878	68	36	11,940
1879*	74	74	25,900
1880	80	80	31,175
1881	78	78	31,010
1882	96	96	35,485
1883	111	111	43,188
1884	138	138	52,368
1885	130	111	54,620
1886	146	135	57,996
1887	146	146	68,836
1888	149	143	73,997
1888–89†	175	137	68,797

Source: Calculated from RNP (Bombay), 19 January 1878; 4 January 1879; 3 January 1880; 1 January 1881; 7 January 1882; 6 January 1883; 5 January 1884; 3 January 1885; 9 January 1886; 1 January 1887; 7 January 1888; 29 December 1888.

* See table 67.
† See table 68.

TABLE 67. *Distribution of Indian-owned newspapers in Bombay, 1878–9*

District and Division	English/Gujarati		Gujarati		English/Marathi		Marathi		Others		Total	
	No.	Circ.	No.	Circ.	No.	Circ.	No.	Circ.	No.	Circ.	No.	Circ.
Ahmadabad	1	450	2	260	—	—	—	—	—	—	3	740
Kaira	—	—	2	268	—	—	—	—	—	—	2	268
Broach	—	—	2	150	—	—	—	—	—	—	2	150
Surat	1	137	4	2,000	—	—	—	—	—	—	5	2,137
Panch Mahals	—	—	—	—	—	—	—	—	—	—	—	—
Total Gujarat	*2*	*587*	*10*	*2,678*	—	—	—	—	—	—	*12*	*3,265*
Thana	—	—	—	—	1	375	3	850	—	—	4	1,225
Kolaba	—	—	—	—	—	—	1	400	—	—	1	400
Ratnagiri	—	—	—	—	—	—	3	535	—	—	3	535
Total Konkan	—	—	—	—	*1*	*375*	*7*	*1,785*	—	—	*8*	*2,160*
Khandesh	—	—	—	—	—	—	3	300	—	—	3	300
Nasik	—	—	—	—	—	—	2	200	—	—	2	200
Ahmadnagar	—	—	—	—	—	—	2	385	—	—	2	385
Poona	—	—	—	—	4	2,100	5	1,475	—	—	9	3,575
Sholapur	—	—	—	—	—	—	3	400	—	—	3	400
Satara	—	—	—	—	2	525	1	85	—	—	3	610
Total Deccan	—	—	—	—	*6*	*2,625*	*16*	*2,845*	—	—	*22*	*5,470*
Belgaum	—	—	—	—	—	—	1	1,300	—	—	1	300
Dharwar	—	—	—	—	—	—	4	750	1	100	5	850
Bijapur	—	—	—	—	—	—	1	125	—	—	1	125
Total Karnatak	—	—	—	—	—	—	*6*	*1,175*	*1*	*100*	*7*	*1,275*
Total Sind	—	—	—	—	—	—	—	—	*1*	*300*	*1*	*300*
Bombay city	—	—	*14*	*8,340*	*4*	*3,525*	*2*	*1,100*	*1*	*175*	*21*	*13,140*
Native States	—	—	*1*	*45*	—	—	*2*	*245*	—	—	*3*	*290*
Grand total	2	587	25	11,063	11	6,525	33	7,150	4	575	74	25,900

Source: Calculated from RNP (Bombay), 4 January 1879.

TABLE 68. *Distribution of Indian-owned newspapers in Bombay, 1888–9*

District and Division	English		English/Gujarati		Gujarati		English/Marathi		Marathi		Others		Total	
	No.	Circ.	No.	Circ.	No.	Circ.	No.	Circ.	No.	Circ.	No.	Circ.	No.	Circ.
Ahmadabad	—	—	3(2)	814	7(6)	2,090	—	—	—	—	—	—	10(8)	2,904
Kaira	—	—	—	—	4(4)	1,650	—	—	—	—	—	—	4(4)	1,650
Broach	—	—	1(1)	300	4(4)	2,114	—	—	—	—	—	—	5(5)	2,414
Surat	—	—	4(3)	1,409	5(4)	3,275	—	—	—	—	—	—	9(7)	4,684
Panch Mahals	—	—	—	—	1(1)	100	—	—	—	—	—	—	1(1)	100
Total Gujarat	—	—	8(6)	2,523	21(19)	9,229	—	—	—	—	—	—	29(25)	11,752
Thana	—	—	—	—	—	—	—	—	2(2)	1,224	—	—	2(2)	1,224
Kolaba	—	—	—	—	—	—	—	—	2(1)	400	—	—	2(1)	400
Ratnagiri	—	—	—	—	—	—	—	—	5(5)	1,534	—	—	5(5)	1,534
Total Konkan	—	—	—	—	—	—	—	—	9(8)	3,158	—	—	9(8)	3,158
Khandesh	—	—	—	—	—	—	—	—	2(2)	230	—	—	2(2)	230
Nasik	—	—	—	—	—	—	—	—	3(2)	250	—	—	3(2)	250
Ahmadnagar	—	—	—	—	—	—	—	—	3(3)	667	—	—	3(3)	667
Poona	2(2)	1,400	—	—	—	—	5(3)	4,200	9(7)	6,846	1(1)	400	17(13)	12,846
Sholapur	—	—	—	—	—	—	—	—	2(2)	510	—	—	2(2)	510
Satara	—	—	—	—	—	—	1(1)	275	15(11)	2,120	—	—	16(12)	2,395
Total Deccan	2(2)	1,400	—	—	—	—	6(4)	4,475	34(27)	10,623	1(1)	400	43(34)	16,698
Belgaum	—	—	—	—	—	—	—	—	4(4)	821	—	—	4(4)	821
Dharwar	—	—	—	—	—	—	—	—	1(1)	700	5(3)	790	6(4)	1,490
Bijapur	—	—	—	—	—	—	—	—	2(2)	310	—	—	2(2)	310
Kanara	—	—	—	—	—	—	—	—	2(1)	100	—	—	2(1)	100
Total Karnatak	—	—	—	—	—	—	—	—	9(8)	1,931	5(3)	790	14(11)	2,721
Total Sind	2(1)	300	—	—	—	—	—	—	—	—	4(4)	1,250	6(5)	1,550
Bombay City	2(2)	1,100	2(2)	3,322	24(21)	12,655	8(8)	5,575	4(3)	1,200	5(5)	2,591	45(41)	26,443
States (incl. Baroda)	—	—	2(0)	—	12(7)	3,113	—	—	7(5)	1,752	8(1)	1,410	29(13)	6,275
Grand total	6(5)	2,800	12(8)	5,845	57(47)	24,997	14(12)	10,050	63(51)	18,664	23(14)	6,441	175(137)	68,797

Congress Resolutions, 1885-8

Below is a simple abstract of the more important Congress resolutions passed during these years; they give a picture of the Congress platform. Roman numerals refer to the number of the resolution in the Congress report.

TABLE 69. *Congress resolutions, 1885–8*

Subject	1885	1886	1887	1888
Reform of the Legislative Councils; representative institutions	III	III and IV	II	I
Simultaneous examinations; raising of age limit for the covenanted service examination	IV	VI	—	II
Demand for a royal commission or parliamentary committee on India	I	V	—	XI
Abolition of the India Council	II	—	—	—
Right to volunteer	—	XII	V	Reaffirmed
Separation of judicial and executive functions; trial by jury	—	IX and XI	III	Reaffirmed
Raising the taxable minimum for income tax	—	—	VI	VIII
Career for Indians as army officers	—	—	IV	Reaffirmed
Need for a system of technical education	—	—	VII	IX and X
Repeal of the Arms Act	—	—	VIII	Reaffirmed
Extension of the permanent settlement of land revenue	—	—	—	XIV
Investigation into police administration: commission requested	—	—	—	V

Source: *I.N.C.* 1885, 1886, 1887, 1888.

Resolutions on the following matters were also passed—that military expenditure be decreased (V and VI, 1885); that Burma be constituted into a separate Crown Colony (VII, 1885); that temperance be encouraged (VII, 1888); that public expenditure on higher education be increased (IX, 1888).

Glossary

ABKARI: the excise on liquors and drugs.

AIYANGAR: subdivision of Tamil Brahmins.

ANDHRA: the Telegu-speaking country.

ANGLO-INDIAN: in nineteenth-century usage, a European resident of India.

ANJUMAN: Muslim association.

ANNA: the sixteenth part of a rupee; the term anna is also used to denote a corresponding fraction of any kind of property, particularly co-parcenary rights in land.

ARYAVARTA: ancient name of north India between the Himalayas and the Vindhyas.

ASHRAF: noble, respectable.

ASSAL MARATHA: a subdivision of Marathas Proper, or pure Marathas.

ATEESUDRA (ATISUDRA): those below the Sudra; also a synonym for Mahar.

AUDICHYA (AUDICH): a subdivision of Brahmins in Gujarat.

AYURVED: traditional system of Hindu medicine.

BABU (BABOO): a title of respect, particularly in Bengal. Sometimes used by the British in India disparagingly to denote Indians educated in English.

BANIA (VANIA, BANYA): a Hindu of the trading castes.

BAIDYA (VAIDYA): a respectable caste of hereditary physicians, found only in Bengal Proper.

BALIJA NAIDU: chief Telegu trading caste.

BHADRALOK: the respectable people in Bengal, mainly but not exclusively recruited from the higher literate Hindu castes.

BOHRA (BOHORA): Muslim sect with two main divisions, the trading Shia Bohra, and the cultivating Sunni Bohra.

BRAHMIN (BRAHMAN): the priestly or highest caste of Hindus.

BRAHMO: a member of the Brahmo Samaj (q.v.).

BRAHMO SAMAJ: a movement formed in Bengal by Rammohan Roy to reform Hinduism.

BRAHMA KSHATTRIYA (BRAHMA KSHATRI): small writer caste of Gujarat, claiming Kshattriya origin.

CHANDAL: a large non-Aryan caste of eastern Bengal, mainly engaged in boating and cultivation. Also known as Namasudra.

CHETTI: Tamil trading caste.

CHETTINAD: the land of the Chettis.

CHITPAVAN: subdivision of Brahmins; synonym of Konkanasth.
COOLIE: a hired labourer or burden-carrier.

DACOITY: a robbery committed by dacoits; a gang robbery.
DAROGA (DAROGHA): a title of official, usually a subordinate controlling officer in police, jail, customs, or excise department.
DAR-PATNIDAR: sub-patnidar.
DAR-UL-HARB: a land of war where Muslims have the duty of struggling against the infidel.
DAR-UL-ISLAM: a land of Islam.
DAS-DAR-PATNIDAR: a subordinate of a sub-patnidar.
DASEHRA (DUSSEHRA): one of the great annual Hindu festivals held for ten days in October; also known as Durga-puja.
DESH: (1) native country; (2) the plateau of the Deccan above the Ghats.
DESHATH: a subdivision of Brahmins.
DEVANAGARI (NAGARI): the classical script of the Sanskrit language.

FARAZI: a reforming Muslim sect in Bengal.
FATWA: a ruling on a disputed point of Muslim law.

GAEKWAR: the title of the Maratha rulers of Baroda.
GADI (GADDI): the throne of (Hindu) royalty.
GANDHABANIK: the spice-selling, druggist and grocer caste of Bengal Proper, claiming Vaisya status.
GAUD SARASWAT: a subdivision of Brahmins.
GOMASTA (GUMASHTA): an agent, steward or confidential representative.

HAKIM: a doctor practising the Muslim system of medicine.
HINDI: a term loosely used to describe forms of Hindustani less influenced by Persian; includes the three chief dialects spoken between Bengal Proper and the Punjab.
HINDUSTAN: India, the country of the Hindus; more specifically, India north of the Narbudda, and exclusive of Bengal and Bihar.
HINDUSTANI: a native of Hindustan or his language. In particular, the language of the people of upper India, which developed out of a mixture of Hindi and Persian and Arabic words. In its Persianised form it is known as Urdu.
HUKKA: the Indian tobacco pipe.

IZZAT: honour, credit, reputation, prestige.

JAINISM: a religion founded in the sixth century B.C. by Vardhamana Mahavira as a protest against the Brahminical monopoly of ascetic orders.
JALIKA (JALIYA): designation throughout Bengal Proper for all classes engaged in boating or fishing; thus, Kaibartta (q.v.) Jalika,

375

or fishing Kaibarttas, as distinguished from the cultivating members of that caste.

JEHAD (JIHAD): holy war.

KAIBARTTA: a large cultivating and fishing caste of Bengal Proper.

KALI: Hindu goddess, wife of Shiva; so named for her black complexion; also known as Durga or Devi.

KAMA (KAMMA): south Indian caste, mainly cultivators.

KANAKAN (KANAKKAN): Tamil accountant caste.

KANARESE (KANNADA): Dravidian language spoken chiefly in Mysore.

KAPU: a large caste of cultivators, and landholders in the Telegu country; synonym for Reddi.

KARHADA BRAHMIN: subdivision of Brahmins in western India.

KARNAM: village accountant in Madras; the term also includes the Korono, or accountant caste, of Ganjam and Orissa.

KAYASTH: writer caste, most numerous in Bengal.

KAYASTH-PRABHU: writer caste in western India.

KHILAFAT: a movement among Indian Muslims in support of the Sultan of Turkey.

KHOJA: Muslim of the Shia Ismaili sect; usually a trader.

KOLI: loose term denoting a number of tribes, mainly in western India, of a status inferior to the Kunbi (q.v.).

KOMATI: the main Telegu-speaking trading caste of south India.

KSHATTRIYA: the second varna in the traditional Hindu hierarchy.

KULINISM: a system of hypergamy best known among the Kulin Brahmins of Bengal.

KULKARNI: village accountant, in the Bombay Deccan.

KUNBI: agricultural caste in western India.

LAKH: one hundred thousand.

LATHI: a stick or pole usually of bamboo and sometimes bound with iron rings.

LINGAYAT: sect rejecting the claims of Brahmanism, and attempting to abolish caste distinctions.

MADRASSA (MADRASA): a college or academy, usually Muslim.

MAHAR: untouchable found throughout the Marathi-speaking country.

MAHARASHTRA: the Marathi-speaking country.

MALAYALAM: language of the Dravidian family.

MALI: gardener caste, with status and customs similar to the Kunbi (q.v.), found mainly in the Deccan and north Gujarat.

MANG: untouchable caste, ranking lowest among Hindus, mainly found in the Deccan and Karnatak.

MARATHA (MAHRATTA): (1) in the most general sense, inhabitant of Maharashtra, in contradistinction to men of other regions; for example, Maratha Brahmin.

(2) more specifically, three castes or classes of the Deccan and Konkan: (a) Marathas Proper or chiefs, landowners, and military

families, (*b*) Maratha Kunbis or cultivators, (*c*) certain Maratha occupational castes.

MARATHI: the language of Maharashtra.

MARWARI: a native of Marwar in Rajputana, but found throughout India as traders, bankers and brokers.

MEMON: Sunni Muslims of the Hanafi school, mainly traders, merchants and dealers.

MIRASIDAR: holder of a superior (mirasi) tenure.

MOFUSSIL (MUFASSAL): the country stations and districts as opposed to the principal town; in Bengal, the country or provinces as opposed to Calcutta.

MOPLAH (MAPPILLA): indigenous Malabar Muslim.

NABASAK (NAVASAKHA): group of nine castes in Bengal, from whose hands a Brahmin may take water.

NAGAR: a subdivision of Brahmins in Gujarat.

NAIB: deputy.

NAMASUDRA: a synonym for Chandal (q.v.).

NAMBUDRI (NAMBUTIRI): a subdivision of Brahmins in Malabar.

NAPIT: the barber caste.

NAYAR (NAIR): south Indian caste of high status, mainly found in Malabar.

NAZIR: officer charged with administration of criminal law.

NECHARI: rationalist; a pejorative term among orthodox Muslims.

NIYOGI: a subdivision among Telegu Brahmins.

ORIYA (URIYA): the language of a native of Orissa.

PADISHAH-I-HIND: emperor of India.

PANCHAYAT: a court of arbitration, properly of five persons.

PANDAL: marquee.

PANDIT: a Sanskrit scholar; adviser on Hindu law in the courts.

PARIAH: community in south India looked upon as untouchable by orthodox Hindus; commonly used as synonym for out-caste.

PARSI: a Zoroastrian of Persian origin chiefly settled in western India.

PATANE (PATHARE) PRABHU: small subdivision of Prabhus (q.v.) living mainly in Bombay city.

PATEL: village headman.

PATIDAR: a subdivision of Lewa Kunbis (q.v.) in Gujarat.

PATNI: subordinate land tenure in Bengal, first formally recognised in 1819.

PATNIDAR: holder of a patni (q.v.).

PESHWA: originally the chief minister of the Maratha power; in the eighteenth century, prince of an independent Maratha state and leader of the Maratha confederacy.

PICE (PAISA): a small copper coin, one quarter of an anna.

PRABHU: writer caste in western India.

Glossary

PRADHAN: common title of the eight chief officers of the Maratha state.

PURBIAH (PURBHAYYA): an immigrant from the North-western Provinces and Oudh in Gujarat and the Deccan.

RAIYAT (RYOT): cultivator, peasant.

RAIYATWARI (RYOTWARI): a system of land revenue settlement made by government with each individual cultivator without the intervention of a third party.

RAJ: a kingdom, rule or sovereignty.

RAJPUT: military caste or clan.

REDDI: synonym for Kapu (q.v.).

RUPEE (RUPIYA): standard coin of the British Indian monetary system. Its exchange value was free to fluctuate until 1899. Until 1873 its value stood at 2 shillings, thereafter it fell, sometimes as low as one shilling.

SABHA: an assembly.

SADGOP: cultivating caste of Bengal Proper.

SAHA: title used by certain castes in Bengal such as Gandhabanik (q.v.), Napit (q.v.), and Teli (q.v.).

SARDAR (SIRDAR): chief, lord, leader, commander, officer.

SARKAR (SIRKAR): the state, government, supreme authority.

SEPOY (SIPAHI): native soldier.

SHAKTI (SAKTI): the female energy of a deity; the worshippers of the Saktis (Tantra worship) are prevalent chiefly in Bengal and eastern India.

SHERESTIDAR (SARRISHTADAR): head native officer in a collector's office or court of justice.

SHIA: Islamic sect advocating the claim of Ali, the son-in-law of the Prophet, to the Caliphate.

SOWKAR: moneylender.

SULAIMANI: subdivision of Bohras (q.v.).

SUNNI: Muslim belonging to the dominant majority group in Islam, usually held to be orthodox.

SWADESHI: literally 'of one's own country'; the name given to the movement to boycott goods not made in India.

SWARAJ: self-rule.

TAHSIL: a revenue subdivision of a district.

TAHSILDAR: officer in charge of a tahsil.

TALUK: a subdivision; in Bombay, of a zila, or of a district; in Oudh, the estate of a talukdar.

TALUKDAR: officer in charge of a taluk, or the holder of a proprietary estate.

TAMASHA: an entertainment, jollification, an event.

TAMBULI: trading caste in Bengal, traditionally sellers of betel.

TAMIL: a Dravidian language of south-eastern India or its speaker.

TAMILNAD: country of the Tamils.

TELEGU: a Dravidian language of south India or its speaker.

TELI: large oil-pressing and trading caste in Bengal, and elsewhere.

TOL: Sanskrit school.

TULU: a Dravidian language of south India.

ULEMA (ULAMA): Arabic plural of alim, a scholar, especially in religious subjects; loosely used to describe the whole Muslim ecclesiastical class.

URDU: the language formed by the mixture of Arabic, Persian, and Turkish words with Hindi, written in Arabic characters.

VAIDIKI: subdivision of Telegu Brahmins.

VAISHNAVISM: worship of Vishnu.

VAISYA (VAISHYA): the third varna (q.v.) whose traditional means of subsistence were trade, agriculture and the keeping of cattle.

VAKIL (WAKIL): in the nineteenth century, an authorised pleader in a court of justice.

VARNA: literally 'colour'; denotes each of the four classical divisions of the Hindu community.

VELLALA: largest Tamil cultivating caste.

WAHHABI: puritanical Islamic sect following the doctrines of Abdul-Wahhab, an eighteenth-century Arab reformer.

ZEMINDAR (ZAMINDAR): landholder, paying revenue to government directly; hence, zemindari.

Biographical Notes

ABDUL LATIF (1828–93). Educated at the Calcutta Madrassa; member of Bengal Legislative Council; founder and secretary of the Muhammadan Literary and Scientific Society, 1863.

AJUDHIA NATH (1840–92). Kashmiri Brahmin; educated Agra College; successful lawyer at Allahabad bar; member of North-western Provinces Legislative Council; prominent member of Indian National Congress; afterwards its joint general secretary, 1891–2.

AMIR ALI (1849–1928). Educated Calcutta University and Inner Temple; member of Bengal Legislative Council, 1878–83, and Governor-General's Legislative Council, 1883–5; founder of National Mahommedan Association, and its secretary, 1878–90.

BANERJEA, KALICHARAN (1847–1907). Educated Free Church Institution; baptised, 1864; professor at Free Church Institution; lawyer; helped to edit *Indian Christian Herald*; member, Bengal Legislative Council, 1877; president, Indian Association, 1906.

BANERJEA, SURENDRANATH (1848–1925). Educated Doveton College, Calcutta; B.A., 1868; I.C.S., 1871; dismissed the service, 1874; professor of English, Metropolitan Institution, 1876; founder and principal, Ripon College, 1882; founder, Indian Association, 1876; proprietor, *Bengalee*, 1878; editor, 1879; member, Bengal Legislative Council, 1893–1901; president of the Indian National Congress, 1895, 1902.

BENGALEE, SORABJEE SHAPURJEE (1831–93). Parsi; educated at Native Education Society's school, Bombay; commercial career; active with Furdonjee in Parsi Law Association; member of Bombay Municipal Corporation; member of Bombay Legislative Council, 1876; sheriff of Bombay, 1881.

BHANDARKAR, RAMKRISHNA GOPAL (1837–1925). Brahmin from Ratnagiri; educated Elphinstone College; educationalist and leading orientalist; member of Prarthana Samaj; social reformer; member, Governor-General's Legislative Council, 1903–4; Bombay Legislative Council, 1904–05.

BONNERJEE, WOMESH CHANDRA (1844–1906). Son of attorney of Calcutta high court; Middle Temple, 1867; successful Calcutta lawyer; acted as standing counsel to government, 1882, 1884, 1886–7; president of Indian National Congress, 1885; member of Bengal Legislative Council, 1893.

380

BOSE, ANANDA MOHAN (1846–1906). Educated Presidency College, Calcutta, and Christ's College, Cambridge; barrister-at-law with mainly mofussil practice; started City School, Calcutta; leader of Sadharan Brahmo Samaj; founder, secretary and president of the Indian Association; member, Bengal Legislative Council, 1886, and 1895; president of the Indian National Congress, 1898.

BOSE, RAJNARAIN (1826–99). Educated Hindu College; headmaster, Midnapore district school, 1851–69; president, Adi Brahmo Samaj.

CHANDAVARKAR, NARAYAN GANESH (1855–1923). Educated Elphinstone College; judge of Bombay high court, 1901; leader of social reform movement; president of the Indian National Congress, 1900.

CHARLU, P. ANANDA (1843–1908). Son of sherestidar of district court, Chittoor, North Arcot; educated at Presidency College, Madras; B.L.; lawyer at Madras high court; one of the founders and secretary of the Madras Mahajana Sabha; attended first Indian National Congress; active on its Madras Standing Committee; president, 1891, and joint secretary, 1892, Indian National Congress; zemindar of permanently settled estates.

CHATTERJEE, BANKIM CHANDRA (1838–94). Brahmin; son of deputy magistrate; educated Presidency College; first Indian graduate from Calcutta University, 1858; uncovenanted civil servant, rising to be assistant secretary to Bengal government; leading Bengali novelist.

CHETTY, GAZULU LAKSHMINARASU (1806–68). Son of an indigo merchant; large commercial fortune; founder and president of Madras Native Association.

DEB, NARERENDRA KRISHNA (1822–1903). Educated at Hindu College; active in Calcutta municipal affairs; vice-president and president, British Indian Association; member of Governor-General's Legislative Council.

DEROZIO, HENRY LOUIS VIVIAN (1809–31). Eurasian poet and teacher at Hindu College; leader of Young Bengal movement.

DUTT, ROMESH CHANDRA (1848–1909). Educated Presidency College, Calcutta, and University College, London; I.C.S., 1871; divisional commissioner, 1894; president of Indian National Congress, 1899.

FURDOONJEE, NAOROJI (1817–85). Parsi; educated at the Native Education Society's school, Bombay; assistant professor at the Elphinstone Institution; leader of the 'Young Bombay' party which established several political, social and religious associations in the 1850s; interpreter, high court of Bombay, 1864; member of Bombay municipality.

GHOSE, LALMOHAN (1849–1909). Kayasth from Bikrampur in Dacca district; younger brother of Manmohan Ghose; Middle Temple; called to the bar, 1873; Calcutta lawyer; Indian Association delegate to England, 1879; attempted to enter parliament in 1884; member of

Bengal Legislative Council, 1893–5; president of the Indian National Congress, 1903.

GHOSE, MANMOHAN (1844–96). Kayasth from Bikrampur in Dacca district; educated Presidency College; founded *Indian Mirror*, 1861; failed I.C.S. examinations twice; first Indian barrister-at-law at Calcutta high court, 1867; active in Indian Association and its delegate to England in 1885; active in Indian National Congress; brother of Lalmohan Ghose.

GHOSE, RAM GOPAL (1815–68). Educated Hindu College; vice-president, Society for the Acquisition of General Knowledge, 1838; active on Bengal Chamber of Commerce; member, Bengal Legislative Council, 1862–4.

GHOSE, SISIR KUMAR (1842–1911). Kayasth; son of Jessore lawyer; with his brothers, including Motilal (1847–1922), founded and edited *Amrita Bazar Patrika*; founder, *Indian League*, 1875.

JEEJEEBHOY, SIR JAMSETJEE 1st baronet (1783–1859), 2nd baronet (1811–77), 3rd baronet (1851–98). Leading Parsi family of Bombay.

IYER, G. SUBRAMANIA (1855–1916). Tamil Brahmin; son of Tanjore pleader; educated St Peter's College, Tanjore; headmaster, Anglo-Vernacular School, Triplicane, 1879; editor, *Hindu*, 1878–98; helped to start a Tamil newspaper, *Swadesamitran*, 1882; associated with Indian National Congress from its inception.

MALABARI, BEHRAMJI MERWANJI (1853–1912). Parsi; editor of *Indian Spectator* and *Voice of India*; social reformer.

MANDLIK, VISVANATH NARAYAN (1833–89). Brahmin from Ratnagiri; educated Elphinstone high school; lawyer at Bombay bar; government pleader, 1884; member of Bombay Legislative Council, 1874–82; member of Governor-General's Legislative Council, 1884.

MEHTA, PHEROZESHAH MERWANJI (1845–1915). Parsi; educated Elphinstone College; B.A., 1864; called to the English bar, 1868; municipal commissioner, Bombay Corporation, 1884–5; additional member, Bombay Legislative Council, 1893; first elected member from Bombay Legislative Council to the Governor-General's Legislative Council, 1893; founder member, Bombay Presidency Association; president of Indian National Congress, 1890.

MITRA, DIGAMBAR (1817–79). Educated Hindu College; assistant secretary, British Indian Association, 1851; later vice-president and president; three times member of the Bengal Legislative Council, 1864, 1870, 1873; zemindar.

MITRA, PEARY CHANDRA (1814–83). Educated Hindu College; secretary, Society for the Acquisition of General Knowledge, 1838; one of the founders of the British Indian Association; member, Bengal Legislative Council, 1867.

MITRA, RAJENDRA LAL (1824–91). Respectable Sudra family; educated Calcutta Medical College; vice-president and president of the British Indian Association; active in second Indian National Congress, 1886; leading orientalist.

MUDALIYAR, RAMASWAMI (1852–92). Son of landowner, Salem district; educated Presidency College, Madras; lawyer at Salem and later at Madras high court; Mahajana Sabha's delegate to England, 1885; prominent member of Indian National Congress.

MUKHERJEE, HARISH CHANDRA (1824–61). Son of poor Kulin Brahmin; assistant military auditor, 1855; editor, *Hindoo Patriot*; prominent in indigo agitation.

MUKHERJEE, JOYKISSEN (1801–88). Large landowner of Uttarpara; helped to found British Indian Association.

MUKHERJEE, PEARY MOHAN (born 1840). Zemindar; son of Joykissen Mukherjee of Uttarpara; sometime president of Calcutta University; honorary secretary, British Indian Association; member Bengal Legislative Council, 1879; member, Governor-General's Council, 1884 and 1886.

MUKHERJEE, SAMBHU CHANDRA (1839–94). Educated Metropolitan College; journalist; assistant secretary, Talukdar's Association, Lucknow; president of Indian League; conducted *Mookerjee's Magazine*, 1872–6; founded *Reis and Rayyet*, 1882.

MULJI, KARSONDAS (1832–75). Member of Gujarati Bhatia caste; educated Elphinstone Institution; journalist; social reformer who attacked Vallabhacharya priests.

NAOROJI, DADABHAI (1825–1917). Son of Parsi priest; educated Elphinstone Institution where he became professor; started *Rast Goftar*, 1851; active in Bombay Association; came to England, 1855; founder, East India Association, London, 1866; prime minister, Baroda, 1874; member, Bombay Legislative Council, 1885; member of parliament for Central Finsbury, 1892–5; president of Indian National Congress, 1886, 1893, 1906.

NATHUBHOY, SIR MANGALDAS (1832–90). Gujarati bania; inherited large fortune; social reformer; revived Bombay Association in 1860s.

PAL, KRISTO DAS (1838–84). Educated Oriental Seminary and Metropolitan College, Calcutta; assistant secretary of the British Indian Association, 1858; secretary, 1879; editor of *Hindoo Patriot* from 1861; member, Bengal Legislative Council, 1872; member of the Governor-General's Council as the representative of the Bengal zemindars, 1883.

PETIT, SIR DINSHAW M. (1823–1901). Parsi baronet and wealthy Bombay businessman.

PHADKE, WASUDEO BALWANT (1845–83). Born in Kolaba; minor government clerk; led unsuccessful rebellion in Poona district.

Biographical Notes

PHULE, JOTIRAO GOVINDRAO (1827–90). Phul Mali of Poona district; educated at a mission school; social reformer concerned with female education and the rights of non-Brahmins.

RANADE, MAHADEV GOVIND (1841–1901). Chitpavan Brahmin; educated Elphinstone College; one of the first graduates of Bombay University; acting professor of English, Elphinstone College, 1868–71; subordinate judge, Poona, 1871; judge, small cause court, 1884; judge, high court of Bombay, 1893; several times member of Bombay Legislative Council; social reformer and politician.

ROY, RAMMOHAN (1772–1833). Leading Bengali reformer and educationalist; one of the founders of Hindu College and founder of Brahmo Samaj, 1828.

SAYANI, RAHMATULLA MUHAMMAD (1847–1902). Muslim; educated Elphinstone College; B.A.; honorary magistrate; president, Municipal Corporation; member, Bombay Legislative Council; member, Governor-General's Council, and president, Indian National Congress, 1896.

SEN, KESHUB CHANDRA (1838–84). Educated Presidency College; joined Brahmo Samaj, 1857; seceded from Adi Brahmo Samaj, 1866; missionary tours round India, 1869; reorganised Brahmo Samaj, 1875–8; religious and social reformer.

SEN, NORENDRANATH (1843–1911). Educated Hindu College, attorney of Calcutta high court; editor, *Indian Mirror*, 1879; attended first Indian National Congress.

SHIVA PRASAD (1823–95). Landowner in Benares and Gorakhpur; educated at Benares College; government career; member of Governor-General's Legislative Council, 1883.

SYED AHMED KHAN (1817–98). Born Delhi; entered service of the Company, 1837; subordinate judge; supported British during Mutiny; Muslim educationalist and reformer; founder of Aligarh Scientific Society and the Muhammadan Anglo-Oriental College, 1875; additional member, Governor-General's Legislative Council, 1878–82.

TAGORE, DEBENDRANATH (1818–1905). Educated Hindu College; joined Brahmo Samaj, 1842.

TAGORE, SIR JOTINDRA MOHAN (1831–1908). Nephew of Prasanna Kumar Tagore; educated Hindu College; president of British Indian Association, 1879 and 1891; member, Bengal Legislative Council, 1870, 1872; member, Governor-General's Legislative Council, 1877, 1879, 1881; large landowner.

TAGORE, PRASANNA KUMAR (1801–68). Educated Hindu College; though possessing considerable landed property made a very large income as government pleader; a founder of the British Indian Association, 1851; president, 1867; member of the Governor-General's Legislative Council, 1867.

TAGORE, RAMNATH (1800–77). Educated Sherborne School, Calcutta; prominent in Brahmo Samaj; one of the founders of the British Indian Association; its president for a decade; member of the Bengal Legislative Council, 1866; member, Governor-General's Legislative Council, 1873.

TELANG, KASHINATH TRIMBAK (1850–93). Gaud Saraswat Brahmin from Thana; educated at Elphinstone College; M.A., 1868; LL.B., 1871; joined Bombay bar, 1872; member, Education Commission, 1882; member, Bombay Legislative Council, 1884; founder member, Bombay Presidency Association, and active Congressman; judge of the high court, Bombay, 1889; scholar, social reformer and politician.

TILAK, BAL GANGADHAR (1864–1920). Chitpavan Brahmin; leading journalist and politician in western India who rose to all-India prominence after 1898.

TYABJI, BADRUDDIN (1844–1906). Bohra Muslim; educated in England; called to the bar, Middle Temple, 1867; leading Bombay barrister; elected to the Municipal Corporation, 1873–83; member, Bombay Legislative Council, 1882–6; founded Anjuman-i-Islam of Bombay, 1876; founder member, Bombay Presidency Association, 1885; president, third Indian National Congress, Madras, 1887; judge of the high court of Bombay, 1895.

WACHA, DINSHAW EDULJI (1844–1936). Parsi; educated Elphinstone College; career in Bombay mill industry; active in Bombay local politics and the Indian National Congress; president of Congress, 1901; knighted.

VARMA, GANGA PRASAD (1863–1914). Leading Lucknow journalist; attended first Indian National Congress.

VIDYASAGAR, ISVAR CHANDRA (1820–91). Kulin Brahmin; educated at Sanskrit College, Calcutta; principal, Sanskrit College, 1851; inspector of schools, 1855–8; managed Metropolitan Institution from 1864; leader of widow-remarriage movement and urged reform of polygamy.

Bibliography

This bibliography is simply intended to provide a list of sources and works cited.

PRIVATE PAPERS

Argyll Papers. Microfilm copy, India Office Library.
Dufferin Papers. Microfilm copy, India Office Library [DP].
Curzon Papers. India Office Library. MSS Eur. F. 111.
Lytton Papers. India Office Library. MSS Eur. E. 218 [LP].
Naoroji Papers. Dadabhai Naoroji Memorial Trust, Bombay [NP].
Northbrook Papers. India Office Library. MSS Eur. C. 144.
Mayo Papers. Cambridge University Library. Add. 7490.
Mehta Papers. This collection is in the possession of Sir Homi Mody, Bombay. Microfilm copy, National Archives of India, and University of Cambridge.
Ripon Papers (Second Series). Special correspondence relating to India. British Museum, Add. MSS 43565–43619 [RP]. Another set of the correspondence relating to India, privately printed by Ripon, is in the British Museum, Indian State Papers 290/5, 290/7, 290/8 [B.M. I.S.].
Salisbury Papers. Christ Church Library, Oxford. (I owe my references to this source to Mr James Cornford.)
Stephen Papers. University Library, Cambridge. Add. 7349.
Temple Papers. India Office Library. MSS Eur. F. 86.
Tyabji Papers. Collection formerly in the possession of Husain B. Tyabji, Bombay. Most of it has now been transferred to the National Archives of India. Microfilm copy, University of Cambridge.

UNPUBLISHED RECORDS OF THE GOVERNMENT OF INDIA

Specific references will be found in the footnotes.

RECORDS, PUBLISHED AND UNPUBLISHED, OF POLITICAL ORGANISATIONS IN INDIA

A Records and publications of the British Indian Association, British Indian Street, Calcutta.

Specific references to this source are given in the footnotes, and the source is indicated by the abbreviation: BIA.

B   Records and publications of the Indian Association, Bowbazaar, Calcutta.
    Specific references to this source are given in the footnotes, and the source is indicated by the abbreviation: IA.

C   Bombay Association.

Minute of Proceedings of the Bombay Association. Established 26th August, 1852. Bombay, 1852.
Minutes of Proceedings of the First Annual General Meeting of the Bombay Association... Bombay, 1853.
Petition to Parliament from the Members from the Bombay Association... Bombay, 1853.
Proceedings of a meeting, held on the 14th December 1867...for the purpose of re-establishing the Bombay Association...together with the Constitution and Rules of the Association. Bombay, 1868.

D   Records of the Bombay Presidency Association, Hornby Road, Bombay.
    Specific references in footnotes.

    The following publications are also cited:

Report of a General Meeting of the Bombay Presidency Association, 29 September 1885. Bombay, 1885.
Bombay Presidency Association. First Annual Report, 1885. Bombay, 1886.
Bombay Presidency Association. Second Annual Report, 1886. Bombay, 1887.

E   Madras Mahajana Sabha

First Conference of Native Gentlemen from the different parts of the Presidency of Madras held under the auspices of the Madras Mahajana Sabha...on 29th and 30th December 1884 and 1st and 2nd January 1885. Madras, 1885.
The Madras Mahajana Sabha: Annual Report for 1885–86. Madras, 1886.

F   Indian National Congress

Proceedings of the First Indian National Congress held at Bombay on the 28th, 29th and 30th December 1885. Bombay, 1886. [*I.N.C.* 1885.]
Report of the Second Indian National Congress held at Calcutta on the 27th, 28th, 29th and 30th December, 1886. Calcutta, 1887. [*I.N.C.* 1886.]
Report of the Third Indian National Congress held at Madras on the 27th, 28th, 29th and 30th December, 1887. London, 1888. [*I.N.C.* 1887.]
Report of the Fourth Indian National Congress held at Allahabad on the 26th, 27th, 28th and 29th December, 1888. Calcutta, 1889. [*I.N.C.* 1888.]

Bibliography

G   Others

The Constitution of the Poona Sarvajanik Sabha and its Rules. Poona, 1870.
Report of the Bombay Chamber of Commerce for the year 1875–76. Bombay, 1877.
Report of the Bombay Chamber of Commerce for the year 1877–78. Bombay, 1879.
Report of the Bombay Chamber of Commerce for the year 1882–83. Bombay, 1884.
Report of the Committee of the Central National Mahommedan Association for the past 5 years. Calcutta, 1885.
Report of the Committee of the Central National Mahommedan Association for the year 1883–84. Calcutta, 1885.
The Rules and Objects of the National Mahommedan Association with a list of the members. Calcutta, 1882.
A Short Account of the aims, objects, achievements, and Proceedings of the Kayastha Conference and letters of Sympathy from eminent rulers and High Government Officers. Allahabad, 1893.

NEWSPAPERS AND JOURNALS

Aligarh Institute Gazette
Amrita Bazar Patrika
Bengalee
Bombay Gazette
Brahmo Public Opinion
Englishman
Hindoo Patriot
Hindu
Indian Mirror
Indian Spectator
Indu Prakash
Journal of the East India Association
Kesari (in Marathi)
Mahratta
Pioneer
The Quarterly Journal of the Poona Sarvajanik Sabha
Sadharani (in Bengali)
Theosophist
The Times
Times of India
Tribune
Voice of India

OFFICIAL PUBLICATIONS

These are listed according to region and subject.

A   India

Sharp, H. and Richey, J. A. *Selections from Educational Records. Part 1, 1781–1839; part 2, 1840–59.* Bureau of Education. Calcutta, 1920–2.
Kirpal, P. N. (ed.). *Educational Reports, 1859–71.* Selections from Educational Records of the Government of India, 1. Delhi, 1960.
Naik, J. P. *Development of University Education, 1860–86.* Selections from Educational Records of the Government of India, 11. Delhi, 1963.

Report of the Indian Education Commission, Appointed by the Resolution of the Government of India dated 3rd February, 1882. Calcutta, 1883. [*EC.*]

Correspondence on the subject of the education of the Muhammadan community in British India and their employment in the public service generally. Selections from the records of the Government of India. No. CCV. Home Department Serial no. 2. Calcutta, 1886. [*Muslim Selections.*]

Croft, A. *Review of Education in India in 1886, with special reference to the Report of the Education Commission.* Calcutta, 1888.

Nash, A. M. *Progress of Education in India 1887–88 to 1891–92. Second Quinquennial Review.* Calcutta, 1893.

Nathan, R. *Progress of Education in India 1897–98 to 1901–02. Fourth Quinquennial Review.* Calcutta, 1904.

India List, Civil and Military, March 1877. London, 1877.

India List, Civil and Military, January 1886. London, 1886.

Abstract of Returns of Indian Civil Establishments on 31st March 1886. Calcutta, 1887.

Report of the Public Service Commission, 1886–87 with appendices. Calcutta, 1888. [*PSC.*]

Papers relating to the provincial service from 1888–96. Selections from the Records of the Government of India, Home Department. No. CCCLIII. Calcutta, 1898.

Report on the Census of British India taken on the 17th February 1881, vol. I. London, 1883 [*1881 Census, India,* I.]

The Indian Empire. Census of 1881. Statistics of Population. Vol. II. Calcutta, 1883. [*1881 Census, India,* II.]

Baines, J. A. *General Report. Census of India, 1891.* London, 1893. [*1891 Census,* India, I.]

General Report of the Census of India, 1901. London, 1904.

Hunter, W. W. *The Imperial Gazetteer of India.* 14 vols. Second edition. London, 1885–7. [*HIG.*]

Imperial Gazetteer of India. Provincial Series. Madras. 2 vols. Calcutta, 1908.

The Imperial Gazetteer of India. 26 vols. New edition. Oxford, 1907–9.

Grierson, G. A. *Linguistic Survey of India.* 20 vols. Calcutta, 1903–28.

Indian Industrial Commission 1916–18. Report. Calcutta, 1918.

Cotton, C. W. E. *Handbook of Commercial Information for India.* Calcutta, 1919.

Land Revenue Policy of the Indian Government (being the Resolution issued by the Governor-General in Council on the 16th January 1902). Calcutta, 1902.

Royal Commission on Agriculture in India. Evidence. 12 vols. Calcutta, 1927.

B Bengal

General Report on Public Instruction in the Lower Provinces of Bengal, for 1870–71. Calcutta, 1871. [*RDPI (Bengal) 1870–1.*]

Bibliography

General Report on Public Instruction in Bengal, for 1871–72. Calcutta, 1873. [*RDPI (Bengal) 1871–2.*]

General Report on Public Instruction in Bengal, for 1875–76. Calcutta, 1876. [*RDPI (Bengal) 1875–6.*]

General Report on Public Instruction in Bengal, for 1876–77. Calcutta, 1877. [*RDPI (Bengal) 1876–7.*]

General Report on Public Instruction in Bengal, for 1882–83. Calcutta, 1883. [*RDPI (Bengal) 1882–3.*]

General Report on Public Instruction in Bengal, for 1883–84. Calcutta, 1884. [*RDPI (Bengal) 1883–4.*]

General Report on Public Instruction in Bengal, for 1885–86. Calcutta, 1886. [*RDPI (Bengal) 1885–6.*]

General Report on Public Instruction in Bengal, for 1886–87. Calcutta, 1887. [*RDPI (Bengal) 1886–7.*]

Report by the Bengal Provincial Committee; with evidence taken before the Committee, and Memorials addressed to the Education Commission. Education Commission. Calcutta, 1884. [*EC (Bengal).*]

Report of the Commission appointed by the Government of India to enquire into the conditions and prospects of the University of Calcutta. 13 vols. Calcutta, 1919–20. [*Calcutta Commission Report.*]

Proceedings of the Public Service Commission. Volume VI. Proceedings relating to the Lower Provinces of Bengal (including Assam). Calcutta, 1887. [*PSC (Bengal), VI.*]

Bourdillon, J. A. *Report of the Census of Bengal, 1881.* 3 vols. Calcutta, 1883. [*1881 Census, Bengal.*]

Beverley, H. *Report on the Census of the Town and Suburbs of Calcutta Taken on the 17th February 1881.* Calcutta, 1881. [*1881 Census, Calcutta.*]

O'Donnell, C. J. *The Lower Provinces of Bengal and their Feudatories. The Report.* Census of India, 1891. Vol. III. Calcutta, 1893. [*1891 Census, Bengal, III.*]

O'Donnell, C. J. *The Lower Provinces of Bengal and their Feudatories. The Administrative Tables.* Census of India, 1891. Vol. IV. Calcutta, 1893. [*1891 Census, Bengal, IV.*]

O'Malley, L. S. S. *Bengal, Bihar and Orissa and Sikkim. Part I. Report.* Census of India, 1911. Vol. V. Calcutta, 1913. [*1911 Census, Bengal, V.*]

Selections from the Records of the Government of Bengal, XLII. *Papers connected with the trial of Moulvie Ahmedoollah*...Calcutta, 1866.

Report on the Administration of Bengal, 1873–74. Calcutta, 1875.

Report on the Administration of Bengal, 1874–75. Calcutta, 1876.

Report on the Administration of Bengal, 1880–81. Calcutta, 1881.

Report on the Administration of Bengal, 1885–86. Calcutta, 1886.

Grierson, G. A. *The Administration of the Lower Provinces of Bengal 1882–83 to 1886–87, being a supplement to the Annual General Administration Report for 1885–6.* Calcutta, 1887.

Hunter, W. W. *A Statistical Account of Bengal.* 20 vols. London, 1875–7. [*SAB.*]

390

O'Malley, L. S. S. *Midnapore.* Bengal District Gazetteers. Calcutta, 1911.
O'Malley, L. S. S. and Chakravarti, M. *Hooghly.* Bengal District
Gazetteers. Calcutta, 1912.
Jack, J. C. *Bakarganj.* Bengal District Gazetteers. Calcutta, 1918.
Government of Bengal. Report of the Land Revenue Commission Bengal.
6 vols. Alipore, 1940–1.
Risley, H. H. *The Tribes and Castes of Bengal. Ethnographic Glossary.*
2 vols. Official edition. Calcutta, 1892.

c Bombay

Report of the Department of Public Instruction in the Bombay Presidency,
for the year 1867–68. Bombay, 1868. [*RDPI (Bombay) 1867–8.*]
Report of the Department of Public Instruction in the Bombay Presidency,
for the year 1869–70. Bombay, 1870. [*RDPI (Bombay) 1869–70.*]
Report of the Director of Public Instruction in the Bombay Presidency
for the year 1875–76. Bombay, 1876. [*RDPI (Bombay) 1875–6.*]
Report of the Director of Public Instruction in the Bombay Presidency
for the year 1877–78. Bombay, 1879. [*RDPI (Bombay) 1877–8.*]
Report of the Director of Public Instruction in the Bombay Presidency
for the year 1878–79. Bombay, 1879. [*RDPI (Bombay) 1878–9.*]
Report of the Director of Public Instruction in the Bombay Presidency
for the year 1879–80. Bombay, 1880. [*RDPI (Bombay) 1879–80.*]
Report of the Acting Director of Public Instruction in the Bombay
Presidency for the year 1884–85. Bombay, 1885. [*RDPI (Bombay)*
1884–5.]
Report of the Director of Public Instruction in the Bombay Presidency
for the year 1885–86. Bombay, 1886. [*RDPI (Bombay) 1885–6.*]
Report of the Bombay Provincial Committee. Education Commission.
Bombay, vol. I. Calcutta, 1884. [*EC (Bombay),* I.]
Evidence taken before the Bombay Provincial Committee, and Memorials
addressed to the Education Commission. Education Commission.
Bombay, vol. II. Calcutta, 1884. [*EC (Bombay),* II.]
Proceedings of the Public Service Commission. Vol. IV. *Proceedings relating*
to the Bombay Presidency (including Sind). Calcutta, 1887. [*PSC*
(Bombay), IV.]
Baines, J. A. *Operations and Results in the Presidency of Bombay*
including Sind. Vol. I. *Text.* Imperial Census of 1881. Bombay,
1882. [*1881 Census, Bombay,* I.]
Baines, J. A. *Operations and Results in the Presidency of Bombay*
including Sind. Vol. II. *Tables.* Imperial Census of 1881. Bombay,
1882. [*1881 Census, Bombay,* II.]
Weir, T. S. *Census of the City and Island of Bombay taken on the 17th*
February 1881. Bombay, 1883. [*1881 Census, Bombay City.*]
Drew, W. W. *Bombay and its Feudatories. Part I. Report.* Census of
India, 1891. Vol. VII. Bombay, 1892. [*1891 Census, Bombay,* VII.]
Drew, W. W. *Bombay and its Feudatories. Part II. Imperial Tables.*
Census of India, 1891. Vol. VIII. Bombay, 1892. [*1891 Census,*
Bombay, VIII.]

Bibliography

Source Material for a History of the Freedom Movement in India (Collected from the Bombay Government Records). Vol. I (*1818–1885*). Bombay, 1957.

Source Material for a History of the Freedom Movement in India (Collected from Bombay Government Records). Vol. II (*1885–1920*). Bombay, 1958.

Memorandum prepared by the Government of Bombay for submission to the Indian Statutory Commission, 1928. Bombay, 1929.

Gazetteer of the Bombay Presidency, ed. J. M. Campbell. 27 vols. Bombay, 1877–1904. [*BG.*]

Enthoven, R. E. *The Tribes and Castes of Bombay.* 3 vols. Bombay, 1920–2.

Report on the Administration of the Bombay Presidency for the year 1881–82. Bombay, 1882.

D   Madras

Report on Public Instruction in the Madras Presidency, for 1875–76. Selections from the Records of the Madras Government, no. LVIII. Madras, 1877. [*RDPI (Madras) 1875–6.*]

Report on Public Instruction in the Madras Presidency, for 1876–77. Madras, 1877. [*RDPI (Madras) 1876–7.*]

Report on Public Instruction in the Madras Presidency, for 1877–78. Madras, 1878. [*RDPI (Madras) 1877–8.*]

Report on Public Instruction in the Madras Presidency, for 1879–80. Madras, 1880. [*RDPI (Madras) 1879–80.*]

Report on Public Instruction in the Madras Presidency, for 1880–81. Madras, 1882. [*RDPI (Madras) 1880–1.*]

Report on Public Instruction in the Madras Presidency, for 1881–82. Madras, 1883. [*RDPI (Madras) 1881–2.*]

Report on Public Instruction in the Madras Presidency for 1883–84. Madras, 1885. [*RDPI (Madras) 1883–4.*]

Report on Public Instruction in the Madras Presidency, for 1884–85. Madras, 1885. [*RDPI (Madras) 1884–5.*]

Report on Public Instruction in the Madras Presidency, for 1885–86. Madras, 1886. [*RDPI (Madras) 1885–6.*]

Report on Public Instruction in the Madras Presidency, for 1886–87. Madras, 1887. [*RDPI (Madras) 1886–7.*]

Report on Public Instruction in the Madras Presidency, for 1887–88. Madras, 1888. [*RDPI (Madras) 1887–8.*]

Report on Public Instruction in the Madras Presidency, for 1888–89. Madras, 1889. [*RDPI (Madras) 1888–9.*]

Report by the Madras Provincial Committee; with evidence taken before the Committee and memorials addressed to the Education Commission. Education Commission. Calcutta, 1884. [*EC (Madras).*]

McIver, L. *Operations and Results in the Presidency of Madras.* Vol. I. *The Report.* Imperial Census of 1881. Madras, 1883. [*1881 Census, Madras,* I.]

392

McIver, L. *Operations and Results in the Presidency of Madras.* Vol. II. *Final Census Tables, Imperial Series.* Imperial Census of 1881. Madras, 1883. [*1881 Census, Madras,* II.]

Stuart, H. A. *Madras. The Report on the Census.* Census of India, 1891. vol. XIII. Madras, 1893. [*1891 Census, Madras,* XIII.]

Stuart, H. A. *Madras. Tables I to XVII–C, British Territory.* Census of India 1891. Vol. XIV. Madras, 1893. [*1891 Census, Madras,* XIV.]

Stuart, H. A. *Madras. Tables A to E...and a Caste Index.* Census of India, 1891. vol. XV. Madras, 1893. [*1891 Census, Madras,* XV.]

Report of the Administration of the Madras Presidency during the year 1885–6. Madras, 1886.

Row, T. Venkaswami. *A Manual of the District of Tanjore, in the Madras Presidency.* Madras, 1883.

Innes, C. A. *Malabar and Anjengo,* ed. F. B. Evans. Madras Gazetteers. Madras, 1915.

Raghavaiyangar, S. Srinivasa. *Memorandum on the Progress of the Madras Presidency during the last forty years of British Administration.* Second edition. Madras, 1893.

E   Other provinces

Report on the Progress of Education in the North-Western Provinces for 1873–74. Allahabad, 1874. [*RDPI (North-western Provinces) 1873–4.*]

Report upon the Progress of Education in the Province of Oudh, 1875. Lucknow, 1876. [*RDPI (Oudh) 1875.*]

Report by the North-Western Provinces and Oudh Provincial Committee; with evidence taken before the Committee, and memorials addressed to the Education Commission. Education Commission. Calcutta, 1884. [*EC (North-western Provinces and Oudh).*]

Proceedings of the Public Services Commission. Vol. II. *Proceedings Relating to the North-Western Provinces and Oudh.* Calcutta, 1887. [*PSC (North-western Provinces and Oudh)* II.]

White, E. *Report on the Census of the N.-W.P. and Oudh...1881... with appendices.* Allahabad, 1882. [*1881 Census, North-western Provinces and Oudh.*]

Report by the Punjab Provincial Committee with minutes of evidence taken before the Committee and memorials addressed to the Education Commission. Education Commission. Calcutta, 1884. [*EC (Punjab).*]

Report on the Administration of the Central Provinces for the year 1883–4. Nagpur, 1884.

Bibliography

PARLIAMENTARY PAPERS. [*P.P.*]

Year	Volume	Command number	Short title
1866	LII	—	Moral and Material Progress, 1864–5
1868–9	LXIII	4178	Statistical Abstract, Third Number
1876	LXXVII	1626	Statistical Abstract, Tenth Number
1878	LVII	2077	Vernacular Press Act, 1878
1878	LVII	2040	Correspondence on Act IX of 1878
1878	LVIII	2071	Deccan Riots Commission
1878–9	LV	2376	Admission of natives to the civil service
1883	LI	3512	Native Jurisdiction over British subjects
1883	LI	—	Extension of local self-government in India
1884	LX	3877	Native Jurisdiction over British subjects: further papers
1884	LXXXIV	4061	Statistical Abstract, Eighteenth Number
1884–5	LVIII	4580	Age of Indian civil service candidates
1886	LXVIII	4730	Statistical Abstract, Twentieth Number
1888	LXXVII	—	Resolution on state-aided education
1889	LVIII	5713	Memorandum on Indian Administration
1890	LIV	5926	Correspondence on report of Indian Public Service Commission
1890	LXXVIII	6123	Statistical Abstract, Twenty-fourth Number

PUBLISHED WORKS AND UNPUBLISHED THESES

Aberigh-Mackay, G. *Twenty-one days in India, or the tour of Sir Ali Baba, K.C.B.* New edition, London, 1882.

Ahluwalia, M. M. *Kukas, The Freedom Fighters of the Panjab.* Bombay, 1965.

Ahmad, A. *Studies in Islamic Culture in the Indian Environment.* London, 1964.

394

Alder, G. J. *British India's Northern Frontier 1865–95.* London, 1963.
Andrews, C. F. and Mukerji, G. *The Rise and Growth of the Congress in India.* London, 1938.
Anonymous. 'Indian Students in England.' *Journal of the National Indian Association in Aid of Social Progress and Education in India.* January 1885. No. 169.
Antonius, G. *The Arab Awakening: the story of the Arab national movement.* London, 1938.

Baden-Powell, B. H. *The Land-systems of British India.* 3 vols. Oxford, 1892.
Baden-Powell, B. H. *A Short Account of the Land Revenue and its Administration in British India; with a Sketch of the Land Tenures.* Oxford, 1894.
Baden-Powell, B. H. *The Indian Village Community.* Reprint of London 1896 edition. New Haven, 1957.
Bagal, J. C. *History of the Indian Association 1876–1951.* Calcutta, n.d. ?1953.
Balfour, Lady Betty. *The History of Lord Lytton's Indian Administration, 1876 to 1880: compiled from Letters and Official Papers.* London, 1899.
Balfour, Lady Betty (ed.) *Personal and Literary Letters of Robert First Earl of Lytton.* 2 vols. London, 1906.
Baljon, J. M. S. (Jr.). *The Reforms and Religious Ideas of Sir Sayyid Ahmad Khan.* 3rd edition. Lahore, 1964.
Ballhatchet, K. *Social Policy and Social Change in Western India 1817–1830.* London Oriental Series. Vol. 5. London, 1957.
Banerjea, S. *A Nation in Making. Being the Reminiscences of Fifty Years of Public Life.* London, 1925.
Barker, A. T. (ed.). *The Mahatma Letters to A. P. Sinnett from the Mahatmas M. and K. H.* 2nd edition. (Eighth Impression.) London, 1948.
Beck, T. *Essays on Indian Topics.* Allahabad, 1888.
Bernard, A. *L'Algérie. Histoire des colonies françaises,* ed. G. A. A. Hanotaux and A. Martineau, Vol. II. Paris, 1930.
Besant, A. *How India Wrought for Freedom.* Adyar, 1915.
Béteille, A. *Caste, Class, and Power: Changing Patterns of Stratification in a Tanjore Village.* Berkeley and Los Angeles, 1965.
Bhate, G. C. *History of Modern Marathi Literature, 1800–1938.* Mahad, 1939. Privately printed.
Bhatia, B.M. *Famines in India: a study in some aspects of the economic history of India, 1860–1945.* London, 1963.
Blunt, W. S. *India under Ripon. A Private Diary.* London, 1909.
Bose, N. K. *Modern Bengal.* Calcutta, 1959.
Bose, Rajnarain. *Atmacharit.* [Autobiography, in Bengali.] Calcutta, 1909.
Buchanan, D. H. *The Development of Capitalistic Enterprise in India.* New York, 1934.

Bibliography

Buckland, C. E. *Bengal under the Lieutenant-Governors.* 2 vols. Calcutta, 1901.

Campbell, G. *Memoirs of My Indian Career*, ed. C. E. Bernard. 2 vols. London, 1893.

'Caste. A Trend Report and Bibliography.' *Current Sociology*, vol. VIII, no. 3, 1959.

Chandra, B. *The Rise and Growth of Economic Nationalism in India. Economic Policies of Indian National Leadership, 1880–1905.* New Delhi, 1966.

Chandavarkar, G. L. *A Wrestling Soul; story of the life of Sir Narayan Chandavarkar.* Bombay, 1955.

Chatterji, S. K. *Languages and Literatures of Modern India.* Calcutta, 1963.

Chaudhary, V. C. P. *The Creation of Modern Bihar.* Patna and Khirhar, 1964.

Chaudhuri, S. B. *Civil Disturbances during the British Rule in India (1765–1857).*Calcutta, 1955.

Chintamani, C. Y. (ed.). *Indian Social Reform in four parts. Being a Collection of Essays, Addresses, Speeches, etc. with an Appendix.* Madras, 1901.

Chiplonkar, V. K. *Nibandhamala.* [Garland of Essays; in Marathi.] 3rd edition. Poona, 1926.

Contemporary Indian Literature. A Symposium. 2nd edition. New Delhi, 1959.

Coupland, R. *India, A Restatement.* London, 1945.

Cowling, M. J. 'Lytton, the Cabinet, and the Russians, August to November 1878', *English Historical Review*, vol. LXXVI, January 1961, pp. 59–79.

Cox, E. C. *My Thirty Years in India.* London, 1909.

Cumpston, M. 'Some early Indian Nationalists and their allies in the British Parliament, 1851–1906', *English Historical Review*, vol. LXXVI, April 1961, pp. 279–97.

Dar, B. A. *Religious Thought of Sayyid Ahmad Khan.* Lahore, 1957.

Dasgupta, S. *Obscure Religious Cults.* 2nd edition. Calcutta, 1962.

Datta, J. M. 'Banglar Jamidarder Katha' ['The story of the zemindars of Bengal', in Bengali], *Bharatvarsha*, vol. XXXI, part 2, no. 6, 1951.

Day, L. B. *Recollections of Alexander Duff, D.D., LL.D, and of the Mission College which he founded in Calcutta.* London, 1879.

de Bary, W. T. (ed.). *Sources of Indian Tradition.* New York, 1958.

Dobbin, C. E. 'The Ilbert Bill', *Historical Studies: Australia and New Zealand*, vol. XII, no. 45. October 1965, pp. 87–102.

Dobbin, C. E. 'The Growth of Urban Leadership in Western India, with special reference to Bombay City, 1840–85.' Unpublished D.Phil. thesis, 1967. University of Oxford.

Dodwell, H. H. (ed.). *The Indian Empire 1858–1918.* The Cambridge History of the British Empire, vol. V. Cambridge, 1932.

Dufferin and Ava, Marquis of. *Speeches Delivered in India, 1884–8.* London, 1890.

Dumont, L. 'The Functional Equivalents of the Individual in Caste Society', *Contributions to Indian Sociology,* VIII (October 1965).

Dumont, L. *Homo hierarchicus. Essai sur le système des castes.* Paris, 1967.

Durand, H. M. *Life of the Right Hon. Sir Alfred Comyn Lyall.* Edinburgh and London, 1913.

Dutt, N. K. *Origin and Growth of Caste in India.* II: *Castes in Bengal.* Calcutta, 1965.

Farquhar, J. N. *Modern Religious Movements in India.* London, 1929.

Faruqi, Ziya-ul-Hasan. *The Deoband School and the Demand for Pakistan.* London, 1963.

Fraser-Tytler, W. K. *Afghanistan; a study in political developments in Central and Southern Asia.* 2nd edition. London, 1953.

Frykenberg, R. E. *Guntur District, 1788–1848: a history of local influence and central authority in South India.* Oxford, 1965.

Fuchs, S. *Rebellious Prophets. A Study of Messianic Movements in Indian Religions.* Publications of the Indian Branch of the Anthropos Institute, 1. London, 1965.

Gadgil, D. R. *The Industrial Evolution of India in Recent Times.* 4th edition. Calcutta, 1942.

Ganguli, B. N. (ed.). *Readings in Indian Economic History; proceedings of the first All-India Seminar on Indian Economic History, 1961.* Bombay, 1964.

Garcin de Tassy, J. H. *La Langue et la Littérature Hindoustanies en 1870. Revue annuelle.* Paris, 1871.

Ghose, D. K. *England and Afghanistan.* Calcutta, 1960.

Ghose, L. N. *The Modern History of the Indian Chiefs, Rajas, Zamindars, etc.* 2 vols. Calcutta, 1879–81.

Ghose, N. N. *Kristo Das Pal: a Study.* Calcutta, 1887.

Ghosh, J. C. *Bengali Literature.* London, 1948.

Ghosh, P. C. *The Development of the Indian National Congress 1892–1909.* Calcutta, 1960.

Ghurye, G. S. *Caste, Class and Occupation.* 4th edition of *Caste and Race in India.* Bombay, 1961.

Gopal, R. *Indian Muslims. A Political History (1858–1947).* Bombay, 1959.

Gopal, R. *Linguistic Affairs of India.* London, 1966.

Gopal, S. *The Permanent Settlement in Bengal and its Results.* London, 1949.

Gopal, S. *The Viceroyalty of Lord Ripon 1880–1884.* London, 1953.

Gopal, S. *British Policy in India, 1858–1905.* Cambridge, 1965.

Govande, V. D. *Tri Murti Darshan.* [In Marathi.] Poona, 1894.

Graham, G. F. I. *The Life and Work of Sir Syed Ahmed Khan, K.C.S.I.* New and revised edition. London, 1909.

Bibliography

Grant Duff, M. E. *Sir Henry Maine. A Brief Memoir of his Life...
with some of his Indian Speeches and Minutes.* London, 1892.
Grierson, G. A. *The Languages of India.* Calcutta, 1903.
Guha, R. *A Rule of Property for Bengal. An Essay on the Idea of a
Permanent Settlement.* The Hague, 1963.
Gupta, A. (ed.). *Studies in the Bengal Renaissance.* Jadavpur, 1958.

Hambly, G. R. G. 'Unrest in Northern India during the Viceroyalty
of Lord Mayo, 1867–72; the Background to Lord Northbrook's
Policy of Inactivity.' *Journal of the Royal Central Asian Society,*
vol. XLVIII. Part 1. January, 1961.
Heber, R. *Narrative of a Journey through the Upper Provinces of India,
from Calcutta to Bombay, 1824–1825 (with notes upon Ceylon), an
account of a Journey to Madras and the Southern Provinces, 1826,
and letters written in India.* 2 vols. London, 1828.
Heimsath, C. H. *Indian Nationalism and Hindu Social Reform.*
Princeton, New Jersey, 1964.
Hourani, A. *Arabic Thought in the Liberal Age, 1788–1939.* London,
1962.
Hübner, Baron de. *A Travers l'Empire Britannique (1883–1884).* 2
vols. Paris, 1886.
Hunter, W. W. *Life of the Earl of Mayo.* 2 vols. London, 1876.
Hunter, W. W. *The Indian Musalmans.* Reprint of 3rd edition,
London, 1876. Calcutta, 1945.
Hunter, W. W. *Bombay 1885 to 1890. A Study in Indian Administra-
tion.* London, 1892.

Ilbert, C. *The Government of India, being a digest of the Statute Law
relating thereto with historical introduction and illustrative documents.* Oxford, 1898.

Jack, J. C. *The Economic Life of a Bengal District. A Study.* Oxford,
1916.
Jambhekar, G. G. (ed.), *Memoirs and Writings of Acharya Bal Gangadhar
Shastri Jambhekar (1812–1846).* 3 vols. Poona, 1950.
Jesudasan, C. and H. *A History of Tamil Literature.* Calcutta, 1961.
Joshi, V. S. *Vasudeo Balwant Phadke.* Bombay, 1959.

Kahin, G. M. *Nationalism and Revolution in Indonesia.* Ithaca, N.Y.,
1952.
Karaka, D. F. *History of the Parsis including their manners, customs,
religion, and present position.* 2 vols. London, 1884.
Karve, D. D. *The New Brahmans. Five Maharashtrian Families.*
Berkeley and Los Angeles, 1963.
Karve, I. *Hindu Society—An Interpretation.* Poona, 1961.
Karve, I. *Kinship Organisation in India.* 2nd edition. Bombay, 1965.
Keer, D. *Mahatma Jotirao Phooley. Father of our Social Revolution.*
Bombay, 1964.

Khatoon, L. 'Some Aspects of the Social History of Bengal, with special reference to the Muslims, 1854–84.' Unpublished Ph.D. dissertation, 1955. University of London.

Kling, B. B. *The Blue Mutiny. The Indigo Disturbances in Bengal, 1859–1862.* Philadelphia, 1966.

Krishna Singh, B. *Lord Ripon's Policy: observations on the Criminal Jurisdiction Bill.* Bangalore, 1883.

Kumar, D. *Land and Caste in South India.* Cambridge, 1965.

Lal Bahadur. *The Muslim League. Its History, Activities and Achievements.* Agra, 1954.

Lamy, E. *La France du Levant.* Paris, 1900.

Latthe, A. B. *Memoirs of His Highness Shri Shahu Chhatrapati, Maharaja of Kolhapur.* 2 vols. Bombay, 1924.

Lawrence, W. R. *The India We Served.* London, 1928.

Leger, F. *Les Influences Occidentales dans la Révolution de l'Orient.* Paris, 1955.

Leroy-Beaulieu, P. *De La Colonisation chez les Peuples Modernes.* 5th edition. 2 vols. Paris, 1902.

Levenson, J. R. *Liang Ch'i-Ch'ao and the Mind of Modern China.* Harvard Historical Monographs, 26. Cambridge, Mass., 1953.

Limaye, P. M. *The History of the Deccan Education Society (1880–1935).* Poona, 1935.

Lyall, A. C. *The Life of the Marquis of Dufferin and Ava.* 2 vols. London, 1905.

Macpherson, W. J. 'Investment in Indian Railways, 1845–1875', *Economic History Review,* 2nd Series, vol. VIII, no. 2, 1955, pp. 177–87.

Madholkar, G.T. *Vishnu Krishna Chiplonkar.* [In Marathi.] Poona, 1934.

Mahmood, Syed. *A History of English Education in India (1781–1893).* Aligarh, 1895.

Maine, H. S. *Village Communities in the East and West.* 3rd edition. London, 1876.

Majumdar, A. K. *Advent of Independence.* Bombay, 1963.

Majumdar, B. B. *History of Political Thought from Rammohun to Dayananda (1821–84).* Vol. I: *Bengal.* Calcutta, 1934.

Majumdar, B. B. *Indian Political Associations and Reform of Legislature (1818–1917).* Calcutta, 1965.

Majumdar, B. B. 'The Congress and the Moslems.' *The Quarterly Review of Historical Studies,* vol. V, no. 2, 1965–6.

Majumdar, B. B. and Mazumdar, B. P. *Congress and Congressmen in the Pre-Gandhian Era 1885–1917.* Calcutta, 1967.

Mallet, B. *Thomas George, Earl of Northbrook, G.C.S.I. A Memoir.* London, 1908.

Mallick, A. R. *British Policy and the Muslims in Bengal 1757–1856.* Asiatic Society of Pakistan. Publication no. 9. Dacca, 1961.

Mankar, G. A. *A Sketch of the Life and Works of the Late Mr Justice M. G. Ranade...* 2 vols. Bombay, 1902.

Bibliography

Marriott, M. *Caste Ranking and Community Structure in Five Regions of India and Pakistan*. Second reprint edition. Poona, 1965.

Masani, R. P. *Evolution of Local Self-Government in Bombay*. London, 1929.

Masani, R. P. *Dadabhai Naoroji: the Grand Old Man of India*. London, 1939.

McCully, B. T. *English Education and the Origins of Indian Nationalism*. Columbia University Studies in History..., 473. New York, 1940.

Mehta, A. and Patwardhan, A. *The Communal Triangle in India*. 2nd edition. Allahabad, 1942.

Metcalf, T. R. *The Aftermath of Revolt. India, 1857–70*. Princeton, New Jersey, 1965.

Mill, J. S. *Principles of Political Economy*. 3rd edition. 2 vols. London, 1852.

Misra, B. B. *The Indian Middle Classes. Their growth in modern times*. London, 1961.

Mitter, R. J. (ed.). *The Speeches of George Thompson*. Calcutta, 1895.

Mody, H. P. *Sir Pherozeshah Mehta: A Political Biography*. 2 vols. Bombay, 1921.

Mohamed Ali. *My Life: a Fragment*, ed. A. Iqbal. Lahore, 1942.

Moore, R. J. *Sir Charles Wood's Indian Policy, 1853–66*. Manchester, 1966.

Morison, T. *The History of the M.A.-O. College, Aligarh*. Allahabad, 1903.

Morris, M. D. and Stein, B. 'The Economic History of India: a Bibliographic Essay', *The Journal of Economic History*, vol. XXI, no. 2, June 1961, pp. 179–207.

Morris, M. D. *The Emergence of an Industrial Labor Force in India*. Berkeley and Los Angeles, 1965.

Mukherjee, H. and U. *The Growth of Nationalism in India (1857–1905)*. Calcutta, 1952.

Naoroji, D. *Speeches and Writings*. Madras, 1910.

Naoroji, D. *Poverty and Un-British Rule in India*. London, 1901.

Natesan, G. A. (ed.). *Indian Politics*. Madras, 1898.

Natesan, G. A. (ed.). *Eminent Mussalmans*. 1st edition. Madras, n.d.

Nurullah, Syed and Naik, J. P. *History of Education in India during the British period*. Bombay, 1943.

O'Brien, C. C. *Parnell and his Party 1880–90*. Oxford, 1957.

O'Donnell, F. H. *A History of the Irish Parliamentary Party*. 2 vols. London, 1910.

Olcott, H. S. *Old Diary Leaves. The only authentic history of the Theosophical Society. Second Series, 1878–83*. 3rd edition. Adyar, 1954.

Olcott, H. S. *Old Diary Leaves... Third Series, 1883–87*. 2nd edition. Adyar, 1929.

Pal, B. C. *Character Sketches*. Calcutta, 1957.

Pal, B. C. *Memories of My Life and Times*. 2 vols. Calcutta, 1932 and 1951.

Parvate, T. V. *Mahadev Govind Ranade. A Biography*. London, 1963.

Patterson, M. L. P. 'A Preliminary Study of the Brahman versus Non-Brahman Conflict in Maharashtra.' Unpublished Master of Arts dissertation. University of Pennsylvania, 1952.

Pavlov, V. I. *The Indian Capitalist Class. A Historical Study*. New Delhi, 1964.

Phatak, N. R. *Nyayamurti Mahadev Govind Ranade. Yance Caritra*. [Life of Ranade, in Marathi.] Poona, 1924.

Philips, C. H. (ed.). *The Evolution of India and Pakistan 1858 to 1947. Select Documents*. Select Documents on the History of India and Pakistan, IV. London, 1962.

Phule, J. G. *Sarvajanik Satyadharma Pustak*. [Everybody's Book of True Religion, in Marathi.] Poona, 1891.

Pierce, R. A. *Russian Central Asia 1867–1917. A Study in Colonial Rule*. Russian and East European Studies. Berkeley and Los Angeles, 1960.

Prasad, B. *The Origins of Provincial Autonomy. Being a history of the relations between the Central Government and the Provincial Governments in British India from 1860 to 1919*. Allahabad, 1941.

Prioyalkar, A. K. *Dadoba Panduranga. Atmacaritra*. [Biography, in Marathi.] Poona, 1947.

Rajkumar, N. V. *Development of the Congress Constitution*. New Delhi, 1949.

Ranade, M. G. *Essays on Indian Economics. A Collection of Essays and Speeches*. Bombay, 1898.

Ranade, M. G. *Religious and Social Reform. A Collection of Essays and Speeches*. Bombay, 1900.

Ranade, M. G. *Rise of the Maratha Power*. Bombay, 1900.

Ranade, M. G. *Rise of the Maratha Power and other Essays*. . . Bombay, 1961.

Ranade, R. (ed.). *The Miscellaneous Writings of the Late Hon'ble Mr Justice M. G. Ranade*. Bombay, 1915.

Ranade, R. *Ranade. His Wife's Reminiscences*. Tr. K. Deshpande. Delhi, 1963.

Ransom, J. *A Short History of the Theosophical Society*. Adyar, 1938.

Reader, W. J. *Professional Men. The Rise of the Professional Classes in Nineteenth-Century England*. London, 1966.

Royle, J. F. *An Essay on the Antiquity of Hindoo Medicine*. London, 1837.

Sarkar, H. C. *A Life of Ananda Mohan Bose*. Calcutta, 1910.

Sastri, H. *Bauddha Dharma*. [Buddhism, in Bengali.] Calcutta, 1948.

Sastri, S. *History of the Brahmo Samaj*. 2 vols. Calcutta, 1912.

Bibliography

Sastri, S. *Men I Have Seen. Being the Author's Personal Reminiscences of Seven Great Bengalis.* Calcutta, 1919.

Saul, S. B. *Studies in British Overseas Trade, 1870–1914.* Liverpool, 1960.

Schwarz, B. *In Search of Wealth and Power. Yen Fu and the West.* Cambridge, Mass. 1964.

Seeley, J. R. *The Expansion of England. Two courses of Lectures.* London, 1883.

Sen, D. C. *History of Bengali Language and Literature.* 2nd edition. Calcutta, 1954.

Sen, S. *History of Bengali Literature.* New Delhi, 1960.

Shaik, Khair-ud-din. *A Brief Report of the Third Muhammadan Educational Congress held at Lahore on the 27th, 28th, 29th and 30th December, 1888.* Lahore, 1889.

Sharan, P. *The Imperial Legislative Council of India.* Delhi, 1961.

Silver, A. W. *Manchester Men and Indian Cotton 1847–1872.* Manchester, 1966.

Singh, H. L. *Problems and Policies of the British in India 1885–1898.* Bombay, 1963.

Singh, S. N. *The Secretary of State for India and his Council (1858–1919).* Delhi, 1962.

Sinha, N. K. *The Economic History of Bengal; from Plassey to the Permanent Settlement.* 2 vols. Calcutta, 1956 and 1962.

Sinha, P. *Nineteenth Century Bengal. Aspects of Social History. A study in some new pressures on society and in relation between tradition and change.* Calcutta, 1965.

Sinnett, A. P. *The Occult World.* 6th edition. London, 1892.

Skrine, F. H. *An Indian Journalist: being the life, letters and correspondence of Dr Sambhu C. Mookerjee.* Calcutta, 1895.

Skrine, F. H. *Life of Sir William Wilson Hunter.* London, 1901.

Slater, G. *Southern India. Its Political and Economic Problems.* London, 1936.

Smith, W. C. *Modern Islam in India.* Reprint from 2nd revised edition, London, 1946. Lahore, 1963.

Spear, T. G. P. 'Bentinck and Education', *Cambridge Historical Journal,* vol. VI, no. 1, 1938, pp. 78–101.

Srinivas, M. N. *Caste in Modern India and Other Essays.* Bombay, 1962.

Srinivas, M. N. *Social Change in Modern India.* Berkeley and Los Angeles. 1966.

Stephen, J. F. 'Foundations of the Government of India', *The Nineteenth Century,* vol. XIV, no. 80, October 1883, pp. 541–68.

Stokes, E. *The English Utilitarians and India.* Oxford, 1959.

Strachey, J. *India.* London, 1888.

Syed Ahmed Khan. *An Account of the Loyal Mahomedans of India.* 2 parts. Meerut, 1860.

Syed Ahmed Khan. *Speech on the Institution of the British Indian Association, N.W.P.* Aligarh, 1867.

Syed Ahmed Khan. *Review on Dr. Hunter's Indian Musalmans: Are they bound in conscience to rebel against the Queen?* Benares, 1872.
Syed Ahmed Khan. *The Causes of the Indian Revolt written by Syed Ahmed Khan...in Urdoo, in the year 1858, and translated into English by his two European friends.* Benares, 1873.
Syed Ahmed Khan. *On the Present State of Indian Politics.* Allahabad, 1888.

Temple, R. *Men and Events of My Time in India.* London, 1882.
Temple, R. *India in 1880.* 3rd edition. London, 1881.
Temple, R. *The Story of My Life.* 2 vols. London, 1896.
Teng, Ssu-yu and Fairbank, J. K. *China's Response to the West.* Cambridge, Mass., 1954.
Thacker's Directory for Bengal, North-Western Provinces...for 1865. Calcutta, 1865.
Thorner, D. *Investment in Empire.* Philadelphia, 1950.
Thorner, D. and A. *Land and Labour in India.* London, 1962.
Thurston, E. *Castes and Tribes of Southern India.* 7 vols. Madras, 1909.
Tinker, H. *The Foundations of Local Self-Government in India, Pakistan and Burma.* University of London Historical Studies, 1. London, 1954.
Trevelyan, C. E. *On the Education of the People of India.* London, 1838.
Tyabji, H. B. *Badruddin Tyabji. A Biography.* Bombay, 1952.

Varma, C. K. N. *Criticisms on Mr Risley's Articles on the Brahmans, Kayasthas and Vaidyas as published in his 'Tribes and Castes of Bengal'.* Calcutta, 1893.

Wacha, D. E. *Rise and Growth of Bombay Municipal Government.* Madras, n.d. ?1913.
Wadud, K. A. *Banglar Jagaram.* [The Awakening of Bengal, in Bengali.] Visvabharati, 1956.
Walling, R. A. J. (ed.). *The Diaries of John Bright.* London, 1930.
'Wayfarer.' *Life of Shishir Kumar Ghosh.* Calcutta, n.d. ? 1946.
Wedderburn, W. *Allan Octavian Hume, C.B.* London, 1913.
Wise, J. 'Notes on the Races, Castes, and Trades of Eastern Bengal.' Privately printed, London, 1883. British Museum.
Wise, T. A. *Commentary on the Hindu System of Medicine.* Calcutta, 1845.
Wolf, L. *Life of the First Marquess of Ripon.* 2 vols. London, 1921.
Wolpert, S. A. *Tilak and Gokhale: Revolution and Reform in the Making of Modern India.* Berkeley and Los Angeles, 1962.
Wright, H. R. C. 'Some Aspects of the Permanent Settlement in Bengal', *Economic History Review*, 2nd Series, vol. VII, no. 2, 1954, pp. 204–15.

Young, G. M. (ed.). *Macaulay, Prose and Poetry.* London, 1952.

Index

Abdul Aziz, Shah, 310 n.
Abdul Latif, **309–10**, 313, 314, 338
Abkari, 26 n.
Academic Association, 196
Afghan war, 248
Afghanistan, 132–3, 147
Agarkar, G. G., 243, 244
Agency Houses, 32
Agra, 327
Agrarian Disputes Act, 212
Agriculture, 32–3, 114–15
Ahmadabad, 154, 262
Ahmadnagar, 241
Ahmed Ali, Nawab, 308 n.
Aitchison, C. U., 151, 153, 158,
 164 n., 180, 186
Aiyengars, 97; see also Brahmins,
 Tamil
Ajodhya, 306 n.
Ajudhia Nath, 321
Akali Dal, 348
al Afghani, 344
Aligarh, 327
 college, 318–19, 321
 Indian National Congress, 324,
  335, 337; see also Syed Ahmed
  Khan
Allahabad, 212, 267 n., 326, 327, 335
Allahabad high court, 305
Amir Ali, Nawab, 308 n.
Amir Ali, Syed, 307, **310–15**, 331–4,
 338, 339; see also National
 Mahommedan Association
Amrita Bazar Patrika, 214, 222, 259,
 367
Ananda Charlu, P. 278
Andhra, 32 n., 93, 101
Anglo-Indian Defence Association,
 261
Anjuman-i-Ahab, Bombay, 330, 335,
 338
Anjuman-i-Islam, Bombay, 229, 300,
 335–6, 338; see also Tyabji,
 Badruddin

Argyll, George Douglas Campbell,
 8th Duke of, 138
Aristocracy, Indian
 army, 14 n.
 British policy, 10-11, 134–5, 141,
  186–7, 188, 192
 education, 109
 employment, 181
 Indian National Congress, 279
 Legislative Councils, 135, 186–7
Arms Act (1878), 146, 148, 162–3,
 172, 173, 280
Army, Indian, 2, 141 n., 172
Arya Darasana, 215 n.
Ashburner, L. R., 144
Assal Marathas, 77, 78; see also
 Maratha caste
Assam, 25, 46 n., 47, 221
Assam Emigration Act, 296
Assamese, 32 n., 47–8
Associations, 14–16, 23, 194–5, 341–2,
 345–6
 caste, 15–16
 communal, 15–16
 English-educated, 23
 national conferences, 176
 regional, 24 n., 195–7, 205–6, 213,
  227–9, 263
 *see also chapters 5 and 6 passim and
  names of associations*
Ayurveds, 119

Babus (baboos), 134, 141, 161, 249
Baidyas, 40–1, 42–3, 110, 207
Balasore, 207
Balija Naidus, 98–9
Banerjea, Kalicharan, 214
Banerjea, Surendranath, 177, 213,
 214, 216–17, 220–1, 252–4, 257,
 260–1, 265, 266, 267, 278, 296 n.,
 316, 348; see also Indian Asso-
 ciation
Banerjee, Guru Das, 216 n.
Bangabasi, 366 n.

Index

Indian Christians, 87 n., 95, 106, 171
Indian Christian Herald, 215 n.
Indian civil service, 4–5, 116, 126,
    136–7, 138, 141–2, 149, 151,
    165, 180–4, 191–2, 193
    entry into, 5, 116–17, 137–43, 166,
    181–2, 203, 221, 230, 238, 280–1;
    age limit, 117 n., 142, 149 n.,
    180, 182, 201, 253, 266;
    simultaneous examinations, 137,
    201, 230, 266, 280, 296–7, 311
Indian Constitutional Reform Association, 256
Indian Councils Act (1861), 184,
    201; (1892), 6, 188
Indian League, 213–15, 222
Indian Mirror, 216 n., 260, 265
Indian Mutiny, 2, 8, 10, 134, 201,
    268, 316
Indian National Congress, 190–1,
    195, 269, 270, 282–4, 294, 341,
    348–9
    Bengalis, 267, 288, 316, 324
    Bombay apathy, 286–7
    British Indian Association, 226,
    289–90
    constitution and organisation, 246,
    277–95
    delegates, 277–9, 285–6, 291–2
    England, propaganda in, 282–5
    finances, 279, 292–3
    genesis, 251–2, 273–7
    government servants, 278–9
    Hume, 287–8, 294
    Muslims, 13 n., 189, 277, 296–7,
    315–16, 320–4, 327–39
    Native States, 190, 279
    North-western Provinces and
    Oudh, 316, 326–9
    Phule, 241
    programme and demands, 182,
    189, 266, 273, 276, 280–2,
    293–7, 324
    sessions; 1st (1885), 176, 265,
    266–7, 277, 292, 329; 2nd
    (1886), 226, 267, 277, 292,
    296–7, 329; 3rd (1887), 277, 292,
    324, 332–3, 329; 4th (1888),
    277, 284–5, 296, 326–9; 5th
    (1889), 279, 292–3
    weakness, 286
    zemindars, 293 n., 294
Indian National Union, 273

Indian Telegraph Union, *see*
    National Telegraph Union
Indian Union, 263
Indigo Planters' Association, 207
Indigo riots, 13, 203
Indu Prakash, 228, 236, 259
Industry, 33, 50, 101–3
Investment, 33–4
Irish party, 258
Islam, 298–300; *see also* Muslims
Iyengar, V. B., 200
Iyer, G. Subramania, 278, 282 n.

Jains, 346
Jais, 306 n.
Jambhekar, Balshashtri, 228 n.
Jaunpur, 318, 327
Jeejeebhoy, Sir Jamsetjee (1st
    Baronet), 82, 198
Jeejeebhoy, Sir Jamsetjee (2nd
    Baronet), 247
Jeejeebhoy, Sir Jamsetjee (3rd
    Baronet), 264
Jeejeebhoy, N. B., 230–1
Jubbulpore, 266, 348
Justice Party, 348–9
Jute mills, 50 n.
Journalists, *see* Press

Kaibarttas, 44, 45
Kaira, 77 n.
Kakori, 306 n.
Kali Prasad, 325
Kamas, 98–9
Kanakans, 98 n., 102
Kanara, 64
Kanarese, 32 n., 70, 101, 104 n.
Kapus, 98–9
Karachi, 68
Karamat Ali, Maulvi, 310
Karnams, 98 n.
Karnatak, 69–70, 84, 347–8
Kayasth associations, 194 n.
Kayastha Conference, 325–6, 328
Kayasth Prabhus, 76
Kayasths
    Bengal, 41–2, 43, 110, 207
    North-western Provinces and
    Oudh, 325–9
Kazis, 119
Kesari, 243–4, 259
Khalsa Darbar, 348
Khilafat movement, 348

Index

Index